LOOKING
FOR
TROUBLE

M AURICE H ICKS

Fulton Books
Meadville, PA

Published by Fulton Books 2023

Cover designed by MiblArt

The content of this book is based on true stories. All the people discussed in this book are considered innocent until proven guilty in a court of law. All the names contained herein have been changed to protect the innocent. Many of the statements in this book regarding murders, shootings, and other violent crimes were related to me by eyewitnesses or suspects. This book is a work of creative nonfiction. The events are portrayed to the best of my memory. While all the stories in this book are true, some names and identifying details have been changed to protect people's privacy. This book is a memoir. It reflects the author's present recollection of experiences over time. In some cases, the characteristics have been changed, some events have been compressed, and some dialogue has been recreated.

ISBN 979-8-88505-086-9 (paperback)
ISBN 979-8-88505-088-3 (hardcover)
ISBN 979-8-88505-087-6 (digital)

Printed in the United States of America

For my family and for crime victims and their families.
I would also like to thank Dr. Ericka White, Ed.S, Ed.D
for her help with the initial editing of this book.

CONTENTS

Introduction..9
Prologue...11

Chapter 1: The Baltimore Way...................................21
Chapter 2: The Few, the Proud, the Marines............43
Chapter 3: Coming Home...56
Chapter 4: The Baltimore City Police Academy........61
Chapter 5: Field Training..64
Chapter 6: Baptism by Fire: The Southeastern Police District....74
Chapter 7: Mickie, the Ticking Time Bomb.............78
Chapter 8: Sergeants Just Don't Understand.............81
Chapter 9: My Old Neighbor Wayman.....................84
Chapter 10: Exiled into Foot Patrol...........................85
Chapter 11: Little Things Matter................................88
Chapter 12: Objective: Put Policewomen through Hell.............91
Chapter 13: Culture Shock..94
Chapter 14: The Couple that Preys.............................97
Chapter 15: Bomb City...100
Chapter 16: Evil Intentions...103
Chapter 17: Drunk and Disorderly.............................107
Chapter 18: Death Valley..110
Chapter 19: Poverty..116
Chapter 20: Green Eggs but No Ham.........................119
Chapter 21: Training Day..120
Chapter 22: The Coffee Boy Rebellion.......................124
Chapter 23: My Lovable Dad: The Burglar................128
Chapter 24: Movers, Shakers, and Haters...................130

Chapter 25: The Wrath of Sergeant Choker 134
Chapter 26: From City Kitty to County Mounty 137
Chapter 27: Indoctrination into the County Police: First
            Days on the Job 143
Chapter 28: Cowboys and Renegades 150
Chapter 29: Pretty Pauly Meets the Naked Green Bean 152
Chapter 30: Fright Night for Real 154
Chapter 31: The Empire Strikes Back 163
Chapter 32: The Howling 170
Chapter 33: The Burning Bush 178
Chapter 34: Living My Best Life 182
Chapter 35: Gun Smoke 185
Chapter 36: The Ride-a-long 189
Chapter 37: BMW Bust 192
Chapter 38: The Inebriated Bodybuilder versus the
            Beer-Bellied Policeman 196
Chapter 39: To Break and Enter; to Protect and Serve............201
Chapter 40: Farewell, Boss Man 206
Chapter 41: Waiting Alone for Death in the Dark................210
Chapter 42: Murder at First Sight 212
Chapter 43: Tough Love 215
Chapter 44: "I Like the Blacks" 217
Chapter 45: PCP and the Bible 219
Chapter 46: Unspeakable Horror 222
Chapter 47: Operation Triple Play 226
Chapter 48: Indiscriminate Drug Sales 228
Chapter 49: Cleaner Mon 234
Chapter 50: DWI Task Force 240
Chapter 51: Let My People Go! 245
Chapter 52: Patrolling Bladensburg 250
Chapter 53: Fast Chase with Pit Bull 254
Chapter 54: Manifest Destiny: Narcotics 256
Chapter 55: One More Large Bust for the Road 264
Chapter 56: The Barksdale Investigation 267
Chapter 57: Working Undercover 270
Chapter 58: Cover Blown 287

Chapter 59: The Prayer of a Drug Dealer amid the Storm........294
Chapter 60: Big Mama versus SWAT 297
Chapter 61: The Devil is in the details 299
Chapter 62: Undercover Yankee 307
Chapter 63: Policewoman 314
Chapter 64: Rookie Detective 316
Chapter 65: Undercover Brother Detector 320
Chapter 66: Undercover Buy with the Jolly Green Giant.........323
Chapter 67: The Wrath of the Lieutenant 333
Chapter 68: The Art of Discouragement 345
Chapter 69: Lone Wolf Detective............................349
Chapter 70: Back to the Gravel Pit.........................359
Chapter 71: Transferred to Homicide.......................367
Chapter 72: Interrogation and Shooting of the Pimp 373
Chapter 73: Driving while Black: PHASE 1 397
Chapter 74: Driving while Black: PHASE 2 402
Chapter 75: Driving while Black: PHASE 3 404
Chapter 76: The Investigation: DAY 7 406
Chapter 77: The Murder of Tony Clark 421
Chapter 78: The FBI Takes Control 428
Chapter 79: The Nightstalker 432
Chapter 80: The Continuing Saga of the Nightstalker 441
Chapter 81: The Colombian Connection.....................447
Chapter 82: The Agony of Defeat 455
Chapter 83: The Breakthrough 458
Chapter 84: No Witness, No Case 465
Chapter 85: The Perfect Mouthpiece 470
Chapter 86: Antoine's Sentencing.............................479

Epilogue...482

This photo was taken in the summer of 1984.

INTRODUCTION

Most of the victims portrayed in this book came from impoverished communities. They did not have the economic resources to
hire private detectives or high-cost attorneys to obtain justice for
their loved ones. So instead, these families—and many other families
in America—must rely on police agencies to obtain justice for their
loved ones.

We live in an era where people hear about violent crime so frequently that they often become desensitized to it. Unfortunately,
police officers do not have the luxury of turning the channel. Each
violent incident has a profound effect on their physical and emotional
well-being. These officers perform their jobs for extraordinarily little
money and often with little recognition.

Many of the officers will relive their nightmares for years to
come. Police officers carry the heavy burden of bringing violent
assailants to justice. No police department in the country can adequately compensate police officers and detectives for enduring these
enormous responsibilities. I want readers to discover one aspect of
police work: the impact of public service on our families.

I commend all the men and women employed by state, local,
and federal law enforcement agencies. These officers risk their lives
daily to bring violent criminals to justice. The police profession rep-
resents a unique subculture that has a strong desire to protect its
members. Like many other organizations, they employ good people
and bad people. In writing this book, my goal is to provide a realistic look at the trials, tribulations, and triumphs of the citizens, suspects, and officers I encountered during my first ten years in the law
enforcement profession.

I bore witness to the inevitable clash among those sworn to protect the community, the lawbreakers, and the citizens caught in between. I witnessed the frustrations and emotional devastation felt by poor people in marginalized communities. There were casualties on all sides. However, the impoverished bore a significant part of the pain.

Sometimes, hunters become the hunted; and sometimes, good people become bad people. If you leave soldiers in combat too long, they experience battle fatigue. Unfortunately, many patrol officers also develop battle fatigue. Some develop an us-against-them mentality. Patrol officers are walking representations of their police departments. Community members often associate the actions of a few bad apples with an entire police department's activities.

Based on my twenty years of experience in law enforcement, my sentiments mimic the words of a great congressman, the late Elijah Cummings: "We are better than this." No matter how difficult law enforcement becomes, we must balance the need to safeguard our communities with the duty to defend the constitution. Lastly, let a man or woman considering a career in law enforcement examine themselves to see if their character is worthy of serving the community.

PROLOGUE

> He returned to the front of the building and shook
> his head as he looked up at the high-rise, which was
> pockmarked by broken windows. "What we have is
> every social problem imaginable concentrated here."
> —Former Baltimore City mayor's
> comment on the scene of a
> police officer shooting at the Flag House Courts
> (excerpt from the *Baltimore Sun*)

I needed help, and I needed it fast. I was trapped in the muggy tiny apartment. The heat and humidity had sweat pouring down my face, obstructing my vision. I was in desperate need of an extraction. I wondered if my backup would find me in that hellhole! I had made a rookie mistake. Now, the laws of the street would prevail.

It all started when I drove up to the Flag House Courts, a public housing project in East Baltimore, to take a date rape report. My partner and I interviewed Vanessa, a caramel-skinned twenty-three-year-old beauty. She was the pride of her community. Everyone there talked about her beautiful, flawless skin, her light-brown hair, and her beautiful light-brown eyes.

Vanessa explained that she had gone on a date with a local man whose nickname was Mistletoe. He was known for kissing any woman he found attractive. Mistletoe behaved like a perfect gentleman when he treated Vanessa to dinner. He walked her to her apartment door and began kissing her. He then pushed her through the doorway and onto her knees, and he told her to suck him off. I was taken aback by Vanessa's candidness and courage to report the incident, primarily because Mistletoe was a known drug dealer.

Vanessa told Mistletoe she did not want to do what he asked. He then lifted her from her knees and drew her face up to his. He wanted her to see the monstrous look in his eyes. He was an extremely dark-skinned African American man who stood about six foot two. He was in his early twenties and had a very muscular frame and unusually long arms. Vanessa described his change in demeanor as similar to that of an animal who was about to devour its prey.

Before Vanessa had time to contemplate her next move, Mistletoe hit her in the head. Then he picked her off the floor, kicked her bedroom door open, and savagely tore the buttons off her blouse. She recalled his repulsive, sweaty body mounting her. She said he looked demonic as he continued his predatory act. After he satisfied his animalistic desires, he delivered a clear warning: "Don't tell anyone what happened." But somehow, Vanessa found the courage to call the police.

I called an ambulance to transport Vanessa to City Hospital. I waited for her doctor to process her with a rape evidence kit. My partner left and partnered up with another officer. I transported the victim back to the Flag House Courts. The Baltimore Police Department had a policy that required officers to escort a rape victim back to their home. The department also had a policy stipulating that no police officer could walk into the projects alone. Standard protocol for handling calls required that a minimum of two officers would go into the designated project and that at least one officer would be dispatched to guard the patrol cars. Members of the Baltimore City Fire Department, including their paramedics, refused to enter the projects without a police escort.

On the way back to the projects, I asked another officer to accompany me on the escort. However, no officer was available. I proceeded to the projects hoping an officer would be available by the time I reached my destination. Once I arrived at the projects, I again called for another officer to accompany me, but everyone was still tied up. It was one o'clock in the afternoon. I had a decision to make. I could enter the projects alone and violate one departmental policy or decline to escort a rape victim to her doorstep and violate a different departmental policy. I also had to calculate the risks of leaving my police car unattended.

The projects were eerily quiet that day. I felt confident that it was safe to escort Vanessa to her apartment door. I looked up at the decapitated building. It was an eyesore for the city. Vanessa walked toward the elevator. She was startled as the elevator door opened. Her woman's intuition was telling her that something was not right. We exited on the tenth floor. Everything still seemed quiet. I walked Vanessa to her door and said goodbye, but I waited for her to unlock the door before departing.

As soon as the door opened, I heard a man's voice say, "I know you didn't call Five-O." I took a step back toward the door. Mistletoe, the suspect in Vanessa's rape, was standing inside the apartment with four other guys. His associates were on edge. They appeared prone to attack at the slightest provocation.

Mistletoe wasted no time displaying his aggression. He looked like a taller black version of Arnold Schwarzenegger. The fact that I was a uniformed Baltimore City police officer seemed to be of no concern to him. It was probably the first time he saw a police officer alone in the projects. The streetwise hoodlum's predatory instincts kicked in. He knew I was a rookie. My neatly pressed white shirt with military creases and my shiny new silver badge gave me away.

The fact that I was only twenty-one years old but looked like a seventeen-year-old kid undoubtedly gave him more confidence. He also had his posse with him. In his mind, he was a big alpha lion, and I was a helpless deer separated from the herd. The pride was about to close in on me. But although I had a youthful appearance, I was not going to rely solely on my academy training. I was a trained United States Marine.

Mistletoe wasted no time getting right up in my face. He believed that the typical rules of engagement did not apply to me because I was behind enemy lines. I knew the odds were against me. It was like David facing Goliath. I knew he would feed on any attempt I made to assert my authority. Backup would have to get there quickly to rescue me. I felt trapped like the citizens living in the projects, whom I was sworn to protect.

Any backup officers would have to wait for the slow elevator once they arrived, or they would be forced to climb ten flights of stairs. Many of the officers were overweight; they were unlikely to take the urine-infested staircase. In the meantime, Mistletoe's posse could wreak havoc on me and get away with it. I made a rookie mistake by violating their territorial integrity. Now they would be the ones imposing sanctions on me. I had to think quickly.

Mistletoe stated, "I know you don't think that you're going to lock me up!"

"Relax, man," I said. "You're saying you did not do anything to her, right?"

"I do whatever the fuck I want to do," Mistletoe replied. He looked at his posse. "Isn't that right, fellas?"

They all replied, "You're the man, Toe."

Mistletoe then asked me whether Vanessa had filed a complaint against him.

"It doesn't matter, man," I said. "I can resolve this for you. Just give me a few minutes to talk to Vanessa in private."

Mistletoe's buddies immediately chimed in. "You aren't going to do anything?"

I was in more considerable trouble than I initially thought. I was outnumbered and probably outgunned. No self-respecting hoodlum would leave home without his gat—his gun. I was dealing with a terrified victim who was standing face-to-face not only with her rapist but also with the rapist's posse. But somehow, I maintained a poker face. I pretended to be calm, although my stomach was in knots.

I referred to the conflict negotiation skills I used to survive as a kid in Baltimore. When I was in elementary school, I talked a group of junior high school kids out of beating me down for joining the school safety patrol. Now I was faced with the same scenario but on a much larger and more serious scale. At last, I had a plan! I would continue to be their legal advocate. I had to convince them there was no need for a confrontation.

I ushered the victim into her bedroom under the auspices of convincing her to drop the charges. I wanted her out of harm's way, but I also fantasized about the enormous satisfaction I would derive from taking down the boogeyman in the very place where he had committed his demonic act. I opened Vanessa's bedroom door and locked it. That was when I got on my police radio and called for backup. I keyed up the mic on the Motorola police radio on the lapel of my uniform shirt and frantically called for help.

"Car 2-2-4, 2-2-4. I need backup."

The dispatcher advised, "2-2-4, I can't hear you."

I repeated, "2-2-4, I need backup at 127 South Exeter Street!"

The dispatcher repeated, "I can't copy. What is your 10-20?"

I replied, "127 South Exeter Street, the same location that I called out on!"

The dispatcher repeated, "2-2-4, I cannot copy. Is there a problem?"

At that point, my mouth was so dry I could hardly get my words out. "Yes, there's a problem. I have a rape suspect on the scene, and I have the rape victim with me. I need priority backup!" I walked over to the window, hoping to get a clearer signal. "I need backup. I have a rape suspect on the scene with four hostiles!"

The dispatcher still could not hear me. Vanessa was staring out of the second bedroom window, trembling. She was trying her best to contain her emotions. First, I saw one tear trickle down her face. Then about thirty seconds later, suddenly, tears came pouring down her face. She started to hyperventilate. Terror stole her words. Fear throbbed inside her heart, and it paralyzed her. The horrified look on her face became etched in my mind, as indelible as ink. She was only a few feet from her assailant. Reality had set in. I was the only barrier shielding her from the muscular beast who had raped her the night before.

Just as I began to think nothing else could go wrong, the deafening sounds of Baltimore's one o'clock whistles crashed through the air. The sirens blocked out any potential radio transmissions and any hopes of calling out the cavalry. At that point, I realized that my worst nightmare had come true. I was trapped alone in the projects with no backup in sight.

Native Baltimoreans knew about that whistle. However, the source of the one o'clock whistle has been debated since the 1960s. At the time, I believed the whistle emanated from the fifteen-story Emerson Bromo-Seltzer Tower in Downtown Baltimore. Forty years later, I learned that the whistle did not come from any single source. Instead, it emanated simultaneously from 112 different locations throughout the city. The city's sirens were tested every Monday as an emergency broadcast system.

They were the debt collectors and wanted me to pay for everything. Yes, pay for Reaganomics and every real or perceived injustice at the hands of the police. I had hope for a positive outcome. However, it was like being an unwitting participant in a horror show. My fate was inevitable. My back was against the wall, and there was no method of escape. It was time for close-quarters combat. One of them had a reputation for being gifted in the art of intercepting fists. My situation was so dire that only the Elite Seal Team Six could have rescued me.

I had visions of Seal Team Six rappelling into the high-rise projects and crashing through the window. However, I was not in the military. I was just a beat cop. Nevertheless, there seemed to be no way to escape the debacle.

At that point, my sentiments mimicked the lyrics from the Geto Boys, "If it is going down, let's get it over with." After that, all I could do was wait for the fist fest to begin.

The tables had turned. The hunter had now become the hunted. The villain and his posse busted down the bedroom door. Mistletoe slammed the door against the wall for effect, as if saying no mere door was going to stop a badass like him and his posse. The battle lines had been crossed, and my fate seemed inevitable. He made a beeline toward me. He was surprised to see me standing by the window.

The suspect defiantly pointed his finger in my face and asked, "What's it going to be, homeboy?" I noticed the brown marijuana burn marks on his fingertips. He took note and said, "What the fuck are you looking at?" I wondered if I should initiate a preemptive strike. Perhaps that might throw them off. But I quickly decided against it. It was too risky. The other scoundrels might try to harm Vanessa. I was running out of options.

My God! I thought. I wondered which one of the hoodlums was going to initiate the attack. June Bug snorted, gritted his teeth, stared at me, and looked at my badge. Ronnie, whose nickname was No Heinie, because of his flat derriere, stood there smiling with his Kangol hat turned sideways. He was chewing on a toothpick. He grunted and looked at my hat. Finally, Cutty, a brown-skinned man in his thirties who had a pick stuck inside his Afro, stared at my gun.

Each of them was examining me to determine which souvenirs they wanted to take after the attack. My gut told me they had previous experience in taking down a police officer. Beating me down and stripping me of my gear would give them enormous bragging rights and would undoubtedly enhance their street cred. They knew their craft. These criminals fought on the streets practically every day.

They were anxious to begin the slugfest. One of the men cracked his knuckles and shook his head. One of the outlaws moved his neck to the side and cracked his neck. He looked at me as if I was the stupidest person on the face of the earth. He seemed to be wondering who in their right mind would sign up for the impending abuse.

The impending attack seemed routine to Mistletoe. He was a gangster, and I was a policeman. There was nothing personal about it. Perhaps in his mind, he was doing me a favor. He was about to give me a free lesson on police work, a lesson I would never forget.

At the time, they knew something that I did not: no one had served time for assaulting a police officer in Baltimore. Still, I remembered hearing one circuit judge say, "It is your job to get assaulted!" His statement now resonated in my mind.

The rest of Mistletoe's crew had a different take on the impending attack. The attack was much more personal for them. As an African American police officer, they viewed me as a defector, a traitor, an infidel, or a turncoat. Therefore, they believed that my punishment needed to be commensurate with my disloyalty to my race.

I thought about the irony of it all. Eight months earlier, I had one of the most straightforward, effortless jobs on the planet: delivering newspapers for the *Baltimore Sun*. I earned the same salary that I made as a police officer; but unlike my police job, there was no stress, no risk, and no danger. My run-in with Mistletoe and his associates occurred during my fifth month of working the streets. It was a hell of a tester. The police academy had not prepared me for this type of test. It was baptism by fire.

Today, I could draw parallels between what I faced in that tiny apartment in the Flag House Courts to what a Marine Corps sniper instructor told his students when they were about to embark to Vietnam, their practical exam to become snipers. "I am about to send each of you out on a real reconnaissance mission," he said. "If you survive, you pass. And if you get killed, you fail. It's as simple as that!" I felt the same way. I was about to start my street survival practical exam. If I survived, I passed.

My heart began pumping rapidly. It took a few minutes for me to regain my composure. But there was one thing for sure: I was not going out without a fight. Before joining the Marine Corps, I was a peaceful person. However, my drill instructor, Sergeant McNair, changed that. He brought the inner beast out of me. If necessary, I would release the beast.

I chuckled when I recalled reciting my Marine Corps prayers for Sergeant McNair: "So I walk through the valley of the shadow of death. I shall fear no evil, because I am the biggest and baddest motherfucker in the valley!" Finally, my attitude mimicked the lyrics of the Geto Boys: "If it's going down, let's get it over with!"

I got angry because Mistletoe had taken away Vanessa's dignity. He was the neighborhood boogeyman. Now I longed to take him down. However, I was not sure I had the skills to defeat Mistletoe or his champion warriors. "It's going to be jail," I told Mistletoe candidly. "You're under arrest for rape. Don't move a muscle, or you'll also be charged with resisting arrest. Turn around and put your hands behind your back."

Mistletoe looked bewildered. I must have seemed more robust and more decisive than when I first entered the apartment. Perhaps he surmised that I had analyzed the situation reasonably and had decided this was the right course of action. To my amazement, he immediately complied, placing his hands behind his back. However, the situation was far from over. I knew I would somehow have to maneuver Mistletoe out of the apartment, past his posse. I also had to get the victim to a safe place.

As I started my way out of the bedroom, the reality of the situation must have settled in Mistletoe's mind. He had other felony convictions on his record: drug charges and weapons charges. He was on probation. He contemplated his options. He recalled that I had ventured out behind enemy lines. That worked in his favor. "I know you all are not going to allow this shit to go down," he said.

Cutty began punching his fist into his open hand. Ronnie looked at me as soon as I cuffed Mistletoe. He, too, seemed to be contemplating his next move. He clenched his fists. I felt a twinge in my gut. I looked back at the rape victim, and then I looked back at Mistletoe's cohorts. They looked at me, and then they looked at my gun. I used one hand to push Mistletoe firmly out of the bedroom and placed my other hand over my standard-issue .38 revolver. I realized that once we reached the hallway, I would be entering a kill zone. I took a deep breath and moved forward.

Suddenly, I heard police radios blasting. A second later, I listened to two kicks on the apartment door and words that were music to my ears: "Police! Put your hands where I can see them." Lord knew I wanted to do a happy dance.

Next, I saw Melvin, the six-foot-four Joel Osteen lookalike, holding his .38 revolver. He had always been a very sharp officer, and that day, he had done what the dispatcher had failed to do: he jotted down the location of the escort. He and four other officers ordered Mistletoe's cohorts to back away. I quickly ushered Mistletoe out of the apartment and signaled Melvin to care for Vanessa, the rape victim.

As I glanced back momentarily to ensure that the victim was okay, I noticed that Mistletoe's men were following me toward the elevator. As I pushed the elevator button, one of them swung at me, catching me on the right side of my head. I spun Mistletoe around and pushed him into my assailant. The assailant fell back against the railing and then lunged toward me, swinging his fists.

All five officers on the scene were engaged in an all-out brawl. Melvin attempted to call for help. The dispatcher called me: "2-2-4, what's going on there?" We were fighting for our lives. The next thing I heard was the alert tone over the police radio. *Ding, ding, ding!* The dispatcher came back on the radio: "Signal 13. Officers in trouble. 127 South Exeter Street. I repeat, Signal 13!"

A Signal 13 was the most severe distress call for a police officer. When a Signal 13 was called, every available police unit in the city was authorized for rescue until the signal was called off. The Flag House Courts was three blocks from Downtown Baltimore, which had an enormous police presence. Therefore, theoretically, every police unit in the city, including SWAT, the mounted patrol unit (horses), the motorcycle unit, and members of the Marine unit could respond to the scene.

I managed to wrestle both my assailant and Mistletoe to the ground. I looked down at the street. About twelve additional police cars were on the road. All of Mistletoe's men were arrested and charged with assault and resisting arrest. I became known as the Sector 4 guy who came to Sector 2 and almost started a riot.

Vanessa, the victim, dropped the charges. Mistletoe walked free and was never convicted of rape. I survived one of my most dangerous encounters. Every time I saw Mistletoe after that, I reminded him he had dues to pay. Eventually, I stopped seeing him down there. I wondered whether the streets had finally caught up with him. I never found out. I knew there would be many more violent confrontations to come. I was just getting started.

CHAPTER 1

THE BALTIMORE WAY

Urge all of your men to pray, not in church alone,
but everywhere. Pray when driving. Pray when
fighting. Pray alone. Pray with others. Pray by
night and pray by day. Pray for the cessation of
immoderate rains, for good weather, for battle.
Pray for the defeat of our wicked enemy whose
banner is injustice and whose good is oppression.
Pray for victory. Pray for our Army, and pray for
peace. We must march together, all out for God.
—General George Patton

Many tourists loved the ambience of Downtown Baltimore's Inner Harbor. However, local Baltimoreans were intimately familiar with another side of Charm City, the side depicted in books, motion pictures, and television series, such as *Homicide: Life on the Street*, *The Wire*, and *The Corner*. My goal was to give readers a glimpse of life as I saw it in Baltimore and, later, in neighboring Prince George's County, Maryland.

Nestled along the Chesapeake Bay and the Potomac River, Baltimore had its share of charm and its own unique set of challenges. Many native Baltimoreans viewed the Chesapeake Bay as a Godsend. The bay was the primary source of the Maryland blue crabs, which helped satisfy the city's insatiable appetite for the delicacy.

Baltimore was a very traditional city that had enormous historical significance. It was the home of Fort McHenry, the place where Francis Scott Key wrote "The Star-Spangled Banner." Baltimore was also the home of civil rights icon Thurgood Marshall and jazz singer and civil rights advocate Billie Holiday, and it was still home to the country's oldest market: the world-famous Lexington Market. It was initially built in 1782, drawing in tourists from all across the country.

Baltimore Orioles baseball fans were quick to boast that Baltimore was the home to one of the world's greatest baseball players of all time: Babe Ruth. It was also the home of one of the most famous poets: Edgar Allan Poe. In the 1950s, limousines occupied by famous actors and musicians lined Pennsylvania Avenue in West Baltimore. The smooth voices of jazz singers Billie Holiday and Cab Calloway thundered throughout the Avenue.

Outsiders identified Baltimore as a place to get your sin on, especially at the world-renowned the Block in Downtown Baltimore. Ironically, the Block was located one block from the Central District of the Baltimore Police Department. It consisted of a few blocks occupied by strip joints and peep shows that fed the perverted appetites of locals and out-of-towners alike.

In the late 1970s, Baltimore's mayor devised a master plan to build up Baltimore's Inner Harbor area. It gave all Baltimoreans an enormous sense of pride. However, lurking less than a quarter mile away from the harbor was an entirely different world. An ugly crime problem in the nearby Flag House and Lafayette Courts scared most tourists out of their wits.

The city police force worked hard to contain the crime. They could not afford to allow the problem to spill into Inner Harbor or into Little Italy, which was located just across the street. At that time, an estimated fifty thousand heroin addicts roamed the city streets. Many of them committed crimes daily to support their habit. There were an estimated one hundred open-air drug markets in the city of Baltimore.

Every community had its sense of culture and values. Some were good; some were bad. We needed to learn both the written and unwritten codes of our culture. It was critical to our survival. My cul-

22

tural education came early in life. I avoided contact with the scores of holdup men, drug dealers, and murderers who wreaked havoc upon our community for most of my life. My strategy had advantages and disadvantages.

In my view, we, the citizens of Baltimore, were living in a lawless land. Criminals were operating with impunity. Most of the brothers on the streets viewed the police as an invading evil army dedicated to destroying their lives. Their view was different from that of their European counterparts. To them, the police were their friends, their helpers, and their heroes.

I became increasingly perplexed about the conditions in which Baltimoreans lived. So many unanswered questions were lurking in my mind. Why were hoodlums hanging out everywhere we went? Why were we always under siege by the inhabitants of our community? Why did we have to walk through an assortment of hard-core criminals to buy a loaf of bread? Where were the police? Why didn't they care about what we were going through? I wondered who they were and where their bosses were. Why didn't they direct their officers to do their jobs? Feelings of hopelessness and despair began to set in.

In the fall of 1972, a group of local hoodlums took over a group of abandoned garages across the street from where we lived. They converted them into shooting galleries, places where drug addicts regularly injected or shot drugs into their veins. The hoodlums sold heroin and partied all night. I distinctly remembered how one night, when I was taking out the trash, I saw David, a local fifteen-year-old kid, standing inside the garage. I watched as a twenty-one-year-old drug dealer stuck a needle into David's arm. David did not make a sound, but he staggered around like a tranquilized animal.

I never knew what horrific sight I might see when I took out the garbage. It was like the night of the living dead. Sometimes, I would see the druggies asleep, bent over in odd positions with needles still stuck in their arms. Those positions were known on the streets as the dope fiend lean. I saw a lot of puffy-handed people staggering around in the garage across the street. The nightmarish episodes made me sick to my stomach. After that, I was committed to never using drugs.

I detested the stench of the urine-saturated sidewalks and urine-infested phone booths. I hated talking to merchants at the corner store through plexiglass. Why were our sidewalks always covered in graffiti? Why were our basketball courts filled with glass and hypodermic needles? I wondered why our basketball courts had bicycle rims for hoops, hoops with no nets attached.

I became increasingly frustrated at never seeing the rollers—the police—drive down the alley near the garages for the entire eight months our neighborhood was under siege. My main goal in life centered on finding a way out of that environment. The only role models I had during that time were my teachers. The only African American teachers I saw in my elementary school years were women. I admired their commitment to their African American culture. They proudly wore their Afros and preached that the children were our future. I remembered listening to Ray Charles singing his version of "America the Beautiful."

Everyone in the community emphasized the importance of education—everyone from the local grocer to the local banker. The security guard at the Food Town Supermarket, which was renamed Food City, told me, "Get yourself a good education, son. You won't be like me, an old man guarding a supermarket."

In the summer of 1972, I found myself glued to the television set, watching several educational programs. I learned valuable lessons in academics in a fun way. I watched *Schoolhouse Rock!*, *Grammar Rock*, *Science Rock*, *Multiplication Rock*, and *Money Rock*. The programs fed my insatiable appetite for learning. They enhanced my knowledge of grammar, economics, science, politics, history, social studies, and math. I also learned valuable life lessons by watching prosocial cartoons like *Fat Albert and the Cosby Kids*. Episodes like "The Fuzz" gave me my first glance at how black officers and white officers interacted with black children living in urban communities.

During my early years, I sought a reprieve from the inner city. The shooting gallery across from our home served as a constant reminder of this imperative. I had only disdain for our local drug dealers. I hated their arrogance and their flamboyant lifestyles. Most importantly, I detested the joy they derived from destroying my esteemed brothers and sisters. They worshipped a god different from mine. They honored their clothes and their cars as their gods. I long desired to see the police remove the perpetrators off the streets, especially off my street. That dream did not come true.

The most critical lesson that Baltimoreans learned was to never become a snitch, a dip artist, or a hot boy. All these street terms were synonymous with being an informant for the police. A snitch was the most despised creature in the jungle. Everyone in the community ostracized snitches. The death penalty was the preferred mechanism when dealing with snitches. I took this lesson with me when I went into the law enforcement profession.

Police beatdown was a frequent and inevitable part of city life for drug traffickers. I often heard young black men bragging about being beaten up by local white narcotics detectives, whom they referred to as the knockers or the jump-outs. For years, I wondered why they were called the knockers. I did not know if it was because they knocked on suspects' doors before they raided their homes or because they struck suspected drug dealers in the head. Although I never witnessed a citizen being beaten up by the knockers, from all the stories I was told, it seemed being beaten up by them was almost a rite of passage for young black men. I thought of the irony of it all. Those young black men learned to identify with their assailants.

I was an introvert who was blessed to have strategically avoided the fate of many of my classmates, many of whom met their untimely deaths before they were fourteen years old. I sought refuge by attending Sunday school at Gillis Memorial Baptist Church. I had a hunger for spiritual wisdom. I was in grave danger of falling into the vortex that sucked the life out of inner-city youth. Plenty of drug dealers, robbers, burglars, and murderers around me provided unconventional wisdom regarding the streets. Unfortunately, my environment was critically short on positive role models. However, God placed an extraordinary person in my life who gave me a fighting chance.

I was raised primarily by my mother with a super-assist from my grandmother and grandfather. My grandmother had a fourth-grade education while my grandfather had a second-grade education. My grandfather always told me, "Boy, get a good education." His stepfather had an entirely different take on education. He convinced my grandfather's mother to "stop sending that boy to that damn funhouse." He was referring to elementary school. As a result, my grandfather suffered from the effects of inferior education.

To the naked and untrained eye, I was just another ghetto child struggling to get by. Conversely, looking through a spiritual lens, my grandfather saw me as gifted and anointed. His background made him seem to be the most unlikely source of support. However, when he came into my life, he was a devoted Christian with an unshakeable faith, a faith he began sharing with me. My grandfather mandated that my uncle and I attended church with him every Sunday. However, when I told him I did not understand all the hollering and screaming in the church, he told me he wanted me to attend Sunday school. That was a life-altering experience. It changed my thinking and my life positively.

My grandfather spent his entire life ensuring that I steered clear of the inner-city minefields that were placed out there to decapitate the bodies and minds of inner-city youth. He made it clear that I had to maneuver through Baltimore's minefields on my own; however, he told me in advance where the mines were. Whether I chose to avoid the minefields was totally up to me. My grandfather drilled into my head the importance of honesty and standing up for what was right.

My first test of honesty occurred a few days later. I was eleven years old. I accompanied my friend to the local Food Town Supermarket at Park Heights and Shirley Avenues. My friend dropped a Kool-Aid packet on the grocery store floor and proceeded to check out. He motioned for me to kick the Kool-Aid in his direction. I unwittingly kicked it to him, not knowing his intentions. He then placed the grocery bag filled with the purchased items on the floor. Simultaneously, he picked up the packet of Kool-Aid. Then he walked out the door. That troubled my spirit. I realized I had helped my friend steal the Kool-Aid. I came back later that day and explained to the cashier we had accidentally picked up a packet of Kool-Aid.

I gave her the five cents for it. She called the manager over and told him what had happened. The manager gave me my first job as a bagger at the tender age of eleven. My grandfather's advice paid off, as it always had. That job was a springboard for another career a few years later at another supermarket.

I realized I needed to refocus my energy. I became an entrepreneur. My first entrepreneurial venture was as a paperboy. This came about after my cousin introduced me to an eccentric black man named Owen. Owen was in his fifties and managed several newsstands in our community. He was a peculiar, Jheri curl-wearing brother who marched to the beat of a different drum. He was the only man I saw wearing a Jheri curl.

Owen loved to talk about money. When I first met him, he proudly held up three identical denim suits he had just purchased. I asked him why he bought three identical suits instead of three different ones. "Because they were on sale!" he said. All righty, then. That made a lot more sense. (Yeah, right!)

God would strategically place us in positions where we could prosper and grow. In the 1970s, Owen set me up with selling newspapers out of a vestibule in Pantry Pride in Mondawmin Mall. By the time I was turning twelve years old, Owen was still paying me about seven dollars per day. By the age of fourteen, I was no longer working for him. I owned the newspaper stand. That meant I kept all the proceeds from my paper sales. I netted fifty dollars per day instead of seven.

I had study hall in that supermarket vestibule every Sunday. Church parishioners from all walks of life stopped by to provide me with inspirational messages, words of wisdom, and promises of hope. They delivered enormous insight into proven strategies for maneuvering through the complicated maze of inner-city life. They were teachers, principals, and church leaders. Some of them were professors at my mother's alma mater, Coppin State University. Eventually, a black Baltimore City police officer got in on the act as well. They made the case that education was the cornerstone of success for young black men.

I spent many hours talking to street taxi drivers—hacks—who stood outside the grocery store waiting to transport customers home with their groceries. My discussions with those hacks and my beloved patrons boosted my immune system, inoculating me from the effects of hatred. There was plenty of hate to go around. Racial hatred and self-hatred seemed to flourish throughout Baltimore.

Owning my newspaper stand provided my first real test at working in customer service. For example, one customer asked me to give him the television guide for free. (In those days, most customers purchased the newspaper for the television guide.) I told the customer I could not do as he asked because I would have difficulty selling that newspaper if I provided the television guide for free. Many of my customers bought the newspaper because they wanted the television guide, so I used the presence of the television guide as my primary sales pitch. I would yell, "Get your *Sun* paper or *News American* with a TV guide inside!"

The customer who wanted the guide for free became irate and started yelling at me. I knew his type. He was one of my many brothers who would pop off at the slightest hint of provocation. He told me he knew I rarely sold all my newspapers. Therefore, in his mind, I could afford to give him the television guide.

The hacks standing around me were watching closely to see how I was going to handle my customer. I decided to negotiate with him. I pulled my eyeglasses down and looked him in the eye. "I'll tell you what, sir," I said. "I will sell you the television guide for twelve cents." That was the commission I received for each paper. The retail price of the newspaper was fifty cents.

The customer got in my face and yelled, "You asshole! You are a little rip-off artist. You are a little crook!" I smiled and stood my ground because I was serious about my money. The customer reached into his pocket and gave me the twelve cents for the television guide. The hacks and the other customers busted out laughing as soon as the angry customer walked away. "Damn, son," one of them commented. "I like you. You drive a hard bargain. You're going to make a hell of a businessman!" From that point forward, my persona as the paperboy was born.

*****

When I was in the fifth grade, I joined the school safety patrol. They elected me to be their captain on my first day on the job. I was floating on air after the bell rang at the end of the day, and I exited the school. Unfortunately, my joy was short-lived. I was immediately surrounded by a group of five junior high school kids.

One of them grabbed me by the collar and told me he and his colleagues had unanimously decided they were going to kick some school safety patrol ass! They aspired to beat down all the members of the school safety patrol they could catch. I thought, *These fellas are off to a good start, because they just grabbed the captain!* I had chosen the worst possible time to join the safety patrol. However, even at the age of eleven, I was good at resolving conflicts.

One hoodlum drew back his fist to punch me in the face. "Wait for a second," I said. "You know something? I just joined today. I was just checking it out to get a feel if I wanted to do it. You know what?" I continued. "This isn't the job for me."

The juvenile delinquent released his grip on my collar, then looked at his comrades. "Good, little man," he said. "I don't want you to grow up and be no snitch!"

"Thank you," I said.

I shook all their hands. Then I picked up my book bag and walked to the corner. I looked back, and then I made a beeline to my house, which was across the street. I was shocked they let me go. I remained on the school safety patrol, but I learned never to wear my badge outside of school. The lesson I learned was important: people harbored a deep resentment for authority figures, even at the lowest levels of society.

My uncle Johnny, who was less than two years older than I was, did not fare as well during an encounter with a different group of junior high school students. A few days after my close encounter, a group of five juvenile delinquents pulverized my uncle during a simple trip to a mailbox across the street from our house. The thugs kicked and punched him just for the thrill of it. Their attack was a practice known then as banking. I guess it was the precursor of the modern-day wilding out. The attack on my uncle earned him the nickname Mailbox.

A few days later, another junior high school kid put a knife to my throat in front of a store at Park Heights and Shirley Avenue, just one block from my house. I made frequent trips to the store for my family and neighbors. I told the robber I only had fifty cents on me and that if he was willing to wait a few minutes, I would give him two dollars. The idiot waited for me to come back. I came back as promised, all right, but I was with my uncle. After the stickup boy noticed I was with Uncle Carlisle, all I could see was his backside and the soles of his tennis shoes. He ran for his life.

After that incident and after thinking about the attack on my uncle, my mind switched to survival mode. I thought it was best to carry a knife to school and the store, but instead, I experimented with hiding large rocks near my school. Like clockwork, a junior high school kid intercepted me after leaving school and demanded my money. I quickly grabbed my hidden rock and told him, "If you come anywhere near me, I will bash your skull in." He walked away.

I told my uncle Carlisle about my skirmish with the would-be robber and that I was trying to decide on the best way to take out future villains. He carefully listened to me. Then he walked me through the worst possible outcomes of carrying a knife and clobbering people over the head with rocks. "Your mother is not raising no little killer!" he said. I agreed. My uncle thwarted my plans to stab young thugs with knives or clobber them over the head with rocks. Thank God for my uncle.

When I thought about my skirmishes and my uncle Johnny's skirmishes with neighborhood villains, I began to realize I had the gift of gab. I also had the skills to deescalate situations. As a result, I was never successfully robbed, attacked, or bullied.

After finishing the fifth grade, my teacher recognized my insatiable appetite for learning, and I was skipped to the seventh grade. I was still only eleven years old. As a fifth grader, I already looked young for my age. My classmates seemed amazed by their baby-faced new classmate. I became affectionately known by my classmates as the Professor. I did not realize it at the time, but they correctly prophesied my future. I would go on to teach at two universities.

I was apprehensive about leaving Louisa May Alcott School's sanctuary and transferring to Lemmel Junior High School, and my concerns were wholly justified. About twenty-five teenage bandits committed robberies and sold drugs openly at school. They also boasted about their crime sprees. I knew that several of them and their younger followers would either commit murder or be murdered themselves. All the kids in my neighborhood wondered how many of us would live through the deadly summer months. One of them, Danny, was killed that summer at the age of eleven. A second kid, Eric, murdered a man when he was fifteen years old.

I initially had problems catching the city bus to school and finding my classes, but I did not experience any difficulties academically. I was happy and living my best life. My mother and I lived at my grandparents' home, which was then the epicenter of social gatherings for our entire family. Because my mother had help from my grandparents, aunts, and uncles, I did not want in any material items.

I wore all the latest fashions—bell-bottoms with my Jack Purcell or Converse tennis shoes. My closet was filled with the most popular pants and blue jeans. In addition, I had an assortment of Lee jeans, Six Pocket Pals, and Screwdriver Six Pocket Pals. If you wore any tennis shoes other than Jack Purcell or Converse, your tennis shoes were referred to as fish heads. If you wore fish heads, you were considered the poorest of the poor, and you were constantly teased.

Like most kids my age, I was obsessed with watching Bruce Lee's kung fu movies and studying karate and kung fu. My dream was to study under Baltimore City karate legend Master Riley Hawkins. Mr. Hawkins was a tenth-degree black belt. However, my goal was never realized. Instead of learning karate in a dojo, I learned karate from two black belts in their homes. It was the homeboy version of the art. To paraphrase Dave Chappelle in *The Nutty Professor*, Reggie studied on the streets! Brother Maurice studied on the streets as well. Their karate and kung fu lessons served me well.

My weekends were always filled with fun and excitement. On Friday nights, I anxiously sat on our porch in 3800 Park Heights Avenue and watched all my aunts, uncles, and cousins pile into my grandparents' house to listen to music, to sing, and to dance. I loved watching my uncle Carlisle's antics. He worked at Whiz Car Wash on Reisterstown Road when the movie *Car Wash* featuring Richard Pryor appeared in movie theaters.

Uncle Carlisle's personality would have been a perfect fit for the film. He was a carefree brother whose pace at work was contingent on the music playing on the car wash's radio. At home, Uncle Carlisle would play the song "I Want to Go Outside in the Rain," grab a can of beer, walk outside, and stand on the median strip in the pouring rain while slowly drinking his beer. He would refuse to come back into the house despite my grandmother's numerous pleas for him to "bring his crazy behind in the house."

Sometimes, it was challenging for my mother to raise me in the forever presence of her siblings. It took a village to raise a child, as other people before me had noted, and that was true. However, each of my extended family members had their own unique teaching style. Sometimes, my mother clashed with my uncle Carlisle and her baby sister, my aunt Sally, over their favorite nephew, yours truly. They each had their way of shaping my behavior.

My aunt Sally talked to me about the importance of keeping my teeth clean. Wearing a gold tooth was a popular fad in Baltimore, and my aunt used that as an incentive to get me to keep my teeth clean. I vigorously brushed and flossed my teeth religiously for three months. One of my junior high school teachers was a dentist who put in gold crowns. I told him my aunt would pay for my gold if he gave her a reasonable price. He quoted me a fee of forty dollars.

When my aunt took me to the dentist to get my gold crown installed, the dentist commented that I had some of the cleanest teeth he had ever seen. My aunt took me back home. When I began talking to my mother at dinner, she dropped her fork and asked me what was on my tooth. I told her Aunt Sally had gotten me a gold crown. I opened my mouth again.

"Look, Mom," I said. "My gold has an *H* for Hicks."

My mom said, "Oh my God . I can't believe she took an eleven-year-old child to get that damn thing in his mouth." She yelled, "Sally, get down here right now!" When my aunt Sally came downstairs, my mother said, "Have you lost your mind? Why would you take my eleven-year-old to get a damn gold tooth in his mouth without my permission? I do not want my child to look like no damn hoodlum! Who in the hell does something like that?"

My aunt said very calmly, "He kept his teeth clean, so that was his reward."

My mother asked which dentist put in my gold crown. When I told her my health teacher installed it, she yelled, "Your teacher did it?"

I said, "Yes, ma'am."

I thought my mother was going to blow another gasket. She was devastated. I was clueless. I had no idea why there was so much fuss. I later learned why my mother was livid about that gold crown.

Soon after my mother accepted she had to see me wearing a gold tooth, my uncle Carlisle added another level of excitement to her life. I was sitting in Uncle Carlisle's car, listening to music with him. I told him I could not wait until I was old enough to drive. Uncle Carlisle had been drinking a little earlier. He turned to me and asked, "Really? Driving is that important to you?"

"Yeah."

"You know what? Here. Take these keys! Get in the driver's seat and go ahead and drive."

"For real?" I exclaimed.

He said, "Yeah, go for it."

I put the car in drive, pulled out of the parking space, drove over the median strip, and stopped. I said, "Oh my God, Uncle, sorry about that."

He said, "No problem. I'll let you try again when you get a little older."

My uncle then calmly told me to put the car in park. He moved over to the driver's seat, and he maneuvered back and forth until he dislodged the vehicle from the median strip. I heard my mother outside yelling, "Carlisle, are you out of your mind, letting my eleven-year-old son drive your damn car?"

To my mother's relief, my aunt Martha had a more conventional way of shaping my behavior. Aunt Martha was a kind, soft-spoken, loving woman whom everyone in the family loved. She was an elementary schoolteacher. She lived in a high-rise apartment in Downtown Baltimore. Aunt Martha had always been my inspiration. She treated me well throughout my life.

When I was still about eleven years old, Aunt Martha asked me a question. She wanted to ascertain if I liked the many acts of kindness she had shown me. I told her I enjoyed all the places she had taken me to and the excellent food she had bought for me. "Good," she replied. "If you want me to keep doing these things, I do not want you to ever use drugs. If you use drugs, I am not going to do anything for you anymore." I believed her with all my heart.

Aunt Martha also explained that alcohol was destroying the lives of all the men in our family. She encouraged me to read about the many ways alcohol could hurt a person. Her stern words resonated with me. The last thing in the world I wanted to do was to have my loving aunt disengage from me.

We loved Sundays because my uncle Johnny and my cousin Roberto would go Super Sunday riding. Back then, we could ride all day on the city bus for about two dollars. We rode everywhere—from the northwest section of Baltimore to Cherry Hill—collecting all kinds of goodies from our relatives along the way. Our favorite stop was Aunt Martha's apartment on the twentieth floor of 222 St. Paul Street. Sometimes, my aunt would let us spend the night. She was always nervous when I spent the night, because she knew I was a notorious sleepwalker.

I loved looking out her windows and watching the activity in Downtown Baltimore. Whenever I looked out of her windows, the theme song from the television series *The Jeffersons* played in my mind. It should have been Aunt Martha's theme song. It always resonated with me, because it adequately described my aunt's ascension from the poverty she experienced in the small town of South Hill, Virginia, to living in a high-rise apartment in Downtown Baltimore, Maryland.

Even as a kid, I was known for going big on all my endeavors. Unfortunately, when I got into trouble, I went big on that as well. Uncle Johnny, my cousin Speedy, and I all developed a curiosity about fire. We enjoyed playing with matches. We would light up old copies of the *Baltimore Sun* tossed in the corner near the trash can, throw them out of the window, and then watch them burn.

One day, we were playing with matches inside my bedroom. I lit up a piece of newspaper just as my grandfather came to check on us. I threw the fiery paper under the bed. My grandfather soon left, but I did not realize the article had not gone out. Soon, I noticed something orange flickering through a hole on the side of the mattress. A fire!

I was too scared to call my grandfather. Instead, I called my uncle Carlisle. I thought he could put out the fire very quickly, but the bed was old with cotton-like material underneath. When Uncle Carlisle flipped the mattress; we saw the bed fully engulfed in flames. My uncle yelled downstairs for my grandmother to call the fire department. My heart sank. I thought *Lord Jesus, please, not the fire department.* Suddenly, I could relate to the line Beaver Cleaver used to say on the show *Leave It to Beaver* whenever he got into serious trouble: "I wish that I was dead." When I saw a fire engine pull up outside the house, I knew I was dead.

I sat on the porch, praying that it would all go away, and I thought about the story in the Bible (John 3:4) when Nicodemus asked Jesus, "How can someone be born when they are old? Surely, they cannot enter a second time into their mother's womb to be born!" Like Nicodemus, I wanted to be born again. I needed a new life in a hurry. Soon, my grandfather came out on the porch. He simply stared at me. He was wearing his standard wifebeater tank top.

Within ten minutes, the fire department extinguished the fire. After the firefighters left, I braced myself for a blow from my grandfather's mighty muscles. I knew it was deserved. Sometimes, the anticipation of a beating was almost as dreadful as the beating itself. I looked up at my grandfather as he stood over me. He said, "You have two choices: either I give you the worst beating of your life or ground you for two weeks."

I said, "Sir, I will take the two weeks."

"Okay," he said. "I don't ever want to see a match in your hand again."

I quickly replied, "Yes, sir!"

I made a wise choice. I was paroled ten days into my sentence.

*****

My neighbor Candy was sitting quietly on her porch and drinking a cold glass of lemonade, watching me sweat profusely while kicking and punching at my perceived invisible opponent. Then the karate expert felt compelled to give me a few pointers. Candy was about nineteen years old and appeared to be a Native American. She held a black belt in karate. She had taken a liking to me. I thought she felt there was something different about me, something unique. I did not know it at the time, but I had an anointing in my life at an early age. I was very enthusiastic about my future.

Candy taught me karate three days a week for free. She convinced her friend Black Manny to teach me karate also. Candy was always exceedingly kind to all the kids in the neighborhood and me. I admired her uncompromising but caring attitude. She was especially good to me. I had a strong desire to reciprocate her kindness. Eventually, the opportunity would present itself.

One thing I understood at the early age of ten was that no one in our neighborhood had confidence in the police. Several members of my family were robbed at gunpoint and had their homes burglarized, yet they never bothered to call the police. In their minds, doing so was useless. The police were long on excuses and short on solutions.

About six months after the hoodlums first occupied the garages across the street, I saw them packing up to leave. I finally had a sense of peace. I thought that perhaps they had gotten a tip that the police were onto them. Whatever the reason was, I was ecstatic they were leaving. That relief would be short-lived, however, as I saw them moving their things two doors down from me and next door to my uncle. *Great,* I thought. *Now, the drug barons are our next-door neighbors.*

They wasted no time embarking on their crime spree. Later that afternoon, I saw the hoodlums carrying a television set out of Candy's house, along with her food and some of her furniture. I stood there in the yard as they cleaned out my good friend's home. Their newest drug-crazed recruit, David, stopped in front of my yard. He pulled up his shirt and showed me his gun. The warning was clear: "If you snitch, you die."

The next day, I saw an emotionally distraught Candy walking toward my house. She told me that someone had broken into her house and had stolen just about everything of value. She asked if I had seen anyone break into her home. I paused for a minute and told her no. I had learned my lesson well on never snitching on anyone for any reason. I felt ashamed of my cowardice. I wished I could put my head in the sand and disappear. To hell with that stupid street code! At that point, I hated the damn code.

I learned a few months later why the hoodlums had selected Candy's home as the first house to hit after they moved down the street. They knew Candy could not afford to call the police because, unbeknownst to me at the time, Candy was allegedly a drug dealer. Candy would be hard-pressed to explain how she had purchased the expensive items the hoodlums had stolen from her house and how she had accumulated the stolen cash.

Some people might have found my naivete about Candy's alleged drug dealing stunning. Most of the drug dealers in my neighborhood were flamboyant, and their activities were transparent. However, the dynamics regarding my interactions with local drug dealers were complicated. The small cadre of drug dealers living near us went to great lengths to hide their illegal activities from me. It was amazing that they cared so much about what I thought of them. I was only a kid. Who cared what I thought? They did.

My grandfather picked up on the change in my demeanor after the burglary at Candy's house. He questioned why I was acting differently. I knew better than to lie to the muscle-bound man; there would be dire consequences if I did not tell the truth. I promptly confessed that David had threatened me with his gun. I immediately regretted the decision when I saw my grandfather dropping bullets into the cylinders of his .38 revolver and slammed the chamber shut. My heart sank as I sat on our porch, watching my grandfather banging on the hoodlums' door as if he was the police. I started to pray.

"God, please look over my grandfather. Do not let any harm come to him. Please do not allow my grandfather to go to jail."

An occupant of the home cautiously opened the door. My grandfather grabbed the hoodlum by the collar and yanked him out of the doorway. My grandfather put his blue steel revolver to the temple of the hoodlum's head. I could not hear what he was whispering to him, but I could tell the hoodlum was repeatedly saying, "Yes, sir. Yes, sir. Yes, sir."

The hoodlums learned the hard way that my quiet grandfather was an OG—an original—gangster. He turned his life around after serving a life sentence for murder. One thing he found intolerable was thugs trying to terrorize me, his grandson. My grandfather was convinced that I would impact the world. No other intervention with the gang of drug-crazed hoodlums was necessary after that. Two years later, all of them met their untimely demise in the same violent manner in which they lived. Problem solved.

I learned that Candy and the hoodlums two doors down the street were not the only people involved in selling drugs. Our next-door neighbors Avery and Wayman, who lived on the first and second floors, paid me to go to the store for them many times. Wayman and I would inevitably collide ten years later when we stood at opposite ends of the law.

Our other neighbor Avery used to pay me to go to the store for him. Once, when I did not see him for about a month, I asked his girlfriend, Wendy, where he was. At first, she told me he was out of town. After another month passed, I asked her again.

Wendy said to me, "You don't know where he is?"

"No."

She said, "You don't know why he drives such a nice car?"

I repeated, "No."

"Don't repeat this," she said. "If Avery knew I told you, he would beat the hell out of me. I promised not to tell. Avery is a big drug dealer."

I was so disappointed. A week later, Avery was back on the scene, looking defeated. He was without his glorious Lincoln Versailles.

The police had seized it. I had never seen Avery distraught before. The next day, I saw Wendy. She was sporting a black eye.

I asked Wendy, "What happened?"

"The same thing that always happens when Avery drinks," she said. "He beats the hell out of me."

At that point, I realized not everything in our neighborhood was what it appeared to be. A few months later, Avery seemed to vanish from the face of the earth. I never saw him again. Perhaps his alleged drug dealing had caught up with him. Wendy moved out, and I never saw either of them again.

*****

When I was in the seventh grade, my mother met a landscaper named Caesar. Caesar made it a point to be very polite to me while he was dating my mother. However, his true character remained unseen. As soon as my mother tied the knot with Caesar, he no longer cared for me. One year later, my mother gave birth to my brother, Caesar Jr.

My brother was Caesar's pride and joy. I thought things would be better. However, Caesar secretly harbored disdain for me. He started on a new campaign of putting me down. He rarely missed an opportunity to offer discouraging remarks. Caesar was a master at it. He explained to my mother in detail why he believed I was retarded. He went on to tell my mother I would never amount to anything. The words resonated in my mind for several years. I began to question my intellectual abilities and my future.

I detested every part of Caesar's existence. He often marched around our apartment bareback, only wearing his blue boxer shorts. He walked around with his fists balled up and his hands in a position as if he was about to draw a weapon. He often stared right through me as he paraded around the house. My nickname for him became Evil Kinevil.

Caesar's motto was simple: "Do not take care of another man's child." He refused to buy me anything, including food. I did not receive anything for any occasion, including birthdays and

Christmases. He was the king who reigned over our household. The king also ordered me to be excluded from family photos.

Two months later, I ran away from home. By nightfall that day, I realized I better find shelter soon. I went to my grandfather's house. My grandfather was on the phone as I walked in. I heard him say to my mother, "I'll call you back." I explained to my grandfather the verbal abuse I suffered while living in the same house as Caesar. My grandfather then picked up the phone and dialed. "That's it, Minny," he said. "He's staying here from now on."

My grandfather sat me down and told me that I had a great heart and a great mind and that I would make a tremendous difference in the world. Tears streamed down my face. I knew this was a turning point in my life. The timing could not have been better. I had long contemplated what I needed to do to get my mother's attention. Now, I felt triumphant. I had cheated death many times. A trip to the corner store or even to the mailbox was always a calculated risk.

My grandparents were reluctant to let me and Uncle Johnny sit out on the porch beyond nightfall for fear that we would be introduced firsthand to a speeding bullet. I was taught essential survival lessons: to never travel alone, to not go to the bathroom in school during class changeovers, and to never snitch on anyone for any reason.

While living with my grandparents, I learned that the identities of most of the suspects committing crimes in our neighborhood were rarely a secret. Their identities were common knowledge. We knew who committed most of the crimes in our community, including murders. It was not uncommon to hear graphic details about a murder in the neighborhood sub shop. No one would dare tell, because that person and their entire family would be in jeopardy.

*****

When I was sixteen, my grandparents, uncle, and I moved to the projects on Billie Holiday Court in East Baltimore. It was considered a luxury resort compared to where my girlfriend Maria lived.

Maria was the pride of the West Side. She was quiet and irresistibly beautiful. Maria appeared to be a mix of Indian, Asian, and black ancestry. She had lovely light skin, an angelic face, coal-black hair, beautiful, full pink lips, and a tiny waist. Her hourglass figure made her the talk of the town.

Maria lived in the Murphy Homes Housing Projects. The locals called it Murder Homes. Each trip to visit Maria came with enormous risks. In retrospect, I had to have been out of my mind as an East Sider to date the West Side beauty. I would never forget the first time I visited Maria at Murphy Homes. I felt the full effect of being in an urban war zone. It was different from where I grew up. Maria lived among some of the most hard-core criminals in the city. I grew up in the northwest section of the city. At least on Park Heights Avenue, criminals were not living together in a fortified structure separated from the rest of the community.

As I drew closer to her building, I noticed what appeared to be the entire population standing on the grounds outside of the building. Police sirens and fire engine sirens were wailing. Flashing blue lights and flashing red lights were reflecting all over the building. Several police cars and ambulances were racing away while others were pulling up. I walked through the chaos, entered Maria's building through the central doorway, and told the security guard I was visiting.

The guard seemed oblivious to the sirens' loud sounds and to the sight of two bleeding men just now exiting a blood-soaked elevator. He recommended that I take the stairs to the fourth floor, stating the elevator would probably be considered a crime scene. I was startled by the buzzing sound of the security door being unlatched by the security guard. It reminded me of the sounds of doors opening and slamming shut in prison movies.

When I finally rang the buzzer on Maria's apartment, Maria's mother answered the door warmly. "You look like you just saw a ghost," she said. I confessed to her that I was alarmed. No one seemed the least bit surprised about all the mayhem going on. I could not imagine walking inside the building with anything resembling a uniform, much less a police uniform.

That evening, we—my grandfather, Uncle Johnny, Cousin Speedy, and I—did what we always did on Wednesday nights. We were glued to the television set, watching our favorite cop show, *Baretta*. We never missed an episode. I always liked Baretta, because Baretta was different from other cops on television. He was a streetwise cop whom everyone admired. Baretta did not hide in the suburbs; he lived right in the community. I liked the fact that people would come directly to his house if they had a problem, and I loved the lyrics to his theme song.

> Don't do the crime if you can't do the time.
> Keep your eye on the sparrow.
> Don't roll the dice if you can't pay the price.

CHAPTER 2

The Few, the Proud, the Marines

We don't promise you a rose garden.
—Former sergeant Charles A. "Sgt. T" Taliano

During the first seventeen years of my life, I was an introvert, and I always looked for the best in people. I believed people were good for the most part. I had an innate desire to challenge myself physically and intellectually. An opportunity to do just that unexpectedly presented itself when my friend Sammy asked me to accompany him to take the Armed Services Vocational Aptitude (ASVAB) Test. I accompanied him to the testing site, but I had no interest in joining the military.

While at the site, the recruiter told me he was glad I wanted to become part of the world's finest fighting force. I explained to him I only came there to keep my friend company. He said, "That's great, son. But while you're here, I want you to take this test." I responded, "Yes, sir," and sat down and took the test. After the test, the recruiter said, "Congratulations, son. You are going to become a United States Marine."

Sammy and I both passed the test. Within two weeks, my mother signed me over to Uncle Sam. I subsequently enrolled in the delayed entry program, which meant I had to report for training immediately after high school graduation. Instead, I was shipped to the infamous Marine Corps Recruit Depot in Parris Island, South

Carolina. Sammy did not enlist in the corps, but I was proud to join the most prestigious branch of the United States military.

On June 22, 1979, I arrived at the Armed Forces Examining and Entrance Station (AFEES) to be processed to enter the Marine Corps. I noticed several lines of young recruits waiting for deployment to basic training. The line for army recruits was practically wrapped around the building. I walked around, trying to find the line for the Marine Corps. When I saw the correct line, only one person was waiting to be deployed to boot camp. Ironically, he did not speak fluent English. I began questioning my decision to join the Marines.

A few minutes later, a recruit from the army line walked over and said, "Hey, man, you got to be crazy to join the Marines. My cousin was in Marine Corps boot camp six months ago. The sergeant had him so stressed out that he killed himself." He went on to say that he had intended to join the Marine Corps too until he received several letters from his cousin.

My indoctrination into the Marine Corps was a rude awakening for my soft-spoken Baltimorean self. I was probably as ignorant as any person could be regarding military customs. I understood nothing about the structure of military rank or military protocols. I realized I would need to receive a lesson quickly to survive the infamous Parris Island. If I had understood the U.S. Marine Corps's resocialization process, I would have been better prepared for what came next.

It was about the break of dawn when the Greyhound bus arrived at the Marine Corps training depot at Parris Island. I was in a deep sleep when I heard the bus door open. Immediately, someone began yelling from the front of the bus. "Get off the bus. Get off the bus!" Whoever he was, he had a distinct Southern accent. "Get off the bus. Get off the bus!" he repeated.

Suddenly, all the recruits on the bus frantically scrambled to get off the bus, all of them at the same time. I hesitated to move forward amid the chaos. Recruits were slamming into one another. It looked like a scene from a Hanna Barbera cartoon. Everyone was going nowhere at the same time. I turned and looked out the win-

THE FEW, THE PROUD, THE MARINES

dow. There stood the stone-faced receiving sergeant. He was a highly dark-skinned black man who stood about six foot three. He looked like he weighed about 170 pounds. He gave me a look of disgust and yelled, "If all of you are not off my bus in thirty seconds, there is going to be hell to pay!"

I patiently waited for most of the recruits in front of me to exit the bus. Then I quickly ran out the door. The sergeant promptly ran over to me and placed his hand on my face, cupping it at a for- ty-five-degree angle. Then he stood there gritting his teeth. It took about ten seconds before words began coming out of his mouth. "So want to buck the system, son?" he ranted. The drill instructor's anger and disdain for me seemed immeasurable. "If you ever defy my orders again, you are going to find yourself in the brig! Get on the yellow footprints with the rest of those maggots."

I looked to my left and saw a series of painted yellow footprints on the ground. I ran over there and stepped on the footprints. The sergeant walked around and looked at the rest of the visibly shaken and bewildered recruits. He began his rant again. "You all are the worst-looking group of maggots I have ever seen on my island." I took a quick peek at the freckled-faced recruit standing to my left. I needed to gauge if I was the only one nervous about my encounter with the receiving sergeant. The recruit was shaking so fiercely that I was afraid he was about to have a heart attack.

The sergeant glimpsed me from out of the corner of his eye. "That is strike number two, scumbag," he said. "Keep your head and eyes to the front. Get inside there and have a seat, scumbags. Do it now, maggots!" We all ran inside the main building of the training depot. I was able to get a quick glimpse at the sign posted above the entrance door: Through These Portals Pass Prospects for the World's Finest Fighting Force.

I wondered whether I came anywhere close to the caliber of person the Marine Corps wanted in their ranks. I was the product of inferior education and a separate and unequal upbringing in the ghetto. I stared into space and reflected on my stepfather's pro- nouncement that I would not make it. I wondered whether his words had spoken my fate into existence.

As we continued through the building, I noticed rows of desks. Each desk had a pencil and a paper. The receiving sergeant directed us to use the stationery to inform our families we arrived safely. "There are only two ways you scumbags can leave my island," he said. "After surviving eleven weeks of training or in a box." My fear was intense. I knew that a drill instructor once marched his entire platoon into a swamp in Parris Island, killing six of them. It was in April of 1956. The Corps had a history of Marines dying in training.

The receiving sergeants directed us to affix the chain to our dog tags. I sat there staring into space, trying to figure out how I could get off the sergeant's shit list. I was close to racking up one infraction per minute. It intensified my nervousness. My hands shook. I struggled with the simple task of getting the chain into the designated slot. I looked up and noticed that all the other recruits had fastened their chains. Their dog tags were already hanging around their necks.

The receiving sergeant looked at me and said, "Somebody help that uncoordinated private with that chain." The term *private* meant I did not have any rank yet or stripes on my uniform. The recruit next to me quickly assembled my chain. The sergeant scanned the room, then said, "Who wants to be the first person to get a haircut?" I quickly looked away. When I turned back around, I saw the sergeant looking directly at me. He pointed at me and shouted, "Michael Jackson, you're up!"

The sergeant grabbed me by my Afro and led me to the barbershop in the next room. He threw me into the chair, then folded his arms across his chest. He stood directly in front of me. He wanted a front-row seat to watch the annihilation of my beloved Afro. The barber glanced at me and smiled. I was perplexed. "How would you like it cut, son?" he asked politely.

I thought for a few seconds, but as I began to speak, I heard the roaring sound of his clippers. By the time I uttered the first syllable, the barber was already handing me a mirror and yelling, "Next!" I slowly glanced in the mirror. I was both astonished and horrified. I was completely bald! I had been transformed quickly into an onion-headed recruit.

I walked back into the main room. I heard the long-haired and bearded recruits gasp as I entered. My official indoctrination into the Marine Corps had begun. Life would be different now. I was no longer an individual. My fellow recruits now began their road to becoming onion-headed recruits like me. Within the hour, we also turned over all our slimy civilian clothing and personal effects. We would not have anything resembling our former lives until it was time to leave the island.

After receiving our haircuts, the receiving sergeants directed us to a bathroom to shave. I had never used a razor blade before, so I took a moment to observe another recruit insert his razor head into his razor blade holder and begin to shave. I followed his lead. I inserted my blade and began to shave. About three minutes later, I glanced over at the recruit. When I first saw him, he had looked like an actor playing a role in a horror movie. Now he had the strangest look on his face. He stood there holding his razor blade while blood gushed down both sides of his face.

Just then, the receiving sergeant walked into the bathroom and looked at the bloody-faced recruit. The sergeant did not seem to be the least bit surprised or the least bit alarmed at the sight of the bloody-faced recruit. He simply got right up in the recruit's face and said, "The next time you decide to kill yourself, cut your dirty wrist first." I wondered if the recruit had escaped from an insane asylum.

Day one passed; we did not get any sleep. Day two passed, and we did not sleep. It would be three days before I would get any sleep. I would never forget how my exhausted body felt after lying on the mattress on the top bunk of my bunk bed. I had been fantasizing about how it would feel to sleep finally.

The sergeant had given us strict orders not to talk. He made it clear there would be dire consequences for violating his order. I closed my eyes while my fatigued body rested on the mattress. I heard a faint whisper coming from a bunk about three beds down.

"Shut up!" one recruit yelled to another.

Another recruit said, "Shh!"

The sergeant entered the room. "Say your Marine Corps prayers. Please repeat after me. Though I walk through the shadow of the valley of death, I have no fear, because I am the biggest and worst motherfucker in the valley!"

One recruit uttered, "Good night, sir."

The drill instructor yelled, "Shut up!"

Within twenty minutes, I drifted into an almost comatose sleep. The lights came on, followed by the sounds of trash cans thrown against the wall. I heard repeated commands coming from all four of our drill instructors: "Get out of the rack! Get out of the rack! Get out of the rack!" We got dressed. The sergeant then yelled, "Get undressed. Get undressed!"

After eight rounds of getting dressed and undressed, we were covered with sweat. The drill instructor said, "Had enough yet, Privates? Recruits, prepare to mount."

We all repeated, "Prepare to mount, sir."

The drill instructor yelled, "Ready, mount!"

We all lunged into our bunks.

*****

While my platoon was in the squad bay, the receiving sergeant rounded us up to prepare to march over to the chow hall to eat. The sergeant herded our sluggish, pathetic-looking platoon to the chow hall. My attention turned to a platoon of seasoned recruits to my left. Their higher status was immediately apparent. They each wore the entire Marine Corps uniform. We were allowed to wear only white T-shirts, camouflage pants, and unbloused combat boots at that stage of our training. The other recruits also sported haircuts that allowed some short hair to remain uncut on the top of their head. They were phase three privates approaching the end of their training.

We watched as the third-phase privates marched past our platoon in unison while stepping in total perfection. In his military cadence, the drill instructor sang, "Lefty right, lefty right left of, low r0dido, lefty right, a left…"

My eyes gravitated to Goliath, a stone-faced, six-foot-five Somalian Drill Instructor (DI). He possessed a perfectly chiseled military body. He was a giant! His biceps were so large; they burst through the sleeves of his shirt. His uniform was perfectly starched. His skin was clean, smooth, and unblemished. He sported a black belt over his uniform, signifying he was not any mere drill instructor; he was a senior drill instructor. That meant he supervised all the other drill instructors. I was mesmerized by his presence. It was as if God had created a perfect military warrior.

Eventually, Goliath glimpsed me looking at him. "Platoon, halt!" he yelled. He waited a few seconds for our platoon to catch up with his stalled platoon. Then he paused again until I passed him, at which point, he yelled, "Get your eyeballs off me!" I thought, *Oh, crap, I am busted again for screwing up.* I quickly looked forward, hoping my drill instructor had not seen where Goliath had pointed, but my drill instructor pointed at me and held three fingers up. It was strike three. I was totally screwed.

We arrived at the chow hall at about 0700 hours. The drill instructor gave us instructions regarding how to conduct ourselves in the chow hall. He said, "No talking. Head and eyes remain to the front." The drill instructor told us to sit with our feet at a for-ty-five-degree angle. I found it challenging to continue looking straight ahead at the bald-headed recruit standing in front of me. Horrific-looking bumps and bruises marked the back of his head.

I knew the drill instructors were directly behind us. However, there were seventy-four recruits in our platoon. I figured the chance of my drill instructor seeing me was slim. I glanced over to see what the recruits in the other platoons who were already sitting down were eating. When I turned back around, the drill instructor was standing right beside me. "I want you to find the ugliest spot on the head of the recruit standing in front of you, and you make love to it!" he said. That was strike number three. I focused again on the bumps and bruises on the head of the recruit in front of me.

By the time I made my way through the chow line, my ner-vousness had subsided. Finally, I felt comfortable enough to engage some of my lunch companions in conversation. First, I asked each recruit where home was. Then I drifted back to my natural habitat. My elbows were on the table, and my feet were placed as I typically put them when I ate. I was surprised by the silence around the table. I glanced up. The drill instructor was standing behind me.

"What is your name, son?" he asked.

I quickly stood up and extended my hand, suggesting a handshake. "Maurice R. Hicks, sir," I said.

No sooner had those words left my mouth than the drill instructor yelled, "Shut your nasty mouth! I don't want to hear your nasty little civilian name. Your first name is Private, you idiot! I cannot wait for you to get your physical, son. Every time I think about this incident, you are going to pay. You're going to become one of my classroom privates. I am going to teach you a lesson!"

It was about 2100 hours when the drill instructor instructed us to line up for a hygiene inspection. As the drill instructor faced us and walked down the line, he stopped in front of the recruit standing next to me. Private Willie Wegman was an eighteen-year-old white man who resembled Leonard in the movie *Full Metal Jacket*.

The drill instructor looked at Willie's stomach and said, "You look disgusting! Suck it in. I don't want to see it!" Willie tried sucking in his sixty-pound stomach to no avail. The drill instructor watched as he struggled. Willie looked at me as if I could help him make his large stomach disappear. He seemed so desperate that I wished I could.

The drill instructor finally said, "Have you lived at Burger King all your life, son?"

Wegman replied with a quick, loud, decisive answer: "Yes, sir!"

*****

The following day, the drill instructor Sergeant Hawk told us to line up in formation. It was the middle of June 1979. I was standing at attention on the infamous Parris Island. I barely managed to maintain consciousness. The relentless heat and humidity of the South Carolina sun were bearing down on me. I tried my best to divert my thoughts and reflect on happier times. A swarm of sand fleas wreaked havoc on my face. They bit the tip of my nose. A few buzzed around my eyelids. Other fleas bit the sides of my face. I struggled to stand still.

The stone-faced Drill Instructor (DI) stood directly before me, watching my every move. The brim of his brown Stetson rested lightly on my forehead. It sported a Marine Corps emblem. The drill instructor dared me to disrupt his beloved sand fleas as they helped themselves to every part of my face. I kept trying my best to stay off his radar. He had made it crystal clear that he would do his best to prevent a "slimy and infectious city slicker" like me from joining the ranks of his beloved corps. Unfortunately, my gold tooth had given me away. He knew that most of the gold-tooth-wearing recruits were from either Baltimore or New York.

Sergeant Hawk looked like a live skeleton. His face was horrifying. He was a twenty-three-year-old white man who looked about thirty-three years old. He was six foot three and weighed about 175 pounds. After letting the brim of his hat linger against my face for what he deemed an appropriate amount of time, Sergeant Hawk stepped to the side and began staring down at the recruit next to me. Sergeant McNair, an African American drill instructor, took his place. McNair made it his mission to break down the gold-tooth-wearing native Baltimorean whom Sergeant Hawk had just left.

The urge to rid myself of the pesky insects was overwhelming, but I knew there would be dire consequences for breaking the position of being at attention. The situation seemed surreal. The swampland was like a foreign country to me. I had never traveled anywhere outside of the city of Baltimore. The DI was enjoying every second of my suffering. However, watching the demise of my face was not gratifying enough. He tormented me further.

The DI smiled at me and asked, "How are you feeling today, Private?"

"Sir, the private is being bitten all over his face by sand fleas, sir!"

The drill instructor replied, "Well, Private, you had your dinner today, didn't you?"

I replied, "Yes, sir."

The drill instructor replied, "Well, let him have his!"

He was referring to the sand fleas.

Just then, I heard the unmistakable sound of someone slapping himself on the face and head. The very muscular recruit from Philadelphia standing behind me went on a flea-swatting frenzy. The drill instructor yelled at the recruit, "You just killed your whole platoon. Everybody, lie on the ground. You are all dead." The DI then grabbed the recruit, pulling him out of formation. "Private," he yelled, "you better find every flea that you murdered and give them a decent burial." The recruit returned to the position he was standing in and began searching the ground for fleas.

The drill instructor explained that if we were in the jungle, we would have all been dead in someplace like Vietnam because one undisciplined Marine had chosen to be an individual. He went on to say that the recruit had chosen his comfort over the life of his entire platoon. Something clicked in my head. I knew then that there was a method to the madness. It started making more sense to me. It was day three of eleven weeks of hell.

After the Philadelphia recruit buried his sand fleas, he stood up and resumed the position of being at attention and looked at Sergeant Hawk with displeasure. Sergeant McNair caught a glimpse of the Philadelphia recruit's expression and immediately got in the recruit's face.

The sergeant said to the Philadelphia recruit, "Say, son, you said you used to be a boxer?"

"Yes, sir," the recruit replied.

"Tell me the names of some of the people that you whipped, son."

The recruit began naming names, but he was abruptly interrupted by Sergeant McNair.

"Shut up. You couldn't bust a grape!" the sergeant yelled. "You couldn't bust your way out of a paper bag!" He continued. "You look like you want to fight Sergeant Hawk. Let me tell you something, son. If you're going to fight Sergeant Hawk, you better have a black belt."

Sergeant McNair walked a few steps away, then turned back around with a facing movement, looked at the recruit, and said,

"Make that a black belt third degree." Then he asked, "Why do all you bald, bullet-headed recruits from Philly think you can box? I'm watching you, son. You understand that?"

The recruit quickly replied, "Yes, sir!"

All the Philly recruits were African Americans, and Sergeant Hawk sensed that they felt singled out because of that. However, he was kind enough to assure them that wasn't why he was so hard on them. "I want you to know something," he said. "I am not prejudiced. I hate all recruits!"

I genuinely believed Sergeant Hawk was, in fact, an equal opportunity harasser. He saw us all as unmolded green slime, and he had to mold us into United States Marines in a short time. The seclusion, the heat, the humidity, and the sand fleas differentiated us from the Hollywood Marines trained in the gentle climate of San Diego, California. The recruit training depot in California sat right next to the airport.

After Sergeant McNair directed the platoon back into formation, he walked back over to me and asked, "You think you are going back on the block wearing my precious Marine Corps uniform?" He could sense I wanted it in the worst way. I began to daydream momentarily. I fantasized about what it would be like to graduate from boot camp and become a part of a tradition of highly motivated men who significantly made an impact on history. I needed a boost to my self-esteem. I thought of the sense of pride it would bring to my life.

Sergeant McNair's head turned slowly toward me like a radar honing in on an incoming plane. It was almost as if he had read my mind. He got directly in my face again. "Forget it, son. You are never going to make it. I am going to make sure it never happens to you. I can see you're not cut out for this, son. Why don't you just quit now, son? You can go back home and not miss a beat. You can be back on the block and hang out with your daddy and your little hoodlum friends," he said.

Sergeant McNair got further up in my face. "What in the hell is that in your mouth, son?"

I explained I did not understand what he was referring to.

"I just saw a glare," he said.

I responded, "That is my gold crown, sir. It has my initial, *H*, on it for Hicks."

Sergeant McNair said, "Shut your nasty mouth. I don't like it! Every time I look at you, I see a glare. I ought to take a pair of pliers and yank that damn thing out of your mouth."

I glanced at him for a moment to see whether he was serious about getting the pliers.

"Get your eyeballs off me!" he yelled.

Looking at him was an enormous insult to him. After all, I was twenty thousand leagues beneath him, just a damn slimy recruit.

It was vital for me to correct the record regarding my father. "No, sir," I replied. "The private never knew his father, sir."

He looked at me with a very analytical eye. "That figures, son," he replied. "Poor Private Hicks. So that's the excuse you are going to use to drop out of my beloved corps."

With enormous conviction, I quickly yelled, "No, sir! Never, sir!"

He looked astonished. It was clear my answer had taken him by surprise. He began to walk away but then turned and looked back at me. He smiled, then sarcastically said, "We are going to see about that, son."

Sergeant McNair's words made me reflect on my stepfather's declaration that I would never amount to anything and that I would never make it in the Marines. That same day, I swore to myself I would become a United States Marine even if it killed me. Both Sergeant McNair and my stepfather said I could not become a Marine; in truth, they now inspired me to become one at any cost. I had already survived living in the jungles of the inner city. I was determined to survive the wrath of Sergeant McNair.

True to my word, after eleven weeks of holy hell, I stood on the parade deck at Parris Island, a man forever changed. That day, I earned the title of United States Marine. I expressed my eternal gratitude to my four heroes: my Marine Corps drill instructors. They instilled in me a sense of pride and integrity as well as mental and physical toughness.

My transformation would last forever. Although I never saw combat, I acquired a lethal combination of spiritual and military training. I was now a force to be reckoned with. I learned I could set my mind to accomplish anything on the planet. Through the grace of God, I developed the mental toughness to bear any burden. I had no idea of the challenges that lay ahead.

The Marine Corps was an expert at carving out prejudice and discrimination. They knew how to break you down and build you back up to their standards. The Marine Corps was a very traditional organization. The organization's customs instilled a lifelong sense of pride and camaraderie not seen in other organizations.

The saying, "Once a Marine, always a Marine," rang true. Wikipedia described the Marine Corps as an organization that honored courage and commitment. The warrior ethos guided Marines through difficult ethical situations and acts as a reminder to provide good order and discipline. I certainly agreed with that depiction of the Marine Corps.

The most important skills I learned in the Marine Corps were adapting to and overcoming any situation, even the most challenging circumstances. In those days, police agencies were inept at ferreting out prejudice and discrimination. The skills I learned in the Marine Corps allowed me to address the biases I encountered in two police agencies maturely and effectively. I sorely needed those skills. Although I did not know it at the time, I was about to enter one of the country's most divided professions.

CHAPTER 3

COMING HOME

"Today you people are no longer maggots. Today
you are Marines. You're part of a brotherhood."
—Gunnery Sergeant Hartman, *Full Metal Jacket*

I exited the Greyhound bus station in Downtown Baltimore
wearing my Marine Corps uniform. It felt good to be back home. A
man pointed at me. I walked closer and noticed he was one of my
newspaper patrons from Pantry Pride in Mondawmin Mall.

He yelled, "Oh my God, is that you, paperboy?"

I replied, "Yes, sir."

He smiled and said, "Man, I knew that you would make it! I am
so proud of you, son."

As always, he provided me with some words of encouragement.
No matter what uniform I wore, my patrons would always refer to
me as either the paperboy or the bag boy. That was a good thing. It
kept me humble.

It was time to bring positive change to the lives of the constitu-
ents in my genealogy. Most of the brilliant and incredibly gifted men
in my family suffered from alcoholism. I watched their lives and their
careers plummet as the long-lasting effects of alcohol took their toll.

I remember intensely watching my uncle for several days as he
desperately struggled to obtain the last drop of Kamchatka vodka

from the corner of his liquor bottle. Despite his relentless efforts, Uncle Roberto concluded it was impossible.

Despite my uncles' struggles with alcoholism, they helped shape my life in very positive ways. I thanked God for all my uncles. Even through their bouts with alcoholism, they never gave up on encouraging me to strive to be the best I could be.

It was hard for me to say which uncle was my favorite. All my uncles played a distinct role in my life. Uncle Carlisle was my protector. Uncle Jay was my life coach. Uncle Johnny was my antagonist, but his role changed in the last years of his life. Finally, Uncle Roberto was my teacher.

Uncle Johnny and I grew up in the same household. We also attended elementary school, junior high, and high school together. He was just one and a half years older than me. My uncle Johnny developed a deeply rooted, subliminal hatred toward me. His disdain for me stemmed from the way people responded to us when we were children. I was light-skinned. He was dark-skinned.

Just about everyone who saw me and my uncle sitting on the steps together seemed excited to see me. They often told my mother and grandmother I was a handsome little boy. They never seemed to compliment my uncle. I believed their actions had a long-lasting effect on Uncle Johnny's self-esteem. Their actions also stirred up anger in my grandmother. She directed her frustrations toward me. She started calling me little red nigger. I did not realize my house was merely a microcosm of society. I learned there was a difference between the way light-skinned people and dark-skinned people were treated.

When we became teenagers, Uncle Johnny started rebelling. Once the realization that his inability to shed his dark skin prevented him from being accepted by society escalated, he began drinking alcohol, getting suspended from school, and committing minor crimes. He also started using drugs. His father, my grandfather, was a disciplinarian. He beat the hell out of my uncle to intervene in my uncle's rebellion. My aunts pleaded with my grandfather not to strike my uncle. Eventually, my grandfather relented but told my aunts cutting back on discipline was a big mistake.

Uncle Johnny was the baby of the family. I believed the dynamic played a significant role in his upbringing. My aunts and uncles were protective of him, because he was their baby brother. Uncle Johnny wanted to see me, his perceived pretty boy nephew, fail, and he knew the perfect vehicle to facilitate my demise: illegal drugs.

Soon after I returned home, Johnny started his campaign to convince me to use drugs. He asked me to smoke marijuana with him. I refused. Initially, he accepted my refusal. When he continued to ask me to smoke marijuana, I realized he had a more sinister rationale for continuing his campaign. He wanted me to fall prey to drug addiction so he could broadcast the information for all to hear: "Maurice is not perfect." Sometimes, he would practically beg me to use marijuana.

My uncle would say, "Please do this for me. I finally dropped the F-bomb." F for you!" I would reply.

My decision not to use drugs and Uncle Johnny's decision to use drugs changed the course of both of our lives. My uncle became a functioning alcoholic and a functioning drug addict. My uncle's drug abuse escalated from marijuana to cocaine, then to heroin, then to pills. Every holiday, my grandfather would call the house from work and tell me, "Put that Negro on the phone." When Uncle Johnny picked up the phone, my grandfather always told him the same thing: "Boy, don't be acting up tonight. I do not want to have to shoot you in the morning!" My uncle's answer was always the same: "Yes, sir!"

Regardless of my uncle's drug use, he was the most lively and fun person you could ever meet. He also had an excellent vocabulary. He was the only person I knew who had twenty places in the city where he could crash, because everyone liked to be around him. If my money was low, I would be pressed to find one or two people willing to allow me to stay with them. Not my uncle. He built about fifty bridges he crossed when he needed a place to crash. Unfortunately, after much effort, he eventually burned every one of those bridges.

I was only the second person in my family line to serve in the military, and I was only the second male in my entire generation to graduate from high school. I was proud of my four-foot-eleven great-uncle Woody. He weighed about 130 pounds. Uncle Woody was a career infantry Marine. He engaged in numerous intense battles in Korea, which included hand-to-hand combat. Uncle Woody also saw action in Vietnam. But what impressed me the most about him was, he was a quiet and humble man. He demonstrated to me that it was okay to be a silent but intense warrior.

After Marine Corps recruit training, I was sent to Camp Lejeune, North Carolina, where I trained for my military occupational specialty. I graduated at the top of my class which earned me a meritorious promotion to the rank of Lance Corporal (E-3).

After leaving Camp Lejeune, I enrolled in college. No male in my family had ever gone to college. If I graduated from college, I would be the first man in my family to obtain a college degree. I worked three part-time jobs during my first semester in college. I took three buses to school, three buses from school to work, and three buses from work back home. My grandfather took notice. "Slow down, son," he said to me. "You're not a locomotive, and some of them break down.

The racially charged environment at the University of Maryland, Baltimore County (UMBC) added stress. Every time I sat down to eat lunch with white students, they would stand up, pick up their food trays, and move to another table. I initially thought their actions were a coincidence; however, after the same thing occurred a couple of times, I realized they did not want to sit at the same table as me because I was black. At that time, only a handful of blacks attended the school.

But my classmates' actions were nothing compared to what I experienced while taking night classes. While waiting for the bus just outside the campus, occupants of vehicles passing by would all yell, "Nigger!" These sentiments came from senior citizens and young children as well. I also recalled one of my UMBC professors talking with students in my class after class. He answered their questions with no problem. However, when I asked him a question about a book he assigned us and I pointed to the paragraph stating the book's principal concept, he slammed the book on my finger and told me to study. I heard another professor telling his class whites were the superior race.

After my first semester, despite being put on academic probation, I continued to work three part-time jobs and did not heed my grandfather's advice to slow down. After the second semester, I failed to raise my GPA. Then came the devastating news. I received a letter from the university indicating I was dismissed.

My free fall from grace was rapid and extremely painful. I was the pride of my family. Everyone had high hopes for me. I had skipped a grade in school. As a child, I lived in the library. As a kid, I could frequently be found sitting on the porch with my head buried inside my uncle's *World Book* encyclopedias. I felt as if I disappointed my family and my entire neighborhood. I had big dreams of becoming a corporate executive and running a multimillion-dollar corporation. Now those dreams seemed forever shattered. I was lost and perplexed as to what God had in store for me.

I humbled myself and enrolled in the Community College of Baltimore. Enrolling in a community college proved to be another defining moment in my life. This stage of my education occurred in a very nurturing environment, one in which my professors gave me enormous hope, support, and encouragement. They got to know me personally. They told me that I had a great mind and that I would do extraordinary things. My management professor was a management guru who encouraged me to be the best manager I could be. I became a man on a mission.

I would get to school many days as the doors opened at five o'clock in the morning. I excelled in academics, earning awards as both a distinguished scholar and a meritorious scholar. I finally got my groove back. Most importantly, I learned the importance of humility.

CHAPTER 4

THE BALTIMORE CITY POLICE ACADEMY

I whizzed down Interstate 83 toward the Baltimore City Police Academy. I was enjoying the fantastic summer day. I proudly rested my arm lightly out the window, displaying the Baltimore Police Department patch on my white uniform shirt. It was June of 1983, and it was my first day of training. I was wearing the official police shirt, badge, and hat. However, I did not carry a firearm, nor did I wear the traditional blue pants. Instead, I wore my standard-issued beige khaki pants. The pants differentiated me from the real police.

I parked my baby-blue Ford Escort near the post office on Fayette Street. The street ran along one side of the infamous Lafayette Court. As I exited my car, I saw a group of men looking at me and shaking their heads. Finally, one yelled, "Rookie!" I continued on my journey. I looked up at the shiny gold-colored headquarters building, took a deep breath, and began hustling up the nine flights of stairs to reach the police training academy. I clenched my police-issued hard black plastic briefcase full of textbooks and took a minute to catch my breath as I reached the ninth floor.

Police recruits were prohibited from using the elevator because of one incident a few years earlier. A group of recruits boarded the elevator with an old white man in his sixties. During the elevator ride, the recruits talked about the jerk instructors in the police academy. The recruits exited the elevator feeling good about having released their frustration. Unfortunately for them, about thirty minutes later, the training division director received a call from the recruits' elevator partner—namely, the police commissioner. From that point forward, all recruits were punished for their predecessors' sins. Recruits could no longer use the elevator to get to the ninth floor.

I sat in my seat in the classroom at the police academy, waiting for our class adviser to walk in. I was elated that the police department was paying me to get an education and to work out. The academy gave me a chance to put my military training to use.

I scanned the room. There was a good mixture of recruits— blacks, whites, men, and women. Soon, a white man about thirty years old walked into the classroom and yelled, "Why are you just sitting there? Get on your feet!" We all jumped to our feet. The officer started laughing. "That was good. I'm a recruit just like you," he said after regaining his composure. He quickly vanished from the classroom.

Our class adviser walked in thirty seconds later. His name was Police Agent Betterment, a very soft-spoken man, much like myself. He was about fifty years old, six foot two, and fit—amazingly fit. Police Agent Betterment was a former Green Beret. He was a very well-educated, humble guy. He was nothing like what I expected. Most of the Baltimore police officers I saw were obese, sloppy, and unprofessional. I realized the Baltimore PD had a lot more to offer than I imagined.

After providing a brief overview of what he expected of us in the academy, he told us about an incident that changed his life. He arrested someone for robbery, he said. The suspect was convicted and sent to jail. While the suspect was supposed to be serving time, Agent Betterment saw him walking the street. Knowing he was still considered to be in prison, Agent Betterment approached the suspect, then placed the escapee against the wall and patted him down for weapons.

Unfortunately, the suspect, a well-buffed, muscular black man in his twenties, was determined not to return to jail. The escapee springboarded off the wall and wrestled Agent Betterment to the ground within a few seconds. He then began pulling on the grip of the agent's service revolver, trying to remove the gun from the agent's holster.

At that point, Agent Betterment told us his greatest fear was not getting shot. Instead, he was more concerned about the enormous amount of paperwork he would have to fill out to explain how he lost control of his weapon. The escapee shot the agent. He, however, was eventually arrested.

I extracted two powerful lessons from Agent's Betterment encounter: If street hoodlums were strong and skilled enough to get the drop on a former special forces commando, I needed to raise my fitness level to an even higher level. Also, the job of a police officer required an overwhelming amount of paperwork.

During our last week at the police academy, my fellow recruits and I watched several videos showing reenactments of fatal police shootings. I distinctly recalled several of the police shootings that occurred in Riverside, California. After watching the last video, our instructor asked us a critical question: "Do you still want this job?" I scanned the room. Some of the recruits seemed deep in thought, including a neighbor of mine who lived across the street.

The day after we graduated, my neighbor resigned. She did not want to do one day on the streets. Her immediate departure after training was not unusual. A fellow Marine quit immediately after graduation too. Our instructor told us an officer quit after clearing his first call on the streets for a man armed with a gun. He handed his badge, gun, and gun belt to the desk sergeant and told him he quit.

Another officer watched his partner being brutally attacked. She ran back to their police cruiser and locked herself in the car. She was so petrified she did not have the presence of mind to call for help. It was another important lesson I learned: Some police officers were cowards. They worked under the false assumption that their authority as a police officer shielded them from danger. They were wrong.

CHAPTER 5

FIELD TRAINING

I graduated from the police academy excelling in athletics and academics. I was fourth in my class, missing the number three spot by one-tenth of a point. After graduating from the academy, I was assigned to a field training officer (FTO). In those days, a recruit initially trained for the field during their twenty-fifth week of training before they graduated. Thus, in our twenty-sixth (and final) week of training, we spent the entire week learning about drugs.

My training officer was a ten-year veteran of the police force. The first time my sergeant introduced me to him, he looked me up and down. Then he stared. Then he frowned. After roll call, he walked toward his car. Then he stopped and finally began talking to me.

"Tell me something, rookie," he said. His disgust for me was no longer masked. "Do you have any college?"

I excitedly replied, "Yes, sir." I thought that meant we had something in common. I was wrong.

He pointed his finger in my face. "Let me tell you something, you stupid rookie," my training officer said. "Don't you ever tell me how to handle my damn calls. I had a punk like you here once before. He tried to tell me how to handle my calls, and I nearly decked the little bastard. Then the bastard went back to the academy and told them all we did all day was eat free food and watch movies. That bastard brought down a lot of heat on us. But I tell you, it's not going

to happen to me again. I told them I do not want any more fuckin'
rookies, but every time I turn around, they send me another one!"

I considered his delusional statements. He believed his police
badge gave him power over me, that I was his dominion. He did not
realize that if the average brother on the streets chose to, he could
pulverize him. I was no different. However, like animals in the jungle, my training officer figured he could bluff his way out of a confrontation if he displayed enough aggression.

Instead of immediately going out on patrol, he immediately
drove to a little diner in Downtown Baltimore. Four more officers
met us there.

"Who the fuck is he?" one of the officers asked. "Haven't you
learned your lesson yet?"

"He's probably with IID," another officer said. He meant the
Internal Investigation Division.

"Come on, man. You should have left the dumb rookie in the
car," a third officer said.

"Hell no, man," my field training officer (FTO) replied. "It
would be my luck somebody would commit a robbery right in front
of the little bastard and then have him go back to the academy and
tell them he should never have been left alone."

The fourth officer said, "What are you going to do about that
rat bastard that dimed us all out to the academy?"

My FTO replied that he had put the word out on him in his
new police district.

The officer frowned. "That isn't enough, man!"

A K-9 officer who had joined our group at the diner spoke up.
"I'll tell you what I'm going to do. I'm going to 10-11. And when he
comes, I'm going to sic my dog on him."

"Are you serious?" my FTO replied.

"I'll just say the dog got away from me," the K-9 officer said,
making it clear he was dead serious.

At that point, I wondered why the department assigned me to
a bunch of psychotic cops.

*****

65

After roll call the next day, my FTO and I walked proudly out of Downtown Baltimore's police station. I was wearing my freshly starched white Baltimore City police uniform shirt with military creases in the front and back, my blue uniform pants, my black chlorofram shoes, and my blue police uniform hat with the shiny silver numbers 884 on top. I was also sporting my fresh Marine Corps haircut.

A traffic accident had occurred near that station. My training officer instructed me to direct traffic around the action. As I directed traffic, two of my customers from my days as a paperboy at Pantry Pride in Mondawmin Mall leaned out of their car windows and yelled, "Oh my God, that's the paperboy! Hey, paperboy, how are you doing?" The crowd turned toward all of us and looked at me. The driver then said, "Hey, paperboy, I knew you would make it!"

I held traffic for a second, walked across the street, and gave both of my old customers—an old lady and her daughter—a hug. The old lady told me that she prayed for me when I joined the Marines and that she would continue to pray for me now that she knew I was an officer. I was so thankful for people like them who had given me so much encouragement during an exceedingly difficult time. It was humbling—and a bit embarrassing.

My field training officer and I drove to a local café for lunch later that day. I was sitting down, enjoying my lunch, when four patrons walked in. One of them looked at me for a few seconds. He then walked closer and looked back at his friend. Then he yelled, "Oh my God, it's the paperboy!" His three companions walked over to our table. One of them, a lady, said, "We knew you would make it, son." I stood up and shook their hands, then thanked them. I looked around and noticed everyone in the café had their eyes on me.

One of my three former customers said to the person who initially greeted me, "I thought he was the paper boy from Pantry Pride."

"Yes," one of the customers said. "That was before he got promoted to bag boy."

I smiled. "I got promoted to cashier before I left," I said.

"Oh God, son," the woman replied, "you are truly blessed."

Their comments were encouraging. They had seen something in me, even as a paperboy. No matter where I went, it seemed people remembered me either as the bag boy or the paperboy. I believed God placed them in my life to encourage me and to keep me humble, so I decided it was best to embrace their remembrances of me as their beloved paperboy and bag boy. They were people God had selected to shape and mold me. They provided me with valuable lessons that lasted me a lifetime.

As I sat back down, I watched the three old police dinosaurs sipping their coffees.

"The department is picking the cream of the crop these days," one of the officers said. "Out of all the people they could have hired, they chose a damn paperboy."

Another officer quickly interjected. "Don't forget, he was promoted to bag boy."

I smiled and finished my lunch. I felt good. I had made it far. Then I reflected on how the dinosaurs were treating me. I recalled a scripture my grandfather once shared with me regarding how to deal with arrogant people. I reflected on Romans 12:3, which said, "By the grace given me, I say to every one of you: Do not think of yourself more highly than you ought, but rather think of yourself with sober judgment, in accordance with the faith God has distributed to each of you." The three police dinosaurs did not know—or did not care about—the Scriptures.

About twenty minutes later, my FTO and I drove through the alleys of Downtown Baltimore. At one point, I saw three silhouettes of men standing in an alley about four streets ahead of our police car. Two of the men were facing the third man. I pointed them out to my training officer. He started to drive in their direction. However, our path was momentarily blocked by cars proceeding down Baltimore Street. Finally, we emerged from the traffic with a good view of the first two men. The third man was clearly in distress. He was yelling for help. My training officer brought his marked tiny AMC Concord police vehicle to a slow stop and directed me to head down the alley.

As the silhouettes of the three men in the dark alley came into focus, I noticed one of them had a shiny object in his hand. Next came a gut-wrenching scream followed by the thud of a lifeless body falling to the ground. As soon as my training officer stopped our tiny AMC Concord, I soared down the glass-filled alley like a leopard. I was breathing through my nose like I was in a track competition. I was in hot pursuit, and failure was not an option.

The echoes of glass breaking beneath the soles of my uniform shoes caused the men to look up. The assailants noticed my white uniform shirt. They ran off and quickly disappeared into the abyss of the dark alley. I reverted to my training by stopping to render aid to the victim. My field training officer yelled, "Go after them right now, rookie!"

The darkness of the alley quickly engulfed me as I raced to catch up with the two assailants. The silence in the alleyway gave way to the sound of a man's labored breath. I closed one eye to help see in the darkness of night. Then finally, the silhouette of a man appeared before me. I pulled my gun up to eye level and took perfect aim in the direction of the sound of labored breathing. It was two against one. The odds were not in my favor.

I was nervous, wondering if I would have to use my gun on my first day. Slowly, one man came out of the shadows. I directed him to walk back to the sound of my voice. I told him to walk back toward the scene where I witnessed the stabbing. He immediately claimed innocence. He asked what was going on. He assured me he was going to cooperate. He claimed he was eager to help me resolve whatever was happening. I partly believed him.

I walked the man about half a block. Several officers were already on the scene. I ordered the man to put his hands on the police car. I began patting him down for weapons. He immediately started playing the race card. He told me how he was glad I stopped him instead of one of those racist white cops. I searched him from the top of his shoulders to his ankles.

After being satisfied he did not have a weapon, I handcuffed him and brought him over to my FTO, who told me the victim positively identified my suspect as the person who had robbed and stabbed him. My training officer asked me whether I combed him. I assured him I had. As I handed the suspect over to the police van driver for transport to the station, the suspect looked at me and said, "Man, this is wrong. I was walking home from work."

I diverted my attention to the ambulance pulling away with the stabbing victim. My training officer told me another officer had caught the second suspect. He then looked at me deliberately. I was happy that I survived my first day on the street. "Not a bad first day," he said. "You collared a felony robbery suspect your first day on the job."

We walked back to our car and headed to the police station to process the robbery suspects. As we walked into the station, the wagon man motioned to my training officer. My training officer began talking to him and told me to wait outside by the car. I waited for about fifteen minutes. Then my training officer walked up to me slowly and quietly asked me whether I had combed the suspect.

"Yes, sir," I replied.

"Okay," he said. He walked behind me, grabbed me by the neck, and put a knife to my throat. "What the fuck is this?" he yelled.

I did not know how the veteran intended to handle the situation.

"This is the fuckin' knife that fuckin' asshole used to stab the suspect, and your dumb ass missed it! Lucky for you, the wagon man never trusts anyone else's searches. He found the fuckin' knife under his balls. Let me guess," my FTO continued. "You didn't want to move his nasty dick to check under his balls?"

I was speechless. My training officer was correct. All I could do was shake my head.

"I'll bet you're never going to make that mistake again, are you?" he asked.

I replied, "Correct."

As much as I hated to admit it, the FTO's nonconventional teaching method was effective. I never missed another weapon during my twenty-year career.

On my third day, I was blessed with divine intervention. Out of nowhere, I was assigned to a new FTO. Even though Officer Dodson was a savvy twenty-year veteran, he was a humble man, immensely different from my first FTO. He was about fifty years old and five foot eight with red hair. His uniform was neatly starched. He politely greeted me and told me he looked forward to teaching me the fundamentals of police work.

Officer Dodson was a welcome relief. Fortunately, he did not verbalize the cliché many rookie police officers received: "The first thing you need to do is to forget everything you learned at the police academy." Although Officer Dodson taught me valuable lessons not included in the textbooks I read at the police academy, he also understood the value of the lessons I learned at the academy. After serving twenty years in law enforcement myself, I could safely say, the lessons I learned at the police academy served me very well.

That said, Officer Dodson's teachings supplemented what I learned in the academy. He taught me the importance of using my discretion and treating people with courtesy and respect. The most valuable insight he imparted to me was the importance of doing the right thing even when circumstances turned difficult. He told me, "Hicks, do whatever you have to do on the street as long as you can justify it. What you do may not be covered by departmental procedure, but if it's the right thing to do, you do it." That powerful lesson served me well while performing police work; it also benefited me in all aspects of my life.

The police academy also emphasized courtesy, professionalism, respect, and discretion. A Baltimore City police officer could be fired for receiving sustained complaints of discourtesy to a citizen. One lesson at the police academy demonstrated that if we citizens were arrested for every crime, most of us would spend at least ten years in jail. For example, expectorating (spitting) on the sidewalk was illegal and carried jail time in Maryland.

I felt blessed to have the opportunity to be trained by a well-trained professional and a very caring person. Officer Dodson was entirely different from the other police officers I encountered throughout my life. He explained he once stopped a woman for speeding and learned she had a suspended license. The woman explained that she knew her license was suspended, but she had nevertheless driven to the store to buy her baby milk and Pampers. Officer Dodson told me the woman's car had several defects in addition to the violations he already noted to me, including a headlight that was out and a broken taillight. He asked me how I believed he handled the situation.

I said I thought Dodson wrote the woman a ticket for each violation. Officer Dodson then explained he did not give any tickets to the woman. Instead, he made her park the car, and he gave her a ride home. Dodson explained the woman was a poor single parent. If he had cited her, his action would have started a cycle from which the woman would take a long time to come out. Moreover, he stated it would have sabotaged any of her chances of ever getting her license back.

I was encouraged and very thankful to learn that a veteran white police officer had so much compassion for people in general. I was particularly impressed by the kindness he had in his heart for poor people. He told me never to lose my compassion for people. He emphasized that even in Baltimore's worst neighborhoods, only a tiny percentage of citizens was the criminal element. Most of the people living in Baltimore were good people trying to survive life in a harsh environment. My experience with Officer Dodson inspired me to want to become a field training officer.

Officer Dodson and I responded to the Greyhound bus station downtown for a disorderly call. Officer Dodson walked in a few seconds before me. I immediately removed my hat as we walked into the building, because Baltimore City officers must wear their hats only when outdoors. Officer Dodson approached a white man in his forties wearing several soiled coats and other soiled clothing.

As I stood and watched him interact with the suspect, I heard the chatter from police handsets coming toward us. Officer Dodson glanced back in the direction of the chatter and noticed I was not wearing my hat. He did not say a word. The officers whose chatter we heard eventually arrived, and Officer Dodson convinced the suspect to leave.

When Officer Dodson and I walked back to our patrol car, my FTO politely asked why I had taken my hat off inside the Greyhound bus station. I told him I took the hat off because we were not required to wear our hats indoors. He told me one of the reasons the other police officers took a while to find where we were was because they were looking through the crowd to spot our hats. He said our hats stood out in groups. That was another important lesson I would not forget. Officer Dodson also told me to carry my nightstick everywhere I went. That included nonviolent calls.

*****

While we were talking, the dispatcher called over the radio. "We have a black male in his early 20s threatening to jump from the top of the shot tower. The man is holding his rejection letter from the police department." I responded, "Car 123 copy, we are enroute.

We arrived at the scene a few minutes and saw about ten police cars parked near the shot tower. My training officer and I grabbed our patrol hats to prevent them from flying off from the large wind circulating us. I heard helicopter blades chopping through the air. Everyone near the shot tower was looking up. I saw Fox Trot, the police helicopter, was hovering over the Shot Tower. I heard an officer shouting over his radio, "Get that damn thing out of here!" referring to Fox Trot. I thought to myself; this is not good. This young African American man was about my age. My mind quickly thought back to a horrific scene that I had witnessed the previous day. I responded to the scene of an accident and saw one of my former classmates from Forest Park High School mangled and trapped in the car. It was one of the many scenes that remained in my mind. That day my FTO allowed me to notify his parents that he was in critical condition and that his chances of survival were in God's hands. I was displeased with watching him take what I believed would be his last few breaths.

The last thing that I wanted to see was that young man's life cut short. Nor did I want to see his body spattered all over the pavement in front of me. I wondered what the hell I had gotten myself into. Fox Trot flew across the street a few minutes later and landed back on the helipad on top of police headquarters. My FTO tapped me on the shoulder. "Do not worry, son; we will get him down." He said. He motioned, and a few officers entered the shot tower. I temporarily felt relieved. My mind worked a mile a minute, thinking what I could say to convince the man to come down. The officers who entered the building looked very relaxed and very confident. The scenario seemed routine to them. Within minutes, the officers had convinced him to come down. I was impressed when two officers brought the man down in handcuffs. Tears were pouring down his eyes. He had his police rejection letter stuffed in his back pocket. I looked at my field training officer (FTO) and said, "I guess he wanted this job bad." My FTO looked at me and replied, "I guess the system worked.

I gained a treasure trove of essential police tactics and ethics by the end of my third day. The information Dodson provided filled in crucial gaps that remained unfilled during my time at the academy. It gave me a solid foundation on which to build my police career. I gave Officer Dodson generous marks on his evaluation when I returned to the police academy. I thanked him for providing me with essential life lessons from which all police recruits could benefit.

CHAPTER 6

BAPTISM BY FIRE: THE SOUTHEASTERN POLICE DISTRICT

> That the trial of your faith, being much more
> precious than of gold that perisheth, though it be
> tried with fire, might be found unto praise and
> honor and glory at the appearing of Jesus Christ.
> —1 Peter 1:7

After field training, I was assigned to the Southeastern Police District. Up until that point in my life, I had spent my entire life avoiding trouble. However, my life changed entirely. Now I embarked on a daily mission of looking for trouble. As the old saying went, "If you look for trouble, you will find it." Unfortunately, I was about to give that phrase a bold new meaning.

I walked into the squad room and began looking at the FBI's wanted posters. The first photograph I saw featured Eric, my former classmate. He was the little terrorist I fought in both elementary school and junior high school. I always knew Eric would kill somebody. His partner in crime, Danny, was killed over drugs when he was eleven years old. The caption underneath the FBI poster read, "Wanted by the FBI for interstate flight to avoid prosecution for murder."

Just then, Officer Mickie, one of my new squad members, walked over to me and said, "What's your name, son?"

"Hicks," I replied.

"You're the black-neck hick, and I'm a redneck hick. If you ever hear a call, go out in my beat, stay away because that is my fuckin' beat." He said. He explained that he never needed backup. He reiterated that he never wanted me "fucking around in his beat."

Just then, Sergeant Harris, my new sergeant, yelled, "Line up for roll call!" We lined up in the hallway and marched into roll call. We remained standing while the shift lieutenant began inspecting us in the roll call room. When he reached the first officer, a short black police officer, he began poking him in the chest to check whether he was wearing his bulletproof vest.

"If you ever poke me again, sir," the officer said, "I will be forced to lock you up!" The lieutenant looked bewildered, but he approached the next officer. This officer was an older white man with gray hair. His name was Sal. Sal drove the paddy wagon. He had twenty-eight years on the force and wore an impeccable uniform.

Sal smiled at the lieutenant, grabbed his crotch, and said, "You want to check my cup too, sir?" Then under his breath, he whispered, "Fuckin' faggot."

The lieutenant inspected the third officer. "Jesus Christ, Harrison," he said, "you could at least iron your uniform shirt."

Officer Harrison continued to look straight ahead while tapping angrily on the back of his shirt. The lieutenant was confused. Harrison tapped his neck harder. Then he tapped his shirt tag. The lieutenant walked behind Harrison to see why Harrison was tapping the back of his shirt.

Harrison said very calmly, "Look at the label and read what it says."

The lieutenant slowly read the words. "Wash and wear."

"That's what I am doing, man," Harrison said, "washing and wearing. Goddamn it, now stop harassing me."

The lieutenant then moved on to the next officer, a short white woman about thirty-five years old. The shoulders of her uniform shirt were sprinkled with dandruff. The lieutenant began poking her stomach with his finger to check for the officer's bulletproof vest. "You can't touch me," the officer observed. "I'm a female officer. I'll sue you for sexual harassment if you feel me again."

At this point, the lieutenant stopped his inspection and headed to the podium to call the roll. As he began reading the roll call notes, two squads headed by two sergeants were present in the roll call room. I was assigned to Sector 4. The squad sergeant for Sector 2 began handing out papers and talking to the officers. The lieutenant then asked the Sector 2 sergeant if he minded waiting until he finished roll call. The sergeant ignored him and kept passing out papers. The lieutenant again asked the sergeant to wait until he finished with roll call. Furthermore, the sergeant smirked at the lieutenant and kept passing out paperwork.

After roll call, my sergeant asked me what my name was. I saluted him and gave him my name. "Son, you are not in the police academy," he said. "Do not go overboard with the saluting." Then my sergeant threw me a map of my post—my patrol area. I stood there a moment in bewilderment. My sergeant told me to make sure I was on time when he called me to turn in my reports.

Sergeant Harris was a quiet short white man with a large bald spot in the middle of his head. He was probably in his late fifties. I said hello to the Sector 3 patrol sergeant, who was walking past. He looked at me as if I was a piece of disposable waste. "I hate patrolmen," he said. He shook his head and walked into his cubicle.

"Don't worry about him," one officer told me. "He's a grumpy old former tank commander with no war to fight."

The former tank commander began venting his frustrations to an obese white officer. The officer weighed about 350 pounds.

"Now the department is hiring all these damn women," the former tank commander said. "They are useless to me. Why in the hell would they even try to get a job with us? This is a man's job. They need to stay their asses at home and take care of their children."

The obese officer chimed in. "You know this is a high-paying job for a woman!" He spoke with a broad Southern accent.

It was clear to me the female officer slated for the squad was going to catch hell. I thought the sergeant should have been more concerned about the obese officer, who could barely get out of his chair, than a younger and likely fitter female officer.

My sergeant then pointed to the exit door. "Roll call is over, son," he said. "Go out there and start handling calls."

Buckle up! I thought. *Prepare for baptism by fire.*

CHAPTER 7

MICKIE, THE TICKING TIME BOMB

> But I say to you who hear, Love your enemies,
> do good to those who hate you, bless those who
> curse you, pray for those who abuse you. To one
> who strikes you on the cheek, offer the other also,
> and from one who takes away your cloak, do not
> withhold your tunic either. Give to everyone who
> begs from you, and from one who takes away your
> goods, do not demand them back. And as you
> wish that others would do to you, do so to them.
> —Luke 6:27–36

The entire squad was out of service, handling calls on the evening shift, when the dispatcher advised me to head to a call for a domestic dispute in Officer Mickie's beat. It had been going on for over an hour. I agreed to go to the call for service if the dispatcher could get the female complainant to meet me outside. The dispatcher convinced the woman on the scene to meet me outside the residence to determine what was happening there.

"The woman said the situation was resolved for now, and she and her boyfriend would discuss their problems the following day," I told the dispatcher. A very short, thin man with dark-brown hair then emerged from the residence. He had a thick beard and mustache and looked like a hippie. It was the woman's boyfriend. He calmly explained that they argued earlier but that now they had settled down.

Just then, Mickie started yelling about me being in his beat. He chastised me for calling out on the scene. He asked me why the fuck I called out on the scene. I reminded him that the required protocol was to notify the dispatcher when the reporting officer arrived on the scene.

"Never let them bastards know how fast you get on the scene," he said. "We lose manpower and money that way." He was out of his mind. I was not going to jeopardize my safety by not calling out on the scene. I was a rookie, but I was not a fool. I explained that the problem had been resolved. Mickie said, "No. I'm tired of coming down here. Somebody is going to jail tonight."

Mickie asked the woman if her boyfriend had hit her. She said she only had a minor shoving match. Mickie then handcuffed the boyfriend and told him he was under arrest. The boyfriend told Officer Mickie that if he was going to jail, so was his girlfriend. He insisted that she had a ton of drugs in the house. Mickie uncuffed the boyfriend and told him to go back inside the house and bring him the drugs.

"We cannot allow this guy out of our sight!" I told Mickie.

Mickie yelled, "Keep your stupid rookie nose out of my business."

That was not going to happen. I knew this type of scenario well from my training in the police academy. One academy instructor always acted like a quiet and cooperative suspect during domestic call practicums. He was notorious for blowing away recruits who allowed him to walk out of their sight.

The boyfriend quickly ran up the steps. The boyfriend's haste was particularly concerning to me. I sprinted up the staircase, ran into the dimly lit apartment, and heard the subject fumbling around in the bedroom. I caught the subject as he picked up a shotgun from the closet. Then I performed a tactic I learned in the police academy called the FBI firearms takeaway. I simply spun the shotgun out of his hand and quickly disarmed him.

Mickie was still standing outside. I ordered the suspect to his knees and called for Mickie to assist me. He slowly walked up the stairs. Mickie was shocked to see me holding a shotgun in my hand. He handcuffed the man and transported him to the station. Mickie's nonchalant attitude almost cost me my life!

While working the day shift, I received another call in Mickie's beat. This call was for a man on a transit bus armed with a gun. I was two blocks from where the bus had stopped. When I arrived on the scene, I pulled up directly behind the bus. I looked in my rearview mirror and saw Mickie pulling up behind me. Now I had to be concerned about two men with guns: the suspect and Mickie.

I began strolling toward the bus's front. By that time, Mickie was five steps behind me. I got about four steps down the aisle of the bus when I was startled by Mickie yelling, "You stupid rookie! I told you not to come into my beat!" His voice momentarily distracted me from searching for the suspect. I turned back, then walked past Mickie and got off the bus. He stepped off the bus and started following me and chastising me for calling out on the scene.

No one knew what was wrong with Mickie. Someone would later become one of his casualties, but not me. From that point on, I left Mickie to his own devices. In my opinion, he posed as significant a threat as any of the criminals on the street. I knew it was only a matter of time before Mickie, the ticking time bomb, would explode. I prayed I would not become collateral damage. In my opinion, he was suffering from an unknown mental health issue.

One year after the incident with the suspect on the bus, Mickie walked inside a convenience store. There, he began talking calmly to a black employee in his twenties. According to initial news reports, Mickie shot and killed the young man a few minutes later. The media reported no argument between the two men before the fatal shooting. Mickie was taken off the street. I was amazed he had been allowed to operate on the road for as long as he did, given that he had unknown mental health issues. I never learned whether the shooting was justified or not.

CHAPTER 8

SERGEANTS JUST DON'T UNDERSTAND

My good friend and colleague, Officer Conrad, called me to impound a car for a woman he arrested for drunk driving. Conrad and I were very close. Conrad was a very sharp, physically fit, light skin African American officer in his early 20s. I admired Conrad, and I enjoyed working with him. We called ourselves the burglary brothers because we caught burglars day and night while riding together. However, that day I was working with Armando. He was a wealthy young Italian officer who was about 25 years old. Armando stayed in tip-top shape. His tight stomach and perfectly chiseled body made him a magnet for beautiful women. He was very conscious of his appearance. He told me he paid $60 weekly to keep his perfectly manicured coal-black hair styled. $60 was a lot of money to pay for a haircut in 1983. Everyone liked Armando on the squad except the wagon man. For some reason, the wagon man could not stand Armando. I always admired Armando because he was a good guy who treated everyone with respect. He never let his wealth or badge go to his head. Armando drove to the scene of Conrad's drunk driving arrest with me riding shotgun. The suspect's car had broken down in the middle of the street. The wagon man pulled up to the scene and took custody of Conrad's prisoner. Conrad headed to the police station.

The suspect's car had broken down in the middle of the street. The wagon pulled up to the scene and took custody of Conrad's prisoner. Conrad headed to the police station while Armando and I chatted while waiting for a tow truck to arrive. Suddenly, we heard the alert tone on our police radios. Ding, Ding, Ding signal 13 officers in trouble. Armando looked at me and said, "That is the next street over." Armando slammed the car into drive and headed to the scene. A few seconds later, we were handcuffing two suspects who assaulted one of our officers. Armando said, "Wow, we were certainly at the right place at the right time." I nodded and said, "Yes, we have to get back to the car to meet the tow truck." Armando said, "Damn, I almost forgot."

We jumped back in our patrol car, and Armando sped off, spinning wheels. When we returned to the scene, we were horrified as the car was gone. Yikes! I immediately called Conrad and asked him to ask his suspect if she knew anyone on the street where she was stopped. He asked her, and she promptly replied, "I am not telling you asshole cops shit!"

"Armando, what are we going to do?" I asked. "We have to call Gunner," Armando replied. Gunner was the acting sergeant who hated my guts. "Oh my God, Gunner will kill me," I replied. "You were not driving, so you do not have anything to worry about," Armando replied. "Yes, I do. He can't stand me. Believe me, and I will take the rap for this," I replied. A few minutes later, Gunner arrived on the scene. I reclined the passenger seat a little, so Gunner could not see me.

Armando explained what happened to the car. "Where is that damn Hicks?" Gunner asked. Gunner continued. "I know he is behind this whole damn thing!" I leaned forward in the car passenger and looked in his direction. I said, "Gunner, I did not do anything but get in the car to go to the 13. I didn't even." Gunner immediately cut me off. He took off his hat, threw it on the passenger seat, and yelled, "Shut up!" I reclined the passenger seat back again and looked away from him. I think Gunner wanted to bite the floor whenever he saw my face. A few seconds later, I straightened my chair up and looked at him again. He sat there staring at me for a few seconds and said, "Damn, Rookie. No wonder I drink!" He leaned forward and pointed at me. "Hicks, if that car does not turn up, you will become the owner of that damn car." He said. I looked at Armando and back at Gunner. "Why me?" I asked. He stared at me again and yelled, "Shut up!" "What are we going to do?" I asked. Armando looked bewildered. Gunner leaned forward, looked at me, and said, "Get a listing on the car, you idiot.?" I ran the listing on the car. "Gunner, it comes back to an address in Baltimore County. "I said. Gunner nodded to Armando, which meant for us to head out there.

When Armando and I got near the address, I thought, *please, God let that car be there.* When I saw the suspect's car at the address, I pointed at the car and said, "Happy days, brother. Thank God the car is here." The car was parked in front of the listed address. I quickly got on the radio and called Gunner. "The car is here. What should we do now?" I asked. He replied, "Get your dumb ass back in the city!" Armando busted out laughing. I smiled, saluted the air, and said, "Yes, sir!" Such was the life of a rookie in Baltimore.

CHAPTER 9

MY OLD NEIGHBOR WAYMAN

I was sitting in my patrol car, waiting at a red traffic light and enjoying an unusually calm summer day, when a car blew past me, hopping straight through the red light. I sat at the light a few seconds in disbelief. The light was steady red when the car blew past me while sitting at the same light. Finally, I caught up with the vehicle, which had stopped at the next red light. I turned on my blue police lights. The driver immediately bailed out of the car and made a run for it. I called the dispatcher. "2-4-5, I am in foot pursuit."

Several officers responded and set up a perimeter around the area where I was chasing the suspect. I chased the subject for about two blocks while hearing the locals yelling, "Get him, Maurice!" Finally, the man tripped and fell. I handcuffed him, then spun him around and listened to a familiar voice say, "Hey, Little Maurice. I didn't know you were old enough to become a cop."

"Oh my God, Wayman," I said. Wayman was my former next-door neighbor and who was allegedly a small-time drug dealer, who used to pay me to go to the store. I felt terrible about arresting my former next-door neighbor, but what else could I do after chasing him around the projects.

CHAPTER 10

EXILED INTO FOOT PATROL

But those who wait on the Lord shall renew
their strength. They shall mount up with
wings like eagles; they shall run and not be
weary; they shall walk and not faint.
—Isaiah 40:31

As crime in the city increased, we were deployed in two-person cars. Officers worked four men to a vehicle when the crime was terrible in certain parts of the city. Working a two-person car allowed me to work with a few younger officers on my squad. But unfortunately, my joy was short-lived, because our acting supervisor would let his buddies off from work right at the beginning of the shift when the sergeant was off duty. That meant the dispatchers were sending us on two-person calls thinking there were two officers in a car, but only one officer was in the vehicle.

Nevertheless, that gave us a chance to bond, because each officer depended on the other to survive. One of my squad mates was a twenty-year veteran named Hightower. Hightower was not part of the clique. He hated the fact that Acting Supervisor Gunner left us in precarious situations. One day, the sergeant left Officer Hightower in charge. He turned the tables on Gunner. He sent two younger officers home and left the veteran officers to fend for themselves. Then he walked over to me and said, "Go home, son. You got diarrhea, don't you, boy?"

Catching Hightower's hint, I said, "Yes, sir!"

It was great to see at least one police veteran had a sense of fairness.

*****

I loved working the midnight shift, because it was easier to decipher who were the bad guys. At that time of night, unless people were on their way to work, we could surmise they were probably up to no good, for the most part. On one particular midnight shift, I called my sergeant, Sergeant Harris, to discuss my delusions of grandeur regarding becoming a detective. It was only a pipe dream for me at that time because I only had six months on the job. Harris established a successful career as a homicide detective before becoming a sergeant.

When I pulled up to his vehicle, Sergeant Harris was reading a book. He rolled his window down while still looking at his book. Sergeant Harris was a very humble guy. His quiet demeanor intrigued me. I picked his brain every chance I had so I could learn what skills I needed to master to become a detective. That night would be no different.

"Sergeant Harris," I said, "what else can I do to become a good detective?"

He slowly looked up at me and said, "You're serious about this. Know this, Maurice. It will probably be ten years before you will become a detective."

"Please let me know if you have any ideas for how I can become a detective sooner," I said.

He smiled. "I like your enthusiasm. I'll let you know if I think of anything," he said.

The following week, on the day shift, I saw my name on the list to work a foot beat. My sergeant walked up as I stood there, staring into space. "What's wrong, Hicks?" he asked.

I looked at Sergeant Harris and reminded him I got some of my best cases working traffic stops. Sergeant Harris already knew I lived to make traffic stops. "Why are you doing this to me, Sarge?" I asked.

Sergeant Harris smiled at me and said, "Your legs are going to be humongous when you get off that foot beat."

I pleaded with him. "Please, Sarge, you cannot do this to me." I hastily explained I could not make any arrests walking around on foot.

He got this grinch-like big smile on his face and replied, "Have fun trying."

After roll call, the beat officer drove me down to the O'Donnell Heights housing project and dropped me off. For a few seconds, I stood there in the alley of the housing project looking like a child being dropped off for his first day of school. As I saw the patrol car driving out of focus, I thought, *What the hell am I going to do out here for the next eight hours?* I heard the voices of veteran officers in my ear saying a good beat officer never got cold, wet, or hungry.

CHAPTER 11

LITTLE THINGS MATTER

Therefore, as God's chosen people, holy and
dearly loved, clothe yourselves with compassion,
kindness, humility, gentleness, and patience.
—Colossians 3:12

Most police work was mundane. Typically, day after day, most officers went through the same boring routine, but I always went looking for crime. As they would say, "If you look for trouble, you will find it." A few days after I started walking my foot beat, I walked around an area close to O'Donnell Heights. I came across a ten-year-old little girl who was crying. She told me someone had stolen her bicycle. I asked her if her mother had called the police. She was not sure. I asked the little girl where she lived, and then I walked her to her apartment and knocked on the door.

The girl's mother opened the door and appeared shocked to see a uniformed police officer standing in the doorway with her daughter. I told her I had just spoken to the girl about a stolen bicycle. Her mother confirmed she did not call the police, because she believed it was a lost cause. I told the little girl I was going to do my best to find her bicycle.

I had no idea where I would start. All I knew was that I wanted to help the little girl find her bicycle. I started my routine by talking to the so-called usual suspects. One of them told me exactly where the bike was. To my amazement, the informant took me to a storage facility in the next building and showed me the bicycle sitting in an unsecured storage bin. I returned the bike and made the little girl's day. Also, by asking about the stolen bicycle, I developed a vital informant.

My next little case came the next day. I was walking foot patrol near another apartment complex. I saw a fragile, wrinkled-faced white woman in her seventies walking out of the laundry room, wiping tears from her eyes. I asked her what was going on. She told me someone had stolen her clothes from out of the laundry room. When I asked her how many people were in the laundry room when she was washing clothes, she told me there was only one lady. I asked her whether she knew what apartment the lady lived in, and she told me she did. She pointed it out.

I went to the apartment with the lady in tow and knocked on the door. I bluffed the lady by telling her management had her on video camera removing the clothes from the laundry room. I explained I would not charge her with any infraction if she gave the clothes back to the lady. She handed over the lady's entire bag of stolen clothes. Case solved. The lady gave me a big hug and thanked me for "caring about an old lady."

I felt good about the bonds I made in the community. Those bonds paid dividends in the future when I began investigating more serious crimes. The last minor crime I worked on was a little case concerning a missing lawn mower. That day, I walked down an alley and waved to an old white gentleman in his late seventies. I asked him how he was doing. He waved back and said he would be a lot happier if he had his lawn mower. I wondered what had happened to the lawn mower, and he replied someone had stolen it. He stated he did not have money to replace the lawn mower.

I told him I wanted to help. I asked him to give me a description of his lawn mower. I asked for any distinguishing features. He described the lawn mower as having paint missing on the right side. I walked through several alleys in the neighborhood, and I went by several front yards, looking for his lawn mower. I finally found a lawn mower that fitted the description; it was in the backyard of a home about three blocks down the street from where I talked with the older adult. No one was using the lawn mower at the time I spotted it.

I headed back to the older gentleman's home. I showed him a photograph of the lawn mower. He immediately confirmed the lawn mower was his. I walked back to the location where I observed the lawn mower. I knocked on the door and asked the man who answered whether he knew who owned the lawn mower in his backyard. The resident stated that he did not know where the lawn mower had come from, that somebody had just put it in his yard. I asked him if he would mind if I removed the lawn mower from his property. He agreed.

After identifying the older gentleman's stolen lawn mower within two hours or so, I returned it to him. The older man's face lit up when he saw me pushing his lawn mower down the street toward his home. I had no idea I would derive so much satisfaction from helping people.

For some officers, these minor cases were probably not worth a second thought. However, I felt solving even the most minor issue could make a difference in their lives. People appreciated me for even making an effort to resolve their problems. It was a good feeling for me too knowing how much my work gratified them. People had a great appreciation for a police officer who demonstrated compassion for them and their families. Also, I enjoyed displaying the police department in a positive light.

Like the crime dog McGruff, I was taking a bite out of crime. Some members of my squad thought what I was doing was hilarious and petty. I agreed it was a small bite, but I was trying to make a difference. Within the police department, my efforts drew resistance from some of my squad members. Some of them did not like me disrupting their cushy lifestyles by calling for backup and asking for assistance. Criminals in the area were taking notice of my crime-fighting efforts as well, and they did not want me taking a bite out of their crime either. The lackadaisical attitudes of a few members of my squad encouraged criminals to operate with no fear of deterrence.

CHAPTER 12

OBJECTIVE: PUT POLICEWOMEN THROUGH HELL

Lieutenant Thaddeus Harris: What
the hell are you doing here?
Cadet Laverne Hooks: I wanna be a police officer.
Lieutenant Thaddeus Harris:
What? I can't hear you-u?
Cadet Laverne Hooks (whispering):
I wanna be a police officer.
Lieutenant Thaddeus Harris: Don't unpack.
—Excerpt from *Police Academy*

In the same way, the women are worthy of
respect, not malicious talkers but temperate
and trustworthy in everything.
—1 Timothy 3:11

I came to realize doing absolutely nothing was the standard operating procedure in Sector 4. I became extremely frustrated. I thought about how the police rarely patrolled my family's neighborhood when I grew up on Park Heights Avenue. The police were always either missing in action or retired while on duty. I had to accept there would be a clash between the worker bees and the on-duty retirees.

To the latter group, I was an annoying little brother who stood in the way of their cushy lifestyles.

It did not take long for me to learn that things around you would change even if you did not. One year later, in 1984, Sergeant Harris was transferred after he stood up against the establishment for mistreating a female officer in our squad. I was devastated when I learned Sergeant Harris was given full-time desk duty. My quiet mentor was reduced to supervising prison intake.

Nevertheless, I extracted powerful lessons from Sergeant Harris's transfer. I learned that hard work, honesty, and integrity did not make you immune to the wrath of upper police management. I also knew some officers held a profoundly ingrained hatred for African American police officers and female police officers. Black police officers were more accepted than female police officers. It took more time for many officers to accept a woman in uniform.

Officers would do everything they could to discourage women. For example, the sergeant who replaced Sergeant Harris wasted no time putting Officer Mancini, a rookie female officer, on foot patrol on the midnight shift in the dead of winter. She had to walk around in thirty-degree weather. The new sergeant did not care. Officer Mancini had three children to take care of. The new sergeant seemed to be a willing participant in the evil plan to break down the 40-year-old white woman. After a patrol officer picked up Officer Mancini and transported her to the foot beat in the cold, the sergeant instructed us not to pick her up until her shift was over.

One night, I drove to the Dunkin' Donuts on Holabird Avenue to get Officer Mancini some hot chocolate and doughnuts. Several members of my squad were there, eating doughnuts. That was their favorite pastime. I told my squad members I would pick up Officer Mancini in thirty minutes and let her eat in my car. They warned me not to let her sit in my vehicle. I asked what the sergeant could do if I allowed Mancini to sit in my car and drink hot chocolate while working her beat.

Two officers looked at me. "You do not know?" they said almost simultaneously.

One of the officers went on to say I missed the full lecture when I was off work. "If you pick her up," the sergeant said, "I am going to put you on foot patrol with her."

I was appalled by the systemic discrimination against women, and I also considered how I would feel if someone in my family were treated as badly as the new sergeant was treating Officer Mancini.

A few minutes after I arrived at the Dunkin' Donuts, Officer Mancini walked into the store and drank some hot chocolate. The officers looked at one another as the sergeant walked in as well. He told Officer Mancini he wanted to talk to her in private. Then the sergeant grabbed some coffee. Officer Mancini waved to us and then followed the sergeant to his car. The next day, we discovered that the sergeant had suspended her for insubordination.

The sergeant charged Mancini with being out of her beat, meaning she was charged with being at the Dunkin' Donuts across the street. The sergeant was trying to get Officer Mancini fired. Officer Mancini had three years in the department. She was not part of the ethnic cliché running the department from top to bottom, and she did not have any advocates.

On the next shift, Sergeant Harris was not working the desk job he was assigned. Instead, the new sergeant was working the desk! Officer Mancini had threatened to call the news media. The commissioner disciplined the sergeant, not officer Mancini.

Another young female officer, fresh out of the police academy, was placed on the midnight shift of foot patrol in the dead of winter. She worked a crime-infested beat where no stores were open. Her only place of refuge was the local firehouse. She devised a strategy to beat the sergeant at his own game in the cold. She called out sick for the remainder of that shift and the rest of the second shift.

Sick leave abuse was one thing the agency had zero tolerance for. I schooled her not to leave her house while on sick leave. I told her to expect a nightly visit from her sergeant. Sure enough, the sergeant showed up at her home. She greeted him nightly from the warmth and comfort of her home.

CHAPTER 13

CULTURE SHOCK

I was loaned to another sector, Sector 2. At that time, I was working in the area near the Flag House Courts. As I scanned the area, I was shocked to realize that none of the officers was wearing their hats. Like the Maryland State Police, we were likely to be written up if we did not wear our hats. Many officers hated to wear their hats, because the hats were causing them to lose their hair, or so they claimed. My mind drifted back to when my field training officer chastised me for not wearing my hat inside the Greyhound bus station, so naturally, the sight of officers not wearing their hats outdoors was inconceivable.

I approached one of the officers and asked, "How come none of you are wearing your hats down here? What's the deal with that?"

The officer said, "Don't worry, son. No lieutenant or captain is coming anywhere near here. This is the jungle. Only combat troops come here."

My mind snapped back to the task at hand. My partner and I entered the Lafayette high-rise's elevator along with five teenage young men. They smirked as we entered the elevator. We made eye contact with one of them. He looked at me and then looked down at my gun. Suddenly, my nostrils detected the odor of urine mixed with heat and humidity. I started to gag. My partner smiled. When the young men had entered the elevator, they made a point to move quickly to the rear. My partner and I both placed our hands over our weapons as we ascended to the eleventh floor.

I noticed our elevator guests did not select a floor on the elevator panel. Instead, they were whispering to one another during the entire ride. As my partner and I exited the elevator, I looked back at the young men, and they looked away. However, as soon as the elevator doors closed, we heard them laughing. I walked ahead of my partner, simultaneously surveying the hallway. You never knew what type of situation you would run into while walking the tiers. It would not be unusual to step up on shootings or robberies. Crime was an everyday occurrence.

As we reached one of the residents' apartment door, I noticed a giant blob of saliva on the back of my partner's uniform coat. I motioned for him to turn around and stand still. I saw a woman sitting outside of the apartment next door. I asked her for some paper towels. Then I cleaned the back of my partner's coat. When he saw the amount of saliva I had removed from his jacket, he said, "I know one of those bastards in the elevator did it. I hate these people here. We come down here trying to help them, and all they do is crap all over us every chance they get. I got to get the hell out of here."

We knocked on the door. A twenty-year-old man answered. I told him we had received a call for a disturbance and asked him what the problem was. He was insistent that there was no problem and that he did not call us. I secured permission from him to check the house.

When we entered the living room, I saw a heavyset, dark-skinned black man in his fifties who weighed about three hundred pounds. He was wearing a T-shirt and shorts while sitting in a chair in front of the television. A black woman in her late forties stood over him, holding a butcher knife to his throat. The man was engrossed in his television program. He acted as if he was in the room alone.

My partner and I both immediately drew our guns and ordered the woman to drop the knife. She gently removed the blade from the man's throat but still stood over him, still holding the knife. We both yelled at her again and ordered her to drop the knife. The woman never said a word, but she kept the knife in her hand.

The man sitting in the chair turned around momentarily and looked at us. "I'm all right," he said. "She goes through this every weekend. I'm fine. You both can leave."

I looked at my partner. My partner asked the man whether he was sure about what he said. The man said he was fine. "Okay, sir," my partner said. "We're leaving."

"Okay, Officers," the man said. "You all be safe. Have a nice night!"

I looked at my partner. "I can't believe he told us to have a safe night."

The man finished watching his television program while the woman put the knife back to his throat. I asked the young man if he believed the woman was going to hurt the man. "No, he's all right," the young man said. Then he announced he was going to bed, because he had to go to work in a few hours. We left the apartment.

I asked my partner, "What the hell was that?"

"Welcome to life in Sector 2," my partner said.

The reality was, most people living in the projects were good and peaceful people trying to survive the best they could amid chaos. Unfortunately, many inhabitants found themselves overwhelmed by an influx of insurgents. I began to look at the situation of the inhabitants involved in criminal activity from their perspective.

They knew we could not protect them from the criminal element. They were caged in and separated from the rest of the community. How could they resist heavily armed and violent men? How could they escape harm if they cooperated with the police? There was only one way in and one way out of the projects.

Criminals often took over residents' apartments and enriched themselves with profits from their illegal drug deals. Criminals preyed on single mothers who had small children. It was a complicated, revolving cycle. I longed to help the good, peaceful residents living there and become their greatest advocate and defender.

CHAPTER 14

THE COUPLE THAT PREYS

I patrolled Sector 2 during the first four days. I walked around the projects and introduced myself to people. I was amazed that citizens would invite me into their homes and converse with me about some of the challenges they faced while living in the community.

On the last day of my assignment, I noticed an attractive, dark-skinned black woman sitting in a lawn chair in front of her townhouse. She was in her late twenties and was wearing an Afro. She had very shapely legs, which told me she took pride in her appearance, but she was holding her head in her hands.

After I approached her, I smiled and cheerfully said, "Good afternoon, miss. How are you doing today?" She slowly lifted her head and made an unsuccessful attempt at smiling. She told me her name was Ms. Cunningham, and she explained that someone had broken into her home and had stolen her stuff. I asked her who was investigating her case.

Ms. Cunningham replied, "Nobody." I asked her why that was, and she replied, "For what? Nobody cares about what happens to black people down here."

I examined her face for a few moments. "I care," I said.

She told me she did not call the police to report the burglary. When I glanced into her living room, I saw her two toddlers sitting on an empty floor. I asked her where her furniture was. "I don't think you understand what I am saying to you," she said. "The burglars stole everything in my house, including all the food in my refrigerator, all of the clothes in my closet, all of my laundry detergent, all of our clothes off the line, my Bible, my kids' toys, and everything else in my house!"

The burglars had emptied her home! I was speechless. It was hard for me to fathom how someone could deliberately leave a single parent with two small children in such a terrible predicament. No wonder she was so distraught when I walked up.

My investigative skills were minimal at the time. All I could do was reflect on my basic academy training. I took a police report and obtained a detailed description of the stolen property. Some of the stolen items included a red wagon with one wheel missing, a red leather coat, a Bible, and refrigerator ornaments that looked like the sun.

I started my investigation by knocking on the next-door neighbors' doors to determine whether they had witnessed the burglary. No one claimed to see anything. I walked across the street to knock on more neighbors' doors. I noticed a window was open at one townhome. I took a quick look inside. I saw a red wagon with one wheel missing, the dinette set the victim described, a red leather coat hanging over a chair that matched the victim's description, and an assortment of refrigerator ornaments matching those the victim described too.

I dashed across the street and asked my victim to peek inside the window to see if she recognized any of the property inside. She came back across the street with me, looked inside the window, and yelled, "Oh my God, those are my things inside there." After obtaining information from a neighbor about the resident's whereabouts, I called my sergeant. After he arrived, I briefed him. Then I left to check out the places where the townhouse's owner regularly hung out. Meanwhile, my sergeant stationed officers in the front and the rear of the townhouse.

I found the suspect within a few minutes. I convinced her to accompany me back to her residence under the auspices of a problem at her home. As soon as we arrived at her place, I told her we had seen stolen property inside her house. I wondered how someone could be so stupid as to leave her window open with an apartment full of stolen property. After obtaining consent to search her home, we located just about all of Ms. Cunningham's stolen property.

Amazingly, within two hours of my initial interaction with Ms. Cunningham, I discovered about 90 percent of her property and returned the items to her. There were still a few missing items, but I arrested the woman who lived in the townhouse, Bertha, and returned determined to find the remaining items stolen from Ms. Cunningham's home the next day. After that, I relentlessly asked everyone I came in contact with about the missing property.

As I was making my rounds on foot patrol, a young white kid in his early twenties said, "Maurice, I know you've been asking around about the other stolen property. If I tell you where it is, will you keep my name out of it?" I agreed. He took me to the woods and showed me a blanket. Underneath the blanket lay the remaining stolen items. I called for a beat car to pick me up. When the sergeant drove up, he asked me what I had in the blanket. I told him Santa came through for Ms. Cunningham again.

I presented Ms. Cunningham with another good news: I had located a witness who had observed the entire burglary. She identified Ms. Bertha and her boyfriend, Tyler, as the burglars. Later, I obtained an arrest warrant for Tyler. Everyone within eyeshot of Ms. Cunningham's home saw Tyler and Bertha take items from the victim's home during her absence. Tyler was never apprehended, but I was able to raise community confidence in the police. Additionally, Ms. Cunningham wrote a letter to the police commissioner expressing her gratitude. As a result, I received my first letter of commendation.

CHAPTER 15

BOMB CITY

His justice knows the Lord; the wicked are
ensnared by the work of their hands.
—Psalm 9:16

About a year into my career, my partner and I talked in front of 200 N. Aisquith Street, the Lafayette Court. By that point, I had become comfortable in my job. As we spoke, I noticed five black men in their early twenties walking past us. One of the men was carrying a large leather case. I tried to study their faces and their demeanors as they passed us. When they noticed us, they all turned their faces straight ahead. I then turned my attention to how the man was carrying the large leather case. I thought it was odd. He was strolling too slowly for someone who seemed to be an agile young man. Moreover, during their journey to the building's front entrance, the other men looked back several times at the man carrying the bag.

I alerted my partner. We followed the group as they entered the building. One of the men made eye contact with me. Dread gnawed at his insides. Fear momentarily choked him. Finally, he whispered something to the rest of the group. They began speaking in hushed tones. Everyone in the group turned around and looked back at us. Panic surged through them. Their faces were encapsulated in fear. Then there was a moment of silence as adrenaline crashed through their bodies. It sent chills down my spine. I knew that something truly sinister was forthcoming. That silence was quickly broken. The men broke out into a full run. Suddenly, the reverberating sounds of their footsteps echoed throughout the building. It sounded like an elephant stampede. I immediately feared for the scores of children standing outside in the hallways. They were trying to get a reprieve from the summer heat. We pursued the suspects across several floors. We saw them again when we reached the second floor and resumed the chase.

Two three-year-old children were standing on the tiers near their apartment. As my partner and I passed them, they looked at us running and said, "Hi, police." I smiled, and I waved at them and continued my pursuit. I was not sure if they realized it was not a game of cops and robbers or if they knew it was the real thing. We caught up with the suspects on two different floors. However, they would flee to another floor whenever we caught up with them. I mentally prepared myself for the moment that we caught up with them. I knew that a fight of enormous magnitude was inevitable. My partner used his radio to call for backup. They heard the radio transmission. They ran to the opposite end of the six-floor and dropped the bag about two doors from where a group of toddlers stood barefoot drinking their bottles. Two of the children, wearing their diapers, walked over to the bag and began trying to unzip the bag. Suddenly, I was startled by the sound of the suspects barreling out the front door of the building. They finally eluded us and made good on their escape. I yelled, "Kids get away from that bag!" One toddler threw her bottle on the ground and tried using two hands to unzip the bag. Several children surrounded the bag. They were mesmerized by the pretty beige carrying bag. By that time, my lungs were scorched. I had run out of steam. I yelled out, "Lord Jesus, please!" It was one of the most terrifying moments I can ever remember—fear pulsed through my heart. Then I realized what absolute terror was. Terror mounted every one of my steps as I slowly headed toward the children. Finally, it was too much to bear.

*****

I finally reached the toddlers. Breathing heavily, I ushered them all inside their apartments. My partner was four doors downs, bent over, trying to catch his breath. I opened the zipper of the bag. I found 12 Molotov cocktails—glass soda bottles filled with gasoline and paper. I also found six cigarette lighters. They were about to firebomb an apartment. My sergeant told me that a hit squad had targeted a drug dealer in the building for failing to pay his debts.

I was thankful my hunch paid off. The magnitude of what the men were planning to do began to sink in. I wondered what could have happened to the beautiful children in the building who cheerfully greeted me every day. What could have happened to their families? The place was a death trap. The residents had only one way out. All families living on the building's twelve levels would have had to escape through the same exit.

It was bewildering to me that the black men we chased would have sacrificed the lives of so many innocent people just to punish one person. Even worse, the fire department's official policy was to never enter the projects without a police escort. That policy meant there might have been a delay in extinguishing the fire.

I learned that God had gifted me with enormous instincts. This gift probably saved the lives of scores of people that day. I was elated to have saved lives and would experience the pleasure of saving more lives as my career progressed.

CHAPTER 16

EVIL INTENTIONS

For wicked and deceitful mouths are opened
against me, speaking against me with lying tongues.
They encircle me with words of hate and attack
me without cause. In return for my love, they
accuse me, but I give myself to prayer. So they
reward me evil for good and hatred for my love.
—Psalm 109:2–5

No call was routine. You must be conscious of that fact when handling all service calls. Police officers must distinguish genuine threats to human life from perceived threats. Police officers needed to have excellent judgment and accurate instincts.

During all my service calls, I weighed those factors. For example, my partner and I once responded to a call for a domestic disturbance. We walked into the tiny one-bedroom apartment and spoke to a petite young black woman in her early twenties named Cora. She was the epitome of an abused woman—soft-spoken and very polite.

My initial conversation with Cora led me to believe that she was a caring person who vigorously pursued peace from the abuse of her boyfriend, Kyle. Her three-year-old daughter stood beside her as my partner, and I tried to determine what was happening. Cora told us her sadistic boyfriend, Kyle, had been terrorizing her. He would slap her around and threaten to kill her. She said Kyle got that way whenever he drank alcohol, and he drank alcohol practically every day.

While Cora was relating the details of the incidents, we heard a knock at the door. My partner answered, and in walked Kyle. He was a mess. His white T-shirt and baggy shorts were soiled and disarranged. The strong odor of alcohol and smoke emanated from his body. He looked like the stereotypical barfly. He kept pulling up his sagging pants as he began to speak. His tone of voice and slurred speech irritated me; it was like the screeching of chalk on a chalkboard. I wondered why he had to talk so damn loudly.

My partner told Kyle why we were there. Then he allowed Kyle to give his side of the story. Remarkably, Kyle said he did not want to share his side of the story. He just wanted us to know he could do whatever the fuck he wanted to do to Cora anytime he felt like doing it. Moreover, he stated he wanted her to know there was nothing she could do about it. He struggled to keep his balance as he insulted every inch of Cora's being. She felt forced to embrace his "Fucked Up Ness."

I could not arrest Kyle, because Cora did not have any physical injuries when my partner and I saw her, but the degradation was too much to bear. I knew the routine. I had seen it many times. Kyle's abusive behavior was going to continue to escalate. Cora's future beatings would come more frequently and become more severe. However, to my frustration, there was nothing I could do about it.

Kyle raised the stakes further by threatening to beat Cora up for calling the police. We told him to leave. "I'm going to leave," he replied. "But when I come back, I am going to burn this fucking place down." I warned him he was inching closer to being arrested. He broke his mug down and gave me the finger for a few seconds, then stumbled downstairs and made his way out of the building.

Kyle's frustration with me was more intense than his anger at my white partner. I was a strong and articulate young black man, exactly the type of person he did not want Cora to know existed. He perceived me as a threat to the psychological hold he had over her. He did not want Cora to get any bright ideas about seeking refuge in the arms of another man.

I encouraged Cora to call us if Kyle came back and started any trouble. Before I left, I took a few seconds to examine her face. Cora looked confused. She was in a terrible dilemma. I looked back at her sweet, petite young daughter. She was still playing with a doll. The doll provided a means of escape. The young girl needed refuge from the darkness surrounding her home.

Seeing children in despair always tugged at my heart. My problem was, I wanted to save everyone I found in distress. I wanted to be everything for everyone. I wanted to be their protector, social worker, and fireman; so I tried to extinguish anything posing a threat to their mental or emotional well-being. My grandfather told me correctly that police work would prove too taxing for me because I cared too much.

I went back on patrol. I knew we would get a call to return to Cora's apartment later that night. I hoped Kyle had gone somewhere to sleep it off. About twenty minutes later, I was driving down Dundalk Avenue. I made a right turn on Holabird Avenue, and I saw Kyle walking toward a gas station. I pulled across the street to watch him. I thought he was probably going to the gas station to buy cigarettes, candy, or other small items. Instead, he walked into the gas station, then came out with a gas can and a glass bottle of soda in his hand. He walked up to the pump and filled up the gas can with gas. He drank the soda and began pouring gas into the empty bottle.

I got on the radio and told my partner that Kyle had made at least one Molotov cocktail at the gas station. I asked him to go to Cora's house to ensure that Kyle was not going there and to be there if Kyle did decide to drop by. In the meantime, I followed Kyle from a distance. Soon, my partner told me Kyle was just entering Cora's street. I watched as Kyle unscrewed the lid to the gas can and set it down. He looked around. I surmised he was looking for more empty glass bottles.

Kyle started whistling as he reached Cora's building. The jerk seemed so relaxed and content. Kyle put the gas can down again and searched in his pocket until he retrieved a pack of matches. At that point, my partner and I quickly converged on him and took him into custody. "I told you I was going to burn this fucking place down!" Kyle yelled.

I wished I had the legal authority to throw Kyle into a pit for a few days and then come back to get him. I was shocked he tried to set Cora's apartment on fire while his three-year-old child was inside. I was glad I followed my instincts. I was joyful beyond measure that we were able to intervene on Cora and her daughter's behalf. I was able to foil several crimes and save a few citizens before things escalated. These were situations you never heard about in the news, but they were things that made a significant difference in people's lives. It was another day that God positioned me to be an armor bearer to one of our citizens.

This photo was taken in 1985.

CHAPTER 17

DRUNK AND DISORDERLY

The difference between stupidity and
genius is that genius has its limits.
—Albert Einstein

I was heading back toward the station about an hour before the end of my shift when I noticed traffic backed up on Eastern Avenue. When I finally made my way to South Ponca Street, I saw a parked vehicle blocking one of the two lanes. I approached the driver and found a man asleep. I had to knock on the window for about two minutes before I could awaken him. I was concerned he might have experienced a medical emergency. My goal was to revive him and send him on his way to relieve traffic. When he finally rolled down the window, I asked if he was okay, because traffic had been backed up for about six miles.

The driver looked at me and said, "Leave me alone, nigger!"

I got him out of the car and said, "Can you repeat what you said in the car? Because I don't think I heard you correctly."

With enormous conviction, the man repeated, "I said leave me alone, nigger!"

I smiled and said, "That is the wrong answer. You were supposed to say, 'Thank you, Officer, for giving me a break.'" Then I said, "I want to give you a field sobriety test if you can stand up on your own." I looked in his car and saw empty beer cans flooding the car's floorboard and seats. The key was in the ignition and in the on position. "You could have walked away with nothing but a verbal warning," I said. "Do you have that much hate in your heart that you cannot tone it down for a few seconds? This whole situation must be killing you!"

When I arrived at the station, the suspect looked up at the grumpy sixty-four-year-old white desk sergeant. "Can you help me get away from this nigger?" he asked. I had to fight back my laughter at the prisoner's desperation to get away from me.

True, the desk sergeant did not like me. He yelled at me every time I brought a prisoner into the station. He would often say, "So what are you going to do today, young man, to fuck up my day?" He interpreted my bringing an arrest into the station as ruining his day. Therefore, I did not know what to expect in response to the prisoner I had just brought in.

The desk sergeant said to the prisoner, "I would keep my mouth shut if I were you. This kid studies the traffic law book like some people study the Bible. All you are going to do is talk yourself into more tickets."

In a very labored voice, my prisoner said, "The bastard did not even catch me driving."

"Wow," I replied. "Now I'm a nigger and a bastard. Don't worry, sir. I am going to give you expeditious police service."

He took a Breathalyzer test and blew two times above the legal limit. I got out my Maryland citation book and began writing tickets. I started presenting him with each citation and asking him for his signature. I thought the sight of all those tickets blew his high. He seemed to sober up. When I saw the defeated look on his face, I felt a little sorry for him. Several of my family members suffered from alcoholism; they were like Dr. Jekyll and Mr. Hyde when they drank.

"I'll tell you what," I said. "I am going to do you a favor. I will call somebody in your family and let them know you messed up big time and need help. I will help you out because you will meet many people who look like me if you go to jail. The only difference is, they may be bigger and meaner than me. To be quite honest, they may want to harm you."

I looked at the prisoner's Virginia driver's license. "Why would you drive down here tanked up like this?" I asked, but he did not respond. I called his mother and told her I had Jimmy under arrest in Maryland.

The woman paused for a minute. "No, you don't have Jimmy," she said. "He's sitting right here. Jimmy is a big executive here. I know who you have. You have that no-good Tom. He is always stealing Jimmy's identity."

I thanked the woman, then said, "Just to let you know, Tom has a driver's license with his face on it but Jimmy's name."

"My God, Officer," the woman said, "you can keep Tom right there in Maryland."

"Yes, ma'am," I replied. "I will see what I can do." When I got off the phone, I turned to the prisoner and said, "Good evening, Tom. I just spoke to your mother. I am going to have a few more citations for you."

I added the following additional charges: possessing a fictitious license, displaying a fictitious license, and false application for a permit. I wrote Tom seven charges in total without even moving his car. This was one of many times I would be called a nigger while in uniform. At least Tom could chalk up his behavior to alcohol abuse.

CHAPTER 18

DEATH VALLEY

A mind is a terrible thing to waste.
—United Negro College Fund slogan, 1972

I was excited when I learned that the police department was paying overtime to patrol the high-rise projects. I immediately signed up to work at the infamous Flag House and Lafayette Courts. These projects were in my patrol district but not in the sector I worked. Now I had the chance to work a job previously reserved for veteran police officers.

Some of them hated the fact that the Baltimore Police Department was actively recruiting minorities and women. I came to realize that I was not always working with the cream of the crop. Instead, I was working with the disgruntled wing of the department. Indeed, not all the officers felt that way. Many of them were helpful and razor-sharp. However, I had the misfortune of working with a few of the department's most skilled and demoralized officers.

Many of them tried to be encouragers. However, some of them needed someone to blame for their lack of success in the department. Female officers, rookies, and young black police officers sometimes became lightning rods for their frustration. But one thing I respected about the hateful veteran police officers was that you rarely had to wonder what they thought about you. First, they told you what they did not like about you to your face. Then they were quick to say that you should not be on the job.

I walked into the Flag House Court to turn my application in to the chief of the Housing Authority Police. However, before I turned it in, one of the officers noticed the application in my hand and questioned me, asking why I was there. I did not say anything. I figured I would speak to him after I handed in my application. However, as soon as the officer saw me pass my application to the Housing Authority Police, he abruptly walked into the office, coming up right behind me.

"Don't hire that rookie," the officer said, getting right up in the police chief's face. "He isn't qualified to work down here." The chief of the Housing Authority Police, who was African American, looked bewildered. The officer continued. "He's a fuckin' rookie. He doesn't deserve to work down here. He hasn't learned how to do police work yet."

My temperature began to rise. I was struggling to take care of my newborn son, who had colic. Therefore, I had to buy Nutramigen, the most expensive baby milk on the market. I put up with the rookie degradation. I accepted it. However, I was growing tired of it. One of the malcontents in the department was affecting my survival. Now things were personal. Everyone who knew me knew I was about my money.

Getting the overtime job would be a double win for me. It would position me to learn more about police work and place me in a much better position to take care of my son. I surmised that the officer's blatant invasion of the Housing Authority chief's personal space indicated the officer's dominance and lack of respect for the black Housing Authority Police chief. I looked at the chief, and then I looked back at the sloppy police officer. My nickname for him at that point was Sloppy Joe.

"Did he not go through the police academy?" the chief asked. Then without listening to Sloppy Joe's response, he said, "This man is qualified, and I'm going to hire him to work down here." The chief directed me to take some other forms into the security office. I was proud he stood up to Sloppy Joe.

I walked into the security office with Sloppy Joe and began filling out the forms. I spun around in my chair to better look at the villain who had tried to sabotage my financial future. The room fell silent as I examined my hater. Sloppy Joe was a giant of a man in his midfifties. He stood about six foot four and weighed about 350 pounds. He had a large gut that hung over his pants.

Sloppy Joe's white uniform shirt and his blue uniform pants were severely soiled. The strong odor of cigarette smoke emanated from his body. He wore huge eyeglasses. His thick, wildly growing mustache flouted departmental regulation. He wore his pistol down at the side like Matt Dillon from the television series *Gunsmoke*.

Sloppy Joe's Sam Browne leather gun belt and holster were beige and dry-rotted. Several bullets were missing from the single-bullet holders on his belt. He looked enormously defeated. He left the police chief's office nowhere nearly as cocky as he entered it. He despised the fact that a black man held authority over him.

Sloppy Joe began throwing papers around the security office. He began snorting and stomping his feet like an antagonized bull. He was about to blow. I considered reaching for my pistol. I did not know what he was capable of. Fortunately, one of the other officers in the room must have felt the same way I did. He escorted Sloppy Joe out of the office.

I stepped into another hornet's nest. In my opinion, the disgruntled Sloppy Joe harbored resentment for years for being confined to uniform patrol. The officer who escorted Sloppy Joe out of the security office assured me it would not take long for him to find someone else to hate. I braced myself for what was going to happen next.

Three days after submitting my application to work the overtime patrol, I walked into the infamous Flag House high-rise projects. As soon as I walked in the door, I saw Sloppy Joe. "They got that fuckin' rookie down here already!" he yelled. "Sarge, please do not put him with me." I also prayed to God I would not have to work with Sloppy Joe.

A few moments later, a second officer, whom I had never met, walked in the door. He was in his late twenties. He stood about five foot three and weighed about 150 pounds. He looked more like a movie star than a policeman. Sloppy Joe's entire demeanor changed as he looked at the pretty boy police officer's name tag. Then Sloppy Joe looked at the sergeant. "I am not working with that coward," he said. He looked back at me. He said Pretty Boy was not fit to work the streets. *Damn,* I thought, *Sloppy Joe does not hold back on anybody.*

Pretty Boy was shot in the line of duty years earlier and was put into a community policing job. While at a community event, he was allegedly flagged down by a citizen regarding a suspect trying to rob him. According to the citizen, when he pointed out the suspect, he confronted Pretty Boy with a gun. Pretty Boy allegedly froze up, then ran back to his car.

The day Pretty Boy and I stood in the same room as Sloppy Joe, I believed Sloppy Joe preferred to work with me. However, his pride would not allow him to do so. Nonetheless, that was the last day Sloppy Joe objected to working with me. He told Pretty Boy to his face that he would "rather work with a stupid fuckin' rookie than a damn coward."

Pretty Boy's placement in one of the most dangerous places in the city was an awful experiment I did not want to be a part of. I found myself in a moral dilemma. I did not want to be like Sloppy Joe. However, I had a family to take care of. I had to survive working in the concrete jungle so my son would not have to live the same sort of life as the people I was being paid to protect. I made my decision.

Ironically, I became part of the resistance from that day forward; I wanted Pretty Boy out of there. When Pretty Boy and I responded to calls for service in the projects, he would turn quiet. I wondered whether it took a few minutes for him to muster the courage to begin moving. We all had to be on guard for an attack; however, he seemed reluctant to start moving toward any threats. The projects were a place where only the strong survived. In my humble opinion, Pretty Boy appeared to be a helpless lamb surrounded by wolves.

I was not sure what ultimately convinced Pretty Boy to stop working in the projects. It could have been peer pressure. Secretly, I concurred that Pretty Boy should not work there. I worried about how his departure would affect his self-esteem. He was a good guy plagued by a horrible experience. I knew it was only a matter of time before the hard-core predators in the projects would identify him as their prey.

After Pretty Boy stopped patrolling the projects, I thought about how I would feel after being shot in the line of duty. How resilient would I be after being shot? Police officers are not superheroes; they do not possess superhuman strength or courage. We were ordinary citizens who had been called to do extraordinary things. However, the job did require people who possessed unique characteristics. It took something special in a person to race toward the scene of horrific violence and mayhem while everyone else ran from it.

I thought about the chilling details of Pretty Boy's encounter with a dangerous suspect who shot him multiple times and left him for dead. He told me he remembered the encounter as if it was yesterday. He vividly explained what it was like lying helplessly on the ground, choking from exhaust fumes, while suffering from multiple gunshot wounds to the chest. There was no way to dispute the fact that his experience was terrifying.

Pretty Boy was not a coward. He had PTSD, a disorder we were all ignorant of. Pretty Boy's intimate encounter with danger was not unique. I would later learn that traumatic incidents like the one he experienced could zap officers of their strength and resolve. I remembered what my Marine Corps drill instructor said to our platoon. He told us we were Marines who received basic training. Yet even with all his training, he said, he was not tested in combat.

My drill instructor then went on to say that no one knew what they were going to do when they were deployed into combat until they were engaged in their first battle. He further stated that some men would freeze up. This stuck with me. "I don't know what I could do," he concluded. "I could freeze up. On the other hand, I hope the hell I don't."

My hard-core drill instructor admitting he could not guarantee how he would respond in battle meant the possibility of freezing up was not merely some whim or a hypothetical nightmare. Instead, my drill instructor's admission showed a vulnerable side to him I had never seen before. If that could happen to my drill instructor, it could happen to anyone. All in all, I was disappointed with how I handled the situation. Nevertheless, it was a lesson learned. My test would come four years later.

CHAPTER 19

POVERTY

> When you surround an army, leave an outlet
> free. Do not press a desperate foe too hard.
> —*The Art of War*, Sun Tzu

I remember staring at the deteriorating eleven-story redbrick building. The building itself told a story. Built in 1955, it symbolized extreme poverty, hopelessness, and despair. The structure was a magnet for crime. Most importantly, it placed failed city and police leadership on Front Street.

I took a minute to survey the building and the surrounding areas. The windows in the apartments in the building center were fenced in, even on the higher floors. About twelve of the windows on the left and right walls of the building were broken. There was a variety of trash lying around the building, including discarded candy wrappers. Small bags of Utz Potato Chips were blowing through the air, and there were several Styrofoam plates with hamburgers, chicken wings, and french fries drenched in ketchup. Melted Good Humor ice cream bars covered a good portion of the playground.

As my partner and I walked toward the building, my partner pointed to it and said, "Keep your eyes on those windows." I looked up at the fenced-in apartments. Several floors above us, a few toddlers peered down at us while holding on to the fences securing each floor. Their faces were lost in fear and despair. To this day, the expressions on those toddlers' faces remain etched in my mind. I wondered what kinds of atrocities the children had witnessed. What subliminal messages had their tiny minds received while watching violent clashes between warring factions in the illegal drug trade? Their minds were longing for emotional freedom.

I thought about my one-year-old son, whom I loved so much. I thought about the excruciating pain the parents in the fenced-in apartments were experiencing and the frustration they must have been feeling for their inability to remove their children from that harsh environment. I felt both thankful and remorseful at the same time. Those families were trapped in a socioeconomic crisis that would have baffled the minds of the most brilliant social scientist.

My heart was heavy. I wanted to rescue the children from their earthly damnation. I tried to find the antidote for their emotional despair. The task seemed impossible to me, a rookie young police officer. I seized every inch of my spiritual heritage to try to comprehend why they were living in hell on earth. I wondered why some families lived blessed, peaceful, prosperous lives while other families suffered so severely.

My partner and I continued our journey. Unfortunately, we fell prey to a coordinated attack when we were within twenty feet of the building's entrance. They hurled the various improvised devices of the day. They bombarded us with a soda bottle partially filled with urine, a tightly rolled piece of paper covered in saliva, and orange metal spikes. I quickly examined my clothing and was pleased to see it was spotless, except for a yellow stain near the hem of my shirtsleeve. My partner's experience served him well. He successfully maneuvered out of harm's way. I survived my first few minutes of combat.

As we entered the building's elevator, my mind temporarily shifted to a few years earlier, when I visited my girlfriend Maria. Then, the West Side beauty lived on Argyle Avenue, at the notorious, crime-plagued Murphy Homes Housing Projects in West Baltimore. The locals called the buildings Murder Homes.

My partner separated, and we started patrolling the building. We were crisscrossing each other on each floor. As I turned the corner of the 11th floor, the heroin dealer I did not realize was being chased by my partner collided with me as I entered the floor. The impact of the collision sent me airborne into the filthy urine-infested concrete staircase. The gazelle-like brother did not miss a beat. He proceeded to step right over me. He cleverly used my body to maintain traction, leaving his boot prints on the front of my white uniform shirt. The back of my head struck the concrete steps causing me to become momentarily disoriented. That created an excellent opportunity for the heroin dealer. He doubled back and stared at me for a second. It was like he was delighting in the helplessness of his prey.

Finally, he leaped into the air. Then I noticed the blurry image of the glass fragments from the bottom of his boots. I regained my composure, caught his foot, threw him down, and gave him a taste of the urine-infested stairwell. My partner and I subdued him and took him into custody. It was another day in paradise. I had only 29 years and five months to go before I became eligible to retire.

CHAPTER 20

GREEN EGGS BUT NO HAM

I stood in the doorway of an apartment in the Lafayette Courts in response to a call about a theft. The woman's face communicated a great sense of urgency.

"Ma'am, what can I help you with today?" I asked.

The woman stated that she wanted to make a theft report.

"What was stolen, ma'am?"

"My little brother ate my boyfriend's ham sandwich," the woman said.

I looked at my partner, then looked back at the woman. "You mean to tell me you called us here over a ham sandwich? Can't you just make another one?"

Her eyes widened. Then in a high-pitched voice, she yelled, "That crazy motherfucker is going to kick my ass as soon as he opens that refrigerator and sees that his ham sandwich is gone. I got to have a report. I need to know where I can get a copy of the report."

I looked at her in disbelief. "Please tell me that you are not serious," I said.

She then became hysterical. She began throwing things around the house. I reassured her I would gladly call her boyfriend and tell him she called the ham sandwich police.

"If you do, he is going to kick my ass for having another man in his house," the woman told me.

I took the report. *My people have some severe problems,* I thought.

119

CHAPTER 21

TRAINING DAY

Most people assumed that because I was born and raised in Baltimore, I understood the drug culture. Nothing could be further from the truth. I stayed as far away as I could from drug dealers. I never experimented with any drugs, including marijuana. Staying away from drugs and alcohol was the key to my survival.

Six months into the job, I walked into the roll call room and saw a grimace-faced new police officer sitting there. He looked totally out of place. He was slumped in his chair; his posture bore no military bearing. He was about thirty years old and had long brown hair. He stood at six foot three. He had an earring in his ear. He looked like a hippie dressed up as a cop.

I walked over and spoke to him. He grunted something back to me that was unintelligible. Then he turned back around and stared into space. After roll call, Sergeant Harris introduced me to my new hippie partner. His name was Richard. Sergeant Harris told me Richard would be teaming up with me. "I'll drive," Richard said.

We entered our patrol car. Richard made a right turn and started speeding down Eastern Avenue. He noticed me watching him strangely. "What's wrong?" he asked. I told him our post was in the opposite direction. Irritated, he abruptly made a U-turn and headed back toward our post. I directed him to O'Donnell Heights.

As Richard drove, he stared intensely at everyone we passed. It was almost as if he was using telepathy to figure out what was going on. About fifteen minutes into our patrol, Richard passed two guys standing on a street corner. He checked his rearview mirror. Then he suddenly made a U-turn and headed back toward the two men. He leaped out of the car, threw one of the men against the wall, and directed me to detain the second guy. I grabbed the second guy. Perplexed, I asked Richard what the hell he had seen.

"I got me a litterbug," Richard said. "And guess what? He happens to have drugs on him." I searched my suspect, who had a twenty-dollar bill in his hand. It was clear we were arresting the men for a drug deal. I was impressed by my hippie partner's ability to detect drug deals. We arrested two drug dealers within fifteen minutes of starting our shift. I questioned Richard again about what had alerted him to the two men. He only said they did not pass the mirror test.

On day two, Richard and I headed to O'Donnell Heights. Richard followed the same routine. He intensely studied two men who were standing together on the street. He reminded me of the lions I had seen on *National Geographic*. When he saw drug dealers, the posture of his entire body shifted. He frowned, looked intensely at the suspects, and then crouched down in his seat like a lion or a tiger. He looked like a predator about to pounce on his prey.

After Richard passed the two men this time, he looked back at them in his rearview mirror. Then he started breathing heavily and snorted through his nose. *Why did the sergeant put me with this damn reptilian?* I thought. Richard's behavior seemed very odd to me.

Richard saw the two men separate. He jumped out of the car and directed me to stop one suspect while he stopped the other. When we immobilized the two subjects, Richard searched his suspect and removed heroin from his pockets. I got the second suspect with the money from the drug deal. That was our third drug arrest.

Richard was not a conversationalist. In those days, veteran officers did not communicate much with rookies. If you had less than five years under your belt, you were considered a rookie. Day after day and week after week, Richard and I arrested subjects for drug violations based on Richard's observations. I kept asking Richard how in hell he knew the suspects were selling drugs. Finally, I confided in him that I never saw the suspects do anything suspicious or illegal myself.

Richard's aptitude for catching drug deals in progress was uncanny, so I asked him again, "What are you seeing?" He never revealed his secret. Instead, he wanted to remain the star of our show. But one day, when I asked Richard how he knew so much about drugs, he paused for a minute, then struck a profoundly severe tone and said something shocking that I can't repeat. However, after that conversation, I clearly understood where his wisdom concerning drugs came from.

Richard revealed to me that he spent the last ten years working in narcotics. He was transferred out of narcotics for reasons never disclosed to me. He had a difficult time adjusting to being back on uniform patrol. He resorted to using the one skill he had perfected over many years: his ability to catch drug dealers. I surmised that Richard had spent a lot of time on surveillance, watching drug activity. That time had allowed him to study the mannerisms of people operating in the drug culture.

Three weeks later, Richard was gone. By that time, I was determined to sharpen my drug enforcement skills. I learned to step away from my patrol car, get out on foot, and watch what was going on from a distance. It did not take long for me to figure out how Richard could zero in on the streetwise hustlers.

Richard did not see the drug deals going down. What he saw was a recurring theme indicative of a drug deal. Two individuals would meet. Briefly, they would look around to see whether anyone was watching. Then they would walk away quickly, often in opposite directions. One person would have dope on them while the other would have the proceeds from the sale in their pockets.

I recalled how after Richard stopped a suspect, he always asked for an ID. In the process of retrieving the ID, suspects would often remove a wad of money from their pants pocket, revealing doper folds—a series of cash in various denominations representative of twenty- and fifty-dollar sales. The purchaser of the drugs would either discard the drugs as we approached them, or the dealer would inadvertently remove the drugs from their pocket in a state of anxiety.

Working with Richard turned out to be a blessing in disguise. He unwittingly provided me with unmanaged on-the-job training. As a result, I refined my skills in catching the most elusive street-level dealers. Moreover, the skills I learned would help me realize one of my biggest dreams: bringing down scores of drug dealers.

CHAPTER 22

THE COFFEE BOY REBELLION

I came to roll call one day and noticed we had a new Japanese patrol sergeant. He was about fifty years old. He introduced himself to me and told me he had spent a good portion of his career as a narcotics detective. Naturally, I was excited, thinking I could pick his brains about narcotics investigations, as I did with Sergeant Harris regarding homicide investigations. He was approachable. However, he was a macho guy with a very authoritative voice.

After roll call, the new patrol sergeant waved to me and told me to bring him and the lieutenant some coffee. I took a deep breath and agreed to get them their coffee, but I had a severe problem with being someone else's errand boy. I hoped the new sergeant would not make this a habit, because I knew I would stand my ground.

When I returned with the two cups of coffee, I noticed coffee stains on my white uniform shirt. Later that day, I saw two of my squad members at a 7-Eleven. They immediately commented on the stains on my shirt. One of the officers said I was turning into a slob, just like the old-timers. That only added fuel to the fire, because I took enormous pride in my uniform's appearance.

Every day for the next two days, after roll call, my sergeant would say, "Hicks, go get the lieutenant and me some coffee." My squad members would look at my face and begin to giggle. Eventually, I had enough. I told the sergeant that I did not mind doing anyone a favor but that I did not like getting coffee at all and that I was partic-ularly upset about getting the lieutenant's coffee.

By then, the squad's contempt for the lieutenant had rubbed off on me, although I never disrespected the lieutenant and never talked about him. However, I did not respect the pencil pusher, who was afraid to come out on the streets with his troops. The episode sparked the defiant side of me. *After all,* I thought, *I'm not their slave.*

I told the sergeant that I did not mind getting coffee occasion-ally for him and only him but that I would not do it every day—or every week, for that matter. That ignited my sergeant's temperament like a firecracker. He lit into me.

"Who in the hell do you think you are?" my sergeant exclaimed. "Even I will get the lieutenant his coffee."

I continued my resistance. "Not me," I said. "I'm not doing it at all."

He pointed at his stripes. "Do you see these?"

I nodded.

"These give me the legal right to fuck with you whenever I feel like it. Do you understand that?"

"Yes, sir," I replied. "I do, but I hope you are bigger than that. I want you to understand that I do not have a problem with you or with doing my job, but I am not somebody's errand boy. I have never been and never will be!"

My hard-core, old-school sergeant stood in the doorway to his office, fuming. The Pacific Islander was going to exact revenge on me for defying his orders to get their coffee. There would be hell to pay for my taking a stand. I wished I were different. People did not know how to take me because I was quiet most of the time. However, certain things fired me up. Once I reached that level, I was not about to back down, which was often to my detriment. But if I hadn't stood my ground, then I would have become their permanent concierge.

I drove to the 7-Eleven and saw the same two squad members sipping coffee. They immediately asked me how coffee duty was going. I snapped back at them and said, "The only coffee I am get-ting is my own!"

The older officer laughed. "Wow, that is a change," he said. "The sergeant got your dander up?"

I told them, "By the way, I don't like dogs. So if we go on a call and a dog is there, let me know before arriving on the scene, because if the dog comes at me, it is not going to be pretty."

Officer Hightower said, "What is your beef with dogs?"

"A group of dogs attacked me when I was a kid," I explained. "I got bitten badly."

The other officer started barking like a dog. "This is unit 2-4-5," he said. "I got a Signal 13. Officer down. Dogs are surrounding me!"

"I knew I should not have said that around you," I replied. "Very funny. You should be onstage."

I decided I would not take any more crap from them because I was already in the doghouse with the sergeant. It was time for me to shed my skin and demand the respect I deserved. I braced myself for what was to come next.

About twenty minutes later, the sergeant walked in and removed the coffeepot from the warmer. As he began pouring his coffee, he looked up and noticed me drinking my coffee. "Why are you here?" he asked.

"Because this is my post, sir," I replied.

"You're not assigned to the 7-Eleven. Head to the street!"

My squad members began snickering as I put a lid on my coffee cup and headed out. "Damn," I whispered. "I'm getting kicked out of here when I'm the only person that is supposed to be here."

Members of my squad eagerly anticipated obtaining the intimate details of my rebellion against the sergeant. Naturally, I would not give them the satisfaction. From that point on, I gave my sergeant a nickname: Sergeant Choker. My sergeant had an obsession with choking people.

As I walked out of the 7-Eleven, I ran into a funny Jewish man in his late seventies. He frequented that particular 7-Eleven, and I always looked forward to talking to him. He enjoyed quizzing me on police scenarios.

"Sonny, I want to ask you a question," he said. "What do you do if a man points a gun at you from a distance but you aren't sure if it's a gun?" Before I could answer, the man said, "Always shoot, Sonny. You can always get another job."

I laughed with him, as I always did, but ironically, the man's joke would serve as helpful advice several years later.

CHAPTER 23

MY LOVABLE DAD
THE BURGLAR

My squad was working the midnight shift on a bitterly cold winter night in January 1984 when we received a call to investigate an alarm going off at a school. The alarms had been going off each night for four nights in a row. Each night, we surrounded the school as a precaution and called for a K-9 officer to check the school building, but K-9 did not find anything out of place during the previous four calls.

On our fifth and final night, we received word of another alarm. We surrounded the school again. It was about three o'clock in the morning. K-9 went into the school to search. I had the heat turned up in my police car, which made me start drifting off to sleep, but I was still glancing at the door I was monitoring. I saw a man peek his head through the doorway. I rubbed my eyes thinking I was dreaming. Then in a flash, the man ran out of the door, full steam ahead.

I drove my car to the end of the parking lot where the man was running. I jumped out of the car just as the man approached the fence. He jumped the fence, and then I jumped the fence and caught him about half a block away. I called for a cruiser to pick him up.

Sergeant Choker was the first to arrive. "The lieutenant is going to love you," he said. "This guy has hit this place four times." He laughed. "Hicks, did you see what just happened?"

"No," I said. "Why do you ask?"

"If you had seen what happened when you jumped that fence, you would have crapped in your pants."

I asked what he meant.

"It went like this," he said. "First, the suspect jumped the fence. Then you jumped the fence. Then the K-9 dog lunged at you as you jumped. I don't know how you didn't see the dog. It was about to take a chunk out of your behind."

"What the hell!" I said. "I never saw the dog."

During the next shift, I saw the son of the man I had arrested for burglary at the school. He told me that his dad had told him I had arrested him for the burglary, but the son said, "You know, the only reason that you caught him was that he was tired from working a lot of hours."

I thought, *I guess doing nighttime burglaries can be taxing.* However, I did not want to hurt the son's feelings. His dad was his hero. It was my place to arrest his dad, but it was not my place to make disparaging remarks about him. Instead, I felt the need to console the son. So I tapped him on his shoulder and said, "I am sure that your dad did the best he could do to try to escape."

CHAPTER 24

MOVERS, SHAKERS, AND HATERS

Sergeant Choker stared at me as I marched into the roll call room to work the 11–7 shift. I knew that look. It meant he had decided it was time for more payback for my coffee boy rebellion. Sergeant Choker told me he was loaning me out to Sector 3. I was guessing he had expected me to whine about it, but secretly, I did not want him to know he just made my day. There were three African American officers on that squad who were close to my age. I had been hoping I would eventually have a chance to work with them.

Two officers on the squad were women; the third officer was a man. I formally introduced myself to the three of them. The first two officers I introduced myself to were very friendly; however, when I held out my hand to shake Officer Brenna's hand, she moved it away. By then, I knew she had officially joined the Hicks Haters Club.

Officer Brenna said, "I know who you are. You like to showboat by putting everything you do on the air." I asked her if she was referring to me making traffic stops. "Yeah, I know all about you," she said. I asked her if she called out when she made traffic stops. She did not answer. I could not understand why she was envious of me, why she found my positive attitude so intimidating. She had a negative vibe. I was disappointed. The other two officers merely shook their heads and said, "See you out there."

A few hours later, my squad members worked together to close in on a suspect during a foot pursuit. We were able to apprehend the car thief within a few minutes. I took the suspect down. Brenna seemed disappointed. I guessed that was the last thing she wanted to see.

About two hours later, a call was dispatched for a stabbing at a bar with multiple victims. It was a bustling night. The dispatcher was shoveling out an array of seemingly never-ending felony-in-progress calls every few minutes. Another call went out for a suspect who was wanted for multiple stabbings. He had fled the scene and then committed several hit-and-run accidents.

As I was about to head toward the scene, I saw a small blue compact car make a wide right-hand turn as the driver turned onto the same street I was on. I turned on my lights and pulled the driver over. However, radio traffic was so busy that I was unable to call in the traffic stop. As I approached the driver on foot, I asked him to exit the vehicle. But instead, he kept yelling, "Officer, I'm hurt! I need your help! Please come to the car! I need your help!"

At that point, I knew something was wrong. The driver was determined to get me to walk up to the car. I ordered him to remain in his vehicle. A few minutes later, the dispatcher described that the suspect was wanted for several counts of attempted murder and several hit-and-run accidents. It was impossible to get on the radio. All hell was breaking loose all over the city for every type of call imaginable—from shootings to bar fights to robberies in progress. I was on my own.

I ordered the suspect out of the car and down onto the ground. The driver slowly got out of the car. He was very intoxicated. I placed the suspect in handcuffs, looked inside the suspect's car, and observed a machete lying on the driver's floorboard. I was glad I had paid attention to my instincts. The suspect had been baiting me. He had tried to lure me to the car so he could stab me with his machete.

I secured his machete and arrested the suspect for drunk driving. As soon as I placed him in my car, the dispatcher came over the radio and described the vehicle and suspect wanted for attempted murder. As soon as the tag number was given, I looked at my suspect's vehicle tag. The tag number the dispatcher provided matched the tag of the car I had stopped.

I could not get on the radio for another ten minutes, as the dispatcher kept updating the situation. As soon as there was a break in radio traffic, I advised the dispatcher that I had stopped the vehicle in question, giving her my location. The dispatcher immediately started asking if anyone was available to assist me. Everyone was tied up. As soon as there was a break in radio traffic, I told the dispatcher I already had the suspect in custody.

In fact, at the end of the shift, when I returned to the station, I saw Brenna. She gave me the same nasty look she had given me at the beginning of the shift. I wanted her to tell me what she had been telling all the officers in her squad: "Hicks is not all that." I wanted to say to her, "Baby girl, this is what an anointing looks like. I am gifted to serve." However, as a rookie, it was vital for me to stay in my place. I had to let the haters keep hating.

I gave Brenna two more reasons to hate me that same night. I made two significant arrests in her beat. I never understood the hate people gave me for just doing my job. I only wanted to make a difference where I could. I was not there to steal anybody else's thunder. But there was one thing for sure: God was going to turn my lemons into lemonade. No matter what the situation, I learned to adapt and overcome.

*****

I saw a six-foot-four African American officer in his late twenties talking to a group of officers in the station's hallway. The officer was telling the group he did not think he could kill anyone. The other officers expressed their concerns about working with him. Eventually, the officer's sergeant convinced him to see the department's psychiatrist, whom the department had hired to help officers deal with stress.

A few weeks later, the officer responded to a call for an animal that had been struck in the street. When he arrived, he saw a cat on the verge of death. The cat seemed to be suffering. The officer took out his knife and stabbed the cat. We assumed it was mercy killing.

Word of the officer's peculiar behavior quickly spread through the station. When I came to work, there was a hand-drawn comic strip on the officer's desk. It showed the officer thinking about the cat. In the last panel of the comic strip, there was a drawing of a Tasmanian devil. The caption above the Tasmanian devil read, "Animal Complaint—No Description."

*****

Everyone who knew me knew my greatest phobia: dogs. When I was a kid, a group of dogs attacked me. I was still not over my fear. My squad used to get a kick out of screwing with me about my fear of dogs. One time, I received a call for an alarm going off at a business. Unbeknownst to me, another officer in my squad had arrived there before me. I checked the back of the building. I heard a large dog barking. The barking sound was coming close to me very quickly. I started backing up and reaching for my gun.

Finally, when the barking stopped, I saw my squad mate laughing like hell. He had been back there, barking. I said, "Man, you are lucky you aren't getting shot right now. I know you are sick. For that barking sound to be so convincing, you must have been practicing that bark for a week. You sound just like a large dog. What do you do, spend your time listening to dogs so that you can screw with me?"

CHAPTER 25

THE WRATH OF SERGEANT CHOKER

I was never perturbed by people who tried to play games with me. I knew I was anointed and that people who wanted to harm others always got their just desserts. Even though Sergeant Choker liked to play games with me, I still liked him. He was hilarious, particularly when he got mad. I also liked him because he carried himself like a Marine. He was very authoritative.

For the next three weeks, Sergeant Choker called me to the station to take reports. He enjoyed screwing with me every chance he could get. He exiled me to other sectors every chance he got. But God transformed each provocation Choker used to harm me into something for my good. I got better-quality arrests and good felony cases instead of minor misdemeanor arrests.

The assigned beat officer was required to take all reports at the station. The station was not in my post. The sergeant made me take all the reports to the station. The sergeant also screwed with me by calling me to Dunkin' Donuts to take reports. By the end of the third week, Sergeant Choker was the acting lieutenant. He called me to Dunkin' Donuts to take a report. The citizen there told me about a theft that occurred about five years ago. I asked what had made him decide to report the theft now. He said that the sergeant had told him to. Sergeant Choker looked at me and smiled. I took the report and began to walk out.

"Have you had enough?" Sergeant Choker asked.

I told him that if he preferred to have me writing reports while the community was being terrorized, that was his decision. I pointed at his sergeant stripes. "It's three to zero," I said. "You have three stripes, and I don't have any." I saluted him, then headed toward the door.

"Wait a minute. I'm not done," he said. "How do you feel about working in Sector 2?"

"You're the boss," I said. "I'll do whatever you tell me to do, sir, as long as it is legal and ethical."

The sergeant knew that lending me out to patrol other areas was more dangerous than patrolling my own. He wanted to rattle my cage a little more, but God always blessed me and turned my lemons into lemonade.

The following week, a member of our squad was stabbed in a nightclub in our sector. Sergeant Choker was off that night. About an hour after the incident was over, I went back on patrol. A few minutes later, I received a call about a disorderly person at a nightclub. When I arrived, I was shocked to see Sergeant Choker yelling at the club owner.

As I drew closer, I heard Sergeant Choker say, "I am going to close this motherfucker down because you stabbed one of my men!" The owner told me he did not know what the man's problem was. Sergeant Choker was in plain clothes. He never identified himself as a police officer. He just came in and asked for the manager and began his drunken rant. I asked him to walk outside with me. He began walking until he saw an attractive white woman cleaning glasses at the bar.

Sergeant Choker pointed at the pretty bartender and said, "Oh my God, she is really good-looking! I'm going to take her home with me."

"That's the owner's wife, sir," I said.

"As I said," he replied, "I am going to take her home with me!"

I reminded him he was married. Finally, I convinced him to leave the bar. I let him know the assailant had already been arrested.

*****

Sergeant Choker worked hard and played hard. He was like Dr. Jekyll and Mr. Hyde when he drank. He was his own worst enemy. During the day shift one day, a call went out for a man choking an employee at a convenience store in Sector 3. A few minutes later, a call went out again saying the assailant was a police lieutenant. I did not go to the scene because it was out of my area; I was assigned to Sector 4.

At the end of the shift, I went to the station and saw Sergeant Choker sitting in the waiting area of the district commander's office. The sergeant had his head down. He seemed to be on the verge of breaking down in tears. I feared that something had happened to someone in his family. I asked the sergeant what was going on. He said, "Maurice, I choked another one." I asked how many people he had choked.

"I think that is my seventh person," he said. "I think that I'm gone this time."

"Where do you think they are going to transfer you?" I asked.

He said he believed he was going to be fired.

The next day, everyone at the station was talking about the incident. They said the sergeant had stopped in his wife's store to talk to her when he saw a male employee smiling and talking to her. That Ignited his fire. Sergeant Choker allegedly walked behind the counter. Several customers were standing there, watching the scene unfold. Choker was wearing his full police uniform and sporting his acting lieutenant bars. Then the sergeant allegedly put the employee in a chokehold and nearly choked him out.

Just then, as the officers at the station were finishing their story, Sergeant Choker walked into the room. Everybody suddenly stopped talking. Sergeant Choker told us he was being transferred back to narcotics. A witty officer threw a quick verbal jab at the sergeant. "Hey, Sarge," he said. "We're going to give you a going-away party. It's going to be Bring Your Own Chokee." The previously confident, overbearing, authoritative sergeant found himself at a loss for words.

Sergeant Choker's little reign of terror against me abruptly ended. I missed seeing him getting hyped up and cursing with his deep accent.

CHAPTER 26

FROM CITY KITTY TO COUNTY MOUNTY

In May of 1985, my partner told me that the Prince George's County Police Department was in town to try and recruit police officers.

I asked him, "Where the hell is Prince George's County?"

He laughed. "Baltimoreans are something else," he said. "You all love to stay in the hood." Then he answered my question. "It's about an hour away, near DC."

I asked him if he would leave the Baltimore Police Department if Prince George's County offered him a job. He told me he was not sure, and then he said that the Wicomico County Police was also hiring. He asked if I would ride up there with him.

Just about then, the sergeant walked up. "Hicks," he said, "you're the low man on the totem pole. Everyone has taken their vacation day. Look at the book and tell me which days you want off." I took the book and marked my days off. The sergeant looked at the book and noticed that instead of taking many days off in a row, I took two and three days off at a time.

The sergeant laughed. "Where are you going for vacation?" he asked. "West Baltimore?"

"Gee, you really know me, Sarge," I said. "Yes, we Baltimoreans love Baltimore."

A few days later, my partner Conrad and I went to a local hotel to test for the Prince George's County Police Department. We were met by a very friendly Prince George's County Police corporal. Remarkably, he had some of the same qualities as my recruiter from the Baltimore Police Department. He, too, emphasized the need to hire good African American police officers. He told us his department was in desperate need of experienced police officers. He said they were grossly understaffed.

He asked me if my partner and I were ready to take the test. Conrad replied he was. I was shocked the corporal was going to give the test right there. He asked if I was ready to take the test as well. I told him that I had simply ridden down there to keep Conrad company.

The corporal said, "Son, since you have to wait for your partner, I want you to take the test for me."

I replied, "Yes, sir."

We took the test with several other applicants. When the testing was over, the corporal motioned me and Conrad over to him. "Sorry, fellas," he told us. "You guys didn't pass it this time, but you're welcome to come to PG County next week to take the test." Conrad told the corporal he was not interested in pursuing the job any further.

The corporal then asked me if I would retake the test. I frowned at him and said, "I don't like failing anything. I'll be there if I can find it." I looked at Conrad and asked him if he would go with me. He told me he was not interested. I stared at him. "How in the hell do I get there?" I asked. Both Conrad and the recruiter laughed.

"Just take 95 and get off at Pennsylvania Avenue," Conrad said. "Follow the signs to the police station."

We both shook hands with the recruiter before leaving.

"I'll see you next week, son, right?" the recruiter asked.

"Yes, sir," I replied.

Conrad asked me on the way home if I was planning to go back out there. I told him that the recruiter seemed like a nice guy and that I did not want to disappoint him.

The following week, I drove up I-95 and got off the highway at Pennsylvania Avenue. I eventually found the county police station in

Forestville, Maryland. I walked into the police academy and looked at the glass enclosure displaying the badges of officers who had been slain in the line of duty through various methods—from being shot or stabbed to being run over by a vehicle. First, there was a short synopsis describing how each of the officers was killed.

A very muscular young black police recruit wearing an all-blue uniform with no badge or police logo on it walked over to me and said, "Excuse me, sir. Please don't put your hands on the glass." I looked at the recruit while thinking, *How dare this damn boot tell me what to do?* However, I was highly impressed by his professionalism, so I also thought, *Wow, if all recruits looked like this, they must have a hell of a physical fitness program.* Several months later, the recruit and I would work together in the same squad.

After leaving the glass display case, I poked my head into a few different offices and found the recruiter's office. As I entered, I saw the recruiter standing up while talking to a female employee. I scanned the room and noticed that two other black officers were working in the recruiting office. I was stunned to see them.

Once the recruiter noticed me, a large smile appeared on his face. He immediately walked over and shook my hand. "It's good to see you, man," he said. "I have you all set up to take the test. Are you ready?" I told him I had already eaten and had gotten plenty of rest unlike the last time.

I took the test and patiently waited for the results. Finally, about thirty minutes later, the recruiter walked over to me and said, "Man, you did it. You passed the test." I thanked him and headed for the door. "Where are you going?" he asked. I told him I just wanted to prove to myself that I could pass the test. He looked disappointed. He said, "I got a job for you if you want it."

The recruiter asked me to sit down while he explained the benefits of working in Prince George's County. He told me I could get a five-thousand-dollar raise to start, and he could guarantee I would receive a take-home police car after graduating from the academy. He also said I could get a free apartment.

After that conversation, I surmised that the job would create better opportunities than working in Baltimore. I learned I would not have to go through a twenty-six-week academy. Instead, the academy for experienced Maryland officers was three and a half weeks. Three months later, I was selected as one of fifteen people out of 550 experienced police applicants to attend the academy.

As always, I consulted my grandfather about switching to the Prince George's County Police Department. He looked distraught and asked me to sit down. Then he asked what my rationale was for changing to Prince George's County. I explained that I would get a five-thousand-dollar raise, a take-home car with free gas, and possibly, a free apartment. He patiently allowed me to make my case. Then he said, "Now you are going from bad to worse."

He knew I had made my mind up, so he did the only thing he could do. He told me where the minefields were. He explained that the city's police were still getting used to accepting blacks; he warned me to brace myself. The Prince George's County Police Department would give me a hard time because I was a black man from Baltimore. His wisdom was astonishing.

It was up to me to maneuver through the minefields my grandfather warned me about. If I had taken the time to explore the history of the Prince George's County Police Department, I would have been better prepared for what was to come.

I had no clue what police work was like in a county police department. The average city police officer learned in one year more than the average county officer learned in five years. However, I eventually realized certain things differentiated the Prince George's County Police Department from the Baltimore Police Department.

The county police department had a hell of a driving course, and their firearms qualifications course was incredibly tough. The good old boys in the county were excellent marksmen and excellent drivers. In the Baltimore Police Academy, we used driving simulators. Thus, the county's emergency vehicle operations course and firearms qualifications course presented severe challenges. I had never owned a speed loader. I wore the Barney Fife-type gun belt in Baltimore; it had holes to house your bullets.

My driving experience at that point was primarily limited to city driving, and I had only driven on the beltway a few times. So when I drove to Prince George's County for the first time, I was shocked to see how fast people drove on the interstate and switched from lane to lane. I thought, *These county people drive like they are trying out for the Indianapolis 500.*

When I arrived at the police driving range off US 301 in Upper Marlboro, I gasped for air as I noted the large array of cones running throughout the lot. The driving lanes were narrow, and the curves were very tight. The second array of cones formed a small box.

The instructor explained that we would be tested on speed control, maneuvering, controlled braking, and parking. That was challenging enough, but what the instructor said next blew my mind. After driving through the course once, he told us that we had to go back our way through the entire course. But he saved the best for last: all driving maneuvers were timed. At the end of the course, we would have to drive in and out of the box. He then laughed and said, "That box is a bitch." I thought, *I'm glad I left the Baltimore City PD on good terms, because I'll probably be back there soon.*

I carefully watched as the driving instructor maneuvered through the course. Another instructor had a bullhorn and a radar gun in his hand. At different points, the second instructor would tell the driver to get up to certain speeds. For example, he would say to the driver to accelerate to fifty miles per hour. Then to my horror, he would randomly tell the driver to brake right or brake left.

I leaned over to a recruit standing next to me. "This driving course is freaking insane," I said. I took a moment to pray, telling God, "I am sure I'm going to need you on this one." My family's future was hanging in the balance. The instructor warned us that hitting cones was like hitting his children and that it would cause us to fail. In addition, there was one more complexity in completing the course: It had to be completed within a short time. If you ran out of time, you failed the course.

When it was my turn, I gave the instructor a half-hearted thumbs-up. Then I climbed into the car and started my journey. As I reached certain places in the course, I had to accelerate when the instructor told me to, just as the other recruits did. At different points, the instructor indeed said, "Brake right!" or "Brake left!" *Oh God,* I thought. *Lord, not again. When in the hell is this going to end?*

Finally, the first half of the test was over. Now I had to go back through the entire course and then park the car in that amazingly tiny box. I was surprised that backing through the course was not as hard as I thought. However, when I reached the little box, my luck changed. I kept pulling forward and then backing up. The next thing I heard was a whistle. My time had run out. The time constraint caused me to go back and park seventeen times before completing the course.

Some recruits were never able to get through the course. I wondered about their fate, but relief came quickly for them. The instructor announced that experienced police officers were not required to pass the course. My mental torture was over. It had to have been by the grace of God that I was able to get through the course. The course was necessarily tricky. I needed to perfect my skills to engage in numerous high-speed pursuits after graduating from the police academy.

Next, I set out to conquer my final challenge: firearms qualification. I lined up for the firing line with the other recruits. We were told, "When the target turns, shoot five times with a strong hand and holster." The target turned. I unsnapped my holster and drew my weapon, but when I aimed at the target, it had already turned back around. I was horrified. The rest of the recruits had already shot their five rounds and holstered their weapons. I received some additional coaching from another firearms instructor. After the coaching, I qualified with my gun. What a relief that was! A few years later, my firearms training would come in handy.

After three and a half weeks, I graduated from the Prince George's County Police Academy. Unlike the Baltimore Police Department, my field training lasted three months instead of five days.

CHAPTER 27

Indoctrination into the County Police First Days on the Job

My first on-duty assignment for the Prince George's County Police Department was at the Hyattsville station. As I walked into the station, a white man in his thirties was asking the station clerk to speak to a supervisor about filing a complaint against a police officer. A few seconds later, a tall white police sergeant in his thirties walked into the station lobby with a stack of complaint forms in his hand.

The sergeant asked the citizen how many complaint forms he needed. The citizen told the sergeant he required only one. The sergeant took the large stack of complaint forms and slugged the citizen in the face with the forms, knocking the citizen down to the floor. *What in the hell is going on here?* I thought. A few years later, that sergeant was promoted to deputy chief.

I walked into the roll call room, anxious to meet my new squad. One cheerful-looking young white officer in his mid-twenties, about my age, introduced himself and extended his hand to give me a handshake. I eagerly shook his hand and felt a buzz in my palm. That officer, Matt, was the first person to prank me.

I sat down in my seat and waited for the rest of the squad to walk in. After a few officers had entered, Officer Matt said, "Hicks, you dropped something on the seat behind you." I looked down and

143

saw a dollar bill just to the right of my foot. I reached down to pick it up. Matt pulled a string attached to the dollar, swiping the dollar into his hand. He laughed. "Two times in ten minutes. I'm going for a record today." He said.

After roll call, the sergeant lined us up for inspection. He looked at my nightstick and asked, "What have you got there, son?"

I feared I was in trouble. "It's my espantoon," I said.

"Your what?" he asked.

Matt was standing next to me. "Oh my God, Sarge," he said. "He has a Baltimore Bomber."

The sergeant looked at me strangely.

"I never leave home without it, sir," I replied.

You would have thought I had a rare gold coin. Everyone in the room seemed mesmerized, marveling at my nightstick. All of them wanted to know where I had gotten my prized Baltimore Bomber. "From Nightstick Joe," I replied. Everybody—from recruits to veterans—bought their nightsticks from Nightstick Joe.

After roll call, I boarded my training officer's take-home car. About halfway through the shift, I heard the sound of someone speaking over the police radio with a deep Southern drawl. "Radio, I got one running!" the speaker said. The officer seemed pleased that someone wanted to run from him; his tone was very inviting.

My training officer floored the gas pedal and began heading to the area indicated by the officer on the radio. I was excited about the opportunity to be engaged in a pursuit; pursuing a suspect by car was not allowed in Baltimore City. But three minutes later, the officer came back over the radio and said, "Never mind, radio. He done wrecked."

We drove to the scene and saw a gray Chevy turned on its side. It appeared to have tumbled a few times before landing on its side. The officer looked at me and said, "If we were down South, I would have shot out his taars. Lemme 'all the faar department 'fore this dang thang erupts into flames. I would have to wait another day to catch a suspect running."

*****

144

My training officer drove to the 5400 block of Kenilworth Avenue, where we saw Officer Mighty Matt talking to a belligerent, freckle-faced fifteen-year-old kid. The kid was asserting his right to be out of school during school hours. He was walking his dog.

Matt was twirling his nightstick and told the kid, "If you keep running your mouth, I'm going to lock you up for disorderly conduct and impound your dog. That's going to be a fifty-dollar dog."

I said, "Matt, I can see you have been practicing your twirl." Matt was amazed by how fast and how well I could twirl my nightstick. Walking a foot beat, I was given plenty of time to practice.

I thought, *These county guys march to the beat of a different drum.* It was clear to me some of my squad members did not care for me. Something about people from Baltimore rubbed them the wrong way. But I had always liked Matt. He was the first and the only person on the force who befriended me during that time. He introduced me to his family. We also washed our police cars together.

He showed me the kindness and courtesy that seemed unattainable from other people on the squad. He did not know it at the time, but I would remember his kindness a few years later when I became a supervisor. Many of the people living in Prince George's County were transplants from Washington, DC. There had always been friction between Washingtonians and Baltimoreans.

*****

My field training officer (FTO) sat in his beloved take-home police cruiser, a shiny Dodge Diplomat. I slid into the passenger seat and took a moment to marvel at the sizable, spacious leather seats, the handheld microphone, and the siren dial that had a series of choices for siren tones.

My FTO noticed my fascination with the interior of his car. "You look like you've never sat in a police car before," he said.

"I haven't seen a police car like this before," I replied.

In Baltimore, my police car was a tiny AMC Concord with a small lever to turn on the only siren tone. Our police cars were driven around the clock from one shift to the next. Unfortunately, our vehicle's air-conditioning systems were often out of service. Therefore, we often suffered during the humid summer months.

My FTO used to drive race cars, and he lived for the opportunity to use his driving skills to chase bad guys, so my nickname for him was Speed Racer. That day, Speed Racer observed an eighteen-year-old kid riding a motorcycle without a tag. When he activated his lights and siren, the kid turned around and looked back at us. Then he accelerated.

Speed Racer looked at me with a big, wide grin on his face—he looked like a cat about to chase a mouse—and off we went. Speed hit the accelerator. My head jerked back. I thought, *This is like an episode of the cartoon* Tom and Jerry. Our car engine roared, and our tires began squealing. My nostrils were immediately filled with the smell of burning rubber. I held on for dear life.

The kid desperately tried to escape. He maneuvered, swerved, and cut down some side streets, all to no avail. All the while, Speed Racer was having the time of his life. The motorcycle driver eventually began to slow down, at which time, Speed Racer told me to get out of the car and start chasing him.

"But your car is still moving," I said.

Speed Racer repeated, "Get out and start chasing him."

I waited a few minutes for Speed Racer to slow down. Then I yelled, "Oh God !" and jumped out. PG County policing was certainly a lot different from city policing.

The motorcyclist attempted to drive through a bush to head into the woods. Unfortunately for him, there was a guardrail behind the bushes. The kid hit the guardrail and fell off the bike. I was right there as he tried to run away. I cuffed him and stuffed him in the cruiser. Then I looked at Speed Racer and said, "Speed Racer, what the hell? You boys are serious about your pursuits!"

*****

My training officer reminded me not to take anybody's crap on the streets. We had to keep the department's reputation going, he said. He emphasized that our reputation as a no-nonsense police department kept us all safe.

After hearing Speed Racer's comments, my sergeant smiled and shifted into a positive, happy mode. He started reminiscing about the good old days when DC residents feared breaching the county line for fear of the warrior county police officers. "When those DC boys came into the county," he said, "as soon as they saw a county policeman, they immediately crossed the street. I was left to fill in the blanks for the rest of the story. Talking about county police superiority was soothing to his soul.

As I listened to the sergeant's story, I thought about Richard Pryor's joke about America's bicentennial celebration. "We are celebrating two hundred years!" the comedian said. He paused for a second, then added, "Of white folks kicking ass!" It was clear that entering Prince George's County created challenges for Washingtonians.

It did not take long to realize that Prince George's County policing was different from policing in Baltimore. There was a lot of bravado in the county police department. They marched to the beat of a different drum. County police officers had a unique set of norms and values. They were part of a subculture that used its unique terminology.

Sometimes, I was perplexed about some county officers' behavior, but not all of them. Some of their behaviors were congruent with the behaviors of the people I grew up with in Baltimore. Sometimes, the officers exhibited gang-like behavior. They had their own set of norms and values. They also imposed sanctions on members who violated the norms of the group. In the inner city, people who provided information to the police were called snitches or hot boys. In police circles, officers who violated norms were called rats. No one wanted to be called by the filthy varmint's name.

Like some of my classmates in Baltimore, some county officers were provocateurs who baited people into premature confrontations so that they could assert their great police powers. If the subjects asserted their rights, they would commit the unforgivable sin: contempt of cop. I wondered why the state's attorney referred to county police officers as cowboys and renegades. However, after listening to their macho conversations, I understood why he had made the statement.

I believed the pen was mightier than the sword, so I would instead put my pen on a suspect any day. I developed a reputation for wreaking havoc on suspects with my pen. Some officers called me Edgar Allan Poe. It was for two reasons: first because Poe was from Baltimore and second because I knew the most obscure laws in the books.

On the positive side, county officers took enormous pride in the appearance of both their uniforms and their vehicles. They were more physically fit than Baltimore City police officers. But one significant difference between the PG County patrol officers and the Baltimore City patrol officers was the former's knowledge of investigations.

In my experience, I noticed that Baltimore City patrol officers' investigative skills were unparalleled. It was outstanding compared to PG cops' knowledge. Patrol officers in Baltimore were skilled at getting both arrest warrants and search warrants. They followed up on many crimes PG officers turned over to station detectives. PG cops often criticized members of the DC Police Department, who had similar problems to Baltimore's police department. However, they were masters of police work. Their detectives were each as sharp as a tack.

In Baltimore, quite often, suspects would not comply with a police officer's commands, even when they were staring down the barrel of a gun. Instead, they fought the police at the drop of a dime. For example, on Garrison Avenue in Northwest Baltimore, two uniformed officers arrested two drug dealers, seized their drugs, and called for the police van. While the officers waited, a group of the suspects' friends beat the officers up, unhandcuffed their two buddies, and took the dope back. In a separate incident, a uniformed officer walking a foot beat in Old Town Mall in East Baltimore was beaten, turned upside down, and robbed while he was on duty.

Those things did not happen in Prince George's County. I guessed that was what my training officer was alluding to when he said, "We have to keep our reputation going."

CHAPTER 28

COWBOYS AND RENEGADES

As promised, three months after training, I was issued a take-home police cruiser. The street term used by the county police for being released from training was being cut loose. Now, I was free to patrol my beat. The problem was, my field training officer rarely allowed me to drive. In addition, I was still struggling to learn my way around.

My training officer had grown up in the area. He rarely needed to consult a map to find the location for our calls. For me, being in Prince George's County was like being in another state. I had no clue how to get to any of the areas. To add to my woes, I had an inferior sense of direction.

One day, soon after being issued my take-home car, Tyler, our supervisory police corporal, joined in on a conversation I had with Mighty Matt in my beat. In his thirties, a slender white man walked up to Tyler and asked him how he was doing.

Tyler frowned at the man, looked him up and down, and said, "Do I know you, son?"

"Yes, sir. Don't you remember?" the man asked. "You locked me up about two years ago."

Tyler asked the man to lower his head. He examined the top of the man's head, then said, "Nope, it wasn't me." We were all perplexed by Tyler's response. "Look, son," Tyler told the man. "If I had locked up a little germ like you, I would have given you a wood shampoo. You would still have a knot and my signature mark on the top of your head. So no, I'm sure it wasn't me."

The citizen walked away while rubbing the top of his head. No wonder some of the officers had gone rogue. They had supervisors showing them the way. A few minutes later, our sergeant drove up and joined our conversation.

An emaciated-looking white man in his early twenties walked up to us, made eye contact, and said, "Huey, Dewey, and Louie."

Mighty Matt looked at me. Then he began whirling his night-stick. Tyler puffed his cigarette and looked at the man's head. "This boy is cruising for a bruising," Mighty Matt whispered to me.

Our sergeant held up his hand, signaling for us not to respond to the provocation, but the man continued to taunt us. "The big, bad county police don't have nothing to say?" he said.

It was summertime, and about everybody was outside, enjoying the nice weather. The man then unzipped his pants and began whis-tling. Next, he raised his penis and began urinating on the doors of the sergeant's take-home police car. The provocateur then redirected his aim and began saturating the sergeant's windshield. By the time the urine reached the windows, I was thinking the sergeant was going to lose it.

The urinating was happening in my beat, so I knew I would be the person who would have to make the arrest. I patiently waited for the man to finish unloading about a quarter gallon of urine on the sergeant's car. Then I had the unpleasant task of handcuffing Mr. Nasty Man after he finished urinating. I cuffed him and took him to my car.

The sergeant walked over to my car and stared at the man from the passenger window. I rolled down my window and asked the sergeant if he had any parting words for the man before I left. The sergeant gritted his teeth and said, "You're lucky people are watching me, you little germ. Now I know why tigers eat their young."

I told the suspect, "If you value your safety, don't ever show your face down here again."

CHAPTER 29

PRETTY PAULY MEETS THE NAKED GREEN BEAN

My training officer, Speed Racer, asked me if I had ever fought with anyone on PCP. I had not. He enlightened me that PCP abusers would get overheated and would start taking off all their clothes. He said, "It takes about five or six officers to take them down. They sometimes act as if they have Superman's strength." I was not looking forward to those encounters. However, I would have my first run-in with PCP abusers sooner than I realized.

A few days later, I heard a squeal come over the police radio. It sounded like a female officer in distress. In reality, it was a male police officer. He was shaken up. It took him a few minutes to communicate what was going on over his radio.

Within a few minutes, we arrived on the scene and observed a naked muscular large black man in his thirties on top of the police car of an officer we called Pretty Pauly. I believed it was wise of Pretty Pauly to have remained inside the car, because the guy looked like he could take about three or four people down.

The PCP abuser leaped off the top of the vehicle as my training officer and I arrived. The suspect ran across the street, and a group of about six officers followed him. It was the middle of summer, and the suspect was sweating profusely. We tried to control him by grabbing his arms, but he kept slipping out of our hands.

We finally got him onto the ground, only to have him slip through our hands again. He started running down Annapolis Road and toward Bladensburg Elementary School. Finally, he tripped on the sidewalk. It was painful to watch. I was pretty sure he would not be using his family jewels for a while. He received a large laceration on that particularly delicate body part. We were able to handcuff the suspect and take him into custody.

Pauly told us he was driving slowly down Annapolis Road when the PCP abuser leaped on top of his car and climbed onto his hood out of nowhere. I could only imagine what the fight would have been like if the abuser had chosen to fight instead of run.

CHAPTER 30

FRIGHT NIGHT FOR REAL

Why must I be like that? Why must I chase the cat?
—"Atomic Dog," George Clinton

I certainly knew better than to follow him into the woods. I was trained precisely on how to handle the situation. However, adrenaline had kicked in, and now I was locked in on him. There was no changing course. I was ticked off. The suspect was screwing around in my beat.

It had been three years since my skirmish at the Flag House Projects. There, I had found myself surrounded by four motivated young men who desired to pulverize me and rid me of the pesty badge and police uniform they hated so much. I was now facing another dangerous situation that was about to spiral out of control. If I had known the danger that lay ahead, I would have been better prepared for what would occur next.

I was drafted into the permanent midnight squad via some sort of lottery. I had to do a four-week rotation on the squad. I respected the six-foot-four mountain of a man who ran the squad, Sergeant Hardcastle. It did not take very much time to learn he was a cop's cop. Hardcastle was a great leader who treated everyone on the squad the same regardless of race, time on the squad, or any other factor. Hardcastle was a tough guy; there was no doubt about that. He was practically a folk hero to some members of the department. However, Hardcastle did not flaunt his tough guy image.

Rumor had it, he once encountered a group of robbery suspects in the middle of a robbery. He was a patrolman at the time. One of the suspects shot him in the stomach with a shotgun. Then the suspect fled. When backup arrived, Hardcastle had his foot on the bumper of his car, holding his guts in one hand and his radio in the other. He was calmly putting out thorough descriptions of each of the suspects. Sergeant Hardcastle was always on the streets with his men, and he was always willing to write you a commendation if you did a good job.

It was the first day of the midnight shift. I left roll call and started toward my beat. After a while, I initiated a traffic stop, and I called the traffic stop into the dispatcher. "Baker 2, traffic." There was no answer. I tried a second time. "Baker 2, traffic Landover and Fifty-Fifth Avenue." Again, no response. I gave the driver a verbal warning and sent him on his way. *Damn, radio problems again,* I thought. Throughout my career, I seemed to have more radio problems than the man on the moon.

I did not want to relive my radio failure nightmare from the Flag House Housing Projects. Therefore, I parked my cruiser in the nearby convenience store's parking lot and called the dispatcher from a payphone. I prepared to tell the dispatcher that my radio was not working and that I was heading to retrieve another radio. Then I glanced to my right and saw a liquor store owner chasing a creepy-looking, emaciated white man in his thirties. The store owner yelled to me, "That guy just robbed us!"

I told the dispatcher I was chasing a white male wearing a yellow football jersey. He was in his thirties, was six foot four with a full beard and mustache, and weighed 165 pounds. He was heading toward a wooded area. I hung up the phone and started my patrol car. I glanced at the suspect and drove directly through three lanes of traffic in pitch-black. I tried again to use my police radio, to no avail. Finally, I maneuvered my police car onto the opposite side of the street.

I observed the suspect running across the parking lot of the theater. I ran after him. I drew my service revolver and yelled, "Stop, or I'll shoot!" I had no intention of shooting. I was simply trying to convince the suspect to stop before he entered the woods. He kept running.

I looked to my left and noticed that an African American couple was close enough to hear my commands. I was very reluctant to enter those woods. I knew the best way to apprehend the suspect was to form a perimeter and call for a K-9 unit. The problem was, my radio was not working. *Crap!* I accelerated my sprint and caught the suspect as soon as he entered the woods. I threw him down to the ground. My intense workouts served me well.

I felt confident. I thought I was in complete control of the situation, although I had no way of communicating with my fellow officers. After all, in my mind, I was a highly motivated United States Marine. No mere civilian could handle me.

I proudly stood over the man I believed was my conquered foe, but when I got a good look at his face, his face terrified me. He looked like the convicted serial murderer Charles Manson. Even the length of his hair and his beard was identical to Charles Manson's. It was unbelievable. I told him the fight was over and to put his hands behind his back. He gave me the strangest look. He had no fear. My heart sank. It was clear to me he was riding on the boat, meaning he was under the influence of PCP.

I quickly got off him, removed my service revolver from my holster, and pointed it directly at him. "I repeat, fella, the fight is over. Turn around and put your hands behind your back," I said. The suspect quickly reached out and grabbed my service revolver. A life-and-death struggle for my weapon was now in full force. The suspect was still on the ground. He gripped my gun so hard that when I tried to pull it back, I began lifting him off the ground. I tried twisting the weapon out of his hand. His grip on it was enormous. I quickly glanced at a tattoo on his forearm. Crap, he had a USMC tattoo. He was also a damn Marine.

Finally, after what seemed like an eternity—realistically, it was about four minutes—I was able to pry the gun out of his hands. I quickly holstered my weapon, then snapped the firearm in place. I gave the suspect a series of punches to his face. He sat there for a second and then smiled at me. That scared the hell out of me. "Oh boy!" I said to myself. My fear intensified as the suspect robotically rose to his feet. He waved his finger at me as if to say, "Son, we are just getting started." I wondered, How do you defeat a damn robot?

I sensed that he wanted to show off his drug-induced new strength. Now it was his turn to inflict damage. He smiled and picked me up and lifted me over his head. With both hands, I clapped his ears and tried to throw off his senses, but I had no luck. "Get your fucking hands off me, you psycho. You messed up big time. I am going to put another charge on you," I said.

He threw me down on a large boulder. I felt intense pain on my back. I looked up at the clouds and the thick darkness that surrounded me. It was horrifying lying there on my back like a helpless turtle. I struggled to rise to my feet. I feared that he was coming back to finish the job, but true to my character, I still had to show confidence and trash-talk.

"You got me, good boy! Now I am going to put another charge on you," I repeated. "This is not over yet," I said. I was relieved when I saw him begin to flee. I watched the football-jersey-wearing villain run through the thorny briar bushes as if he was trying to score a touchdown.

I was relieved no one saw me being thrown down in the woods. I would have never lived that down. I quickly scrambled to my feet. The thought of lying helpless in the woods was horrifying. However, I was ticked off, and the desire to catch the suspect trumped any common sense. Like the TV cop Tony Baretta used to say, "He had dues to pay."

I carefully made my way through the briar patches and caught up with the suspect as he came out of the woods. I said, "What we got here boy is a failure to communicate." I had wanted to use the line for years. I tackled him, spun him around, and pulled his football jersey over his head. I heard sirens all around me. However, my colleagues did not seem to be able to find me. Finally, I felt myself being lifted off the ground.

Sergeant Hardcastle said, "Relax, son. We got him." Two of my squad mates came on the scene with their Baltimore Bombers (their nightsticks) slung over their shoulders. "Damn." I thought the officer was disappointed the suspect was under control. Crazy Matt nicknamed the duo the Bruise Brothers. He probably wanted to get some stick time in. Did Officer Byrd and Swartkopf, aka the Bruise Brothers, deserve their nickname? The jury was still out on that. Even after a month on the midnight shift and working with them, it was still hard to tell. Engaging nightly with numerous crazed PCP abusers was certainly not for the faint of heart. Sometimes, it was like being in an episode of *Night of the Living Dead.*

Our patrol commander always questioned the sergeant about the actions of the Bruise Brothers. When I heard the lieutenant scolding the sergeant about the duo's activities, it reminded me of a James Bond episode where the spy's boss expressed her frustration with Bond. She asked, "Why do you have to kill everybody you come in contact with, 007?" He never answered. I wanted to answer his boss for him. I wanted to say, "He does it because everywhere he goes, people are jumping out of hiding and trying to attack him."

I searched Johnny Boy on the scene and found three watches and three wallets on him. I learned that he had robbed three black men in their twenties about three hours before he robbed the liquor store. He observed three black men sitting in their car and talking. Then he struck all three of them in the face, then robbed them of their watches and wallets.

I began brushing off the shrubbery from my uniform shirt. The sergeant started hitting the back of my shirt to remove the dirt. I adjusted my Sam Browne duty belt, bloused my shirt into my pants, adjusted my military alignment, and put my Sam Browne belt back on.

Another squad member looked at me. "Damn, Hicks. You all must have been brawling fiercely."

Finally, I said, "I had enough of this jungle warfare bullcrap. Next time, I will wait for K-9 to hunt the suspect down."

I charged Johnny Boy with four counts of robbery. One charge was for the liquor store robbery. The sarge wrote me a commendation for the apprehension. I thought my skirmish with Johnny Boy was over. I was sadly mistaken.

The next night, I rode with Officer Byrd and related my adventures with Johnny Boy. We drove around, staying within a two-block radius of where I fought with Johnny. As I went through my beat, I saw Johnny Boy walking down the street, free as a bird. Byrd was driving at the time.

I pointed Johnny Boy out to Byrd. "There's that nutjob I fought with last night," I said. It was four o'clock in the morning, so what the hell was Johnny Boy doing now? "Let's jack that boy up and get some answers," I told Byrd. No sooner had the cruiser slowed down that Johnny Boy took off running. "He's heading toward those same woods again," I told Byrd.

We exited the car, and Byrd yelled for Johnny Boy to freeze. Johnny Boy turned around quickly, assumed a combat stance, and lifted his hands, pointing in our direction. We quickly ducked behind a brick wall for cover. Then Johnny Boy ran into the woods. We realized he had only pretended to have a gun. We went back on routine patrol. I did not want to pursue Johnny Boy in the woods. I already made that mistake the previous night.

The next night, I stopped to back up another officer at a traffic stop. I noticed a thin white man staggering as he got out of his vehicle. It was Johnny Boy. I told the officer who had stopped him, "This is the green bean I was telling you about. This is the guy I was fighting with. Oh my goodness, it drives!" Johnny Boy was arrested for driving under the influence of drugs.

*****

I had just started the third night of my midnight shift when I heard a call for a burglary in progress. A couple had come home a few minutes early and noticed their door was propped open. They saw a white man in his thirties drinking their beer and watching television as they entered the house. Officers from the evening shift responded to the call first. When I arrived, they had the building surrounded. They called the residence and convinced the suspect to come out.

A few minutes later, I observed a white male walking backward into the abyss of the police lights with his hands in the air. One very stern-sounding officer quickly ordered the suspect to his knees and told him to put his hands behind him. The officer promptly handcuffed the suspect and lifted him to his feet using the suspect's belt. The officer's actions appeared to be that of an abusive father disciplining his son. When the officer brought the suspect near my cruiser, he told me I had a friend who wanted to say hello.

The suspect said, "Hey, Hicks, USMC man. You all got to put a stop to all this crime, man."

I looked at the suspect. "What the hell?" I exclaimed.

Johnny Boy was just getting started. It seemed as if my nightmare with him would never end.

*****

One month later, Sergeant Hardcastle was driving down Annapolis Road when he saw a nineteen-year-old black man standing in front of a run-down storefront for a trucking company. He got out of his vehicle and asked the black man why he was standing there. The young man replied, "It's nothing, sir. I'm just waiting here while my friend breaks into trucks in the back." The sergeant directed the man to slip into his handcuffs. Then the sergeant called for backup. It was my beat, and I was the first to arrive.

I walked to the back of the trucking company and shone my flashlight around the premises. Unable to locate anyone, I called for K-9. Soon, a veteran K-9 officer named Blaster arrived on the scene. I was delighted. Blaster volunteered to perform the search. He was an excellent K-9 officer. If anyone was out there, Blaster would find them. In my opinion, Blaster had a dark side.

Blaster gave his Rottweiler the command to search with a distinct accent in his native language, Japanese. I always enjoyed hearing him give dog commands. I never knew what the hell he was saying, but it always sounded cool. The search went on for about fifteen minutes. Suddenly, I heard the dog barking, and then the dog started whimpering. I ran down the fence line and shone my flashlight in the area where I heard the dog whining.

I illuminated a spot under one of the trucks. The first image I saw was the facial expression of Blaster's dog. He was clearly in distress. Johnny Boy was repeatedly punching the dog in the face while holding the dog in a headlock. "Blaster," I yelled, "come quickly. He's punching your dog in the face! Come to the location where you see my flashlight."

When he arrived, Blaster crawled under the truck to a point near the fence line. Once he reached the suspect, he yelled, "Get the hell off my dog!" Then he hit the suspect with his flashlight, yelling, "Why did you hurt my dog?"

I turned off my light so I would not blind Blaster. After hearing the unmistakable sound of a flashlight hitting skull, I said, "Stop, Blaster. You're going to kill him!" After two more sounds of flashlight to skull, I saw Blaster drag Johnny Boy out of the yard. When I reached the front of the yard, Johnny Boy was lying on the ground, awaiting the ambulance. His blood-soaked head looked like a jelly doughnut.

About thirty minutes later, I drove to Prince George's County Hospital to check on Johnny Boy. Blaster was already there. He was marching back and forth around Johnny Boy's hospital room, his hands clasped behind his back like a military general contemplating his next strike. The macho, chain-smoking mammal was wearing his dark-blue K-9 police uniform and Vietnam-era combat boots. When I asked Blaster if he was okay, he just stood there, staring into space. Any further conversation with Blaster would have been useless. He was in another zone.

Blaster was indeed fighting his own set of demons. His temper could erupt at any second. First, he began mumbling in Japanese. Then in his heavy Japanese accent, he said, "Nobody messes with my dog. That is my family! You fucked with my family. Nobody fucks with my family. You understand me, asshole?"

I looked toward the doorway. The attending physician just got an earful of Blaster's rant. Before the doctor had a chance to speak,

I walked out of the room. A few minutes later, the doctor called the station to complain about Blaster.

Johnny Boy was in rough shape, but Blaster's dog had sustained only minor injuries.

*****

Three months later, I was working the midnight shift when I received a call around four o'clock in the morning to investigate an alarm at the Exxon gas station on Annapolis Road in Bladensburg. When I arrived, I checked the doors at the front of the station and found them secure. I walked around the back and saw a man sitting on the ground adjacent to the wood line. I walked down to him to identify who he was. He held a book up high over his head. I saw the title: *Marine Corps Land Mine Warfare and Booby-Traps*. I remembered reading the book while training as a combat engineer at Camp Lejeune, North Carolina.

I removed my weapon from my holster and directed the subject to place the book on the ground and raise his hands above his head. The man raised his hands and said, "Hicks, I am going back in the corps, man." I called for backup.

Sergeant Hardcastle arrived within two minutes. I directed him to the back of the gas station. He walked up and asked, "What you got, Moe?"

I took a deep breath and said, "You have to be my witness to this, Sarge, because no one would ever believe this." I pointed at drug-crazed Johnny Boy. "Look at him, Sarge, and look at what the hell he was reading."

The sergeant looked at the book, then shook his head. "Damn, son," he said. "For some reason, this boy loves your beat."

"What the hell, Sarge?" I exclaimed. "I hope he finds someone else's beat to terrorize. I am too through with this guy."

Johnny Boy committed five felonies in less than a month, all within a four-block radius. Thankfully, that morning at the gas station was the last time I ever saw him.

CHAPTER 31

THE EMPIRE STRIKES BACK

If your enemy is secure at all points, be prepared
for him. If he is in superior strength, evade
him. If your opponent is temperamental, seek
to irritate him. Pretend to be weak, that he may
grow arrogant. If he is taking his ease, give him
no rest. If his forces are united, separate them.
If sovereign and subject are in accord, put a
division between them. Attack him where he is
unprepared, appear where you are not expected.
—*The Art of War*, Sun Tzu

After roll call, I followed my routine. I headed directly to the notorious Fifty-Fifth Avenue and Quincy Place. As my patrol car descended the 3500 block of Fifty-Fifth Avenue, I scanned the streets like a bat using radar. By that time, my skills in detecting narcotics deals had been honed almost to a science. My time with the Baltimore Police Department served me well. County drug dealers were good at their craft. However, their street-level drug-dealing skills lacked the sophistication of a Baltimore City drug operation. To me, the county boys' drug-dealing routine was like amateur night at the Apollo.

I immediately noticed the usual cast of characters lurking in the shadows as I scanned the landscape. To the left, I saw Mustache Molly and Dirt Quake. To the right stood Nightmare on My Street and the flamboyant Senator Dee. Dirt Quake was wearing his signature orange T-shirt and blue jeans. Unfortunately, bathwater had eluded Quake once again. As usual, his outfit was covered with dirt and filth, hence the nickname Dirt Quake.

At the beginning of my shift, Dirt Quake walked out of the station holding his arrest paperwork, which was called statement of charges. He had been arrested by the station's narcotics unit called the ACTION Team. He was just released on bond. My colleagues were the overlap squad, which meant we were not the primary patrol unit handling calls for service.

*****

I needed an extraction, and I needed it fast! On that day, my squad was working in plain clothes. When the coast appeared clear, an officer dropped me off in an unmarked car to set up surveillance in a vacant apartment on Quincy Street. As soon as I poked my head out of the apartment window, I saw a group of local drug dealers assembled in front of the building and pointing up to the apartment where I was about to set up surveillance.

Eight of them started singing the lyrics of a popular rap song. They sang, "We got the police on the premises…" They sang, and they clapped their hands. There was joy and excitement in the air. The Caucasian drug dealers across the street howled and rejoiced with their African American and Hispanic American brothers singing their song. But, when they broadcasted my location to the rest of the drug dealers, it was like them throwing chum into shark-infested waters. Now, every killer and their brother were heading toward the apartment. Their heads were probably filled with delusions of grandeur to either partake in or witness my annihilation.

My heart began racing. Then I heard a knock on the apartment door. My fear level rose to pucker factor number 9 as more thugs gathered in front of the building. I refused to acknowledge whoever was knocking at the door. I began transmitting on my police radio. "I am being surrounded. The crowd is getting larger!" I exclaimed. I paced back and forth around the muggy apartment. Suddenly, I felt overwhelmed by the effects of the blistering summer heat. The apartment lacked air-conditioning and airflow.

I finally decided that I needed to take a stand. I stood to the side of the door, sweating while holding my issued 9mm Baretta in both hands. I was prepared to engage with anyone who breached the door. By that time, the crowd was getting hyped up. They wanted to make me their sacrificial lamb; moreover, they wanted to finish the ceremony before backup arrived. I wondered what it would take to quell the rebellion.

I went back to the window and peeked out. One hoodlum gave me the one-finger salute. Another hoodlum defiantly pointed at me and grabbed his crotch. I saw one European drug dealer doing the Cabbage Patch dance. I saw an African American man in his early twenties doing the Michael Jackson spin dance move. I lifted the blinds higher and began studying their faces. I looked at them with a psychotic smile. They knew they had ticked me off.

Within a time that seemed like an eternity, I heard a siren getting louder. It had probably only been about four minutes. Within a few seconds, Mighty Matt's police cruiser came to a screeching halt. When Mighty Matt exited his vehicle, he started walking toward the crowd, twirling his nightstick. He had a commanding presence. The crowd separated and started to dwindle. They knew reinforcements were on the way. I took a deep breath and hastily took the walk of shame. The thugs began cheering, for they had triumphed over the man. No sooner had I walked out of the door than the drug dealer Dirt Quake waved a copy of his statement of charges at me. He had a wide grin on his face.

"What is up, Hicks?" Dirt Quake said.

I smiled and said, "Good work, man. You all got me this time."

We drove off. I did not realize the drug dealers had recognized my walk as I entered the building. Kudos to them for doing their homework. I told Mighty Matt, "I ain't going to lie, man. That was the scariest and most humiliating thing I ever experienced in my life." I met with the sergeant and the rest of the squad a few blocks away.

The sergeant smiled. "Are you okay, Junior?" he asked.

"No, Sarge," I said. "My pride hurts badly."

"I guess the gig is up for our operation today," he said.

"No, sir," I said. "It's time for a little payback."

"I'm scared to ask," he said.

I said, "The manager gave me keys to another vacant apartment directly across the street from the apartment where I took the walk of shame. Look, Sarge, they're convinced our operation is blown. All we need you to do is have the rest of the squad round them up while Matt and I sneak through the woods to the apartment."

The sergeant reluctantly agreed. My squad swarmed down on all the guys hanging out on the street while Mighty Matt and I snuck into the vacant apartment. After chastising them about blowing my cover, the officers took off while activating their lights and sirens to create the illusion that they were all going on an emergency call.

No sooner had their cars left than the dealers set up shop as if they were running a legitimate business. They each took their specified positions as if they were in a stage play. Matt and I were stunned by the swiftness with which they put their operation into play. Lookouts were placed in each direction. Dealers were standing in different places along the entire block.

Members of our squad quickly set up their patrol vehicles a few blocks away, covering all the customers' locations after buying their drugs. I heard a whistle and watched as a sixteen-year-old lookout pointed to Dirt Quake, a local drug dealer. A white compact car drove to Dirt Quake's position. Dirt Quake leaned in toward the passenger seat with a big grin on his face. I tapped Mighty Matt on the shoulder and said, "This boy has got the nerve to be flashing his arrest paperwork." Any astute drug dealer would have completed the sale quickly, but instead, Quake was advertising to his customers that the criminal justice system was a joke.

About two minutes later, Quake reached into his pocket, pulled out a rock of cocaine, and handed it to the female client. Then he walked away and pointed to another drug dealer, whom I knew as Flash. The white male driver remained in the same spot while Flash collected the money and then resumed his position.

Mighty Matt called in the description of the vehicle. Officer Frazier radioed back saying he was behind the car. Frazier stopped the vehicle, seized the cocaine the female client had purchased, and arrested the driver and passenger for possession of cocaine. We continued the same routine until we had enough evidence to arrest all the choirboys who had sung, "We got the police on the premises."

Now, it was time for our grand finale. I looked at Mighty Matt and said, "This day turned out better than I could have imagined. We got enough to charge Quake and Flash with felonies, and guess what, Matt."

"What?" he asked.

"We have a front-row seat to see the rest of the squad take them down."

Mighty Matt replied, "No, we need to get out of here."

I pleaded with him to wait. He eventually agreed.

We stood at opposite ends of the window, peeking out down below. "Flash is going to get away like he always does," Matt said. Flash was a gazelle-like brother who used to run track in high school. He was a master escape artist. I told Matt it did not matter, because we could get a warrant for Flash if he escaped.

We watched our squad converge on all five suspects. When Flash saw the officers approach his other comrades, he slowly started walking about six houses down to his home. Just then, two officers began to close in on him from each side. Flash ran back and forth between the two officers like a baseball player caught between first and second base. I heard the distinctive sounds of his tennis shoes sliding on broken pieces of glass as he played his usual game of cat and mouse with the street troops. We all knew Flash had enormous speed. However, he was usually closer to his house when the police pulled up.

Suddenly, Flash leaped across the street, throwing the officers off, because we all knew exactly where Flash lived. He lived on the same side of the road where the officers had initially tried to apprehend him. I braced myself for Flash's inevitable escape. As soon as both officers crossed the street to apprehend Flash, he faked heading back across the street toward his apartment.

Another officer pulled up and got out of his car and began running toward Flash. Flash leaped toward the steps of his apartment. As he jumped, I saw a Rottweiler leap toward him. It was Blaster's K-9 dog. I heard Flash yell so loudly that the sound echoed inside the apartment building where Mighty Matt and I were standing. The K-9 dog had bitten Flash. I immediately walked away from the window.

"What's wrong, Moe?" Matt asked.

"I got attacked by a dog when I was a kid," I told him. "That K-9 dog gives me flashbacks. That was horrifying!"

"I can't believe that Hard-Core Hicks has a weak stomach."

"Yes, I do when it comes to them damn dogs!"

We made our escape through the woods. I let the squad know we made it back to our patrol cars. Two of my squad members called me over the radio and told me to come down to the scene. The squad still had Dirt Quake handcuffed outside. My squad mates encouraged me to transport Dirt Quake to the station. They got me all psyched up.

"Hicks, that will be the ultimate payback. You can parade him around Quincy Street in a triumphant celebration," one officer said.

I smiled. "Yes, that would be the ultimate payback," I said.

I was anxious to regain my pride. I grabbed Dirt Quake and started walking him back toward my car. I noticed members of my squad whispering and watching as I strapped him in the seat belt in my vehicle. As soon as I shut the passenger door, they all started laughing. I asked them what was so funny. "I hope you enjoy your ride to the station," one officer said.

I got in my car and notified the dispatcher I was on my way to the station. I noticed Dirt Quake kept looking at me, smiling. I remember asking him, "What is so funny? You got two felony charges in one day." A few seconds later, I began gagging. "What the hell? What in the hell is that smell?" It was the most horrific odor I ever smelled.

Dirt Quake had eagerly anticipated the moment when I got a total whiff of his body odor. I was sure that in his mind, he was thinking, *Wait for it. Wait for it. You got it?* He kept smiling and said,

"You didn't know? That's why no one ever arrests me. I got caught by narcotics detectives, but the beat cops didn't want to arrest me because they didn't want to transport me in their take-home cars."

My squad members began taunting me over the CB (citizen's band) radio. "Felony Moe meets Peppy Le Pew!" one officer said. Pepé was a Warner Brothers cartoon character who sought love from a cat with a white stripe but did not understand that the cat was a skunk, nor did he understand the effects of the skunk's odor.

"You guys set me up!" I replied over my CB radio. They continued to taunt me during my entire ride to the station. Finally, I had to learn the hard way that Dirt Quake's horrific odor had provided him with immunity from arrest. He wore his distinctive odor as a badge of honor. Dirt Quake proved that only the most dedicated officer would take him into custody.

When I brought Quake past the court commissioner's office, the commissioner looked at him and said, "Not you again." I thought that the commissioner had released him earlier that day because he could no longer handle Quake's distinctive odor.

CHAPTER 32

THE HOWLING

The next day, I was back in uniform, patrolling my beat. As always, I was in apprehension mode. I turned my attention to Mustache Molly. Molly's nickname was becoming on her. Her fully developed mustache and partial beard set her apart from the rest of the female drug dealers. Her reluctance to trim her mustache gave a clear indication of her priorities. All her energies were devoted to securing the next rock of crack cocaine. That was her only job. After all, crack could not smoke itself.

Molly's emaciated accomplice, Nightmare on My Street, was known for her scarecrow-like hairstyle and paranoid facial expression. Nightmare's legs were often covered with mud. She looked as if she took daily mud baths, poor lady. At the top of the hill stood Senator Dee. The self-proclaimed street senator was a Jamaican who had an affinity for politics at one point in his life. He often wore a sports coat and jeans, a bright-green Polo shirt, and green tennis shoes. Finally, there was a crack dealer named Cynthia. To each dealer's credit, he or she was the most cautious dealer out there, because much like zombies, all of them came out only at night, and they always hid in the shadows.

Local drug dealers had nicknames for us as well. The elusive drug dealer Cynthia gave me the most unflattering nickname of all the officers who worked the area. My nickname was Sewer Rat. After watching me appear out of nowhere in the shadows at night, Cynthia came up with the nickname, especially because I confronted local dealers right in the middle of making their drug deals. The other officers' nicknames were Curly, Monty Hall, Cary Grant, and the Bruise Brothers.

That day, as the numbers of my patrol car—123—came into focus, I heard the usual whistling and howling. I got on my CB radio and asked Mighty Matt if he was listening to the wolves and the orcas hiding in the shadows. He confirmed that he could hear them. The unrest warned that the police (5-0) were on the prowl. Drug dealers had different sounds for different patrol squads.

I wanted to catch Cynthia. She was a grand prize. She was one drug dealer who had a sixth sense about the presence of the police. She had very cunning instincts. She admitted to me that I had almost caught her in the middle of a drug deal. However, she had managed to crush the drugs on the ground before I could see her. Cynthia still held the title of most elusive drug dealer in my beat. I never caught her making a drug deal. Drug dealers who paid attention to their instincts were exceedingly difficult to catch.

The dealers knew that when my squad was out, we would be on the prowl for them, so the challenge for all of us was to catch the dealers between our calls for service. That day, I decided to drive away because I did not have any other officers in service. Besides, they were all spread too far apart.

Before driving on, I shone my spotlight on some would-be dealers, hoping to discourage them from selling drugs. I drove two blocks down the road and checked out my other favorite fishing hole: the infamous Fifty-Fifth Avenue and Quincy Place. I quickly navigated through the area and noticed it was filled with new faces. Unfortunately, none of them lived in the area.

I parked my car a block away, walked down the street on the side of the woods, and focused on what appeared to be a game of catch with a football in the middle of the road. I had been there for two minutes when I saw a vehicle drive down the street. The guy holding the football threw it in the direction of the car. Another guy in the road caught the football, ran over to the vehicle, and spoke to the driver. The catcher then waved at the thrower. The thrower threw the football in the direction of a tree near where I was standing. I ducked behind the nearby building briefly.

The catcher reached behind the tree, removed something from a bag, and placed it in his pocket. Then he waved to a third guy, who started running toward the car. The catcher threw the ball toward the vehicle, and the third guy caught it and retrieved money from the car driver. He moved away from the vehicle and threw the ball to the guy holding the drugs. The person holding the dope caught the ball and handed the drugs to the driver. They repeated this routine for about twenty minutes.

By this time, other officers in my squad had come back into service. They all got out of their vehicles and approached each suspect on foot. None of the dealers ran, as they were confident their sophisticated plot to sell drugs had gone undetected. My comrades questioned each of the dealers separately. Their answers were the same. They claimed they were playing football and enjoying a fantastic summer night.

I walked over and removed the bag from which I watched the dealers remove the drugs from; it was still behind the tree. It was a surprisingly good return for the dealers' forty-minute investment. That day, we netted forty-seven baggies of crack from behind the tree, almost one thousand dollars in cash, and three arrests. Their ingenuity was impressive.

I put one of the dealers in my car to transport him to the station. First, however, I needed to send a message to the scores of drug dealers waiting for us to leave so they could get back to work selling their wares. So I reached down and grabbed the microphone on my public address system and drove the dealer around three times while playing "White Lines" by Grandmaster Flash.

A businessman is caught with twenty-four kilos
He's out on bail and out of jail
And that's the way it goes, raah

I played the entire song. My message was clear to drug buyers and dealers: the drug business was a losing game, particularly for low-level drug dealers. I was determined to do everything in my power to restore peace to the people living in the community. In my beat, my relationship with some of the local drug dealers resembled the relationship between the cartoon characters in the Looney Tunes cartoon *Ralph Wolf and Sam Sheepdog*. The cartoon depicted skirmishes between the two blue-collar workers, who carried their lunchboxes and punched in on a time clock.

Ralph Wolf spent every day trying to abduct the helpless sheep but inevitably failed. The main lesson from the story was that the wolf's job was to try to catch the helpless sheep, and the sheepdog's job was to protect the sheep. There was nothing personal about the skirmishes between the two main characters. To them, they were only doing their job.

Most of the criminals in my beat were the same. They understood that selling drugs came with certain risks they were willing to take. They also understood that we were going to be aggressively pursuing them practically every day. They did not have a problem with us as long as we did not break the law or police rules. They respected us for doing our jobs. Officers who broke those norms made the skirmishes personal. I believed beating up suspects and insulting them personally were not only morally and ethically wrong but were also cowardly. This type of behavior could be hazardous to officers' health.

The relationship between police officers and the inhabitants of their beats constantly evolved. My beat was no different. One day, a person in your beat might be a suspect in a robbery or homicide. The following week, the same person could be the victim of a shooting or another violent crime. The following week, they might be a witness to a crime. Therefore, having good rapport with everyone in our communities was critical to our success.

Policing was an ongoing learning process, and I was grateful for the school of hard knocks I went through as a Baltimore City police officer. County police officers spent most of their time in their patrol cars, because their beats were much larger than those in most city police departments. For example, my beat in Hyattsville encompassed an area almost as large as the entire patrol district in

Baltimore. I would often ride through my beat to look for suspicious activity. I did not realize I was becoming like the former narcotics officer I worked with in Baltimore. I found myself unwittingly taking on the same lionlike posture as my former partner Richard when hunting for drug dealers.

When I passed through the Bladensburg area, I noticed two extremely obese black men looking at me. They always gave me the evil eye. I always studied their demeanor as I passed through. One day, I stopped, walked over to the men, and asked, "What is it?" Instead of staring at us, they told me that I needed to catch the block full of drug dealers who were out selling drugs every day. I explained that I was trying to figure out who lived there and did not know when I drove through. I apologized to the men if I made them feel uncomfortable. I assured them that my main goal was to do just what I had told them. I wanted to establish who was part of the drug operation. I also explained to them that I understood what it was like living under the siege of drug dealers.

The two black men and I spoke to one another and exchanged pleasantries every day from that point forward. We established mutual respect. I had to relearn what I was taught in Baltimore: Only a tiny percentage of people in the neighborhood was in the criminal element. Most people in these neighborhoods were good people caught up in a bad situation.

A few days later, I worked foot patrol on Fifty-Fifth Avenue in Bladensburg, Maryland, when I ran into an older black woman in her sixties. She joked about my parading a drug dealer around in my car while playing Grandmaster Flash's "White Lines." A few minutes later, her demeanor turned sad. She told me that her son had been murdered in Bladensburg and that the case was never solved. I could tell that she still felt excruciating pain as a result of her son's murder. I felt the same sense of uselessness I felt when I patrolled the Lafayette and Flag House projects. I was just a patrol officer, not a detective or a supervisor. Nonetheless, I wanted to help.

I prayed many nights for the old Lady, Ms. Cora. I wanted to heal her pain. I wanted God to keep her safe. I prayed for divine intervention. I asked for strength and wisdom to make a difference in her community. Sometimes, I wished I did not care as much as I did about people. My grandfather was my best mentor, and he had warned me that I cared too much about people and their situations. He did not want me to be a police officer because he knew I was a bleeding heart at my core. Whenever I identified someone in need, I was locked in. This characteristic haunted me both in my personal and professional life.

Ms. Cora told me that while cleaning the grounds, she heard drug dealers talking about how I was a pain in their behinds. She told me I would never know how much she appreciated me for trying to make a difference. I told her I grew up in the same kind of neighborhood and would do all I could to make her community safer. I also told her I would talk to homicide detectives to see if they had any leads on her son's murder.

I forged a long-lasting bond with Ms. Cora. She worked at an apartment complex, and I checked on her as often as I could. When I spoke to the homicide detective who investigated her son's murder, he casually told me her son's murder was what police called a whodunit. He added that the murder of Ms. Cora's son would probably never be solved. That was a punch in the gut. I had no hope to give Ms. Cora. The crime, the violence, and the murders had again become very personal for me.

Many other families would eventually find themselves grieving as a result of the crime spree in the area. I had to endure watching the bullet-ridden bodies of many of the young teenagers. I desperately tried to run off as many drug thugs as I could before I left the beat. I knew most of the murders in that area could be traced to one organization. I had a strong hunch about who had killed Ms. Cora's son. Years later, I would get a chance to bring the man to justice.

*****

Evenings and midnights were some of the most exciting times for police. Those hours were when most of the action occurred. Unfortunately, we would often catch the same criminals time and time again in the middle of their crime sprees. One night, I was making traffic stops on Kenilworth Avenue near the Washington, DC, line. I pulled over a vehicle with a taillight out.

As always, I took a few minutes to observe the driver before I approached the car. I noticed he was reaching under his seat. I came to the passenger side without him seeing me. By then, he had stopped reaching down. I switched to the driver's side and asked for the man's driver's license. I walked back to my car and was about to call for backup.

The man's name was Vincent. Before I had a chance to finish running his license, I received an emergency call. I gave the license back to the suspect and responded to the call. I had a bad feeling about the suspect, but I did not have a chance to check him out.

The next night, two other officers responded to a hotel for three men armed with guns. One officer stopped the same suspect, Vincent, whom I had stopped on Kenilworth Avenue. Vincent started reaching into his waistband. The officer grabbed him and removed a .357 Magnum from his waistband. Then the officer arrested him.

I was off the next night when my sergeant and Monty Hall staked out the house of a local drug dealer named Devon. They were waiting to light up his bedroom again at precisely 5:00 a.m. when a car pulled up and stopped directly in front of the house. They drove up and turned on their police lights. The suspect started reaching under his seat. They ordered him to stop, but he kept reaching under his seat as though he could not find whatever he was looking for.

The driver suddenly leaped out of his vehicle, made a beeline toward the two officers, and knocked them to the ground. He was on PCP. He began dragging them down the street. He switched the channels on their radios and dropped them on the ground. The channel switch caused the officers' radios to send their emergency signal to another channel.

The suspect attempted to flee, but when he tried to rush past a newspaper boy out delivering newspapers, the paperboy football-checked the suspect, causing him to fall to the ground. The officers gathered their composure and arrested the suspect. They searched his car and found a large bag of PCP and a .357 Magnum under the front seat. The suspect was the same Vincent I had stopped a few nights earlier on Kenilworth Avenue and whom another squad mate had arrested with a different .357 Magnum.

Monty called me to tell me what had happened. I was moonlighting at the time, but I came to the station after work. Monty proudly pointed Vincent out to me. He said, "This is the same boy you stopped and the same boy Officer Leslie locked up at the hotel. And guess what? He had a load of PCP on him and a .357 Magnum." Then he said, "Don't worry, Hicks, I tamed him down."

The suspect's head was bandaged. Monty taunted him, saying, "Now you know not to fuck with the county police, don't you?"

The once arrogant but now subdued villain nodded in agreement and said, "Yes, sir."

CHAPTER 33

THE BURNING BUSH

Strategy without tactics is the slowest
route to victory. Tactics without
strategy is the noise before defeat.
—*The Art of War*, Sun Tzu

As a county officer, you never knew which officer was going to
get you into trouble. We all had our quirks, but some of our peculiar-
ities were worse than others. For example, some officers did not have
a cut card. They did not understand that there were limits to what
one could say or do on the streets. One thing was for sure: 98 percent of the time, when an officer's behavior was out of the ordinary,
the supervisor backed the officer unless the officer's conduct received
extensive media scrutiny.

It was about 3:00 p.m. when I received a call for a man wanted
on a warrant. The subject was described as being in his early thirties,
six foot two, 170 pounds, and with a slender build. He was wearing a
short-sleeved brown shirt, beige khaki pants, and tan boots. Mighty
Matt and I arrived at the local bar in separate vehicles. I parked out
front, and Mighty Matt parked in the rear.

As soon as I exited my vehicle, I saw someone who fitted the
description walking out of the front door. He took one look at me
and ran back inside. He popped his head out of the back door, then
ran inside again. Mighty Matt and I communicated each time we saw

him. Finally, as Mighty Matt walked toward the front door, I walked to the back door. The suspect broke into a full run out of the back door and got away.

About twenty minutes later, we received another call from the dispatcher stating the suspect was bragging about escaping from the police and had headed to another local bar to celebrate his great escape. We headed to the bar where the suspect was supposed to be drinking. To our amazement, he played the same game. He appeared out of the front door, then ran back inside. However, this time, the suspect chose to make his escape by the back door, where Mighty Matt was stationed. The suspect ran across the street to the marina. I stood at my patrol car, smiling momentarily, as other officers arrived on the scene.

Finally, officer Stanley stopped and asked, "Hicks, why are you standing there smiling instead of chasing him?"

"That varmint is a great runner, but the boy isn't Aquaman. He is not going to swim across the marina." All the officers on the scene walked over to the marina. I nodded my head. "He is right there across the street, hiding in the tree. Do me a favor. Please do not look over there. Follow my lead," I said. "Point to those boats over there. We'll pretend we think he's there. I want him to think we're a bunch of idiots. In the meantime, I'm going to walk over to my car and call K-9."

I got back in my car and called a K-9 unit. My goal was simple. I wanted the suspect to know that the next time he ran, he would not only have to outrun us, but he would also have to outrun the K-9 dog. When the K-9 officer arrived, the dog immediately tracked down the suspect in the tree. However, when the dog reached the tree, the dog could not climb up the tree where the suspect was now hiding because the brush at the top of the tree was thick. I could not believe it. Within the short time since the K-9 officer's arrival, the suspect got through the brush and concealed himself near the top of the tree. The K-9 officer called the dog back.

"My goodness," I said, "we're going to have to find a way to cut through the brush."

The K-9 officer looked at me and asked, "Do you have any flares in your car?"

I quickly said no even though I had a whole box of flares, but I thought, *This cannot be good.* The K-9 officer asked Mighty Matt for a flare. I stood behind the K-9 officer, shaking my head at Matt and waving my arms, trying to discourage him from giving the K-9 officer any flares.

Finally, Mighty Matt perked up, smiled, and said, "I sure do."

"Oh my God, fellas," I said, "let's see if we can come up with a different solution."

As Matt handed the K-9 officer a flare, I ran to my patrol car and got on the loudspeaker and said, "Sir, we know that you are in the brush, so I am giving you a final chance to surrender." There was only silence. I turned my attention back to the K-9 officer, who was already trying to light the flare. I asked him to give the suspect a few minutes to come out.

The K-9 officer lit the flare and started walking toward the brush. He suddenly tossed the flare to the bottom of the brush. Unfortunately, the flare went out before it even reached the brush. The K-9 officer looked at Matt and said, "Give me another flare." I reiterated that using a flare was a bad idea, but the K-9 officer lit the next flare and tossed it. As soon as the flare hit the brush, the entire tree lit up in flames. The suspect instantaneously leaped out of the tree. By the time he walked twenty feet from the brush, it was already fully engulfed in fire. I stood watching in horror. I envisioned myself wearing an orange jumpsuit and standing behind bars.

The suspect walked over to my car with his hands up, signifying his surrender. I examined him from where I was standing. Thank God he was not harmed. I snapped back into reality and called for the fire department. Then I walked over to the suspect and said, "Are you out of your Vulcan mind? What took you so long to come out of there? How many warrants do you have on you?"

"None, sir," the suspect said.

I told him I was aware he had at least one warrant out on him. I searched his pockets and retrieved his driver's license. I stood there for a moment, staring at the license. The K-9 officer noticed that my facial expression changed after I examined the suspect's driver's license. I turned and looked at him.

"What's wrong?" he asked.

It took me a few moments to get the words out of my mouth. "This might not be the right guy," I finally uttered.

"What?" the K-9 officer exclaimed. "You have got to be kidding me."

Just then, the sergeant pulled up. I briefed him. The sergeant told me, "At this point, I don't care who the hell he is. Take his dumb ass to the station, have him sign a waiver, and send him on his way."

At the station, I asked the suspect why he ran when he saw us. He said he was told when he moved to Prince George's County to run fast when he saw the police, and if not, he was going to get his butt kicked at the highest level. He explained that he believed his girlfriend had set him up by calling the police and telling them he was his girlfriend's ex-boyfriend who was wanted on drug warrants. He thought his girlfriend did it because they were having problems in their relationship. She vowed she would screw with him if he did not come back to her.

Just like my days growing up in Baltimore, I always went big. This included screwing things up when I went after something: I always went big there as well. The incident had me scared straight. So that night, I prayed, thanking God and asking him to deliver me from any more antics like that.

CHAPTER 34

LIVING MY BEST LIFE

My mission in life is not merely to survive but
also to thrive; and do so with some passion, some
compassion, some humor, and some style.
—Maya Angelou

By my third month, I led the station in criminal arrests. I
remained the top stat person for my entire three years at Hyattsville.
One day, in about my fourth month, the captain was in the office,
handing out paychecks. When I asked for my check, he asked me
my name. When I told him, he said, "Good stats last month."
Interestingly, he did not know me by my face; he knew me by the
quality of my work. It gave me hope, because it was clear my senior
corporal, sergeant, and lieutenant did not care for me. I did not know
whether it was a black thing, a Baltimore thing, or a combination of
both.

Two months after that, they were all gone. We were assigned
a new senior corporal, a new sergeant, a new lieutenant, and a new
captain. It did not take long for me to realize that you lived and died
by your stat sheet under new management. Overnight, I went from
being their stepchild to their golden boy. God was showing me favor
once again, but I wondered how long it would last.

My new lieutenant called me into the office one day and told me
that he was impressed with my work and that he wanted to reward

me. I was still a private. He told me to go down to vehicle services to pick up a police cruiser. I thought I would get a model a few years newer than the one I had, but when I went down to vehicle services, they handed me the keys to a brand-new Chevy Celebrity with the new light bar package. It was an excellent attaboy for doing a good job. I was astonished and pleased beyond measure.

When I drove my cruiser around the county, officers did double takes when they saw that the person driving the car did not have any stripes. When I parked my car in front of stores where I moonlighted, officers would stop, look at me, and stare at my car. It felt good to know my hard work was appreciated. I loved being a patrol officer. I loved the freedom of being outdoors. But a lot of my friends began to ask me when I was going to make detective. That offended me because I was living my best life working the street.

After working with my new sergeant, Bradshaw, for about two months, he sat me down to talk. He said that the previous sergeant had given him an overview of the squad. He also said the old sergeant did not speak very highly of me. I told him I knew the old sergeant didn't like me from day one. Sergeant Bradshaw told me he found my work to be the opposite of what my old sergeant, Lorring, had told him. It seemed Sergeant Lorring had classified the good officers as useless and the bad officers as the good ones.

I knew that Sergeant Lorring had liked the two other black officers on the squad because they sucked up to him and smiled in his face. I explained to Sergeant Bradshaw that some people did not take to me because I was quiet. Sergeant Bradshaw told me that he was impressed with my work and that I had my act squared away.

I did not know more good news was coming. I was selected to become a field training officer (FTO). I was still a private at the time, which seemed to cause some resentment. Before I became an FTO, most of the officers were against becoming FTOs. They did not like the idea of having to babysit somebody for three months. But I was enthusiastic about the job. That was easy for anyone to see.

After I became an FTO, I identified something that brought enthusiasm back to officers. It was a little gold pin that had the initials FTO affixed to it. That was the first time an FTO pin was worn on a police uniform in Prince George's County, but it was nothing new to me, because FTOs in Baltimore had already worn the pin for years.

As a rookie, I hated the pin, because it identified me as a rookie. But now because of that little pin, everyone wanted to become an FTO. A field training officer was an officer who had received detailed schooling on training new officers in the field. An FTO evaluated new police officers after they graduated from the police academy. FTOs were not supervisors.

When I picked up my rookie from the police academy, he told me he had shot a 99.7 on the pistol range. I told him that was great, but there was a big difference between shooting paper targets and shooting at real people. "Targets do not shoot back!" I told him. I did not realize that in two short days, he would understand precisely what I meant.

In Prince George's County, my patrol squad was like many frat boys having fun while trying to learn their way. We were all excited to come to work to embark on our next adventure. Unfortunately, we were oblivious to the real dangers that lay ahead.

It took me only a few days on the job to realize black officers were treated like stepchildren while our white counterparts were treated like biological children. We were all a part of the family, but we did not have other white officers' privileges. That was clear from the day I walked into the police academy. The trainers smiled and greeted my white counterparts warmly and graciously and invited them into the family. However, their interactions with the black recruits in the class were businesslike and half-hearted.

CHAPTER 35

GUN SMOKE

Never tell people how to do things.
Instead, tell them what to do, and they
will surprise you with their ingenuity.
—General George Patton

I was in a great mood while walking down the hallway to roll call beside Officer Dylan when a tall white man in his early thirties passed by me. I noticed that his head was bleeding, and several glass fragments were still in his hair. He asked Officer Dylan if he knew where the court commissioner's office was located. Just then, the sergeant walked up to see what was going on. Officer Dylan took a puff of his cigarette and blew smoke in the man's face and said, "I don't talk to the maggotry." Then he proudly walked into the roll call room.

The sergeant and I looked at each other for a second. Then I told the citizen where the commissioner's office was located. I asked the man if he had considered going to the hospital before obtaining a warrant for whoever had assaulted him. But before he answered, I said, "Let me take a guess. You want the court commissioner to see the blood and glass in your head so he would not deny you a warrant?"

"Yes, sir," the man said.

"I'm sure your plan will work," I replied. "But next time, go to the hospital first and take pictures of yourself so you don't endanger your health."

I walked into roll call. After it was over, the sergeant gave us all our performance evaluations. I noticed that I was marked down one level for communication. I laughed and signed the assessment, but I commented to the sergeant, "I get along with people." I had no idea—nor did I care—why the sergeant had scored me as good but not very good in communication. However, my attitude changed a few hours later.

After handling a few calls, Officer Dylan asked me to meet with him. He immediately began bragging about his evaluation. "Look at this, Hicks," he said. "I got a perfect evaluation."

"Oh!" I exclaimed. "You buck the sergeant, and you get complaints practically every week, but you're rewarded with a perfect evaluation? How is that possible?" He put a giant smile on his face. That evoked my curiosity. From that day forward, I was on alert for other injustices.

*****

On my recruit's second day of training, we took a report for a shooting victim at Prince George's County Hospital. The victim explained that her Jamaican husband had accused her of sleeping with a white man and had begun shooting at her while she was lying in bed. A bullet had grazed her head. My acting supervisor devised a plan to arrest her husband. My squad set up a perimeter around the suspect's house. One officer called the suspect's home and pretended to be a neighbor to lure the suspect outside so we could arrest him. The acting supervisor directed me and the rookie officer to apprehend the suspect.

A few seconds later, the suspect exited his house, shirtless and shoeless. He began circling his van, which was parked about sixty feet away from us on a curve. I did not see anything in his hands. When he emerged from behind his van, I saw him lift both of his arms, begin to assume a combat stance, and then point his arms toward my rookie. Everything seemed to go in slow motion from that point forward.

I unsnapped my holster, grabbed my gun, and raised it waist high. The suspect's hands were fully extended by this time, and his feet were firmly set in a full combat stance. He was standing in front of a motorcycle parked on the sidewalk. I fired one shot from my department-issued .38 revolver. The shot struck the motorcycle, which startled the suspect. I saw something black fall out of his hands.

We advanced on the suspect at gunpoint. When I was an arm's length from him, he lunged for his gun lying on the ground. I took my left hand and backhanded him in his face, hurling him a few feet off the ground. He landed on top of a car a few feet away from us. The rest of my squad suddenly emerged. K-9 Officer Blaster immediately engaged the suspect, striking him on the head. Blaster's K-9 dog also attacked the suspect.

I reached down and picked up a loaded 9mm handgun with the trigger already pulled back. It gave me pucker factor number 9. The creature tried to take me out. I beat him, pulling the trigger by a fraction of a second. My rookie did not fire his weapon. I was thankful we survived the deadly encounter. The suspect had a superior weapon and a tactical advantage over us, as he was standing at a position of greater height.

As I walked back to my car, I reflected on my conversation with the old Jewish man who frequented the 7-Eleven in Baltimore. He was the person who told me that if I saw someone pointing what I believed was a gun at me, I shouldn't ponder it. He said, "Always shoot, Sonny. You can always get another job." His advice served me well, because I had no idea whether the shirtless, shoeless man that day had a gun. I did know he was pointing something at me. However, I could not tell what was in his hand.

Mighty Matt called me Quick Draw McGraw. They were all amazed by how fast I was able to unholster and fire. I thought about my first day of firearms training, when my draw was so slow that the target had turned back around before I had a chance to unholster my weapon, much less aim and fire. All I would say was, glory to God. It was one thing to get yourself hurt or killed; however, it was different when your mistake caused someone else to lose their life.

A few months later, I got caught in traffic and walked into the station about eight minutes late for roll call. After roll call, the sergeant wrote me a counseling form for being late for roll call. He said he had to write me up. He explained that it was essential to set an example for the other officers on the squad. I agreed that I deserved to be written up, because walking into roll call late was disruptive. He then asked me to take the counseling form and place it in my personnel file in a cabinet in his office.

I found my personnel file and placed the counseling form in my file. Then I remembered that Mighty Matt was late every day for the entire week about a month prior, so I looked in his file and noticed that there were no counseling forms. I took out both files from the file cabinet and immediately confronted the sergeant. When he saw I had two files in my hand, his body language told me he knew the jig was up.

I asked him why in the hell he would write me up for being eight minutes late one day while allowing Mighty Matt to be late five days in a row. The sergeant replied that Mighty Matt was late many times because he had been picking up his rookie. That enraged me even further. "That's even more a reason why he should be written up," I said. "He was setting a bad example for his rookie." The sergeant shrugged his shoulders. I walked out of the roll call room and drove down to my beat. Injustice, I realized, was baked into the system.

CHAPTER 36

THE RIDE-A-LONG

I saw an eighteen-year-old Asian kid sitting in the sergeant's office. He was about five foot four, was wearing black glasses, and had a pocket protector with three ink pens inside.

"Who is the kid, Sarge?" I asked.

"He is your ride-along," the sergeant replied.

I smiled at him and looked at the rest of the squad. "Are you kidding me?" I asked. My squad members started chuckling. They all knew I was a magnet for trouble.

*****

I stopped a black 1974 Toyota Corolla covered in mud. A man exited his vehicle and started walking toward mine. I scrambled out of the car to intercept him. The knife case on his belt was open, but the knife was gone. He kept walking toward me. I backed away from him to create some distance and pointed my service weapon at him. The suspect complied and put his hands on the car. He was sweating and twitching. I quickly patted his waistband and his pockets. Both of his pockets were filled with rifle ammunition. I asked him if he had any weapons. He started chattering. "Of course I have my rifle with me," he replied. I thought this was not going to turn out well.

"Excuse me, sir. My ankle itches. I need to scratch it real quick," he said. He removed his hands from the car and started scratching his head.

"Put your hands back on the car," I said.

When I picked up my radio to call for backup, he reached down to his right ankle. I dropped my radio and quickly removed his hands from his ankle. I saw he was trying to pull an ice pick out of an ankle holster. I wrestled him down to the ground. "Whoa, Rambo, not so fast!" I exclaimed. I looked into his eyes. He was another man riding the boat—under the influence of PCP.

The ride-along got out of the car. "Sir, what do I do?" he asked.

"Stay the hell away from this guy!" I yelled. God only knew what the green bean might have done to him.

I unsnapped the ice pick holster and threw the ice pick on top of the hood of my car. The kid quickly picked up the ice pick and got back inside my cruiser. I scrambled to pick up my radio, which was a few feet away. The suspect leaped up and tried to get back inside his car. The knife and the rifle were sitting in the front passenger seat. I grabbed Rambo, and then I started slipping on the rifle shells that had fallen out of his pockets.

I guided Rambo away from the loose rifle slugs and onto the front passenger side of my car. He began banging on the passenger-side window, where the kid was sitting. Rambo started slobbering on and licking the front passenger-side window as my ride-along watched in horror. "Are you having fun yet?" I asked the kid. Rambo stopped licking the window and decided it was more fun to get inside my vehicle's front passenger seat. I was hoping my backup would get there before the sergeant did.

Rambo pushed off the car and tried to elbow me, but he had picked the worst possible time to restart the fight. My backup, the Barbarian, reached my car's driver's side, which was within his arms' reach. The Barbarian swung his nightstick, striking Rambo on the top of his head. Blood spattered on the front windshield on the passenger-side window. The ride-along cringed at the sight and was struggling not to vomit. Finally, Rambo fell to the ground and surrendered. When I was handcuffing him, the kid still had his eyes closed. "You can open your eyes, son. He is in custody," I said.

I called an ambulance to transport Rambo to Prince George's County Hospital for treatment. When he arrived at the hospital, the doctor who treated him was laughing while examining him.

"You must have fought the officers hard," the doctor said.

"Yep. My nickname for him is Rambo, because he had a knife, an ice pick, and a rifle," I said.

"Seems to me that we ought to switch names, because you and your boys did a number on me," Rambo replied.

I looked at the doctor. "I never hit him, Doc, I swear," I said.

"Sure. You did not hit him, Officer," the doctor said and winked at me. The ride-along looked at me and shrugged his shoulders.

"That is a damn shame. The doctor does not believe me," I said.

CHAPTER 37

BMW BUST

The next day, after my reality check about injustice, I drove out to my beat. As soon as I arrived at Fifty-Fifth Avenue and Quincy Place, I noticed a very youthful-looking man driving a red BMW very slowly. He stopped momentarily in the roadway because he was having a conversation on his car phone. Car phones were few and far between back then.

The driver made a left turn without using his turn signal. I followed the red BMW for one block, turned my lights on, and stopped the vehicle in the 5300 block of Quincy Street. I approached the driver and thoroughly examined his face for stress indicators. I noticed he kept licking his lips. His hand was also shaking as he handed me his driver's license, and he tried to avoid eye contact with me.

I took a second to scan the faces of his passengers. They were fidgety and nervous. I obtained identification from all of them and called for backup. I learned long ago to call for backup whenever there was the slightest hint of trouble. A good officer always paid attention to his instincts. I was a firm believer that your instincts would tell you everything you needed to know. There were clues to danger that were often present. However, people very often did not act on their instincts.

I ran the driver and the two occupants for warrants. Before backup arrived, the dispatcher came back with some troubling news.

She advised me that the driver and the front-seat passenger had priors for murder in Washington, DC. She also announced that the rear-seat passenger had two outstanding warrants for his arrest. One warrant was for obstruction of justice for a case involving the murder of a Prince George's County police officer.

I quickly got out of my police car and positioned myself in the back of it. First, I unsnapped my gun and rested my hand on it. Then I waited for backup to arrive. I had learned at the police academy that the safest place to position myself was behind my vehicle, because the engine block could help repel incoming shots.

When backup arrived, I gave Officer Dylan a quick briefing on what we had. I walked back to the red BMW and motioned for the right rear-seat passenger to exit the vehicle. When he stepped out of the vehicle, I handcuffed him and put him in the passenger seat of my car. Then I explained to him that two warrants were out for his arrest. I never let a suspect one-up me, and I never told them in advance if they had warrants or if I had seen drugs or other contraband in their vehicles. The fight-or-flight syndrome kicked in when they discovered that an officer was aware of those things. That often resulted in an officer getting assaulted.

Then Officer Dylan and I got the driver and passenger out of the car. I put the driver's hands up against the trunk of his car. Dylan searched the passenger and directed him to the rear of the vehicle. I kept guard on both suspects as Dylan searched the vehicle. Within a few seconds, Dylan looked in my direction with a shocked expression on his face. He came back and told the front passenger he was under arrest. Then he attempted to handcuff the suspect. Suddenly, the suspect leaped away from the car and took off running. Dylan took off after him.

The driver pushed off the car and tried to make his escape. He swung at me with everything he had. However, he could not quite maintain his balance. I took out my Baltimore Bomber and began striking him on his kneecaps. I knew that if he could not stand, then he could not fight. He buckled at the knees and fell to the ground. I shook my head and stood over him with my nightstick slung over my shoulder, watching him struggle to get up to resume the fight.

"Wow, I got you good, didn't I? Look at yourself, man. Pathetic!" I exclaimed. I handcuffed him and called for reinforcements.

Before backup arrived, I saw Dylan walking back toward his car with the handcuffed suspect. The suspect looked winded and submissive. I asked Dylan how he caught him so quickly. Dylan said, "It is hard to escape from the long arms of the law." I told Dylan it was interesting to see how calm the suspect was acting. "I took the fight out of him," Dylan replied.

"How?" I asked.

"He took a swing at me, and then I busted him in the head with my radio," Dylan said.

"You sure know how to improvise, you damn barbarian!" I exclaimed.

"Did your guy try to fight?" Dylan asked.

"He sure did," I answered.

"And?" Dylan asked.

I smiled and looked in the direction of my handcuffed suspect. "Let's just say that he did not have the skills to launch a successful attack." My suspect looked defeated, as his pride was deflated.

For the next three months, every time I saw Dylan, images of barbarians would pop in my head. We were happy to have survived the encounter. Both suspects could have taken our lives. Dylan found over a pound of marijuana in the shoebox on the front seat, and I found nineteen baggies of cocaine in the trunk.

The driver and the passenger were brothers who had murdered someone in Washington, DC. They were released from prison under the district's Youth Rehabilitation Act. The act allowed for alternative sentencing for people under the age of twenty-five. They served only three years for murder. They were released when they turned twenty-one years old. They had been out of jail for only six months. So much for rehabilitation. When the young men were in jail, they earned enough money to buy a luxury car. The men expanded their résumé to touting drugs and fighting with the police.

The rear-seat passenger was not much better. He was believed to be the chief architect of a gruesome robbery murder at a convenient store involving one of our officers, but he was given immunity to testify against the triggerman. He had brought a map and notes concerning the planning of the robbery to court for the state's attorney to present as evidence. According to the state's attorney, he and the accomplice were discussing the accomplice's testimony when the accomplice tore up the robbery map and refused to testify, hence the warrant for obstruction of justice.

There was no such thing as a routine traffic stop, so that traffic stop for a simple turn signal carried more risk than I could have ever imagined, and there was a lot more danger to come.

CHAPTER 38

THE INEBRIATED BODYBUILDER VERSUS THE BEER-BELLIED POLICEMAN

"Champions aren't made in gyms. Champions are made from something deep inside them—a desire, a dream, a vision. They have to have the skill, and the will. But the will must be stronger than the skill."
—Muhammad Ali

We received a call about a guy drinking liquor outdoors and using profanity. As I pulled up in my patrol car, I saw a muscular white guy drinking a beer in his backyard, near the end of his fence. I approached him and asked him what he was doing. "None of your fucking business, asshole," he replied.

The sergeant was with me. He asked me, "What's this guy's claim to fame?"

I said, "This guy must have a serious malfunction if he's calling a uniformed police officer an asshole." The sergeant always got a kick out of watching my exchanges with street lawyers who thought they understood the law.

The man looked at the sergeant and said in a raunchy voice, "Aye, fuckin' right, man, and you are an asshole too!"

I looked at the suspect. "Wow," I said, "you are two for two."

THE INEBRIATED BODYBUILDER VERSUS
THE BEER-BELLIED POLICEMAN

I explained to him that it was illegal to have an open alcoholic container outside of his residence. He threw his head back, chugged down another beer, and crushed it in his hands. He looked at me as if to say, "Now it's time for me to turn into a super jerk!" He balled up his fists, placed his arms in front of his body, and flexed his muscles.

"Now, I am going to kick both your asses and then drink some more beer!" the man said.

I looked at the sergeant. "It will be interesting to see if he can get over that fence to receive his beatdown," I said.

The man pointed at the sergeant and said, "First, I am going to kick your ass." Then he pointed at me and said, "Next, I am going to kick yours!"

I looked at the sergeant and said, "Damn, Sarge, why do you get to go first?"

Billy Bob quickly attempted to climb over the fence, but the alcohol had affected his balance. By his third attempt to climb the fence, I was standing a few feet away, holding my nightstick over my shoulder. "Sir, are you going to make it over that fence anytime soon? My shift ends in an hour." I laughed at him while twirling my nightstick. His breathing became increasingly labored as he made his fourth attempt to climb the fence. "Sir," I told him, "if you make it over that fence, you're going to have a really bad day."

On his fifth attempt, he tried to balance himself on the fence before climbing over. His body was shifting back and forth. He continued trying to get over the fence while breathing heavily. Finally, he stopped briefly, caught his breath, and said, "Two ass-whippings coming up."

I put my nightstick in my holster, looked at the sergeant, and said, "Watch this." I took one finger and gave the man a slight shove. He fell to the ground, back on the other side of the fence.

"Damn, that hurts!" Billy yelled.

I started up my cruiser. "Thank you, sir, for the show. It was a pleasure providing you with police service."

As I began to pull off, I heard Billy's exhausted voice say, "Your ass is mine next time I see you."

I backed up. "Sorry, Billy," I told him. "But this is my last day of work. I'll be back on Tuesday. Hopefully, you'll be off the ground by then."

*****

On Tuesday, we started our day shift. We left the 7-Eleven—the police substation—and headed to our favorite fishing hole to look for Riverdale Road drug dealers. I drove into the parking lot of a local apartment complex, and lo and behold, who should be there? Billy Bob, the rowdy drinker from our last shift! He was walking with his girlfriend.

I got on my CB radio and said, "Officer Dylan, remember the guy I was talking about that promised me and Sarge butt whippings? We just passed him." The next thing I heard was the sound of tires squealing. Officer Dylan, who had pulled his vehicle into the parking lot earlier, backed up at full speed. I got on my CB radio and tried to convince him to just let it go, but there was no use. Dylan was determined to confront Billy. After all, he relished any opportunity to educate criminals regarding the well-established pecking order of his beloved police world. I made a quick U-turn and walked up just as Dylan began talking to Billy.

Dylan wasted no time initiating his investigation. "It is my understanding that you got a beef with my boy Hicks," he said.

Billy Bob stood there with a bewildered look on his face. "Who the hell is Hicks?" he asked.

Dylan replied, "I'll ask the questions around here, sir."

Billy Bob asked again, "Who the hell is Hicks?"

"Now, you're becoming disorderly, sir," Dylan said.

The suspect did not recognize me as I walked up. Dylan pointed at me and said, "That's Hicks. If you have a problem with Hicks, you have a problem with me. So you call yourself a police fighter? Okay, then. Put them up."

I looked at Dylan, who had a caved-in chest and a giant beer belly. Then I looked at the suspect. He looked as if he could lift five hundred pounds with his teeth. I noticed that the suspect's girlfriend had kept walking as the two men began to square off.

The suspect was a bodybuilder, and he was happy to oblige Dylan. He put up his hands. Dylan approached the suspect with his fists up. When Dylan was about ten feet from the suspect, I saw him reach for his mace. He balled it up in his fist. The suspect closed in on Dylan. Dylan sidestepped the suspect and unleashed a quarter can of mace into Billy's face. The suspect grabbed his face, then began swinging his fists blindly. I thought, *If Billy connects one of those punches, it will knock Dylan out.* That prompted Dylan to do his version of the Ali Shuffle. I almost died from laughter.

"What the hell are you doing, Dylan?" I asked.

"I'm going to teach this boy a lesson he's never going to forget," Dylan replied.

While Billy was still holding his face, Dylan assumed a karate stance, so I thought, *Now, he's switching from boxing to karate.* I wondered what my potbellied companion was going to do next. "Kiai!" Dylan yelled, delivering a karate chop to Billy's neck, followed by a slow and flicked-looking roundhouse kick. The kick knocked the suspect to the ground.

Billy held his face, yelling for help. Just then, his girlfriend rounded the corner of the apartment building. Billy's clueless, drug-crazed girlfriend finally noticed Billy was no longer with her. She doubled back to see where he was. She looked at him on the ground and yelled, "Oh my God, what happened to you?"

It took Billy about twelve seconds to speak. "Mace, baby, Mace."

The emaciated girlfriend quickly became combative. "Why in the hell did you do that to him?" she asked. Then she ran full speed toward Dylan. Dylan reached for his mace again.

I yelled, "No! Please, no more of that!"

Dylan quickly grabbed Billy's girlfriend and threw her on the ground. He stood boldly over Billy and his girlfriend and proclaimed, "He needs to learn not to fuck with the police. Tell all of your friends about me." I thought, *Now, Dylan thinks he's Batman.*

When I walked back to my car, I saw a small cardboard sign taped to my bumper saying I Brake for Felons. I wondered how long the sign had been on my car. I looked at Dylan and told him I knew Mighty Matt had done it because he smiled too many times when he passed by me earlier today. I called Mighty Matt on the CB and said, "I found your little sign, Matt. You're trying to ruin my image." Matt started laughing. I knew right then that he would plant more signs on my cruiser.

CHAPTER 39

TO BREAK AND ENTER; TO PROTECT AND SERVE

We proceeded to our destination, an apartment complex on Sixty-Fourth Avenue. The apartment complex had recently been plagued by drug trafficking. A wave of Jamaican drug dealers had essentially taken over the complex. Officer Dylan and I had arrested scores of drug dealers there. At night, we would put green raincoats over our uniforms, put on ball caps and tennis shoes, and walk up to drug dealers selling their wares. We would quickly place them under arrest and seize their drugs.

On this day, a suspect standing in a corner noticed us walking up, and he began running. The foot chase was on. We quickly removed our caps and pulled our raincoats back, exposing our uniforms. We yelled, "Police! Freeze!" The suspect glanced back quickly, then switched into overdrive.

"Hicks," Dylan yelled, "call for backup!" I stopped momentarily and called out a foot chase on my police radio. I ran in the direction where Dylan was chasing the suspect. I found Dylan standing in front of a building. I asked him what had happened to the suspect. He explained that the suspect had run into the top apartment. I asked whether the suspect threw any drugs down.

"No," Dylan said.

"Oh well. We'll catch him another day."

"No, Hicks," Dylan said. "I'm going to get that little bastard today. Nobody makes me run and gets away with it!"

"Dylan, running is not a crime, man," I said.

"It is to me, Hicks," Dylan replied.

I said to myself, "Lord Jesus, help this man with his frustration."

Dylan quickly ran up the stairs and reared back to get a running start.

"Dylan, what the hell are you doing, man?" I asked.

"This is a hot pursuit," Dylan said. "I'm breaking down the door."

"God, no, please do not do that," I said.

Before I could get the rest of my words out of my mouth, Dylan had broken down the door. I thought, *I could not let him go in there and get shot.* I ran into the apartment to find a couple quietly sitting on their living room sofa, watching television. I stood there a moment, wondering which news channel would air the fiasco first. I looked at Dylan and shook my head.

Dylan looked at the couple on the sofa, then quickly spoke up. "Drug dealers are taking over this apartment complex. Hicks and I were chasing a drug dealer, and he ran into this building. I thought it was this apartment, but now I know I was wrong. Did you see Hicks and me out there?"

I thought, *Oh my God, he even gave the people my name.*

The couple slowly began shaking their heads. Dylan continued. "Hicks and I are out here every day trying to eliminate this problem for you. Nobody else in the police department cares about this but Hicks and me. We are out here because we want this community to be safe so you all can raise a family here. I'm sorry we broke down your door, but we were just trying to do the job that nobody else wants to do."

Of course, I wanted to say, "What do you mean we, white man? I didn't kick the damn door down."

Dylan continued his plea. "Don't worry. I'll get your door fixed."

At this point, I wondered how in the heck we were going to get the door fixed. After all, we were patrol officers. We were subject to getting another call any minute. We did not have time to fix the door. Dylan then called the building's rental office. "Hey, Hicks and I just kicked in the door to an apartment." I was thinking again, *Why does he keep saying we?*

To my amazement, the rental office sent someone over to repair the door. The couple shook our hands, and off we went. The funny thing was, several officers, including Dylan, Mighty Matt, and Curly, all individually proclaimed that I was the only person they could work with. I thought, *Son, working with this cast of characters, you are in big trouble.*

*****

On a cold winter night in October 1998, Matt and Dylan responded to an alarm at a county school in Landover Hills, Maryland. Several men ran out of the school and were immediately arrested by Mighty Matt and Dylan. I caught the third suspect a few blocks away. He was a muscular twenty-five-year-old black man. He had the physique of a boxer. Upon seeing him, I lunged from my patrol car and ordered him to put his hands on a vehicle. Instead, I spread his legs apart and began searching his pockets. He was wearing a thick leather coat.

When I opened his leather jacket, I was surprised to see he had large, deep inside pockets. I reached down inside his pockets and felt something hard; it turned out to be a thick wallet. I kept reaching down inside his pockets. I felt a large plastic bag. There must have been at least eighty tinfoil packs of PCP. I was mesmerized and momentarily looked down at the bag of PCP for a fraction of a second. *Damn, he caught me sleeping.*

He quickly spun around and swung with such force and speed that someone would have thought he was trying to knock out the heavyweight champion of the world. I leaned back almost like Keanu Reeves did in the movie called *The Matrix*. I leaned back just far enough that his fist barely touched the edge of my nose. I got a brief look at his paranoid stare. He was on the boat. If his punch had connected, he would have knocked me out.

I was hot as hell! Unfortunately, everyone on the squad had a burglary suspect in custody. I was hyped up. I locked in on the suspect's movements like a cheetah pursuing its prey. I did not have the good sense to stop chasing him. I was heading for the second round of my fight with Hercules. This was very unwise. I got on my radio and started calling for help.

"Baker 2, I am on a foot pursuit with a suspect who is wanted for assault on a police officer and for possession with the intent to distribute PCP."

The dispatcher replied, "Is any unit available to assist in capturing a suspect wanted for an assault on Baker 2?"

There was no answer. I continued pursuing the suspect and called out his locations. "The suspect just passed Cooper's Lane. Now, he is crossing Warner Avenue," I said. A few minutes later, I was closing in on the suspect when I heard a roaring engine heading in my direction. It was Monty Hall barreling down Warner Avenue. The suspect leaped down a hill and into an apartment complex. I jumped down the hill in pursuit and slid down the grass.

I heard a loud breaking sound and looked up to find Monty Hall's cruiser airborne. His cruiser plummeted and crash-landed on the top of two cars in the parking lot. Monty leaped out of his car, jumped on top of another vehicle parked in the parking lot, and joined me in the foot pursuit. *Who in the hell does something like that?*

The suspect stopped at an apartment wall and told us he was surrendering, but it was a fake-out. He pushed off the wall and tried his knockout punch on Monty Hall, aka the Barbarian. Big mistake. The Barbarian sidestepped him, at which time he and I both swung at the suspect. You would have thought we practiced boxing together. Both of our fists connected with each side of the suspect's face. I thought we were going to be in a prolonged knockdown and dragged-out fight. I was wrong.

Our punches connected simultaneously, which threw off the suspect's senses. He was happy to surrender at that point. I asked the Barbarian what he did with his prisoner before he joined my pursuit. When he pointed to his car, I was shocked to see his prisoner sitting in the passenger seat with his seat belt on. "The sergeant is going to have a hissy fit when he arrives," I said. The Barbarian had his issues, but he was there for me when I needed him.

The next day, there was a full moon, and any officer who had worked the evening or midnight shift could tell you that people acted nuts when there was a full moon. You could count on dispatchers spitting out calls for service every few minutes. It was a great time to be off. I took off the last four hours of a ten-hour shift to take my girlfriend to the movies. Less than an hour later, Johnny, a thin Italian police officer, got a call for a theft report.

When I sat down in the roll call room, Johnny gave me the evil eye and said, "You are an asshole, man."

I asked, "Why did you say that, Johnny?"

He replied, "When you took off four hours early yesterday, I had to go to a call in your damn beat. That damn Baker 2 jerk tried to light me on fire."

I said, "Sorry, buddy. I know that you wished it were me."

I left the station and headed out to my beat. While driving down the street, a few pretty girls in different cars drove close to me, smiled, and blew their horns. I thought that was strange. Then Mighty Matt asked me to meet with him at the Cheverly Theatre on Landover Road. When I pulled up to his vehicle, he had a great big grin on his face. "How is your day going, Moe?" he asked. He pulled off quickly and went about his business.

About an hour later, another woman pulled up beside me and blew her horn and pointed to the back of my car. I pulled over and saw a piece of cardboard taped to my bumper that said, "Honk if you're horny." I got on my CB radio and said, "Matt, you got me again. I should have known something was not right." Matt always knew how to change the mood. I appreciated him.

CHAPTER 40

FAREWELL, BOSS MAN

"Don't count the days, make the days count."
—Muhammad Ali

Just about everyone considered him a good man. He wanted to serve his family and serve his community.

When I worked a beat, I established close ties with many of the merchants. Many small mom-and-pop operations couldn't afford to hire private security to guard their stores. Instead, they had to rely on local beat cops to be their informal security.

After leaving roll call one morning, I stopped at a little convenience store called the 7-Market located at Annapolis Road and Bladensburg Road. I introduced myself to the store's Korean owner, who was nicknamed Boss Man. I explained to him that his store was in my beat and that I would be checking on him from time to time. The store sold subs and grocery items.

I ordered a hot turkey sandwich with American cheese, mayo, lettuce, relish, hot peppers, Utz barbeque corn chips, and a diet Dr Pepper. I proceeded to the back of the store, slid back some canned goods, and set my chips and soda down. Then I began eating my sandwich.

Two officers from the squad came in and ordered their food. They looked back at me and asked what I was doing back there. "What does it look like?" I asked. "I'm eating in the dining room."

Boss Man heard me and began laughing. The officers came back and joined me in the dining room. This became our routine. Whenever possible, if we ordered food at the 7-Market, we ate in our makeshift dining room.

Every day, I made it a point to come into Boss Man's store and order a hot turkey sandwich. In the evenings and near closing time, I parked my patrol car in front of Boss Man's store and wrote my reports. Boss Man would come over to my car with a big smile and say, "Good evening, Mr. Hick. Would you like a turkey sandwich?" He always called me Hick instead of Hicks. I always got a kick out of hearing him call me that, and I never corrected him.

Many of the merchants in my beat had a great appreciation for my Baltimore City community policing style. I got to know all the merchants in my beat and most people living there as well. My former Baltimore City police sergeant's master plan to expose me to foot patrol turned out to be a master plan to position me to make a significant difference in the communities in which I served.

*****

One day, I walked into the 7-Market with two officers and immediately greeted Boss Man. "Hello, Mr. Hick," Boss Man said.

Boss Man's wife said, "Mr. Hick, you want turkey sandwich with extra, extra, extra?"

Every day, Boss Man, his wife, or his son-in-law would greet me the same way: "Hello, Mr. Hick. You want extra, extra, extra?" So my squad members began to call me Extra, Extra, Extra. I was the extra turkey man.

*****

A few months later, I made a traffic stop near the 7-Market. My sergeant pulled up behind me to provide backup. While waiting for a warrant check on the suspect to come back, I heard a knock on my window. I rolled down my window. Then Boss Man handed me a bag containing a hot turkey sandwich with extra meat and American cheese, mayo, lettuce, relish, hot peppers, Utz barbeque corn chips, and a diet Dr Pepper. I thanked him and watched him run back into the store.

My sergeant walked over to my car and asked, "What the hell was that about, Junior? Are you getting curbside service now on traffic stops?"

I laughed. "I'm like Detective Axel Foley in *Beverly Hills Cop*," I said. "I'm here teaching you, boys, how to do police work."

That was a result of Baltimore City-style policing. I looked out for them, and they looked out for me. I had intense care and concern for Boss Man and his family and the many merchants in the community. Their businesses served some of the kindest and some of the most violent people living in the community. A Baskin-Robbins stood about fifty feet down the street from the 7-Market. On weekends, the store was staffed primarily by young teenage girls. The store was robbed so many times I lost count.

As a patrol officer, I dreaded the day I would respond to a robbery at the store and find that the robber had killed any of the people I cared so deeply about. I came to realize how right my grandfather was when he talked about my caring too much. I took my responsibility as a police officer seriously. I viewed myself as a shepherd looking over my sheep.

*****

After retiring, I maintained contact with one of my rookie officers, who contacted Boss Man. The officer told me that Boss Man was constantly complaining about the officers who worked in the area of his store. "There were no problems like this in my store when Mr. Hick here!" he would tell them.

One officer had said, "My God, how long has Hicks been retired? If I hear Hicks's name one more time, I'm going to scream!"

I was devastated when I learned that Boss Man's sister-in-law was killed in the store in 2002. The news in 2011 was even worse. My rookie called while living in Las Vegas and told me my good friend Boss Man was murdered. He was robbed, stabbed with a box cutter, and beaten with a chain saw. The suspect then set the store on fire.

The officer knew how much I cared about Boss Man. The news was devastating to me. I had been telling stories about Boss Man for over thirty-five years. I wish I could have been there to save him. May God rest his soul.

Many officers took for granted the difference they could make in people's lives. I hoped my diligence in being at Boss Man's store so frequently at closing time had given him some feeling of peace, safety, and security.

After leaving the 7-Market, I often parked my car at the bus stop a few feet away and waited for a beautiful, studious-looking black woman in her twenties who wore glasses while waiting for the bus. I would always wave to her, but I did not make contact.

Then one day, at about two thirty in the afternoon, I was driving in the 3500 block of Fifty-Fifth Avenue in Hyattsville when I saw the young lady. She waved me down, introduced herself, and told me how much she appreciated my waiting for her at the bus stop so many nights. I explained to her I wished I could have been there more often. Unfortunately, I further explained, I had to take calls, which prevented me from being there many nights.

The reality of the situation was, I believed police officers should do what they could for our citizens. I was trying to find a way to make a difference in people's lives. I felt blessed to have a job where I had a chance to do that. Citizens needed officers to be compassionate when they became victims of crimes.

CHAPTER 41

WAITING ALONE FOR DEATH IN THE DARK

Live every day as if it were your last because
someday you're going to be right.
—Muhammad Ali

Many of the good things police officers did went unnoticed. We were in the life-saving business. Each day on the job presented an opportunity to make a difference. The difference might deter a criminal from continuing a crime spree. It might entail rescuing someone who was hurt. I used the same sixth sense to catch criminals and to locate victims.

On this particular day, I was driving on Kenilworth Avenue near Greenbelt Road in pitch-black at about 9:00 p.m. As I passed by this intersection, I caught a glimpse of something white on the hill. Most people would have ignored it, but my senses were telling me to investigate further.

I had to drive quite a bit of distance and perform quite a bit of maneuvering to get back to the spot where I was before. I turned around and double-parked my car in a very hazardous part of the road to check out whatever was on the hill. I climbed about thirty feet up the hill and found a Hispanic man's mangled body.

The man appeared to be in his twenties. To my utter amazement, he was still alive. I called an ambulance, and the man was taken to the hospital. He had been struck by a car and had been lying there helplessly for over six hours. I made a mental note to myself: *Maurice, you are making a difference out here.*

CHAPTER 42

MURDER AT FIRST SIGHT

Hate the sin; love the sinner.
—Mahatma Gandhi

I began my patrol in Riverdale hoping to capture some street dealers. I looked to my right and saw Ronnie, a seventeen-year-old drug dealer, standing on a street corner. He was playing hooky from school as usual. However, this time, he had a snake around his neck. I said, "Ronnie, why aren't you in school, and why do you have a snake around your neck? You know I'm not having that. I'll tell you one time: do not be out here during school hours, and do not let me catch you selling drugs in my beat, because it will ruin your future.

"Drug dealing is a losing game bound to catch up with you sooner or later. I do not want to come out here to see your baby face riddled with bullets one day. Do you know how many people have been shot standing out here? Too many. Get yourself an education, and get your family the hell out of this neighborhood and make something of yourself."

A few months later, Ronnie was selling drugs in front of his building. We chased him into the apartment. Ronnie quickly made it into his bedroom. In my mind, I thought that if he had the snake with him, the snake would be dead meat. Ronnie ran full speed toward me and threw a kick at me. I sidestepped him and returned with a dropkick of my own. However, I was out of practice, and my kick was a little too slow. He caught my foot and pushed me back. The other officers put an end to the mini kung fu match and hand-cuffed him.

Ronnie started foaming at the mouth. I asked him what the hell was going on. I realized he had swallowed some cocaine. My instincts told me not to wait for the ambulance and take him straight to the hospital. I made the risky move of throwing him in the back of my car, then driving less than a quarter mile to Prince George's County Hospital. They took him in and started pumping his stomach. He appeared to be in excruciating pain.

"Hicks, I swear to God," Ronnie said, "when I get out of here, I'm going to kill you the first time I see you."

"Ronnie, I hope that you are going to be all right, man," I replied.

I knew the kid needed some guidance. I did not want to see any harm come to him. However, I never slept on any threat against me. I was going to be on guard the next time I saw him. About a month later, I was in Upper Marlboro's courthouse when I heard someone yell, "Aye, Hicks." I turned around and saw Ronnie pointing me out to a female companion standing beside him. They were standing on the other side of a metal detector, waiting for screening.

All of a sudden, Ronnie ran through the metal detector without being screened. A deputy sheriff tried to stop him. I braced myself for the inevitable attack. I thought it was going to be *The Karate Kid Part II*. I was beginning to raise my fist to defend myself when Ronnie suddenly grabbed me, pinning my arms to my side. He began crying.

Surprisingly, what I thought was an attack turned out to be a hug. Ronnie told his girlfriend I was the man who had saved his life. He said the doctor had told him that if I had not acted immediately to save his life, the amount of cocaine he had swallowed might have killed him.

"Thank God we were able to save you," I said. "I was really worried about you. When I saw you, I thought the worst, because when you were in the ER, you vowed to murder me at first sight."

"Sorry, Hicks," Ronnie said. "I was so out of it. I cannot remember anything that I said."

"Look, man," I replied, "you're here with this beautiful young lady. Life can be good if you just let that other stuff go."

The beautiful young lady shook her head and grabbed Ronnie's arm. Ronnie said, "You're right, Hicks. I'm done with that crap."

"Good. Make something of yourself, man. God has given you a second chance. Perhaps that was a sign to you to change course."

To my amazement, I never saw Ronnie out there selling drugs again.

CHAPTER 43

TOUGH LOVE

Love recognizes no barriers. It jumps
hurdles, leaps fences, penetrates walls to
arrive at its destination full of hope.
—Maya Angelou

Sometimes, single mothers must make tough choices to ensure that their children would not get consumed by a life of crime. Unfortunately, Ms. Johnson was faced with such a choice. I met her while patrolling my beat. She left me a message at the station, asking me to call her regarding her son. When I spoke to her, she told me her son, Sheldon, was dealing drugs. Of course, this was something I already knew. She also told me to pick up her son's drugs and take him into custody.

When I walked through the door of their home, Sheldon got the shock of his life. He looked on in horror as I spoke to his mother. "Let me show you something," Ms. Johnson said to me. She walked into Sheldon's room, reached under his bed, and removed about a gram of crack cocaine. She then handed it to me.

"God, Ma, what are you doing?" Sheldon yelled.

"Sheldon, put your hands behind your back," I said. When I handcuffed Sheldon, Ms. Johnson began to cry.

"I hate you, Ma!" Sheldon yelled.

Ms. Johnson started crying. "But I love you," she said.

The episode was so emotional that I still fought to maintain my composure whenever I thought about it. It was a terrible choice to have to make. However, I was proud of Ms. Johnson's courage in deciding to send her only son to jail.

"I know this is hard for you," I told her. "But in the long run, you are saving his life."

"I certainly hope so," she said.

Ms. Johnson learned how flawed the criminal justice system was. I spoke to her about a month after I arrested Sheldon. She told me she received notice from the court that she was required by law to hire an attorney to represent her son. The letter threatened to find her in contempt of court if she did not hire a lawyer. Ms. Johnson, a person with limited financial resources, was ordered by the court to hire an attorney. This was for a case she initiated. The situation with her son turned out to be a double-edged sword. In the end, she hired an attorney. Her son pleaded guilty but was able to avoid jail time.

I wondered how the episode was going to affect Sheldon moving forward. I ran into him about three years later in the supermarket. He was dressed professionally and had a beautiful lady with him and a newborn baby. He smiled when he saw me, which warmed my heart. He introduced me to his lady friend and told her about me. She showed me their beautiful little girl. I told Sheldon I was happy to see him doing so well. I asked him how his mother was doing. His demeanor changed. He took a few seconds to compose himself. I looked at his girlfriend for clues regarding his change of demeanor. Sheldon began to tear up. He told me his mother had died the previous year from cancer.

"Your mother was a good, kind, strong woman who loved you very much," I said.

"I know she was a good woman," Sheldon said. "She made a decision that no mother should ever have to make. What she did changed my life, and I'm a better man because of it."

CHAPTER 44

"I LIKE THE BLACKS"

> Hating people because of their color is
> wrong. And it doesn't matter which color
> does the hating. It's just plain wrong.
> —Muhammad Ali

Like most county police officers, when I wasn't working for the police department during the day, I spent many hours working part-time at local businesses. Many of us earned another twenty thousand to thirty thousand dollars yearly working this way. I enjoyed working at the Hong Kong Club and watching Latinos dancing and having a good time. Many of them were friendly regulars who came there every weekend.

One night, I was working when a very intoxicated short Latino man smiled, tapped me on the shoulder, and said, "I like the Blacks."

I said, "Thank you very much."

He smiled and said, "My best friends are the blacks. I like to buy you a Coca-Cola!"

I told him I appreciated the gesture, but I explained I received free drinks at the club. He was very persistent. He continued to blow his beer breath in my face, repeatedly saying, "I like to buy you a Coca-Cola!" I reminded him three additional times that I got free drinks at the club. When he got back in my face for the fourth time, my patience and tolerance for the odor of the alcohol on his breath wore thin. "Just buy the damn thing!" I exclaimed. I did not have the patience to explain that I could not drink Coca-Cola anyway.

When he finally bought the drink, I took it from him and placed it on the bar. Then he walked back toward the dance floor. About ten minutes later, I was sitting down, enjoying some Chinese food, when an employee said, "Aye, Hicks, your friend that bought you that Coke is harassing everyone he encounters."

I went over to the man and tapped him on the shoulder. "Hello, old buddy, old pal," I said. "I have to ask you to leave the club, because customers are complaining about you harassing them.

"Shut up, nigger!" he said.

I had to laugh. I was always amazed by how fast alcohol could change people's personalities. I reminded the man that he had said he liked the blacks. He refused to leave; instead, he stood there with his arms folded. Finally, a few patrons volunteered to convince him to go to prevent him from getting arrested. A few minutes later, they escorted him out of the club.

I felt relieved. I did not have to go hands-on to remove this man from the club. My relief was short-lived, however. As soon as the other men left the club, the man who had been escorted out attempted to walk back through the door. I tried to reason with him again.

Finally, I said, "Hi, good buddy. You cannot come back in."

He again said, "Shut up, nigger. I'll tell you what to do!"

"Friend, old buddy, old pal, let's not go there," I said. "Please leave."

He tried to swing at me. However, his reflexes were extremely slow because of his level of intoxication. I moved out of the way and swept his legs with my foot from his side, hoping I could take him down without injuring him. He was so light on his feet that his feet went up almost as high as he stood. He fell to the floor and hit his head. Some other Latinos picked him up and drove him off the parking lot.

CHAPTER 45

PCP and the Bible

A new and more addicting drug made its way into Prince George's County. Crack cocaine came to town. It was a much more potent version of cocaine. The euphoria experienced from smoking crack was undeniable. I remembered talking to one crack addict who told me how difficult it was to stop using crack. When I explained to him I couldn't understand how anyone would want something that bad, he explained it to me this way: If he had the choice between having sex with the most beautiful woman on the face of the earth and a chance to use crack cocaine, he would take crack over the woman every time. I said, "Now, it's clear to me that crack cocaine is a potent drug."

In the mid-1980s, the crack epidemic was really in your face. One could go on any street corner and see scores of drug dealers lined up, openly selling their wares. The epidemic disrupted the lives of many of the county's hardworking families. Their quality of life was never the same once a member of their family started on crack. These violent offenders would encamp themselves in their community and take over many people's apartments. Sometimes, they would take over entire floors and sometimes entire buildings. Drug dealers stationed themselves in the hallways of apartment buildings.

In addition to dealing with scores of crack cocaine dealers, citizens also had to endure the occupation of a cadre of armed PCP dealers and their customers. PCP was a hazardous drug that caused the user to hallucinate. Three or four drug dealers would block the hallways in many apartment buildings while tending to an endless stream of customers. These events were occurring while families were taking their children in and out of the buildings.

Phone lines at the chief's office rang off the hook during this period. Calls came in from the governor's office, the county executive's office, and church and community leaders. They all wanted the same thing: to disrupt the indiscriminate sale of drugs and curtail the death and destruction associated with it all. Illegal drug sales, illegal drug usage, and crime were on a deadly collision course. The impact of the collision would be on a level no one could have ever anticipated. Two incidents involving female PCP users would personally rock my world as well as the entire Prince George's County community.

*****

My partner Jim's voice cracked over the police radio. I ran out of the station, started my cruiser, yanked my car into drive, and sped off the station parking lot. Within a few seconds, I was barreling down Baltimore Avenue with blue lights on and the siren wailing. I was dodging in and out of rush hour traffic while simultaneously reaching down and switching my siren tones.

As I turned right onto East-West Highway, my heart was pounding almost out of my chest. I was oblivious to the sounds of my wheels squealing and my cruiser sliding sideways. I had tunnel vision. I was on a mission to get there as quickly as possible. I did not know Jim had found a man leaning on a car who was suffering from multiple stab wounds inflicted by his girlfriend until I arrived. Our squad had warned Jim numerous times to stop going on calls without backup.

There was a twenty-three-year-old female suspect who began walking toward Jim, totally naked, with a butcher knife in one hand and a bible in her other hand while the man was still leaning on Jim's car. She mumbled something about Jehovah. There was nothing that could have prepared me for what happened next. It was something so horrific that it haunted me to this very day.

When Jim looked up from the man, he saw a naked twenty-six-year-old black woman looking at him through the window. As she walked toward Jim, she stopped and began stabbing herself while mumbling something about Jehovah. Finally, after stabbing herself a total of twenty-nine times, she raised the knife and advanced toward my friend Jim. By this time, the K-9 officer had arrived on the scene. He discharged his weapon to keep the woman from advancing. The woman fell to the ground, got back up, and then stabbed herself a few more times before collapsing.

When I arrived on the scene, the woman was lying on the ground, suffering from multiple stab wounds and gunshot wounds, but she was still alive. She did not die until she reached the hospital. As disturbing as it was to see her lifeless body, I could only imagine what it must have been like to witness the woman's attack on herself in real time.

We cleared the scene. Within a few hours, my friend Jim was back to handling calls. Later, I saw him on a call. He appeared visibly shaken. When I asked him if he was okay, he said something I had never given a second thought about until he mentioned it. "No," he said, "I am not okay. Who in the hell can see something like that and not be affected by it? The woman stabbed herself twenty-nine times in front of me. The woman cut her eye out in front of me. She stuck the knife in her chest and in her fucking groin! They didn't even give me the rest of the fucking day off."

As Jim's close friend, I felt ashamed, as I did not realize how intensely the incident had affected him. More than that, I realized people in management thought we were robots with no feelings or emotions.

CHAPTER 46

UNSPEAKABLE HORROR

Submit yourselves, then, to God. Resist
the devil, and he will flee from you.
—James 4:7 (International Version)

As if the first incident with a PCP user was not enough, the following incident shook me to my core. I was moonlighting at a business in Takoma Park, where I became friends with an employee who worked there. She was an extremely ambitious college student who worked as a waitress at a restaurant to put herself through college. She was a beautiful, light-skinned girl in her early twenties. I was about twenty-four years old at the time. I enjoyed talking to her. I was impressed by her intelligence, her ambition, and her undeniable beauty. We finally managed to coordinate our schedules once and broke bread together. I had no idea how her life would be affected by PCP.

Two months after breaking bread, I was listening to my police radio when a call went out for a murder. The location of the homicide was out of my area; therefore, I did not respond to the scene. When the details of the horrific murder came out a few days later, everyone in the community was terror-stricken. The previous night, we had received a call concerning a man armed with a gun. When one of my coworkers knocked on the door of an apartment in the apartment complex, responding to the call, the mother of a five-year-

222

old child told the officer he did not want to see what was inside the apartment. As a result, the officer left the scene. The following day, the woman threw a brick through her apartment window; she went to church afterward.

Several people at church asked the woman where her son was. They knew the woman was close to her son, and she always brought him to church. The woman told the church pastor she no longer had to worry about her son, because the demons were finally out of him, and he was at rest. The following day, the child's aunt visited her nephew and found parts of his body lying on the sofa. He was dismembered, decapitated, and disemboweled.

The next day, I was moonlighting again at the restaurant where I saw my friend Sheila. I told her about the murder of the five-year-old child and how PCP was ruining people's lives. In an incredibly soft voice, she told me, "I know. That was my nephew. I was the one who found him on the sofa and called the police." I was stunned beyond measure.

The drug war could not have become more personal for me. I had to do my part to prevent such horrible things from happening. The most seasoned police officer and the most seasoned fireman would tell you that it stayed with them for life when they saw a child dead or murdered. I remembered talking to a fireman who said to me, "I don't want to pull another dead child out of a pool. It's screwing up my mind." What happened to my friend's nephew renewed my resolve to take down as many menacing drug dealers as I could.

The murder of the five-year-old child and many other instances like that led to a call for action. The police chief allocated two ten-man squads of detectives and two sergeants to attack the problem head-on. Thus, our agency was officially enlisted in the war on drugs.

Drug sales were becoming indiscriminate. There was so much money to be made that most drug dealers became careless about to whom they sold drugs. In many cases, drug dealers did not have a particular client base. Therefore, a drug user did not have to know their local dealer to purchase from them for the most part. Drug barons and drug buyers did not feel deterred from openly selling and buying drugs. A new strategy was needed to deal with the surging PCP and crack cocaine epidemic.

The next day my beat partner and I were talking outside our cars in Bladensburg when we saw a 20-year-old drug dealer standing on the corner talking to some men. My partner noticed that he was wearing a colostomy bag. "Oh no, I feel bad seeing someone so young wearing a colostomy bag. I guess the game finally caught with him." My partner said. I turned toward my partner with a stern look on my face. "I do not feel sorry for him. This is a freaken war, man. He got what he deserved. He is selling death to other people. He is lucky that he is still alive!" Once the words left my mouth, it reminded me of the time when the rooster crowed after Peter denied Jesus three times. I immediately reflected on what a field training officer in Baltimore said to me, "Never lose your compassion for people." My training officer was a 20-year patrol veteran. He had maintained clarity of purpose through all the storms of working Baltimore's cold good harsh streets. I immediately felt ashamed. I realized that I had become battle-hardened. I had been thrown off course. I had to get back on message. I reflected on a Sunday School lesson from Gillis Memorial Church in Baltimore. Colossians 3: 12. Therefore, as God chose people, holy and dearly loved, clothe yourself with compassion, kindness, humility, gentleness and patience

I got back in my car and slowly moved the mirror toward me. However, I was afraid of what I was about to see. I examined my face closely. It was a timely awakening for me. Then, I realized how important it was that I never lose focus. Moreover, no matter what horrible things I saw on the streets, I had to maintain my compassion for people.

The liquid PCP and marihuana were recovered from
the scene of an armed home invasion.

CHAPTER 47

OPERATION TRIPLE PLAY

> When strong, avoid them. If of high morale, depress
> them. Seem humble to fill them with conceit. If
> at ease, exhaust them. If united, separate them.
> Attack their weaknesses. Emerge to their surprise.
> —*The Art of War*, Sun Tzu

The department developed a new strategy to take control of the problem. It was called Operation Triple Play. The purpose of Operation Triple Play was to cause disruption and confusion among drug dealers and buyers. The goal was to prevent drug dealers and buyers from knowing who the real dealers and the actual buyers were. The agency sent undercover officers in to buy drugs on the streets and inside people's homes. After they busted real drug dealers, undercover officers sold their customers a placebo resembling cocaine.

Drug barons filled the hallways of many apartment buildings, forcing residents to pass groups of armed men to get to their homes. Some barons took over entire apartment buildings. Some were willing participants in the drug trade; others were unwilling participants. Drug dealers liked to prey on single women living by themselves. They manipulated these women either by offering money or by making them fear for their lives.

Drug dealers commonly used children as young as ten years old to look out for the police. Some of them were paid as much as five hundred dollars a day to be a lookout. I remembered executing a search warrant and reading seized documents laying out the pay structure for recruits in a drug operation. The sheet showed that one hallway lookout site paid five hundred dollars per day, a second different hallway lookout site paid five hundred dollars per day, a mobile lookout paid five hundred dollars a day, and a stationary lookout paid five hundred dollars a day.

The drug operation's pay schedule demonstrated the difficulty in keeping young kids from selling drugs. Juveniles under sixteen could get out of jail immediately after their arrest by obtaining their parents' signatures. Therefore, it was exceedingly difficult for them to take a job at McDonald's or other fast-food restaurants with lower pay because the money earned from working in drug organizations was just too good to resist.

50 and 100-round magazines were recovered from the home
of a 21-year-old in Upper Marlboro, Maryland.

CHAPTER 48

INDISCRIMINATE DRUG SALES

You knew that your jurisdiction had a severe problem when dealers tried to sell you drugs wherever you went. I found it ironic that I was always looking to root out crime whenever I was on duty, but I couldn't seem to escape it even when I was off duty, and one of the most frustrating things was people trying to sell drugs to me while I was off duty. It did not matter if I was in Prince George's County or Baltimore; people were always trying to sell me drugs. In Prince George's County, things were so bad that people tried to sell me drugs even while I was in uniform. I just ignored them; if not, I would never have gotten a minute of peace.

It was amazing that my off-duty skirmishes with people were almost equal to my on-duty altercations with suspects. I started moonlighting at many different places because the department allowed police officers to work security jobs in uniform for extra income. For some reason, people treated us as if we were security guards instead of police officers even though we were fully armed.

People constantly tested my patience while moonlighting at a variety of different businesses. It was as if they knew I had no desire to arrest them when I was moonlighting. A patron at the International House of Pancakes on New Hampshire Avenue did his best to torment me by walking over to the counter and grabbing a plate that didn't belong to him. Then he began munching on the french fries, daring me to do something. I kicked him out. Another IHOP patron slapped me on the shoulder and asked when he was going to "get some justice around here!" I guessed he was asking when he was going to get some service. I told him never to put his hands on me again.

The patron turned to his friend and said, "I hate people like this. I make more money than him anyway!"

"You can make more money than me outside of here," I told him, "because you're not eating in this joint tonight!"

With that, I escorted him outside. When we got outside, he completely changed his tune. He begged me to allow him back inside the restaurant. His party watched intensely as we held our discussion. Then to ensure that his friends understood our interaction precisely, I closed my fist, extended my thumb, and raised my hand quickly, gesturing as though I was an umpire ejecting the patron from a baseball game. He was out! The man patiently waited outside while his ego had a chance to deflate.

*****

I worked security at the apartment complex where I lived in exchange for free rent. It was another reason I could not get any peace while I was off duty. At first, I was excited about getting a free apartment with free utilities. However, it did not take long to learn that I lived among the most annoying people, including privileged students who attended a local university. I did not know who was more annoying: the students or the criminals who lived in the apartments.

I was the victim of more crime during the six months I lived in my apartment building than in my twenty-plus years in Baltimore. I had a rock thrown through my window the second night I lived there. I had my Police Only parking sign ripped out of the ground right in front of my apartment. I had all four tires on my car stolen. Someone even lit off about twenty firecrackers in front of my apartment.

The people I dealt with were trying to terrorize me, and I had to admit, they had me shaken. At that point, whoever was trying to scare me awakened a sleeping giant. I started staking out the parking lot. I was able to arrest several of the perpetrators for tampering with vehicles and other minor crimes. After I turned the tables on them, suddenly, nobody wanted to screw with me.

One day, I was getting dressed for work when one of my neighbors knocked on the door. He told me his wife was beating him up. My girlfriend was in the apartment at the time. She just shook her head. I asked the man to wait a few minutes while I finished getting dressed. I shut the door, tucked in my uniform shirt, and put on my gun belt. I grabbed my radio and opened the door. Now, his wife was at my door, arguing with him. I asked her to calm down. She yelled, "Fuck you and your little girlfriend!"

I told the woman to get away from my apartment with that nonsense. She had been drinking. She was incapable of toning it down. She reared back and coldcocked her husband right in front of me. I was embarrassed for the guy. I immediately cuffed his wife and asked my girlfriend to give me my lunch box. It was summertime. My neighbors watched me parade the man's wife to my marked patrol vehicle with my lunch box tucked under my arm. The neighbors merely shook their heads. I thought, *Good. Now you all know I am not playing with you.*

By the time I arrived at the station, I was late for roll call. I stopped past the roll call room to let my sergeant know I had a prisoner in lockup. "What do you have now, Moe?" he asked. I explained what had happened. After that, everyone on the squad started laughing.

The sergeant said, "You are the only officer I know who constantly brings prisoners to work with you. What is wrong with you, Junior? How many prisoners have you brought to work, Moe?"

I became a little defensive. "Maybe four or five," I said.

One officer responded, "That is bullshit, Hicks. I can count about ten off the top of my head!"

"What can I say?" I replied. "I live around a bunch of assholes, man!"

"Let's be real," the sergeant said. "You're always looking for stuff to get into."

"That is not true," I said. "This annoying little drunk provoked me and hit her husband right in front of me. What else was I supposed to do?"

"How about those four guys in the stolen car you brought in last week?" the sergeant said.

"That was different," I said. "I saw four juveniles driving on the Beltway in the fast lane, doing the speed limit. When I looked at the driver, he looked straight ahead. That was a dead giveaway. I initiated a rolling stolen check, and the car came back stolen. State police and county officers boxed them in, and we took them into custody. That one does not count."

"Jesus, Moe!" the sergeant replied. "Go take care of your prisoner."

I realized right then that I was working on my sergeant's patience. He did not understand the hell these criminals and college students living in my apartment complex were putting me through. My next call for service would stretch my sergeant's patience even further.

In July 1987, Mighty Matt and I responded to a call for a disturbance at an apartment complex in Hyattsville. I knocked on the door, and a white woman in her thirties named Rebecca answered the door while holding a six-month-old baby in her arms. First, I explained that we were investigating a complaint for a disturbance. Then I asked if my partner and I could step inside and speak to her. Once inside, I noticed a white male in his early thirties standing by the window. He was pretending he was climbing the curtains.

"Who is that guy, and what in the hell is he doing?" I asked.

Rebecca said, "He is my baby's daddy. We just smoked a little Love Boat."

Mighty Matt and I looked at each other. "How do I know that you are not going to start tripping out like him?" I asked.

She yelled, "Get out of my house!"

I said, "Don't screw with me. I will take your baby."

She pointed at the door and said, "I told you to get the fuck out of my house."

I called the dispatcher and asked her to call protective services to respond to the scene regarding the baby. After an hour of waiting, protective services still had not arrived. In the meantime, Mighty Matt and I patted down her baby's daddy and directed him to sit on the couch after verifying that he did not have any weapons. He started moaning and saying some words we could not understand. He had a bad high. We kept a careful eye on him. We did not know what he was capable of doing.

Things were quiet for the next few minutes until Rebecca started her rant again. "Get the fuck out of my apartment. Both of you are trespassing."

I said, "Very well! If I leave, the baby is coming with me." I said, "Matt, please grab the baby's car seat. She is going for a little ride."

Rebecca exploded. "You are not taking my baby, you fucking asshole cop!" she exclaimed.

I grabbed the baby and began walking out of the door. Matt followed me with the car seat.

"I am going to sue you and the fucking police department," she said.

"You might want to call the sergeant first," Matt said. "I am not going to take the chance of the child getting hurt. I will talk to the sergeant when I get to the station."

I transported the child to the station and brought her into the clerk's office. Just then, the sergeant walked past the station clerk's office, looked at the clerk standing over the baby and then at me, and did a double take.

"Junior, what is a baby doing in the station?" the sergeant asked.

"Don't worry, Sarge. I have her in protective custody for now," I said.

"Where in the hell is protective services?" he asked.

I said, "Your guess is as good as mine. I waited for them at the woman's house. However, they never called or showed up."

"Jesus Christ, Moe, why didn't you call me?" he asked.

"What was I supposed to do, Sarge? Should I have let those two green beans cut Matt and me up and feed us to the baby?" I asked.

He said, "You violated a general order, Junior. You know that you are going to be charged with violating department policy."

I said, "My FTO in Baltimore City taught me to do whatever I have to do on the street even if it goes against the general orders as long as I could justify my actions. Sarge, that is the code by which I operate. However, if they burn me, they burn me. At least I can sleep at night knowing the child is safe."

The protective services worker arrived at Rebecca's house about one hour after we left. The worker did me a disservice. She got Rebecca fired up by telling her she had good cause to file a civil case against me and the police department. She urged Rebecca to make a formal complaint against me. The worker also made a complaint against me. When I returned to work, the sergeant broke the news that two complaints were lodged against me. "Whatever, Sarge. Let those bozos have at it. I still stand by my decision to take the child," I said.

The sergeant took a written statement from me. In the statement, I went into detail about my observations of Rebecca and her baby's daddy. I talked about how Rebecca admitted that she had taken PCP, a hallucinogenic drug that could cause highly violent behavior and memory loss.

The sergeant looked at me and said, "You are working hard to cover your ass, Junior."

I said, "It is what it is, Sarge. I guess you all want to crucify me for doing my job."

When the sergeant concluded his investigation, I was cleared of all allegations. I also received a letter of commendation from the director of protective services. In her letter, she wrote, "I want to commend the officer for deciding on a course of action in complicated circumstances. In my view, the officer acted bravely and in the best interest of the child. Officer Hicks's actions set an example for others to follow." It felt good to be exonerated. I also thought I taught Sarge something about decision-making on that day.

CHAPTER 49

CLEANER MON

On a cold winter night in November 1988, several officers headed down to Kenilworth Avenue. We received a report that ten young men were hanging around the 7-Eleven. We all exited our cars wearing our dark-blue uniforms, dark-blue sweaters, and black gloves. It was about forty degrees outside. We were hoping to snag a quick drug arrest. We figured that one of the ten suspects had drugs on them or that drugs were within an arm's reach. We knew Jerry's Subs's rainspout, and the pizza shop was one of their favorite hiding spots.

I approached the suspect standing closest to the rainspout and said, "Break out some ID." The suspect handed me a folded-up birth certificate that looked as if it had been washed about twenty times. "What the hell is this?" I replied. "I can't make out anything! Okay, name, address, date of birth, and age. Have you ever been arrested?

The suspect replied, "I had a breaking and entering problem back in 1983."

"Wow, a B and E problem? What the hell is that? Most importantly, is it a curable disease?"

Right then, a burly officer named Hercules from Squad 22 walked up and told me, "Don't worry, Hicks. It's curable, all right." He then looked directly at the kid and said, "If you break into my house, I will shoot you so that you won't have that problem anymore." Then he walked away. He looked delighted to have gotten those words out of his system. I thought he fantasized about shooting one of the so-called scumbag drug dealers working on Kenilworth Avenue.

The suspect asked me if Curly Top was working.

"Who is that?" I asked.

"It's that crazy white cop making deals with people down here."

I was perplexed. He evoked my curiosity. "What kinds of deals?" I asked.

"They are calling him Monty Hall—you know, like the game show host on *Let's Make a Deal*," he said.

"Why?" I asked.

He said, "He be giving people down here options."

"What kinds of options?" I asked.

So he searches everybody down here. When he finds something, he says stuff like, 'Do you want to go to jail or get two or three lumps?' Some people asked for the lumps since they are on probation. I cannot confirm nor deny the validity of his story.

"Wow!" I replied. "That is a heck of a story."

Just then, Officer Dylan, aka Monty Hall, pulled up to the scene.

The suspect whispered to me, "That is the crazy cop that I was telling you about."

Monty looked at the suspect whom I was talking to and said in a very authoritative voice, "Where did you put the drugs?"

The suspect looked terrified. He did not realize that Monty Hall was watching him before the rest of the squad had pulled up. Monty had a general idea where the drugs were hidden, but not precisely. The suspect walked out of sight for a few seconds. Monty Hall started his negotiations with the suspect. He asked the suspect if we wanted to make a deal. The suspect tried to negotiate with Monty. He selected door number two.

The suspect said, "Sir, if I tell you where the drugs are, will you promise not to lock me up?"

Monty stared at him for a few seconds and said, "I promise. Scout's honor."

The suspect walked behind the trash can in front of the convenience store and handed Monty Hall a large bag containing about fifty tinfoil packs of PCP.

Monty Hall said, "Cuff him, Hicks!" I handcuffed the suspect.

The suspect started jumping up and down, saying, "Sir, you promised that you were not going to lock me up!"

Monty Hall said, "I know, but I did not say anything about Hicks."

I patted him down for weapons and quickly caught a glimpse of a green BMW with New York tags flying down the street. The driver raced through a puddle of water, causing water to wet the back of my uniform pants and shoes. The driver and front-seat occupants were smiling at me while sporting their Kango hats. I looked at my sergeant, O'Malley, and said, "Them boys are in big trouble! I got to go. Would you mind handing this prisoner back over to Monty? I am going after those guys who were flying down the street in that green BMW." O'Malley handed the suspect back over to Monty.

While pursuing the guys in the BMW, I accelerated and nearly caught up with them as they entered the intersection of Kenilworth Avenue and East-West Highway. Unfortunately for them, they were oblivious to my presence. They blew straight through a red light. I wasted no time lighting them up. I studied the suspects' movements in the BMW while parked behind them, waiting to exit my vehicle. I always watched the movement of occupants intently for signs of danger before leaving my car. First, I would position my spotlight to hit the driver's exterior mirror. Then I would unsnap my standard-issue 9mm Beretta handgun and make my way over to the driver's side of the car. I would turn the volume down on my police radio and stand beside the driver's door.

My former FTO in Baltimore always told me my instincts would tell me everything I needed to know. My instincts never steered me wrong, and at the time, my instincts told me to watch the driver for about five seconds. I saw the driver remove a beige shaving bag from under his seat and hand it to the passenger. The passenger placed the bag under his seat.

Sergeant O'Malley pulled up behind me. I was pleased to see her there. She was an excellent street cop when she worked the streets. She had good instincts. She was also a wonderful patrol supervisor who had the respect of everyone in the station. She quickly maneuvered to the passenger side of the suspect's vehicle. I was not sure whether the sergeant had seen the passenger hiding the bag, and I did not want to telegraph to the suspect what I had seen. I told the sergeant we needed to get them out of the car.

Once the driver exited the vehicle, I directed him to place his hands on the back of the vehicle. I was shocked by how tall and muscular he was. He was about six foot four and packed with muscles. I gave him a quick shove to lead him and let him know I meant business, but his physique was so imposing that his body did not move an inch when I pushed him. "Damn," I said. Sergeant O'Malley removed the passenger and began patting him down for weapons. She signaled to me that she had seen them hide the bag.

I began to question the driver. "What's that bag that you handed your partner?"

He replied, "It's cleaner, mon. I am a cleaner, mon."

I detected a heavy Jamaican accent. "Where are you from, mon?" I asked. "Jamaica?"

"No, mon," he said. "Me from the Dominican Republic."

I directed him to count to five.

"One, two, tree," he said.

I told him that if he was from the Dominican Republic, then I was from Ireland. I knew he was lying. I felt a large wad of cash in the inside pocket of his leather jacket. I estimated it was about four thousand dollars.

"Where did you get this money, mon?" I asked.

"My mama gave it to me," he said.

"You must have been a good boy," I replied.

I looked behind me and noticed Officers Matt, Vader, and Jim Boy were driving up. *Great,* I thought. *We outnumber the bad guys.* Now, we could dig deeper into what was going on with these guys.

I asked the driver, "Mind if I look inside the bag under the seat?"

"No worries," the driver said. "It is cleaner."

I opened the shaving bag and saw a silver can of Vanish.

"I told you, mon," the driver said again. "It is cleaner."

I looked at Vader, then looked back at the suspect. Why in the hell would he have hidden Vanish? The facts did not add up. I had difficulty trying to get the can to open.

"I will open it for you, mon," the driver said.

I removed my gun from the holster and took a step back. "No funny stuff," I said.

He opened the can slowly. "See? I told you, man. I am a cleaner."

I was surprised to see that the can contained some Vanish. I got frustrated and threw the can back in the car. Unfortunately, the side of the can split open. I took a quick second look at the can and noticed something white inside the middle of the can. Vader quickly grabbed the can and started cutting it open with his knife. "Hicks," he said, "I am telling you, the shit is in here." He was right. The can was filled with about one hundred baggies of crack cocaine.

That was our first time seeing crack cocaine. Crack had made its way to our county. I turned and looked at Sergeant O'Malley. She smiled. I said, "This is what I call a patrolman's delight, Sarge." She gave me a thumbs-up.

The two suspects were arrested and received five-year sentences. After serving their time, they were both deported back to Jamaica. However, it would not be the last time I had contact with the driver after his deportation.

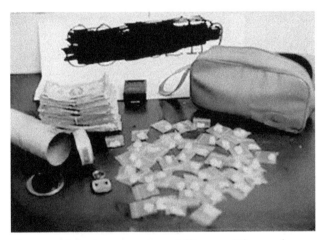

Recovered during a routine traffic stop. The crack was
hidden in a can of Vanish that had a false bottom.

CHAPTER 50

DWI TASK FORCE

Nobody can hurt me without my permission.
—Mahatma Gandhi

It was a beautiful autumn night in September 1988 with a harvest moon. I absorbed the tantalizing effects of the evening breeze. I momentarily glanced at the freshly placed drunk driving decal on my sparkling-clean Chevy Celebrity police cruiser. At last, I landed a spot on the drunk driving task force, to the dismay of our Special Operations Division members. They took a lot of pride in making the overtime federal money for drunk driving enforcement.

To my amazement, I learned that the chief of police had been looking at the drunk driving arrest statistics when he learned that I made more arrests on patrol than the Special Operations officers did on the task force. The chief called the Special Operations Division (SOD) commander and told him he wanted me on the drunk driving task force. The Special Operations Division sergeant despised the idea that I, a regular patrolman, would get some of their cheese. I read it in his face when he briefed me about the assignment.

They assigned me and the members of our Special Operations Division (SOD) to Route 5. While there, I made three traffic stops on the pitch-black road. Cars were flying down the road like it was the Indianapolis 500. None of the members of SOD backed me up during those traffic stops. It was clear to me that they were rebelling against me for getting some of their overtime money.

I was out there alone with no backup. I thought, *And I am not a damn state trooper. I did not sign up for this lone wolf crap!* I got into my patrol car and headed to Hyattsville, my patrol station. I drove onto Baltimore Avenue and then onto Bladensburg Road. I made a U-turn and headed back toward the station. It was time to catch a drunk.

A white man in his fifties accelerated slightly past me. He briefly glanced at my drunk driving decal depicting a wineglass and a car with a red line through it. Then he suddenly slammed on the brakes, nearly coming to a complete stop. I took one look at him and knew he would become the fresh catch of the night. I patiently waited for him to start driving again. Finally, I lit him up with my blue lights. He pulled over and struck the curb—error number two.

I politely asked him, "What happened back there, man?" He rolled down his window less than half an inch. As soon as I made eye contact with him, I could see he was wasted, so I tapped on the window and told him to roll it down further. Then I asked him again, "What were you doing back there, sir?"

"I don't know, sir," he replied. "I just got confused."

"Have you been drinking tonight?" I asked.

He turned his head away and replied, "No, sir."

"Why, then, sir, do you smell like a beer brewery?" I asked.

I got him out of the car and proceeded to give him a field sobriety test. The driver's floorboard, front passenger seat, and passenger floorboard were littered with beer and wine bottles. The bottles on the driver's floorboard rattled as he exited his vehicle. I examined him thoroughly to assess the level of his intoxication. The driver was a very pale-looking white man in his late fifties. He had breadcrumbs on his lips and hot sauce on his beard. He was wearing a red-and-black checkered flannel shirt and a pair of Levi jeans. I tried to give him the walk-and-turn field sobriety test. However, he could barely walk.

"Sorry, buddy," I said. "But you failed your test miserably." He asked me to please give him one more try. He tried his best to convince me he could do it. I gave him one chance simply to amuse myself. He started out by holding on to my cruiser. I told him he could not use my car as a crutch. I handcuffed him and placed him in the front seat of my cruiser. I sat in my cruiser for a few minutes, waiting for a chance to notify the dispatcher regarding my arrest. I could tell he was staring at me. Finally, I asked him if there was something wrong.

The man gritted his teeth and said, "I hate you people."

"Who, the county police?" I asked despite knowing full well what he was talking about. However, he could not answer. I reached down to grab my radio microphone to call the dispatcher and slightly touched his knee in the process.

The man turned his face, gritted his teeth, and with a broad Southern accent, said, "Get your nigger hands off me!"

I laughed and said, "Don't tell me that you are prejudiced?"

He repeated, "I hate you people."

I said I had kind of figured that out by the way he was looking at me. "Let me ask you a question," I said. "Does me barely touching you bother you that much?"

He continued to grit his teeth. If looks could kill, I would have been annihilated. I took the tip of my finger and touched his shoulder and head. He pulled away from me as if I was placing a poisonous spider on him.

"This whole situation must be killing you," I said.

"Are we ever going to get to the station?" he replied.

"Right, right, right," I said. "I am sorry, man. I am just so intrigued by you. I do not meet people like you often. You are the real deal. You do not pull any punches."

He yelled, "Goddamn it, let's go!"

"Right, right, right," I said again. "Let us get this party started."

I drove to the station, where I read him his rights regarding taking a Breathalyzer test. He stared at me the whole time.

"What is wrong now, sir?" I asked.

"You mean they taught you how to read?" he replied.

I disguised my voice to sound like a Southern slave. "Yes, sir!" I exclaimed. "Yes, Master! They also taught me how to read, and they also taught me how to write, so I am going to write Master Mosley a whole bunch of tickets."

As soon as my master sat down, he started coughing, wheezing, and sneezing.

"Achoo! Achoo, achoo, achoo, achoo. Achoo!"

"Jesus, man, you must have sneezed twelve damn times. You are about to sneeze your confounded brains out," I said.

"When am I getting out of this joint?" he asked. Again, five minutes later, he asked, "When am I getting out of this joint?" Then twenty minutes later, he again asked, "When am I getting out of this joint?"

I finally said, "I swear, if I hear those words one more time, I will go berserk on you."

"When am I getting out of this place?" he replied.

I started taking short, deep breaths. "Shut the hell up, man! I can't take it anymore," I said.

I sat at the opposite end of the table, pinching my nose with my two fingers. The horrific smell of his beer breath was taking its toll on me. Finally, one of my former coworkers, Officer Johnson, walked into the prisoner processing area.

"Are you okay, Hicks? You look like you are in distress," he said.

"This fellow is driving me out of my Vulcan mind. I am about to turn into Captain Insane O. He is the most irritating person on the face of the earth, man!" I exclaimed.

Then came the hiccups—hiccup, hiccup, hiccup. The bad thing was, I could not give him any water to cure his hiccups until he took his Breathalyzer test. I had at least thirty more minutes to endure his hiccups. I was thinking, *I cannot wait until this night is over.* Next came his irrational tirade. He stood up and started grinding his hips as if he was having sex.

"I am tired of the police fucking me, the prosecutors fucking me, and my boss fucking me," he said.

"Okay, okay. I get it! Please set your drunk behind down, man, and act like you have some sense," I said. Master sat down and started crying.

"I hate myself!" he yelled.

I wanted to hold up two fingers and say, "Make that two people that hate you, sir." However, I could not bring myself to add fuel to the fire. Officer Johnson looked at me and looked at my prisoner and smiled. "Mr. Moe, the big DWI task force man, I guess you love your fancy little task force job now, don't you, boy?" he said. I did not utter a word. I proceeded to cite Master Mosley with every traffic citation I could think of.

CHAPTER 51

LET MY PEOPLE GO!

If my mind can conceive it, and my heart
can believe it—then I can achieve it.
—Muhammad Ali

"Car 2, Baker 2, and 2-Baker 3, start priority at Fifty-Third Street and Quincy Street for two black males. One of them is armed with a shotgun, and the other one is armed with a handgun. Complainant states they are threatening to shoot several citizens in the area. Complainant states that the two suspects are Kevin Barksdale and Pit Bull."

"Baker 2, copy," an officer answered.

"Baker 3, copy," a second officer answered.

"10-4, Baker 3, I copy," the beat officer said.

Two minutes later, eight police cruisers converged on a small gray Chevy. Several police officers quickly approached the vehicle. It was clear they considered the two individuals as a severe threat. The officers' eyes were laser focused on the occupants of the car. They all assumed a combat stance, and their weapons were raised at eye level. Finally, one officer yelled, "Barksdale, do not move a muscle, or I'm going to warm your ass up with some hot lead."

The driver, a slender, brown-skinned six-foot-four nineteen-year-old with a slightly muscular frame, slowly opened the driver's door. His hands were in the air. He laid prone on the steaming-hot, tarred street. Another officer yelled to the front passenger, "Okay, it's your turn." A few seconds later, a short, obese eighteen-year-old exited the vehicle's passenger side with his hands raised. He went directly to the urine-infested sidewalk and laid down fully prone without the need for additional instruction.

The suspects had picked the wrong day to terrorize the community. An enormous police presence was in the area. It was an overlap day. That meant two different squads were working the same day. Also, it was just before shift change. Therefore, four squads consisting of fifteen officers were working. Another group of officers swarmed the car, converging on it like ants on watermelon.

The officer on the car's passenger side began removing shotgun shells from the vehicle and placing the shells on the car's hood. After a burly, agitated officer saw the shotgun shells, he lifted Barksdale off the ground by the back of his belt and placed him against a car.

"Where is the fuckin' shotgun, asshole?" the officer asked.

Barksdale smiled and said, "You'll never find it."

Officer Janson, one of the officers who had responded to the call, spun Barksdale around and nodded to two other officers at the scene. The police duo walked to the trunk of their cars while adjusting their black gloves. They quickly handcuffed both suspects. After exchanging glances with the gloved officers, Janson uncuffed Barksdale. He took Barksdale's keys out of the ignition, then drew his arm back and threw the keys on top of the roof of a nearby apartment building.

"You guys are free to leave," Janson told Barksdale. It killed him to release Barksdale and his partner, Pit Bull, but he had no choice. The officers did not find any weapons in the car. That was my first contact with the two leaders of the Barksdale Gang.

Three hours later, a second call went out for the same suspects. "Baker 2 and Baker 3, start priority Fifty-Fifth Avenue and Macbeth Street. Complainant states that Barksdale and Pit Bull are back and threatening to kill him for calling the police." My former training officer, Speed Racer, and I were working a two-person unit, so we responded.

"That boy is a pain in the ass," Speed Racer said. "We get calls for him day in and day out."

"Why don't they lock him up for something?" I asked.

"The sucker never has anything on him," Speed Racer replied.

When we arrived on the scene, Barksdale and Pit Bull were standing near a wooden railing in front of some apartments. They lifted their hands as we exited the vehicle.

"You officers are wasting your time," Barksdale said. "You're never going to catch us with anything. My hands don't touch anything but money."

Speed Racer replied, "I know you think you're the big man on campus, but you'll probably only live to the end of the summer. Enjoy the time you got left, man." He turned to me. "Moe, get his horsepower."

I got their names and ran a warrant check on them. The dispatcher said, "Baker 2, 10-35." Speed Racer put the two suspects against the fence and had them spread their arms and legs further. The dispatcher came back on. "Suspect has priors for attempted murder."

I nodded and replied, "Thanks, radio." I said, "Let me tell you something, son. If Officer Tyler or members of Squad 22 find you out here, you might not make it through the night."

Later, I asked Speed Racer, "Who the heck are these guys?"

"They are little gangster wannabes," he said. "This is your beat. They are now your problem. Watch your ass when you're down here. For the most part, they only kill each other, but I would not put it past one of them to fire a shot at one of us under the cloak of darkness."

Speed Racer just prophesied something that eventually was to be proven true.

*****

I was patrolling the 3500 Club around ten thirty in the morning at 3500 block of Fifty-Fifth Avenue. A fellow squad member, Officer Vader, and I parked side by side. I looked over and noticed a seventeen-year-old kid named Marty Cantor standing on the wood railing.

"Look at this, Vader," I said. "They must not know there's a new sheriff in town."

"Damn, man," Vader said, "I'd take that personally. All these little knuckleheads know I will not lock them up because I hate handling drugs. I'll stomp that crap on the ground before I spend the entire shift in the station papering that crap.

I approached Marty. "Hey, son, how are you doing today?" I asked. Silence. "I got a question for you. Aren't Prince George's schools in session today? Did I miss a holiday or something?" Again, silence. "I may not be Columbo or anything like that, but my instincts tell me today is a school day. And you are school-age, but you're not in school.

"Also, you have been standing on the same spot, watching and waving to cars as they go down the street, so bear with me a little while longer here. This is a drug corner, correct? You know something. Some people like me might conclude you are a drug dealer. What do you think of my theory?"

Marty said, "I'll warn you, man. You do not know who you are dealing with. You do not know who I work for. You do not understand I could have someone like you killed."

"Wow," I said. "Did you hear that? Man, this is a bad kid here. Son, let me tell you something. I know exactly who you work for and exactly why you are out here. You are out here making Barksdale rich while simultaneously throwing any chance of having a respectable life for yourself down the toilet."

"Watch yourself, man," he said. "I could make one phone call and…"

I put my hand on his shoulder and said, "Son, the only person you can get killed is yourself. Get out of the business while you can. Think about this, son: Suppose someone robs you out here and you come up short on Barksdale's money. He's not going to tell you to use Mommy's Visa card to pay him back. He is going to kill you, son.

"Here is something else that I want you to think about. If you sell out here every day in front of these folks' windows, don't you think somebody will call the police and get you locked up? What grade are you in, son? Do you know anything about probability? Think about this, son. What is the probability you will get caught by one of the officers on these three shifts who are trying to catch you every day? The next time I see you out here, Mommy will have to pick you from the station." I knew the kid was heading for calamity.

*****

Barksdale was a smooth and handsome criminal. He stood six foot three or maybe a quarter of an inch bigger, but he was known on the streets for his hair-trigger temper.

He stood at the top of the hill, staring at his empire like a mighty lion. He was indisputably the king of the jungle. Even the most dangerous criminals feared him.

Barksdale's upper lip curled in disdain as I exited my patrol car. His hostility toward me was off the Richter scale. More than anything, he despised the black history lessons and my college boy words.

I approached Barksdale and said, "Let my people go," He elbowed the Murder Boy, AKA Jungle Jim, and began laughing. He grabbed his crouch and asked, "What did you say?" I removed my mirrored shades and said, "Let my people go." Barksdale, Jungle Jim, and Pit Bull kept laughing. "What would Dr. King say about what you are doing if he were alive? These young men are magnets for enemy fire. Your little foot soldiers are entangled in a path of hopelessness, death, or destruction." He cut me off, looked around at his posse, and said, "I don't understand that shit. I only understand money." I put my shades back on and said, "Very well, gentlemen, have a nice day."

I knew then that he would never stop his ruthless ambitions because he loved it too much. Barksdale had unwittingly set the stage for a 10-year epic battle that would take me from Street Patrol to the FBI in the relentless pursuit of the aspiring Drug Kingpin.

CHAPTER 52

PATROLLING BLADENSBURG

I was patrolling my beat the next day when I came across a local drug dealer named Buckwheat standing on a notorious drug corner in Bladensburg.

"What's up, Buckwheat?" I asked.

"What's up, Hicks?" Buckwheat asked.

"Man, you are trying to make me look bad. I'm trying to detoxify this neighborhood, and you're out here trying to sell on my favorite street on my favorite day," I said.

He said, "I ain't selling drugs today, Hicks."

"Buckwheat, what is wrong with doing your homework or going to see your girl or something after school? Don't you know that two-thirds of the brothers in this area are in jail or on probation? What would Martin Luther King say about what you are doing? Don't you know people died so that you and I can go to school?"

"Hicks, this is all I know, man," he replied.

I said, "Come on. You can do anything you put your mind to. You're only seventeen years old. Give it a chance."

"I ain't book-smart, Hicks," he said. "I cannot learn that stuff."

"You know that boy Barksdale is nothing but trouble," I said.

Buckwheat replied, "I don't mess with that crazy nigger, man. I deal with Pit Bull. We have been friends since high school."

I asked, "Can Pit Bull control Barksdale? That brother is trying to get rich by enslaving our young brothers. Barksdale is just as bad as the slave masters from the South, man. Just think about what I am saying."

"I know you love your job, Hicks," he replied.

"Yeah, I do," I said. "But I hate having to take a young brother's freedom from him. I'd much rather be recommending you for a job."

The next day, I saw Barksdale and Pit Bull back on the same street where I stopped them the previous day. I immediately engaged them in conversation.

"Are you here on my streets trying to corrupt all these young black men?" I asked. "Don't you have any shame, man? Are you trying to obliterate these young men through the distribution of death?"

Barksdale said, "Man, I do not understand that shit." He looked at Pit Bull and said, "The only thing I understand is money."

"Let me tell you this, my brother," I replied. "I will get you fitted for my handcuffs sooner or later, and what a good day that will be. Then the brothers will be free at last! Let my people go."

Later, I asked Speed Racer when he arrived on the scene, "How connected is this boy?"

Speed Racer said, "I think most of these little knuckleheads do work for him."

As it happened, we received calls regularly that Barksdale was threatening several people with a gun. Then came another call from the dispatcher. Finally, I heard a radio squelch; the dispatcher said, "Cars Baker 2 and Baker 3, start priority Fifty-Third Place and Quincy. Barksdale and another black male are brandishing firearms and terrorizing the neighborhood."

When I arrived on the scene, I saw Barksdale and a black man standing on the street. "Barksdale, you and your homeboy, grab a piece of that wall," I said.

"What are you harassing us for now?" he asked.

"Let's not play that stupid game, Barksdale," I told him. "You know that you are public enemy number one down here. Here's how it works. Most people, unlike you, have real jobs and pay taxes. They pay taxes for the privilege of calling the police on gangsters like yourself that want to terrorize the neighborhood. When that happens, I come because this is my beat, and I get the joy of patting your disruptive ass down to ensure you don't shoot anyone for at least a few hours until you become some other officer's headache. By the way, who's your boy? I've never seen him down here before."

"This is my homeboy Antoine," Barksdale replied.

I said, "Pleased to meet you, Antoine. Since you may be new at this thing, let me break down the protocol for you. When I approach you, I assume you are armed. Therefore, do not make sudden moves so I do not have to shoot you and spend the next two days writing reports. Got it?"

Antoine nodded and said, "Yes, sir."

All righty, Antoine. Great, I thought. "Antoine is it?" I then asked. "Give me your horsepower."

"What's that?" he asked.

"Your name, address, DOB, and stuff like that."

Once Antoine gave me his information, I got on the radio and said, "Baker 2, 10-29 on Barksdale and Antoine."

The dispatcher came back quickly and said, "Baker 2, 10-35, Mr. Antoine has several priors for attempted murder and witness intimidation."

"Wow, Mr. Antoine," I said, "I understand now. You are Mr. Barksdale's enforcer. Are your services expensive?"

"I don't know what you are talking about, sir," he said.

"I understand," I said. "Okay. You're free to go. You don't have to go home, but you got to get out of the B-2 beat. Just drive to the other side of Landover Road, past Route 50. That's G Sector. It's out of my patrol district."

"Hicks," Barksdale said, "I am getting tired of this shit, man. This is bullshit. I'm going to kill that fucking Beaver. I know he's doing the fucking snitching."

"Beaver who?" I asked.

"That bitch-ass and snitching-ass Beaver Johnson."

"Thanks, Barksdale," I said. "I'll pass this information on to our station detectives in case Beaver should find himself staring at the barrel of that shotgun you ditched a while back." I added, "I have some other bad guys I need to check on now, so if I get another call tonight, I'll make a traffic stop on the way here and let you have a little chat with the Bruise Brothers instead. Capisce?"

I would repeat this routine many times over the next three years, documenting every stop and every conversation with Barksdale and his cohorts.

CHAPTER 53

FAST CHASE WITH PIT BULL

"Vader, guess who is out driving around in a BMW with no license?" I asked. "It is our favorite foe Pit Bull," I continued. I watched as Pit Bull zoomed past me. "Start my way. I know he is going to run as soon as I get behind him," I said. Pit Bull looked in his rearview mirror and floored the accelerator. "Too late. He is running," I said.

I grabbed my police radio. "Baker 2, I got one running!" I told the dispatcher. "It is a black BMW being driven by suspect Pit Bull." I grabbed my CB radio to update Vader directly. "Damn, my cruiser is slow. I think I lost him already," I said to Vader.

A Cheverly town officer grabbed his radio to acknowledge he was monitoring the chase. "Tell Baker 2 that I think he just passed me on Cheverly Avenue," the town officer said.

I was concerned the town officer and I might collide during the chase. "Do not pull out yet. I am about a block behind him, doing about fifty," I informed him.

When I arrived on the scene, Pit Bull jumped out of his vehicle while it was still running. The vehicle crashed through a white picket fence of a single-family home. The BMW started sliding sideways on the wet grass, ruining the well-manicured front yard. It finally came to a stop before hitting the front steps. I saw the head of a sixteen-year-old girl in the front seat. She was holding a baby. Town officers caught Pit Bull while I checked on the child and the baby.

254

Later, when I approached Pit Bull, I asked, "What were you thinking, man? Were you trying to kill folks for a traffic stop? Don't you know that I could have just given you a ticket if you had stopped?"

"I had a BMW, Hicks," Pit Bull said. "What did you expect me to do? If it weren't for the town cops, you would have never caught me."

"Well, Pit Bull, when you run from me, you run from all my homeboys, who are going to try to catch you." I said.

CHAPTER 54

MANIFEST DESTINY
NARCOTICS

Do not be anxious about anything,
but in everything by prayer and
supplication with thanksgiving, let your
requests be made known to God.
—Philippians 4:6

Our squad's numerous drug arrests caused frustrations to members of our newly formed narcotics unit, the ACTION Team. Everyone on my squad was furious I was not selected to be part of the team. The team was far more furious than I could have ever been. I always led the station in drug arrests. The ACTION Team got off to a terrible start. It seemed they could not get a quality drug arrest to save their lives, and unbeknownst to me, my squad took every opportunity to rub the team's lack of success in their faces.

One evening, we were in roll call when our sergeant directed me to remove the drugs seized from the drug vault. The timing could not have been more perfect for my vindictive squad members. Mighty Matt looked at one of the narcotics detectives and yelled, "Hey, Bedwetter. Come here for a minute. I want you to look at the plastic evidence bag sitting on the table here. Hicks seized that stuff at a traffic stop. You see that white substance inside the bag? That is what cocaine looks like." Of course, that irritated the hell out of the detective.

On the detective's way out, Mighty Matt took his second swipe at him. "Bedwetter, why can't you all find any drug dealers on Kanawha Street when patrol officers catch people every day?"

The detective looked at Mighty Matt and said, "My name is not Bedwetter."

After roll call, we saw the narcotics sergeant laying out a drug dealer. He was up in the man's face. He looked at him as if he wanted to banish him from the face of the earth. "You rotten son of a bitch!" he yelled. "Why would you sell to everybody down there besides us?" One of the detectives was doing his best to calm the sergeant down. Finally, Mighty Matt began chuckling and said, "These boys are pathetic."

I was different. I was always cautious not to criticize the ACTION Team, as I longed to do undercover work. Instead, I wanted to get payback for all the drug dealers who had us living under siege in Baltimore.

*****

About three months later, Mighty Matt and I were walking down to the station when we passed one of the station-level narcotics detectives. I spoke to him, but he kept walking without acknowledging me.

I looked at Matt and asked, "What was that detective's malfunction?"

"I guess they are tired of embarrassing themselves by coming up empty," Matt said.

After roll call, I tried to speak to three other narcotics detectives in the clerk's office, but they also gave me the cold shoulder. I walked down the hallway and passed their office. I took a glance at a picture hanging on their door. I was shocked to see it was a photograph of me. I had a big grin on my face, and I was holding up a significant seizure—crack cocaine, cash, and a handgun I had seized during a traffic stop. A caption was written underneath: "How do you like me now?" I thought, *The narcotics sergeant is never going to let me in the unit.*

I immediately ripped the photo off the door and proceeded down the hallway. Two narcotics detectives saw me walking with the picture in my hand and gritted their teeth at me as I passed them. It reinforced my belief that I would never get into the unit. They were convinced I posted the photo. Now, I knew why they were not speaking to me. I wondered how many similar images had been posted on their office door without my knowledge.

I asked Mighty Matt, "Why did you do it, Matt?" He pretended to be confused. He continued his denial, which I believed was a charade. Mighty Matt adamantly denied putting the photo there. I polled the rest of the squad to see who else might have posted it.

Mighty Matt finally smiled and said, "You need to talk to your sergeant."

"What do you mean by that?" I asked.

He laughed again and said, "You need to talk to your sergeant."

The next day, I questioned Sergeant O'Malley about the photos.

"Do you want to know who posted those photos?" she asked.

"Yes," I said. "I want to know."

She hesitated for a moment, then said, "It was me."

"What the hell?" I exclaimed. "Are you kidding?"

"No, but I only posted the last photo. The rest of the squad posted all the rest."

"How many?" I asked.

"Let me put it this way," she replied. "Every time you got a good drug seizure, the photo got posted on their door. That has been the protocol for the last two months or so."

"Oh my God," I exclaimed. "Why did you do that to me, Sarge?"

"Those bozos are not going to let you in there anyway. They know you're going to show them up."

About one month later, in an apparent act of desperation, the narcotics sergeant came to our roll call. He had concluded that he needed our help. He humbly asked us to provide any information on drug dealers operating in the district.

Mighty Matt would not let up. He leaned over and told me in a voice loud enough for the sergeant to hear, "See, Hicks? They know they need us now." As soon as the narcotics sergeant left the room, Mighty Matt said, "Fuckin' defectives." Yes, he said *defectives*, not *detectives*. "They don't know shit from Shinola."

I stored the sergeant's plea for help in my memory bank.

*****

I was patrolling near Parkview Garden Apartments three days later when I observed a Chevy Cavalier making a broad right-hand turn without signaling. I immediately pulled the vehicle over. A young kid who appeared to be about fourteen years old was driving the car. A twenty-year-old was sitting in the passenger seat.

As soon as the driver opened his window, I smelled a chemical odor I recognized as PCP. I took one look at the driver's face and saw he was terrified. I directed him to hold tight for a minute, saying I just received a call.

I walked back to my car and called for backup. Mighty Matt pulled up within three minutes. We approached the car together. The driver quickly admitted he did not have a driver's license. I smiled and looked over at Mighty Matt, who was standing on the vehicle's passenger side. We handcuffed both suspects, and I searched the car.

I found a vanilla extract bottle containing an ounce of liquid PCP and fifty tinfoil packs containing marijuana-laced PCP (street name: Love Boat). Once I showed the passenger the drugs I seized, he quickly spoke up. "It's my stuff, sir. Please don't charge my little brother. My mother would kill me."

My mind reflected on the narcotics sergeant's plea for help with developing informants. I asked the older brother where their trip to Riverdale originated. He said they left their home in Washington, DC. I looked at them and shook my head.

"You boys are in big trouble," I said. "You just imported drugs into another state. You all are not just drug dealers. You guys are drug smugglers. That is a mandatory sentence. Your little brother is going to go to real jail for at least five years. You guys messed up," I told them.

I transported the older brother to the police station, and Mighty Matt transported the younger brother. The older brother constantly questioned me on the way to the station regarding how he could get his little brother out of trouble.

When I arrived at the station, I let the older brother sit in an interview room for an hour. I kept walking over to the small interview window during that hour, looking at the older brother and shaking my head. I finally entered the room and said, "For some reason, I feel for you and your little brother. This is going to break your mother's heart."

I told him that if he was willing to give information on the person who had supplied the drugs, I might have someone who could help him. I put him back on the ice, walked upstairs to the narcotics unit, and asked to speak to the sergeant. I found the narcotics sergeant standing over a twenty-three-year-old drug dealer. The sergeant appeared to be very agitated. Two of his detectives were standing near him, looking at the suspect with their arms folded.

Finally, the sergeant put his finger in the drug dealer's face and said, "You son of a bitch. We watched you for over an hour. You sold drugs to everybody but us." The suspect simply smiled. That agitated the sergeant even more. "We're going to see how funny it is when you get the ten-year mandatory for being a two-time loser!" he said.

The sergeant grabbed the suspect by the back of his shirt. Then he noticed me standing by the door. He looked at me with bewilderment and said, "This son of a bitch sold to everybody but us!" I told the sergeant the suspect probably had his clientele—people he knew well.

"Yeah, right," the sergeant said.

Then I cheerfully asked, "How are you today, Sarge?"

He slowly lifted his head, shook my hand, and said, "I'm fine, man. How can I help you?"

I told him I had some good news, that I had caught two brothers with a lot of PCP. Both of the suspects were terrified, I said, and were willing to do just about anything to get out of it. So I told the sergeant I would not charge them with the dope if they came up with some good narcotics cases.

The sergeant and one of his detectives talked to the older brother. He agreed to cooperate in exchange for us not charging him and his little brother. The sergeant came up to the clerk's office and told me the older brother had a "treasure trove of good information" that could help them catch "a lot of drug dealers."

One month later, the narcotics sergeant, Johnson, came to our roll call again. This time, my patrol sergeant let him read a letter of commendation to our squad. The letter he read commended me for providing the narcotics team with an informant who had provided vital information leading to the arrest of several drug dealers, the seizure of several weapons, and the seizure of a large amount of cash.

My squad members yelled, "Yeah! Hicks is the man! Now you all need to take him in narcotics." I wanted them to shut up. I did not want there to be any hard feelings. The narcotics sergeant walked over and shook my hand. I was beginning to believe I had a slight chance of getting into the unit.

*****

Four months later, the police department announced the formation of a countywide street narcotics unit. Narcotics sergeant Tom Johnson's old team and other station-level narcotics workers applied for the newly formed unit. The sergeant's nickname, Sergeant Tom "Motherfucking" Johnson, came from his affinity for using the word *motherfuckin'*.

The announcement of the new narcotics unit was the day I was hoping for. I put in my request to become a detective in our Street Narcotics Section. They scheduled me for an interview. As I stepped into the Bowie police station, where my interview was to be held, my mind was racing a mile a minute. I had developed an outstanding reputation for catching drug dealers both on foot and during traffic stops. However, now I had to articulate my skills in front of an interview panel.

I wore my favorite dark-blue interview suit supplemented with a blue-and-white tie and my freshly polished black shoes. In addition, I sported my regular faded Marine Corps haircut. I was a little nervous, as I had never interviewed for a position in the department before. To add to my worries, I was concerned some detectives would not recommend me for the job because of the numerous photographs my squad members had posted of me profiling with my seized drugs, money, and weapons.

I was about thirty minutes early for the interview. I walked over to the glass window and hit the buzzer. An old white station detective wearing an old-timey gray suit asked if he could help me. I explained I was there to interview for Street Narcotics Section. He asked me to show him my identification. I reached into my jacket pocket and tried to retrieve my police identification. It took me about three seconds to realize I hadn't grabbed my police identification in my haste to arrive early. I explained I had inadvertently forgotten it.

"I can't help you, son," the station detective said. I told him that I had driven my patrol car to the station and that I would show him I had the keys to the marked patrol unit. He smiled and said, "I can't help you." He walked away and left me sitting in the lobby. I felt like an idiot.

Three minutes later, I remembered one of my squad members lived about ten minutes away, so I called him, and he agreed to bring his badge to the station. While waiting in the lobby, Sergeant Tom "Motherfucking" Johnson walked into the clerk's office and looked at me. "Why are you sitting out here?" he asked. I did not say a word, and he buzzed me into the office.

I was taken into a room with the sergeant, the lieutenant, and one narcotics detective. After my interview, the sergeant said he appreciated my turning in to them an outstanding informant. He said I had given them the best informant they had ever had. He told me things turned around for the unit based on that one informant. He said they made several significant seizures based on the information the informant gave them.

One month later, I saw many patrol officers looking at a clipboard in our station clerk's office. I asked one of my coworkers what information on the clipboard was of interest. "The teletype is out with the new transfers," he said. I quickly made my way to the board. I was shocked to see my name on the transfer list. I was being transferred to Street Narcotics. I was astonished because this was my first try.

CHAPTER 55

ONE MORE LARGE BUST FOR THE ROAD

I was anxious to work another good drug case before my transfer took effect in ten days. Three days before the transfer became effective, I was sitting in my patrol car, talking to one of my coworkers who was also in his patrol car, when I observed a black Toyota 4Runner whiz past us. I glanced at it and noticed that the vehicle did not have a front license tag, as required by Maryland law. I told the other officer I had to go. I always had a sixth sense when something was out of place.

I slowly maneuvered my vehicle away from my coworker's patrol car and hit the accelerator. My coworker called me on the CB radio. I told him something was not right. I followed the car about six blocks, then pulled the driver over on Kenilworth Avenue, about half a mile from Washington, DC. I saw four people in the car. I saw the front seat passenger pass an object to the back of the vehicle.

Just then, another officer pulled behind my cruiser. I motioned to him, pointing two fingers toward my eyes to indicate I had seen something. He nodded, and we both instinctively unsnapped our holsters. We carefully studied the movement of the occupants as we came closer to the car. I stood slightly behind the driver's door for about three seconds to prevent the driver from successfully timing my approach. In addition, standing behind the driver gave me a psychological advantage. It was difficult to turn and shoot if you could not see what was behind you.

I looked at the driver carefully and studied his facial expressions and lack of eye contact. I noticed he was licking his lips. When he did look at me, he looked as if he had seen a ghost. I asked to see his driver's license.

The driver made a half-hearted effort to locate his driver's license and then said, "I think I left it home, sir."

I looked deep into his eyes and said, "Very well. I'll be right back."

My coworker and I slowly walked back toward our cars. We stood behind our cars, watching the suspects' every move. I immediately called for backup. No sooner had I finished my radio transmission than I heard the driver calling out to me. "Excuse me, sir!" he yelled. "I got to go to the bathroom!" The last thing I wanted was a four-on-two confrontation, but just then, my attention was momentarily drawn to the sounds of a car coming to a squealing stop. The backup had arrived.

My coworker and I briefed the two officers on what was going on. We got all four of the suspects out of the car and made them sit on the curb. Their faces could not mask their fear. They were hiding something in the car. The driver renewed his request to go to the bathroom. "Please, sir," he said again, "I have to go real bad."

My partner directed the driver to a wooded area, but I quickly intervened. "Hell no," I said. "The driver is not going anywhere. Stay right there. Put the man in cuffs. He is too antsy." Once the driver was handcuffed, I said, "Okay. Now, let's search the car." The remaining three suspects immediately looked at one another. I searched the back seat of the car, and I found a quarter kilogram of crack cocaine. I was floating on air. Finally, all four suspects were arrested. I could not think of a better way to end my patrol career.

*****

While waiting for my transfer, I could see one of my squad members hating on me. He told the rest of the squad I was a little too happy to be going to what he called JV, or junior vice. He was also telling some people on the squad I was the glory boy. The other officers said to me he was also calling me golden boy.

No matter how good a relationship I had with the people I worked with, petty jealousy always emerged. I decided the best way to deal with that squad member was to message the dispatcher to let the squad member know I was aware of his rumblings. I had the dispatcher call the station to speak to Officer Golden, followed by my badge number. He picked up the clue, called the station, and apologized for talking about me behind my back.

Another squad member could not resist taking a parting shot at me before I left for the narcotics team. He said, "Have fun over there at JV." I asked him what he meant by that. "You're transferring to junior vice," he said. Despite the JV label, we were the pride of the department. Street-level drug sales had reached epidemic proportions. Most of the street corners were littered with enterprising young drug dealers.

CHAPTER 56

THE BARKSDALE INVESTIGATION

As I prepared to start my new job in the Street Narcotics Section, detectives in the Major Narcotics Section and station detectives were zeroing in on the Barksdale Gang's criminal activity. They had received information that Barksdale, Pit Bull, and a third suspect named Donnie were to make a drug run to New York to pick up several kilos of cocaine, which they would then bring back to Prince George's County.

In 1988, they made a run to pick up two kilograms of cocaine. After bringing the drugs back to Barksdale's apartment with his nephew, Barksdale became preoccupied while talking on the phone to a woman of interest. After the phone call ended, Barksdale began weighing the drugs. He soon discovered that about fifty grams of cocaine were missing.

His nephew Chris was present when Barksdale arrived with the drugs. He first questioned his nephew about the shortage, and the nephew confirmed he did not remove any of the cocaine. Barksdale concluded that Donnie had somehow removed some of the cocaine from the bag. Barksdale then set out to kill Donnie. He planned to catch Donnie when he was off guard.

They met up a few days later on Martin Luther King Jr. Boulevard. Within a few minutes, Barksdale pulled out his gun and tried to shoot Donnie in the car. Donnie's survival skills kicked in, and they began to wrestle for the gun. Eventually, Donnie was able to make his escape. Within a few days, he called Barksdale and apologized. As a peace offering, he gave him back the dope he had taken and a handgun.

*****

One day, Barksdale and three of his henchmen were sitting on a porch when a rival drug dealer named Kevin Johnson passed by and gave Barksdale the evil eye. Barksdale said to himself, "He's next on my list." Later, he saddled up with four of his henchmen and shot Kevin Johnson several times. Finally, he directed Manny to take Kevin's vehicle and burn it.

The next day, Barksdale probed Manny regarding the details of the murder and asked him how he disposed of the vehicle. Manny stated that he did precisely what Barksdale had told him to do: he burned up the vehicle to destroy any evidence linking them to the crime.

When Manny gave the details to Barksdale, he mentioned he had left the windows up in the car. That set Barksdale off. He began yelling at Manny, calling him a freaking idiot. He was supposed to leave the windows down so the flames would fully engulf the vehicle.

Manny was killed a few months later in a shootout with DC police. The other henchmen died a few weeks later of a drug overdose. Barksdale's nephew became concerned about all the other employees dying around him. As a result, he sought to distance himself from his uncle Barksdale. When Barksdale's nephew expressed his desire to go straight and narrow to Barksdale, Barksdale became incredibly quiet. A few days later, Barksdale's nephew came outside and noticed that his vehicle was full of bullet holes. His nephew believed it was a sign of his uncle's displeasure with his attempts to distance himself from the organization.

*****

The war on drugs officially began in 1971 when the then-president Richard Nixon, aka Tricky Dicky, formally announced it. Nixon proclaimed that "drugs were the country's greatest enemy." However, some people questioned his true motives for initiating the so-called war on drugs: Nixon was a corrupt and overbearing leader who did not consider the interests of minority members in any decisions he made. In 1973, he formed the Drug Enforcement Administration (DEA). The agency was formerly known as the Federal Bureau of Narcotics.

The term *war* conjured up different images for different people. For some people, it meant police officers were free to use any method necessary to combat drugs. By the 1980s, the war on drugs had risen to new heights. In Colombia, South America, hundreds of people were killed, including news correspondents, prosecutors, politicians, and even presidential candidates, as the battle waged on.

By the time I joined the Prince George's County Police Department in 1985, crack cocaine had made its way to the state of Maryland. By 1988, I was officially engaged in the war on drugs. Soon, the moment I was waiting for would finally arrive.

CHAPTER 57

WORKING UNDERCOVER

In November 1988, I was enjoying the cool fall breeze while driving my rusty old burgundy 1983 Buick Regal down US 301, Crain Highway, in Bowie, Maryland. It was the perfect day to start my new job as a detective in the newly formed Street Narcotics Section. I had officially become a jump-out, or what Baltimoreans called a knocker.

The reality of the revelation sank in for a few minutes. It was hard for me to believe it was happening. I was quiet, a bit nerdy, and as clean as they came. I detested drug dealers, and I never experimented with drugs. I believed convincing streetwise drug dealers to sell drugs to a person like me who had a military bearing might be challenging.

Most of the people in the unit had already worked in narcotics for about a year at the station level. Now, we all became a part of the centralized narcotics unit working the entire county. I was anxious to get to work. Before the Street Narcotics Section was formed, the Vice Control Section unit handled large and small drug violations.

I had to make the mental and physical transformation from my military and paramilitary mannerisms to a drug addict. I had to resist getting the military high and tight haircut I had worn since I was seventeen. My walk and my speech had to change as well. I could no longer enunciate precisely when I spoke, and I had to get out of the habit of speaking in police jargon or police code. I had to make this transition without any training.

By this time in my career, I had arrested scores of drug dealers and too many drug buyers for counting. I had testified in scores of narcotics cases, giving the people I arrested more time to get a closer look at me. Whenever I pretended to be a drug dealer or drug buyer, I knew I risked getting my cover blown.

I initially resisted growing a beard, but I realized I had to wear a beard within two weeks to go into crack houses to buy drugs. It did not take long for me to develop my undercover attire. First, I put a black do-rag on my head. Second, I went to the bottom of my closet and pulled out a pair of old tennis shoes, and I put some mud on them to give them a rugged appearance. Then I put on my floppy, wide-brimmed camouflage-green bush hat. Next, I took out an old camouflage jacket and tore off one of the lapels. I partially tore the second lapel but left it on the coat. Finally, I put a little dirt around my coat, and a drug dealer was born. I called it my stickup boy attire.

I boarded the back of an old beige Oldsmobile Cutlass Supreme with three other black Street Narcotics detectives. I headed to the infamous 2100 Alice Avenue in Oxon Hill, Maryland. At that time, the apartment complex was a notorious open-air drug market.

I had never had the pleasure of venturing out of my patrol district, and I could not hide my excitement. The detective sitting next to me looked over at me and said, "You look too motherfucking happy to be doing this stuff. You need to look more serious, man." I laughed and broke my mug down. Then I asked the detective if that was any better. "Keep working on it," he said.

When we arrived at the apartment complex, we saw a group of about eight black teenagers inside the building intensely watching every car passing by. The detective who was driving asked, "Everybody got your buy money?" We all nodded our heads. Everyone on the squad carried one hundred dollars in preregistered bills at any given time.

We all touched our 9mm Beretta handguns and ensured that they remained hidden under our street clothes. The driver instructed us to try to buy from a different dealer in the group if we could. Then we walked into the building. Within two seconds, the dealers were offering each of us handfuls of crack cocaine. I bought mine from a sixteen-year-old kid who was standing in the back of the group. He seemed a little aloof.

Each detective bought from a different drug dealer. After we left the building, the arrest team swarmed down and arrested all the juveniles in the building. When I interviewed the kid I bought drugs from, he said, "I should have known that you were a cop, because you looked like you were mad at me for having the drugs. Most people are glad to get it." I realized then that my undercover persona needed a lot of fine-tuning.

*****

I figured my ascension in the unit would be difficult. Some of my new coworkers were former members of the Hyattsville ACTION Team. I was sure they remembered the images of me grinning beside my drug seizures in the pictures posted on their office door. The same sergeant from the Hyattsville ACTION Team was now one of the sergeants in Street Narcotics. He was now my sergeant. I would never forget my first meeting with him.

"Son," he said, "the first thing you need to know about me is that I drink Hennessy."

An interesting fact to know, I thought. He asked me what I drank. I told him Mountain Dew.

The sergeant smiled and spun around and looked at the rest of the squad. "Mountain Dew!" he said. "How can I trust a motherfucker that drinks Mountain Dew?"

I looked at him, bewildered. "On a rough day, I drink Dr Pepper," I said. They all laughed.

"This motherfucker is as geeky as they come," the sergeant said. "But this little motherfucker is about catching them drug dealers."

I learned that my sergeant's affinity for the word *motherfucker* had given him the nickname Tom "Motherfucking" Johnson.

*****

Everything was going fine. One day, I saw Lynette, one of the prosecutors assigned to the narcotics unit, walking into the station. When I asked what she was doing there, she told me she screened felony drug cases for court. I told Lynette I was just about to make an appointment to have my case screened. She told me she would review the case for me.

Later, I noticed that a detective in the Major Narcotics Section was sitting next to assistant state's attorney Lynette. He was gathering his documents to screen his drug case. I asked Lynette to screen mine as well. I began providing the details regarding my last traffic stop before coming to narcotics, the stop that had just netted me a seizure of a quarter kilogram of cocaine.

A Major Narcotics detective turned his head and stood over me, pointing his finger. It took about three seconds for him to get his words out. "You little motherfucker, that was my case. My informant called that guy up. He was on the way to sell that quarter kilo to me. You fucked up my case, you little asshole. Do you know how long I worked on that?"

I looked at him and shrugged my shoulders. Then I looked at the state's attorney. I told her I had no idea where the guy was heading. The detective pressed me on why I had stopped the suspect. I told him that because the vehicle the suspect was driving had a missing front tag, I had a hunch he was probably transporting drugs. He looked at me as if he wanted to rip my head off. *What a great first day,* I thought. I had already pissed off a detective in the Major Narcotics Section, so I figured the chances of my working my way up to that unit were severely diminished.

It did not take exceptionally long for another conflict to begin brewing between me and my coworker. His name was Francois. He was a former member of the ACTION Team. He worked in narcotics at my former station. In my view, Francois was a legend in his own mind. He was a tall, slinky, light-skinned guy who dressed like Jeannie. I knew two weeks would not pass by before we had an encounter.

On the last day of our first week together, we made an undercover buy of narcotics. Later, we were in the office together. First, I

273

watched Francois read the newspaper. Then I asked him if he planned to help with the paperwork for the arrests we made. "You rookies can handle that," Francois said. I asked him who had died and made him boss. Francois replied, "You've got to pay your dues, rookie!" I insisted that he helped, because one of the arrests was his. He refused and continued to read the newspaper.

I spoke to Tom "Motherfucking" Johnson about the situation. He told me I needed to respect Francois's seniority. When Francois heard about me ratting him out to Sergeant Motherfucking Johnson, he said, "Okay. I'll help process the drugs for the damn rookie." I finished the paperwork and left for the weekend.

On Monday morning, I found Francois's newspaper thrown all over my desk when I arrived at work. I lifted the newspapers and saw several tiny rocks of crack cocaine fall onto the floor. I was bewildered for a moment. *How did the drugs get there?* Francois was sitting at the desk next to me. He leaned over and said, "You better watch yourself. You can get yourself in the trick bag by not processing that stuff."

I hesitated for a moment. Then I remembered that Francois's only responsibility amid the mounds of paperwork from the arrest on Friday was to process the drugs. "That's it, Francois," I yelled. "We need to talk!" We walked into a large closet.

I asked, "Francois, what the hell was that, man? You were supposed to take care of that. So what's your deal, man?"

"You know what your problem is?" Francois said. "You thought you were the shit at Hyattsville. Your lieutenant used to sing your praises. You can't handle the fact that you are not shit here. You are a fucking zero here. You must earn your stripes!"

I stood there with my mouth open for a moment. I was in disbelief that the little wannabe narc had talked to me that way. He would never have guessed that although I was quiet, I was highly skilled in the use of profanity from my teenage years. I grew up with people who cursed so much that they were physically unable to express themselves without using vulgarity.

"Let me tell you something, you tall, non-narc MF," I said. "You could not find a joint if it were lit and burning up your ass. You were a loser in patrol, and you are still a loser. I don't know how you got here, but I ain't going to take up your slack, you fuckin' slug!"

"Remember what the sergeant said," Francois replied. "I'm a senior officer. You need to sit your rookie ass down and try to learn something."

"Learn something from you? You don't even know your ass from a hole in the ground," I said.

At that point, I opened the closet door to leave. But instead, I found the entire squad outside, listening in on our whole conversation.

"Damn," one detective said, "you guys were going at it."

I looked at him and said, "Somebody needed to take him down a few notches."

*****

About a month later, the entire squad was deployed to an open-air drug market on 3500 Dodge Park Road. I was shocked to see about eight drug dealers working one corner. One dealer was so bold that he had his gun openly displayed on the outside of his waistband. I pointed out the dealer to Detective Barry. "Look at Billy Badass Junior. What is this, the Wild West? Is this Dodge Park Road or Dodge City?" I asked.

Dodge Park Road was in the jurisdiction of the District 3 station. It was the busiest district in the county. Patrol officers seized 355 guns off the street the previous year, which meant they caught someone with a gun almost every day of the year. I was never in that part of the county. I experienced culture shock. It was as if we had walked into the most lawless part of the county.

Our first mission was to buy drugs from drug dealers. Then we were supposed to take over the corner. We would then pretend to be drug dealers. Within twenty minutes of our arrival, we had bought drugs from all dealers and had taken over the corner. Later, our drug laboratory provided us with a placebo that looked precisely like crack cocaine. Each detective in our squad had an ample supply of it.

We could not resist having fun with some new drug dealers who came over to our area to sell drugs. One of my detectives walked over to a heavyset drug dealer and asked, "Did you pay toll, man?"

The dealer looked bewildered. "What the fuck are you doing on my corner, man?" he yelled. "Get the fuck out of here unless you are going to pay me two hundred dollars an hour for this corner!" He gritted his teeth at the undercover detective. The detective simply pointed at us. We all lifted our shirts to display our guns. Then the wannabe dealer took off running.

We saw a relatively new red Corvette drive past us a few minutes later. Then it stopped. The driver waved twenty-dollar bills out of his window. The vehicle had a personalized license tag. But, I thought, *who would bait homicidal drug dealers over to a car by waving a stack of twenty-dollar bills in his hand?* The driver briefly got out of the vehicle and handed the money to a local drug dealer. Then finally, we were able to see the driver. To our amazement, it was Detective Francois. He drove his red Corvette with its personalized license plates to make a drug buy. Eventually, for some unknown reason, he was transferred out of narcotics.

After Francois was transferred out of the unit, it was time to show the troops on the well-orchestrated team that I had the skills to catch drug dealers. The remaining members of the squad had distinguished themselves in their previous assignments. I was proud to work with all of them. Two detectives impressed me. One was an extraordinarily effective and smooth-operating black female detective who previously worked for Baltimore PD. I am also fond of a young white detective named Tyler. He was a good, kind country boy who always treated people with enormous respect. He always maintained his integrity no matter what the circumstances were.

Tyler and I went out and bought drugs from a small-time drug dealer the next day and brought him back to the station. I sat down with the tall, slender drug dealer who was about forty years old, maybe six foot one, and 170 pounds. He sported a beard. The dealer could see I was anxious to talk to him, so he sat there and studied me in the interrogation room for a few seconds.

"I guess you want to get a good look at me so you can know who I am next time," I said.

He smiled. "I got caught by 21 Jump Street," he said.

I assumed he had said that because I looked so young. I shot him a stern look. His smile quickly dissipated. Then I looked him straight in the eye.

"You are lucky, my friend," I said. "If you were arrested for rape, robbery, or murder, I couldn't help you, but you were arrested for drugs. What would you say if I could get this charge off you with no lawyer, no money spent, and no jail time?" *As if the charge is an actual object he could touch and hold.*

"Stop playing, man," he said.

I was sitting backward in my chair. I moved my chair closer to him. "I am serious as a heart attack," I said. "You can be back home tonight. First, I need to know who supplied you with the dope. Second, I need you to buy some more dope for me."

This time, he said, "You're trying to get me killed."

"What if I tell you that they will never know it was you? I will not mention your name or the day you bought the drugs. All you must do is go back tonight and buy me some drugs."

"Oh my God . Can I think about it?"

"No, you got to act now," I said.

"Calm down, baby boy!" he said. "I guess you want to make a name for yourself bad."

I said, "Look, man, you're a small fish. I want to let you swim, man, and catch the bigger fish."

That night, he went back to the house where he bought his drugs, and he brought the drugs back to me. So I was able to flip one of my first arrests, and I was on my way to getting my first search warrant.

I could remember taking my first narcotics search warrant to a judge's chambers to be signed. I was excited while watching the judge read my application for the warrant. Then he reached for his pen, signed the warrant, and said, "Good luck." I quickly headed to the narcotics unit and told Sergeant Tom "Motherfucking" Johnson that I had obtained my search warrant. I could hardly contain my excitement.

The sergeant looked at me and said, "Damn, son, you look like you are about to have an orgasm. You love this shit, don't you?"

"Yes, sir, I do," I replied.

The sergeant reminded me that obtaining the warrant was just half the battle and that I needed to time the raid correctly to make sure I seized some dope. He reminded me that although he knew I had had a lot of success seizing dope in uniform, seizing drugs as a detective was an entirely new ball game.

Three days later, we met with our Emergency Services Team (EST), the SWAT team. I gave them an overview of what I knew about the suspect, which was extraordinarily little. I knew only her first name and that she lived in her home alone. The SWAT team sergeant seemed unfazed by the lack of information. I learned that most of the street-level cases we investigated were based on minimal information. We often knew only the nickname of the person who was selling the drugs.

The EST sergeant explained that I had to ride in the van with him and the rest of the team. My job was to fall behind him and point out the correct door for the apartment we would be raiding. This procedure protected them from raiding the wrong apartment. Pointing to the door was necessary because sometimes, the numbers on the apartment doors were missing.

I boarded the van and watched as the team secured their helmets, checked their weapons, and adjusted their body armor. Two men on the team had machine guns capable of being fired as automatic or semiautomatic weapons.

Once we arrived at the apartment building, we exited the van and began ascending the apartment stairs. Then I pointed out the right door and stood back as a team member began using a rabbit tool—a hydraulic ram—to separate the door from the frame. Another team member bent down and held a large metal shield by the door, protecting the team member using the tool. A few seconds later, a third EST team member took the battering ram and broke down the door.

"County police!" one of the team members yelled as the team entered the residence with their weapons drawn. About six minutes later, a team member gave us the all clear to enter the apartment. As we entered the residence, the EST team sergeant slapped me on the shoulder and said, "Sorry, buddy. There's nobody here."

We began a search of the apartment. After killing scores of roaches and sifting through soiled underwear and saliva, we came up empty-handed. No drugs were found, but I was able to seize drug paraphernalia, such as crack pipes, smoking bongs, baking soda, which was used to convert cocaine to crack, and plastic baggies.

As I stood there bracing myself for the sarcasm from my fellow detectives, I could feel the sergeant's eyes peering at me. I finally lifted my head and accepted my fate for my first investigation. I knew they all remembered how my patrol buddies teased them about their inability to seize drugs while working station-level drug investigations in Hyattsville.

"You okay, man?" Sergeant Johnson asked.

I shrugged my shoulders. "This is not how I envisioned my first search warrant," I replied.

"I told you that this shit is not an exact science," the sergeant said. "In street-level narcotics, we don't have the luxury of putting a lot of time into the investigations. The chief needs as many of these places shut down as possible. Here, we don't worry about seizing a lot of drugs. Instead, we want to disrupt this shit as best we can. You know they're going to ride you about this. Now, you know how they felt back at Hyattsville."

I gathered up the evidence, and we headed out the door in plain clothes. As we reached the bottom of the stairs, we met a brown-skinned, pimpled-faced black woman about thirty years old walking with a very muscular, dark-skinned black man about forty, and both cheerfully greeted us.

The woman smiled at me and asked, "Where are you all coming from? Raiding my apartment?" She began laughing. I smiled and asked her what apartment was hers. She replied, "202."

I asked, "Are you Felicia?"

"Yeah," she answered. "What do you need?"

I replied, "I'm pleased to meet you, Felicia. I'm Detective Hicks. Yes, we just raided your apartment."

I heard a gigantic fart followed by a horrific smell. Felicia had soiled her pants. Also, she dropped the bag she was carrying. About 2.5 ounces of crack cocaine fell out of the bag. Within a fraction of a second, I turned and looked at her companion. He touched his waistband area, and I heard metal hit the ground.

The sergeant ordered the man to step back and place his hands in the air. He picked up the man's 9mm semiautomatic handgun that had fallen to the ground. The sergeant looked at another detective. "Can you believe this shit?" Then he looked at me and said, "You lucky first-time motherfucker." It was another excellent opportunity to use his favorite word.

We discovered that the woman's companion had an active arrest warrant for murder. The sergeant said, "Well, son, you made homicide happy today. You did a good thing. I'll give you this. You're quiet, but you're about your business. You are an unusual dude. I'm still trying to figure you out. You don't drink, smoke, or chase women. So maybe when we go out drinking, I'll treat you to your ever-loving Diet Mountain Dew." I smiled and attended to my two prisoners. My earlier feeling of despair had quickly turned to hope for a successful career as a narcotics detective.

*****

A few months later, I met a *Washington Post* reporter named Debbie. Debbie had secured permission to ride along with us and to write several stories. It did not take long for her to get her first story. I went over to the drug lab to obtain some placebo. Unfortunately, the placebo looked just like crack cocaine. We then broke into two-person teams and drove to Palmer Park. Debbie watched from our police van as we stood in a corner with the placebo in our pockets. We were anxious to sell our freshly baked cocaine look-alikes to unsuspecting drug buyers.

It took about two minutes before a buyer approached me. He walked up to me and asked for a fifty (translation: a fifty-dollar rock of cocaine). I pulled out a large piece of placebo and watched the buyer's face light up like a Christmas tree. He smiled and said very happily, "Glory to me." I handed him the rock. Then I gave the bust signal to the arrest team and took two steps back as the detectives stormed out of the van with their guns drawn, aimed at the suspect.

The man looked bewildered as one detective grabbed his arm and placed it behind his back. The placebo fell to the ground. The suspect quickly grabbed for it. He was mesmerized by the beauty of my placebo. He fought with the officers and yelled, "Please give it to me!" At that point, I realized the placebo was my lucky charm.

Within a few minutes, new customers were approaching us. I proudly displayed my lucky rock to a new customer. I sold it to him for fifty dollars. I repeated the bust signal, and the arrest team tended to his arrest. However, the customer wanted to fight as well. He looked me in the eyes and begged for the placebo. I asked him if he was nuts. "We cannot give you drugs to smoke," I said.

This behavior was repeated several times. The last person we arrested had also attempted to buy my beautiful placebo, and he fought so hard that he knocked the placebo out of my hand. After the struggle, we could not even find it. Finally, Debbie looked at me and said, "That is the most amazing thing I have ever seen. It was like the rock had magical powers over these people." I said the fighting was too much work for an arrest.

After observing the enormous success of selling placebos on street corners, we decided to employ the same strategy after our drug raids. We raided an apartment in Oxon Hill. We arrested about fifteen people during the raid. While we were still searching the apartment for drugs, we heard a knock on the door. I answered the door wearing my police raid jacket, gun belt, gun, and radio.

A twenty-year-old woman handed me a twenty-dollar bill and told me the money was for the last time. Then she gave me another twenty-dollar bill and asked me to buy another twenty, which was street terminology for twenty dollars' worth of crack cocaine. I was bewildered. She appeared unfazed that I was wearing my raid jacket with the county police patch on the front.

I looked back inside the apartment and glanced at one of the detectives. Then I asked for a twenty. The detective looked at me, bewildered, so I told him again to get me a twenty. The detective finally handed me a small placebo. I stepped out of the apartment and gave the young lady the placebo.

"Wait a minute," the young woman said. "You have a police jacket on and a gun and a radio. Are you the police?" she asked.

I looked at her and tapped the temple of my head. "Think if I were the police, would I be selling you the twenty?"

"No," she said.

I sold her the placebo. Then I told her she was under arrest, and I took her into the apartment. That day, we arrested about fifteen more people by selling them placebos. Later, we moved our operation to Langley Park. We went down to the infamous Fourteenth Avenue and Kanawha Street. This was an area where you could find a drug dealer on almost every corner.

Our friendly *Washington Post* reporter Debbie watched intensely as we set up our dragnet. We followed our routine: arresting all the drug dealers and setting up shop on their street corner. We carried fifty pairs of regular handcuffs. Within an hour, we were out of handcuffs. We sent a detective to the station to obtain fifty pairs of flexcuffs. In less than an hour, we were down to thirteen pairs of cuffs.

*****

What I loved to do as an undercover operative was raid a crack house, take over the place, and pretend to be the drug dealer. Usually, when we raided crack houses, we arrested between seventeen and twenty-one people inside who were smoking crack.

One day, we took so many suspects into custody that we chose not to reverse the house. Suddenly, I heard a knock on the door and went over to answer it. I was again wearing my police jacket with my badge and name tag, gun, gun belt, and police radio. I answered the door and saw a white woman in her twenties. She told me that she had given her boyfriend fifty dollars to buy some crack but that he did not return. I tried to discourage her by telling her he had probably burned through the money and had left through the back door. However, she was insistent.

She told me she wanted her dope or her money back. I told her no refunds and no exchanges. She started getting indignant, yelling at me and telling me she wanted her dope. Finally, I decided to make a case out of our interaction and asked her to describe her boyfriend. She was placed under arrest for attempting to buy crack cocaine. However, when she came to court, she had an entirely different story. She told the judge that her friend had been tossed out of her house and that she had gone over to the crack house to look for her friend. She was an attractive-looking white woman, and she wanted the judge to believe I was an overzealous detective trying to frame her. I was curious to see how the judge was going to handle it.

The judge paid close attention to the details of the suspect's reason for being at the crack house. He did not tell her he initially believed her. When asked to repeat her story, she contradicted herself. He was agitated that she had lied to him. She was using her privilege to discredit me. Her testimony could have diminished my credibility every time I testified in court from that point forward. Some people could lie their way out of anything. I was certainly glad she did not prevail.

The next customer who came to the door of the crack house after the young white woman was a young black man in his thirties. He did not know who the person was who sold drugs out of the house, or else maybe there were so many people that he could not keep track of who was who. He handed me forty dollars. He told me the money was from earlier today. Then he gave me another forty dollars and told me he wanted to buy more.

I said, "Okay." I took the man's money, then threw my badge on the table and asked him, "Will this cover it?" He looked at me. Then he started laughing, and I asked him why he was laughing. He asked me where I got the toy badge. I told him to turn around and look behind him. Two police officers with their badges hanging on a chain around their necks were standing there. The suspect was taken into custody.

The next customer came to the door. She was a young black woman in her twenties, and she was a little sharper than the previous customer. She asked me for a twenty. I told her I would be right back. She hesitated for a minute.

"Hey, the word *police* is on your jacket, and there's a badge around your neck. Are you the police?"

I stared at her for a second and said, "Would I be selling this to you if I were the police?"

She looked at my police radio and the gun on my gun belt and said, "I guess not."

I handed her a placebo of crack cocaine, and then I placed her under arrest.

*****

When we worked operations in Langley Park, there was never a shortage of suspects to lock up. At that point, we did not allow any suspects to escape after we sold them the fake cocaine. We explicitly set up a perimeter to cover any possible escape route.

One day, I was working with four other officers. We were standing near a van where we had our arrest team. We waited for customers to approach us on foot to buy crack cocaine, and we sold to them whatever quantity in the form of a placebo they wanted. Then we stepped back and watched the arrest team snatch them into the van. It was the invasion of the body snatchers.

Sometimes, we had customers coming to us so quickly that we sold placebo to them, badged them, told them they were under arrest, and stood right there as the arrest team stepped in. Sometimes, we had four arrestees standing beside us, waiting to be taken to jail, even as we serviced other customers.

My next customer drove up and got out of his car. He was a white guy in his twenties. He walked up to me with a big, wide grin on his face and asked, "Can I get a twenty from you?" I reached into my jacket pocket and handed him a placebo piece in exchange for a twenty-dollar bill. I was surprised he did not leave immediately after receiving the drugs like most customers did. Instead, he said, "I'm very cautious when I come down here to buy drugs. I always check my surroundings first. Today, when I drove down here, I saw police cars stationed at every exit out of here. Something's going on down here."

I said, "Your intelligence is amazing."

Just then, two detectives walked behind him and started hand-cuffing him. He had the wisdom to know we were setting up an operation, but he couldn't put two and two together. He did not realize it was our operation he had seen set up! He subsequently fell right into our trap.

Some of my customers pulled up in cabs to buy their drugs. Other customers drove to the site of our operation in their company vehicles. The diversity of drug buyers always astonished me. Before he knew I was an undercover operative, one customer commented that he was satisfied with the ease in which we sold the crack cocaine. He told me the last time he bought drugs, the drug dealer inter-viewed him at gunpoint to verify he was a legitimate customer.

The customer said he was an employee at a fence company, at which point the dealer asked him what hours he worked and his job location. I put my arms around him and replied, "You never have to worry about going through that with me, old buddy, because I am a police officer. I prefer to take you to jail instead of shooting you." I whipped out my badge and told him he was under arrest. He stood there for a few seconds with his mouth open in utter disbelief.

My next customer decided he wanted to fight. Young white kids fought us the most. They fought because the thought of going to jail was terrifying to them. After selling the placebo to this customer, I flashed my badge and told him he was under arrest. He pushed me and tried to make his escape. One member of the arrest team grabbed him from behind and told him to settle down. However, he was determined to try to get away—that was, until my friend Tony joined the act and said, "Meet the nine." The next moment, he slugged the guy in the head with his 9mm handgun.

That was the bad thing about being a jump-out narc. Often, when we jumped out of the van and found a group of drug dealers, we only had our guns to defend ourselves. We always pointed our guns at the suspects to gain a tactical advantage; therefore, we used our guns as clubs to protect ourselves if they engaged us in hand-to-hand combat.

I had never thought about how painful clobbering someone on the head could be. However, God always had a way of getting our attention. I stored my gun on a top shelf in my closet. Unfortunately for me, one day, my gun fell and struck me on my head. It gave me a little lump, and I had to laugh. From that point forward, I understood how painful being struck by a gun could be. Eventually, when I became a supervisor, I ended using a gun to hit suspects on the head.

My last customer had gotten away from us. The suspect was a master sergeant in the army who had managed to escape when she drove off while the stop team was tied up with other activities. We were packing up, about to leave, when she drove back, exited her car, and walked up to me complaining that what I had sold her wasn't dope. That decision cost her dearly. She had to notify her commanding officer that she had been arrested for buying drugs while in uniform and on duty.

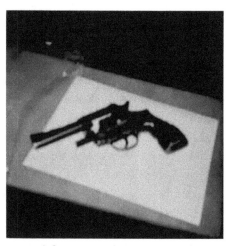

Gun recovered from murder suspect while executing
my first search warrant in Glenarden, Maryland.

CHAPTER 58

COVER BLOWN

I was making an undercover buy in Palmer Park. As a group, we had already arrested about 200 to 250 street-level dealers on this particular night. I walked over to a group of about six guys who was selling crack cocaine. I asked for twenty—twenty dollars' worth of cocaine. The inexperienced young dealer was anxious to get a sale. Unfortunately for me, one person in that crowd recognized me. "Yo, yo, yo!" he said. "Do not sell to him. He's 5-0."

The young dealer looked confused. By that time, we had already exchanged money for the drugs. The person who recognized me reiterated to the young dealer that I was 5-0. I started getting nervous. I did not recognize the homeless-looking man who was identifying me as an undercover operative. He looked like a bum. I had no idea how he knew I was working undercover. He then clarified his point to the young dealer to erase any doubts the dealer might have been having. "He is jumping out vans on MF every day out here!" he said, pointing to me.

While the dealer was trying to figure out how to resolve his dilemma, I scratched my head, giving the arrest team the bust signal. However, the spot we were standing in made it difficult for the arrest team to see me. I started scratching my head very quickly as if I was trying to get fleas off me. I started scratching my head harder, and then I started scratching the rest of my body like I had an insatiable itch. I must have looked like a nutjob! Finally, the arrest team saw my signal and jumped out, surrounding the group of men. To my amazement, the streetwise bum escaped, probably in hopes of blowing my cover again another day.

*****

I still had not converted from patrol officer to undercover agent at that stage of my career. I had not learned the importance of controlling my body language and facial expressions. One day, a group of about seven juveniles was selling drugs out of an apartment building hallway. My partner and I walked into the building.

As soon as we broke the plane of the door, all seven juveniles showed us handfuls of crack cocaine. I was astonished that they had taken over the apartment building hallway. I was also surprised that they had so much crack available for sale and that they didn't have enough sense to only show one or two crack rocks. One of the stickup boys in the area could have easily robbed them.

When I asked for fifty—fifty dollars' worth of crack—I had difficulty picking out which rock I wanted to buy because there was so much dope in their hands. So in the end, my partner and I each picked a separate person to buy from. Then we headed out of the building. Once we were safely outside the building, we gave the thumbs-up, and the rest of the team converged on the group of juveniles at lightning speed, guns drawn. They apprehended all seven kids. Each kid had crack on them; one of them also had a gun. Now, it made sense why they were so bold.

When they were taken to the station for processing, I interviewed the kid who had sold me drugs. He said to me, "I should have known you were a cop."

"Why do you say that?" I asked.

"Because you looked like you were mad at us for having it. Most people are happy to get it."

*****

I had been working in the Street Narcotics Section for nine months when I got a most unexpected visitor. It was the commander of the Major Narcotics Section. He was a very charismatic, competent, and upbeat leader. I had enormous respect for him. He was admired by everyone I knew in the department.

The commander told me that he had asked all the detectives in the Major Narcotics Section for the name of an excellent candidate to replace an outgoing detective in his unit. He said that just about everyone had suggested me for the job. I was stunned. The commander asked me if I wanted to be a part of the unit. I said, "I would love that, sir!"

The situation was surreal. I had only nine months in the Street Narcotics Section. Several other people in my unit had seniority over me. I was truly blessed. I was in awe. Such a well-respected commander had asked me of all people to come there. I was not part of the original station-level detectives, and I had never spoken to anyone about going over to the Major Narcotics Section. I found it difficult to believe that it was going to happen. I thought politics would overshadow any of my chances of getting into the unit.

I went over to the Major Narcotics Section to speak to the detective leaving the unit. He warned me that the sergeant was a micromanager who believed in keeping African American detectives on a short leash. He said he could no longer work for someone who tracked him every minute of the day. I found myself hoping that the situation was not as bad as he was making it out to be. However, as I eventually found out for myself, his analysis was right on point.

Ten days later, I was transferred from the Street Narcotics Section to the Major Narcotics crime unit. It was an entirely new ball game for me. No longer would I be making street-level buys from local drug dealers. Now, I would be investigating large-scale drug dealers and kingpins. I would have to learn how to operate sophisticated surveillance equipment, body wires, and covert video cameras. I would no longer be evaluated by the number of arrests I made. Instead, I would be assessed based on the quantity of drugs and the amount of money and assets seized.

We were expected to seize large quantities of drugs, large sums of money, luxury vehicles, luxury homes, and other assets. I also had to transform myself into a different character. I could not walk around looking like a crack addict. I had to act like a financially secure drug dealer. I had to wear designer clothes and plenty of jewelry. I had to use the jargon large drug dealers used. I had to develop more sophisticated cover stories about my life. There was a lot I needed to learn. I was essentially a rookie all over again.

When I started working on major cases, I knew I would significantly enhance my knowledge. Working major narcotics cases was a lot more sophisticated than working street-level narcotics. I had to learn how to conduct long-term surveillance, seize assets, and interact with clever, large-scale drug traffickers. An excellent, veteran narcotics detective was assigned to train me. He was a well-respected, low-key guy whom I admired. However, it was always my nature to go out of my way to learn my job. I never left anything to chance. I thought about who the best person was to speak to and learn about new investigative techniques' legality.

I turned to an assistant state's attorney named Veronica. I quizzed her on everything I wanted to know about the most complicated investigations. Veronica was a beautiful person inside and out. I often wondered what kind of man could land a beautiful, sophisticated, and intelligent woman like that. I mentioned these facts to my training detective. He concurred that she would be a good catch. I thought I had planted a seed in his head, because he married her a few years later.

Veronica was brilliant and very dedicated to her craft. She was a classy, professional petite white woman with beautiful long brown hair. Veronica's quiet, librarian-like demeanor was deceiving; she was a tiger in the courtroom. When I met with her, I picked her brain for about six hours. Other investigators wondered how I learned so many things so fast, but between what I learned from my training detective and Veronica, I was sufficiently armed to take on the most complicated drug cases.

From my days working in Baltimore City, I learned that not many people were willing to help me. Officers knew knowledge was power. But every time Veronica and I met, she came thoroughly pre-pared. She had sample search warrants. She taught me how to seal search warrants and file criminal information so suspects could not discover details relating to confidential investigations. I learned all that vital knowledge beforehand. I did not want to get into a situa-tion where I did not know how to handle something when it came up.

I knew interrogations would play a crucial role in catching the big dealers while in the Major Narcotics Section, and I knew that the exact person to talk to about it would be Detective Coppenheimer. He obtained a confession from every suspect he ever interviewed. He was a legend in the unit. I was thrilled that he took the time to share his interrogation tactics with me.

Coppenheimer explained the importance of talking to a suspect immediately after their arrest and playing the good cop. He explained that immediately after detectives jumped out of their vehicles, drew their guns, got in the face of the suspect, and arrested them, he would offer the suspect consolation. He would wipe grass or weeds off the suspect's clothes and tell them they did not have to talk to any offi-cers. Then he would say, "I'll see you at the station."

At the station, Coppenheimer would say to the suspect, "Did you remember what I told you? Do not talk to anyone but me. You have rights." About an hour later, Coppenheimer would read the sus-pect their rights. He told me that when a suspect asked him if he was their lawyer, he would say to them, "I am your legal officer."

I looked at Coppenheimer and started laughing. "You are kid-ding, right?"

He looked bewildered. "I'm serious," he said. "I'm not telling them I'm their lawyer."

Fortunately for him, it was exceedingly difficult for a suspect to beat a case based on a verbal understanding with an undercover officer. It took about two years before judges noticed a disturbing pattern. Suspects were pleading guilty to selling drugs. However, at their sentencing, several of them said words to the effect of, "I admit I sold the drugs, but I thought the guy who took my statement was my lawyer." Coppenheimer retired just before receiving disciplinary action, so I thought, *How could a veteran detective have operated that way for so long without a defense attorney challenging him on his actions?*

*****

On my first day in the Major Narcotics Section, I was eager to meet my new squad. My new sergeant, Sergeant Martin, was the ultimate micromanager. He was not cut out to work in narcotics. Unfortunately, everyone knew that but him. I hoped he was a better sergeant when overseeing detectives than when he was managing patrol officers.

Sergeant Martin smiled as I walked into his office. He quickly reached out his hand and said in a very raspy voice, "Welcome to Major Narcotics, pal."

I smiled back at him and said, "It's good to be here, Sarge."

Sergeant Martin's attention was momentarily distracted by a video on the television in his office. He watched a dashcam video of a traffic stop. Three petite Hispanic men were jumping a much larger white Texas police officer. The men took the officer's gun from him and killed him with it. As the video played, Martin started yelling, "Fucking spics!" I was shocked by how uninhibited he felt while making that statement. I knew that if he held hatred in his heart for Hispanics, he probably hated other minorities. First impressions were lasting impressions.

Martin introduced me to my new squad. First, I met my training detective. He was a very well-respected detective who had been in narcotics for fourteen years. (He was in the department for a total of twenty years.) He had trained the chief of detectives during his patrol days. He was an incredibly quiet and humble guy whom I came to admire.

I was anxious to see how I would fare with investigating large-scale drug traffickers. I knew that one of my most significant challenges would be dealing with Sergeant Martin. My predecessor on the squad had already told me that Martin was prone to micromanaging blacks; he also explained that was why he left the team. Since I had an excellent reputation for being a hard worker, I hoped Martin would take a different posture with me. I would be disappointed.

Our commander was quite a character. I would watch the tall mountain of a man make comments to our clerk, Sheila. I liked Sheila. She was a quiet, petite nineteen-year-old police clerk. One day, the commander looked at her and told one of our detectives, "I'll be glad when one of you fucks her and gets it over with." The next day, I asked Sheila how often he behaved like that. She told me practically every day. I asked her if she had explained to him how his behavior affected her. She said it would not do any good.

A few months later, the department devised a policy on sexual harassment. The commander told Sheila and the other clerk about the policy. He asked if Sheila had any questions or comments. Before Sheila had a chance to answer, a black detective took his pencil, leaned over her, and rolled the pencil over her breasts. Sheila yelled, "Yes, I'm sick of your detectives, and I'm sick of you. I have a problem with you and your detectives harassing me every day!"

The commander looked bewildered. He walked back into his office. I was astonished that he had not realized the hell he was dragging this young lady through. I made up my mind that day that if they asked, I would dime them all out. I despised seeing women treated that way. I was determined to expose any type of harassment if I ever got promoted.

Note to self: the code of silence was real. That was precisely what I broke years later, at which time I was shunned by everyone in the chain of command, including the chief of police.

CHAPTER 59

THE PRAYER OF A DRUG DEALER AMID THE STORM

I was very excited. I was working with investigators to tap the phones of a group of drug dealers. It was my first Title III (wiretap) case. I followed the suspect for a week. Now during our second week on the case, we were working twelve-hour shifts. While monitoring the dealers' phone calls at the listening post in our office, we watched some of my favorite police shows on television. I was enjoying Steven Seagal's movie *Above the Law* when a call came through. Our main target, David, was heading to New York to resupply.

I notified the supervisor of the surveillance team. They all gassed up their surveillance vehicles and geared up for the four-and-one-half-hour journey to New York City. One of the detectives in the unit took a lesson straight out of our surveillance book. Before the suspect left for New York, he busted the suspect's taillight. The broken light helped investigators follow him from a distance.

It was a very successful surveillance operation. The surveillance team followed David directly to the home of his drug supplier. While there, the group oversaw David stashing two kilograms of cocaine into his Mercedes-Benz. Then they followed the suspect back to Maryland.

When David reached Prince George's County, investigators called patrol officers to pull him over on I-95. By law, we could not tell patrol officers we had tapped the suspect's phone. Only investigators assigned to the suspects' case were allowed to communicate details about the case. The patrol officers were told that the suspect had a taillight out and that his license was suspended.

When an officer spoke to the suspect, he explained he had a taillight out. The suspect debated with the officer, then got out of his car and was astonished to see his taillight out. The officer ran his name and placed him under arrest; he then brought him to the station.

After previously following him, I walked through the station's lobby to talk to the clerk about the impounding of the suspect's vehicle. I was shocked to see the suspect standing there, out of jail within an hour of being brought in. He looked at me for a minute, scratching his head. He knew he had seen my face somewhere before, but he could not place it, so I played it off, asking the clerk if she had my friend Knucky under arrest. The clerk laughed and told me she needed a real name.

I went back to the office and called the clerk, telling her not to enter the suspect's car into the computer as being impounded. I quickly hung up and went back to monitoring the suspect's phones. Just as I was putting on my headphones to listen to calls on the car phone in the suspect's other Mercedes, I heard the suspect calling his girlfriend from the payphone in the station's lobby.

I knew the call would be interesting, because the lead investigator had directed me earlier to tickle the wire, a phrase in law enforcement circles meaning we should stimulate conversations between suspects. In this case, I told the clerk not to enter the suspect's Mercedes-Benz as impounded into the computer because I knew it would cause the suspect to panic and talk about the ordeal either on his car phone, payphone, or the station lobby phone.

The suspect told his girlfriend to pick him up at the station and check whether his car was still parked on Interstate 95 before picking him up. As she drove along the Beltway, I listened as she gave him a blow-by-blow description of her location. Finally, when she passed Annapolis Road, she said, "Baby, it's not here."

The suspect immediately turned around and looked at the station clerk. He was almost in tears. He felt overwhelmed. He was tired from the long trip to and from New York, and now the beautiful Mercedes-Benz he had worked so hard for by selling drugs was nowhere to be found. Even worse, his two kilograms of cocaine were no longer at his disposal. He had loyal customers waiting for the product. He was desperate. I was sure he was thinking his girlfriend did not look in the right place.

A few minutes later, his girlfriend pulled into the station. Surveillance detectives watched as the suspect boarded his other Mercedes-Benz with his girlfriend. Initially, I wished I were working with the surveillance team that day. However, I felt differently now. I had the pleasure of monitoring the suspect's phones! I wanted to hear how the smooth-talking drug dealer managed a crisis.

The suspect wasted no time in getting on his other car phone after passing Annapolis Road and the Beltway. I wished I could have seen his face when he did not see his beloved Mercedes-Benz. He started calling his closest associates. The first call he made had me in stitches. "This is the worst day of my life," he said. "I have two kilos of cocaine in my car, and I can't find my car!"

After calling four of his associates and repeating the story, he yelled, "Lord Jesus, what have I done to deserve this? You know I am a good person!" Three times he repeated, "Lord, what have I done?" The Bible said prayers of the righteous availed much, but not of the unrighteous. I wished I could have called him and said, "You are a rotten drug dealer. That is what you have done."

CHAPTER 60

Big Mama versus SWAT

As soon as I saw Major Narcotics sergeant Stryker walking in my direction, I knew what it meant. The team needed a black man to conduct surveillance or other activity in a black neighborhood.

Stryker had told me that the day before that, the surveillance team had followed one of the suspect's cohorts to an apartment complex, and he had discarded a paper bag into the dumpster. Immediately, I braced myself for what I believed would be a fairytale.

First, he claimed they had retrieved a paper bag containing traces of cocaine from the dumpster. They also recovered some mail addressed to an apartment where one of the suspects lived. Then he told me to go into the urine-infested building to get the names written on the mailbox.

Later that day, I went into the building and got all the mailboxes' names. When I handed Stryker the information, he looked disappointed. I think that my report did not fit into the narrative that seemed to me to be concocted. He asked me if I was sure the information was correct. I threw him my usual sarcastic look and said, "It is what it is, Sarge." The sergeant walked over to the lead investigator. They huddled for a while.

The next day, the lead investigator obtained several search warrants for locations we planned to raid simultaneously. They gave my sergeant the search warrant for the building from which I got the mailbox names. I told my sergeant not to take the warrant because we were being bamboozled, but being the genius that he was, he ignored my warning.

At about seven o'clock in the morning, our SWAT team crashed down the door to apartment 4B. No sooner had they breached the door than they knew something was wrong. A song from Mahalia Jackson was playing softly in the background of the dimly lit one-bedroom apartment, and the sweet smell of several candles wafted all around the space. Several Bibles lay strategically placed about the living room, dining room, and kitchen.

A few seconds later, a light appeared from the direction of the bedroom, and a dark figure emerged from the shadows. An obese African American woman in her late sixties stood there soaking wet and completely naked. Water was dripping all over the floor. "Jesus, help me!" she cried. She knew her Bible well. She called on the name of Jesus. She continued calling on Jesus as men wearing dark clothing converged on her. "Jesus, please give me strength!" she yelled standing in the hallway while the SWAT team tried to grab her arm to handcuff her.

Jesus answered her prayers. She punched, kicked, and elbowed each SWAT team member who tried desperately to gain control over Big Mama. SWAT members began slipping around the floor because it was so wet. Finally, the SWAT team leader yelled over his police radio for our squad to come inside the apartment to help. It was the first time I ever heard him call for help.

We rushed into the apartment and saw the humiliated members of the squad struggling to keep their balance. It was like watching Disney on Ice. I looked at the humiliated woman's face and asked a SWAT team member to bring her a towel. I looked at her and said, "Ma'am, those are police officers." She temporarily came out of her daze. Then she walked over to her bed and put on her robe.

Later, the lead investigator said, "Even though we hit the wrong place, she isn't going to get any compensation for what we did because we followed the four corners of the warrant." I thought, *How can he not have any compassion for the elderly black woman? Are female black senior citizens devalued that much here?*

CHAPTER 61

THE DEVIL IS IN THE DETAILS

The following week, my squad met with a tall, goofy internal affairs lieutenant who briefed us about a case he needed help with. The case involved a police officer who was suspected of using crack. The officer was buying crack in his beat while he was on duty. When the lieutenant gave us the officer's name, I remembered I had talked to him a few days earlier. He had confided in me that he was under so much stress that his hair was falling out. At this time, my surveillance skills were minimal at best. Most of the surveillance conducted in the Street Narcotics Section was short-term surveillance that lasted just a few hours. I learned quickly that my surveillance skills needed a lot of fine-tuning.

Later that night, I drove to the officer's apartment complex to see his apartment building and understand the layout. It was about eleven o'clock at night. I thought no one would be out. When I arrived there; the parking lot and building were dark. I stopped my car in front of the building and looked up to see the apartment building number. When I looked down again, I saw the figure of a man standing by a tree. As the man started walking toward me, I realized it was the officer I was investigating. His marked police car was parked in his assigned parking spot in front of the building.

I quickly sped off, hoping he would not get into his police cruiser and pull me over. When I looked back, I was relieved that I did not see his police cruiser behind me. I struggled to find the nearest exit out of the dark parking lot. When I looked in the mirror, I noticed a black compact car following me. "Oh my God," I said aloud, "this crazy, armed crack monster is following me now!" I finally found an exit and drove out of the parking lot. Unfortunately, the black compact car was right behind me. I looked at the officer in my rearview mirror. "You better be doing warp 9, boy, if you want to follow me!" I exclaimed.

I put the pedal to the metal and blew through traffic lights to make sure I lost him. I made a couple of right turns after that. Once I was convinced he was not following me, I headed home. I realized I needed to up my surveillance skills quickly. I was operating on an entirely different playing field.

*****

It did not take me long to draw parallels between my experience as a rookie police officer in Baltimore City and my experience in the Major Narcotics Section. My sergeant was a henpecked husband interested in taking care of personal business (PB) when working. PB always took precedence over investigations; this was the norm for the squad. As a result, we were forced to conduct our investigations after our sergeant's or another squad member's PB was taken care of in its entirety. This wore on me after a while. Finally, I learned that the only way to make a case was to do a lot of surveillance on my own.

I asked the sergeant to send an investigator to check another lead for a drug case one day. As usual, he was too busy taking care of his PB. He also did not want to inconvenience the other black detective by asking him to come with me. I was alone again. I drove to Hyattsville to conduct surveillance on a Jamaican drug operation. I pulled into the parking lot just after it turned dark. I sat quietly with my car engine, lights, and police radio off. My eyes were peeled on the apartment building where my suspect lived.

It was a hot and humid summer night. I had my driver's window down on my cozy burgundy Chrysler New Yorker Fifth Avenue. After waiting for about an hour, I was startled by the appearance of a very dark-skinned, dreadlocks-wearing Jamaican. He was standing over me and holding the flame from a lit cigarette lighter and a lit cigarette to my face. "Why are you sitting here, mon?" he asked. I had already learned to always have a cover story ready if someone approached me while on surveillance.

I took a second to compose myself. I reached down to ensure my gun was still under the newspaper on the front passenger seat. I said, "I followed my wife to this apartment complex yesterday. I saw her park somewhere near here. I know she's sleeping with some Mexican dude named José. I swear to God, man, if I find her down here, I am going to blow her away, man." Then I showed him my gun. I described my supposed wife as a Mexican girl in her twenties, and I asked the man if he had seen her.

As quickly as the man had appeared, he disappeared into the night. He was creepy as hell. I scanned the area around my car, looking for him for a few minutes, and then I drove off. I was amazed by the man's stealthy approach to my vehicle from behind. I was beginning to believe I was not going to survive long enough to make my case.

A few nights later, narcotics detectives from the Montgomery County Police briefed my squad regarding Jamaican drug dealers being investigated. They had followed the dealers to an apartment complex in Chillum. The narcotics detectives described the vehicle the dealers had used and the tag number. I was assigned to follow up on the case. I asked my sergeant for help. He told me to call him once I got to the apartment in Chillum and let him know if I spotted any activity there.

When I drove up, it was about nine o'clock that night. As soon as I entered the apartment complex, I saw the dealers' vehicle double-parked in the parking lot. I drove past the car and parked in the parking lot. Because the vehicle was double-parked, I believed I would, at a minimum, get my first glance at the suspects. I took to heart the lesson I had learned from my previous experience with the cigarette-lighter-happy Jamaican: I parked a reasonable distance away from the dealer's car and carefully watched the car, the apartment, and the surrounding area. I was a rookie detective who should never have been tracking the Jamaican posse alone. Nothing could have prepared me for what would happen next.

I tried to call from my bag phone. However, I could not get a signal. I waited for about thirty minutes and drove to a phone booth outside of a shopping center half a mile away. Unfortunately, the tiny strip mall was closed. I double-parked in the fire lane, then walked over to the phone booth to call the station's sergeant. I left my gun under a newspaper on the front seat. No one was walking around the shopping center, so I felt pretty comfortable.

While I talked to the sergeant, I noticed a compact car drive into the parking lot at an average pace with the high beam lights on—the car passed by my car. Suddenly the driver made a U-turn in the parking lot. The driver started riveting the accelerator. Finally, he floored it and made a beeline in my direction. The driver slammed on the brakes in the middle of the parking lot, and almost on cue, two soldiers leaped out of the car. My heart began to palpitate.

*****

It dawned on me that the posse had used their double-parked as bait. I felt like a sitting duck. I had fallen squarely into their well-orchestrated trap. I thought to myself; Buffalo Solider get in the fight. I steadied myself for the race. My mission was to grab my Smith and Wesson semi-automatic handgun from the front seat, outflank the two soldiers, and get a few shots before they could shank or shoot me. One of the soldiers yelled, "Bloodclot!" the other soldier yelled, "Bumbaclot!" You did not have to be the sharpest tool in the toolbox to recognize that those words were not precisely terms of endearment. I knew that the yell was a form of psychological warfare. Nevertheless, it still had me rattled.

Before I could move, the driver startled me by blowing his car horn. It was a diversion done to distract me. The posse had cleverly outmaneuvered me. I released a battle cry of my own. "Marine Corps," I yelled. It was survival of the fittest.

I wondered how my sergeant would explain to his commanders how I met my demise without having any backup. Lord knows that I was ticked off at my pencil-pushing sergeant.

I dashed over to the passenger seat, retrieved my gun from the front seat, and moved to the front of my car to use my engine block as cover. The driver signaled the other members of the posse. The men retreated to their car. "Are you through snooping now, Mon?" The driver asked. The front seat passenger slapped the side of the car and waved forward. They all began laughing. The driver immediately sped off simultaneously while away, giving a series of celebratory horn blows. Beep, beep, beep, beep, beep. "Yeah, mon, cool runnings!" I yelled.

The car turned left and headed back toward the apartment complex where I initially spotted them. I stood by the car for a few seconds and took a deep breath while clutching my gun tightly. Then, finally, I sat down in my car and began repeatedly hitting the steering wheel. I wondered if their goal was to scare the living daylight out of me; *if so, they did an excellent job.*

Later, when I returned to the station, the sergeant said very casually, "What happened on the phone, pal?"

"I almost got shot by a car full of Jamaicans," I yelled. "And the worst part of it was, I left my gun on the front seat." I then asked the sergeant if he would send the other black detective to go on surveillance with me, but for some reason, he just did not want to.

The job was quickly becoming *Mission: Impossible*. When I spoke to the Montgomery County Police sergeant the next day, I told him about my experience with the Jamaicans. He said, "Oh, I forgot to tell you. When we followed the Jamaican suspect to the apartment complex, a rookie detective had the eyeball on him as the suspect pulled into the parking lot."

The Montgomery County sergeant had told the rookie not to follow the suspect to the building, which was a dead-end, but the rookie had already followed the vehicle in there, so the rookie began backing out at full speed, which drew suspicion. The sergeant's minor omission could have cost me my life. I learned the importance of probing for exact details when being briefed about a case.

*****

I developed a third case involving a Jamaican drug dealer wiring hundreds of thousands of dollars to Jamaica through Western Union. He, too, was living in an apartment complex in Chillum. Again, I had the suspect's building number, vehicle description, and tag number.

This time, I chose to look for the vehicle in the middle of the night. For about three weeks, I looked for the car but could not find it. Finally, a Drug Enforcement Administration (DEA) agent asked to meet with us to help with their investigation of a local drug dealer. As the DEA agent was briefing us, the other members of the DEA team showed us photographs of the suspect's vehicle. They only had a nickname for the suspect, but they had surveillance photographs of the building and the vehicle. When they showed me a picture of the vehicle and the building, my jaw dropped.

"What the hell?" I exclaimed. "I've been searching that parking lot for this vehicle for three weeks, but I could never find it, so how did you all know this was his vehicle?" They said they had learned from an informant that the streetwise drug dealer always switched his tags at night. I was pissed off to the highest level of pissificity. Damn streetwise villains!

I renewed my energies. I turned my attention to a Nigerian heroin smuggler. He was the perfect target. The DEA and Customs Service were also investigating him. About five years earlier, he was previously arrested by Customs Service with the mother lode—over two thousand grams of heroin. His name was listed in Interpol's database. Several other countries were investigating him as well. I had dreams of catching him with the mother lode and distinguishing myself as a veteran narcotics detective. Instead, I was shocked to learn he still hadn't been deported even though his record included a conviction for smuggling heroin.

The suspect's enormous wealth was not the only thing keeping him in the United States. He foiled a robbery, which he pointed to as evidence that he had reformed. He was so wealthy that he had parties where he gave money away. His arrogance was mind-boggling. Twelve vehicles were registered under his name, and all of them were usually parked on the street near his home.

I asked U.S. Customs agents to help me by corroborating some information I had developed about the suspect. I gave customs specific instructions. The suspect was heading back to the U.S. from Nigeria. Customs was to stop the suspect when he returned to the United States and inventory the items he was carrying in his bags.

I made it clear that I did not want customs to raise suspicion that he was under investigation. He did not personally smuggle drugs; instead, he used mules to smuggle drugs into the country. I developed information about the suspect's travel plans and alerted customs about what items he would bring back. He was into voodoo. He brought his voodoo dolls back with him.

The rationale behind stopping the suspect was to establish the reliability of one of my informants. About one week later, I received a call from a customs agent, who informed me that customs had intercepted the suspect at JFK International Airport in New York. I asked if the suspect had the items the informant had told me about. They confirmed he had the items. I was excited. I knew my informant had inside information. But my joy was short-lived when I learned the rest of the story. The agent said that customs had x-rayed the suspect and detained him until he made a bowel movement. Then after examining his excrement, they let him go.

"What the hell?" I exclaimed. "Why did you all do that? You all were given specific instructions not to do anything to arouse his suspicion."

"Sorry, buddy," the agent said. "The notes in our computer had specific instructions on what we were supposed to do when we contacted him."

I called the customs agent I had asked to help me. He admitted that he had deliberately omitted my instructions to try to make a good case for himself. I assured him I would never again share any information about a smuggler with him. That was the last straw for me. Between my unmotivated, pencil-pushing sergeant and the backstabbing feds, I was at my wit's end. I wondered whether I was cut out to be a detective in the Major Narcotics Section. Perhaps my anointing was gone. Had I lost my sixth sense?

I had a lot working against me. Besides not having the support of other investigators, I had difficulty getting the lieutenant to give me money to make undercover buys. The most money he would let me spend or let walk was $250. I repeatedly explained how difficult it was to convince someone I was a big drug dealer if I worked with a baby budget. I once told him, "I could have the acting skills of Al Pacino and still not convince someone I was a big drug dealer." He did not seem to care.

CHAPTER 62

UNDERCOVER YANKEE

I received a call from agents at the Immigration and Naturalization Service (INS), now known as the Immigration and Customs Enforcement (ICE). They had an informant who was connected to a large-scale drug trafficker. I got together with the agents at INS, and they introduced me to their informant.

The lead INS agent, Bernstein, was a tall, slender white man with black hair. He was in his late forties. He dressed like a preppy college student. He spoke the most proper English I ever heard. His speech was so sophisticated that he seemed incapable of using everyday words. I quickly surmised that he would have difficulty communicating with the average street hoodlum. The informant was a former Jamaican gang member. My initial assessment of him indicated he was a master manipulator.

Agent Bernstein explained that our goal was to have the informant introduce me to members who were lower down in the organization. I would buy increasing quantities of drugs and then work my way up to the dealer at the top. In addition to posing as a drug dealer, I would also be an illegal supplier of green cards, which the organization desperately wanted.

I had a very uneasy feeling about the informant, and my instincts never led me wrong. What also troubled me was, the ICE detectives seemed to put too much trust in the informant. One of the lessons I learned while I was in undercover school was to never trust an informant.

The informant set up our first meeting at an apartment ICE had set up. The informant arranged our first meeting with a drug dealer connected to the suspect within a few days. We had a briefing before making the deal. I had to wear a wire for safety and to record our conversation. When my sergeant told me that another Sergeant, Stryker, would be fitting my body wire, I threw a tantrum. "Martin, I don't trust him. I told him.

Sergeant Martin pleaded with me to calm down. I asked him to check behind Sergeant Stryker to ensure that the body wire was working. Sergeant Stryker did just about anything to make his squad shine. He justified holding back information on cases to the detriment of other investigators. He confessed to the lieutenant that there was a competitive spirit throughout the office. I reminded my sergeant that Sergeant Stryker's competitive spirit was the kind of spirit that could get me killed.

I drove to the undercover ICE apartment to meet with the informant, Desmond, and a drug dealer. I arrived at the apartment early and followed my usual routine by aggressively reading the riot act to the informant about following my exact instructions. When he introduced me to the dealer, I discussed the dos and don'ts—what he should and should not do. I specifically told him not to speak any Jamaican dialect during the deal. My undercover school training had left me paranoid about dealing with drug dealers who were foreign nationals.

A few minutes later, the drug dealer knocked on the door. The informant, Desmond, led him into the kitchen, where I was standing. The dealer quickly removed a plastic bag containing crack cocaine and handed it to me. I asked if it was an 8 ball—street terminology for an eighth of an ounce of cocaine. He nodded, and I handed him the money. After the dealer left, I weighed the drugs at the station and determined it was only half of the weight it was supposed to be.

One week later, the same dealer came to the apartment and followed the same routine. When I asked him if the drugs were the correct weight, he replied, "Sure, mon." I broke out a portable scale in the drawer and weighed it. It was less than half of the weight again. I pointed to the scale. "Sorry, man," the dealer said. "I'll make it up to you next time."

I paid him half of the price we agreed on. Then I looked at the informant and said, "I can't do business anymore with your friend. I want to purchase a lot more, but I want to deal with someone else." I walked into the bathroom. While in the bathroom, I heard the suspect ask the informant, "Where did that Yankee get all that money from?"

I walked out of the bathroom, and their conversation ended. I used the dealer's shortchanging me to justify my need to meet someone in the organization who was trustworthy enough to buy large quantities of drugs from. "I have green cards for sale in exchange for some good-quality stuff, but I can't be dealing with this shortchange shit. I need to meet with the main guy exclusively before I make any more purchases," I said. The tactic worked. I was set to meet with the top guy the following week.

Sergeant Stryker wired me up again. This time, he used a different kind of body wire. I asked my sergeant to make sure he understood how to manage the signal for the wire. Then I asked my team to set up surveillance before I arrived at the prearranged meeting site. I was afraid my sergeant would be taking care of his usual personal business before attending to his official police duties. As it would turn out, they were late in setting up surveillance. I arrived to make the deal about an hour after Sergeant Stryker wired me up.

When I walked up the steps, I saw Emmanuel AKA Larry, the manager of a local restaurant where I used to moonlight. Larry loved his liquor, Therefore, my nickname for him became Liquor Loving Larry. Whenever he was in his drunken stupor, he had the irritating habit of greeting me in a way that was hazardous to my health. "Officer Hicks," he would say, much to my horror, "are you still working undercover?" I had warned Liquor Loving Larry several times not to greet me as a police officer when he saw me.

As I walked up the steps to the undercover apartment, I saw Emmanuel coming down the steps. We passed each other on the steps. We were so close that our shoulders almost touched. I could smell the alcohol all over him. I breathed a sigh of relief when Emmanuel kept walking as he passed me without saying anything. By the grace of God, somehow, he did not recognize me that day. When I reached the top of the steps, I saw Erroll, the top Jamaican drug dealer with whom I was doing an undercover buy. I could tell the Jamaican was wearing a gun in a shoulder holster. He had come early to quiz the informant about me.

I used my key to enter the apartment. When I opened the door, the informant was sitting on the couch, trembling and smoking a cigarette. He looked paranoid. He explained that the main guy had just left after quizzing him about me for thirty minutes. The informant confessed that the suspect lived in an apartment in the same complex where the ICE agents had set up our undercover apartment. However, the informant had previously told me he did not know where Emmanuel lived. My antennae went up. I had caught the informant in a blatant lie.

I knew Jamaican drug traffickers were extremely surveillance-conscious criminals. Many of them had a sixth sense, much like the police, so I wondered whether Erroll had surveilled us at the ICE apartment. I peeked out the window to see if any of my cover team was noticeable. I immediately picked out two of our team members in the parking lot. I walked into the bathroom and tried to communicate with the team members via my body wire. I asked one of the detectives to call my phone and hang up if he could hear my body wire. My phone did not ring.

I went into the living room and reminded Desmond not to speak with Erroll in his Jamaican dialect. He told me the main guy was probably going to search me before making the deal. My phone began to ring. I walked back into the bathroom.

An African American detective called me and told me he did not hear anything over my body wire the entire time I was in the apartment. Finally, he told me to rattle it. I did, to no avail. "Be careful, man, and watch your ass," he said. My greatest fear had come true. I was defenseless with no eyes and no ears trained on me. I could tell this would be one of those days when everything that could go wrong would go wrong.

*****

I was happy that I had finally worked my way up the Jamaican posse chain of command. Erroll stared at me for a few minutes and then began his examination. He was looking for any clues that I was a cop. Although he was eerily calm and reserved, I could tell he could pop off in a fraction of a second. The first stage of the examination was my eyes. People knew the eyes were clues to the soul.

Desmond began biting his nails. The stare-down was particularly frightening for him because he had made the introduction. Erroll pulled his jacket back and displayed his loaded .357 Magnum. He wanted to show his dominion over me. My life depended on passing the test, so I fought desperately to conquer my fear.

Erroll examined my clothing next. He looked down at my tennis shoes. Unlike real drug dealers, Erroll knew that cops wore cheap tennis shoes. I didn't think I fared well on that test. Erroll told the underling to follow him into the bedroom. He began yelling at him in their Jamaican dialect. Then they started whispering. Finally, I heard him say, "Where did that Yankee get all that money?" I prayed that greed and the hope of eventually getting those green cards would override his well-developed instincts.

I contemplated walking out of the door. However, before I had a chance to move, he walked back into the room and motioned me to raise my arms. I anticipated the search; therefore, I was not wearing my gun. When he closed in on me for the examination, the enormity of his size and stature crystalized for me. I realized I would probably have a difficult time defeating him in hand-to-hand combat. He was six foot two with a muscular physique. I had to consider that in case shit hit the fan. I tried to manage my breathing, hoping he would not locate my body wire.

Erroll's attention was momentarily diverted to something he had seen out of the window. He walked over and examined the parking lot. When I looked out too, my heart dropped suddenly. My sergeant, a white man, was climbing out of the back of the surveillance van, adjusting his eyeglasses. Errol examined the sergeant's mannerisms like a computer. He studied his dufus walk and his clothing. The sergeant was wearing a blue jean shirt, its collar buttons fastened, with his beige khaki slacks. He had cop or federal agent written all over him.

When he reached the parking lot in front of our apartment building, he opened the trunk of the surveillance van parked directly in front of the apartment where we were making the drug deal. He opened the trunk so high that Erroll could see the Motorola electronic device sitting inside. The sergeant twisted a few knobs on the surveillance equipment, closed the trunk, and climbed into the back of the van. I wanted to choke the crap out of him.

Erroll looked me up and down. Finally, he looked directly at Desmond, who was now biting his nails. Erroll snatched the bag containing the cocaine off the table. Desmond appeared frozen in a fear-induced stupor, contemplating Erroll's next move. Erroll stood there for a minute, staring right through me with his fist clenched. Then he reached inside his shoulder holster and touched his weapon. I braced for the blast from his .357 Magnum and the smell of carbon from the explosion in the air. I felt as helpless as a lamb. I was totally at Erroll's mercy.

For the next few minutes, the room was silent. I felt a lump in my throat. *Will he kill me or Desmond or both of us? Will my life end this way, or will Erroll take this opportunity to cripple me for the rest of my life?* Finally, after some very intense moments, Erroll's fury seemed to subside. He just walked out the door. Within a few minutes, Desmond began crying. His death seemed inevitable.

A few minutes later, I heard wheels spinning. I looked out the window and saw Erroll speeding out of the apartment complex parking lot in a new brown Mercedes-Benz. The vehicle disappeared into the simmering summer sun. No one attempted to follow him.

After the undercover fiasco, I sat down with the two ICE agents to discuss discrepancies in what Desmond was telling us. For example, Desmond knew that the top guy in the drug operation lived in the same apartment complex as the ICE undercover apartment. I had caught him in about thirteen different lies.

We shifted our attention back to Desmond. It turned out that he was still cutting side deals with Erroll. I had long suspected it. Desmond was a double agent. I knew he was holding out on me. The boy smiled too damn much. He was also allegedly battering and torturing two women he was dating. Desmond was so out of control that he allegedly set both of his girlfriends' hair on fire.

ICE scheduled Desmond for a one-way trip back to Jamaica. The long-term snitch had known his fate was inevitable. He had set up a lot of Jamaican drug dealers, so the ICE agent asked him what he thought would happen to him when he arrived back in Jamaica.

The informant said, "They are going to kill me, mon!"

The agent smiled. "We all will say a prayer for you, Desmond," he said. He was as cold as ice.

I was disappointed. It was another failed case. I wasted all that time for less than desirable results. Erroll disappeared from the face of the earth. I needed to revive my reputation.

CHAPTER 63

POLICEWOMAN

I was pleasantly surprised when a new detective named Rebecca transferred to our squad. She was a baby-faced short, tiny white girl in her twenties who had a lot of grit. She was transferred from patrol duty straight to the Major Narcotics Section. It did not matter to me how she got there. I was thrilled to have a squad member who wanted to work.

Within a few weeks of starting in our unit, she made her first drug case. When we executed the search warrant, I told her, "Here comes the hard part: trying to locate the drugs." But when we walked into the suspect's bedroom, we found a quarter kilo of cocaine, several thousand dollars in cash, and a handgun sitting on the dresser.

We all looked at one another, and I said, "You've got to be kidding. Who in the hell gets a large seizure like this on their first search warrant where all the drugs are sitting right out in the open?" The drug dealer's nickname was Lucky, so I looked at Rebecca and said, "You bad girl. Lucky's luck ran out when you got on his case." Rebecca distinguished herself right off the bat.

Rebecca was a pioneer who opened doors for other women to shine within the Major Narcotics Section. What I loved about her was, she was always willing to help me with my cases. She also dared to go out with me in the middle of the night to do trash rips—digging through a suspect's trash to find evidence of their drug dealing.

Once, Rebecca and I were out stealing trash at three o'clock in the morning. We removed the lids off several trash cans. Then suddenly, we heard a noise coming from the suspect's house. Out walked about six Jamaican drug traffickers. I put the lid back on the trash can and motioned for Rebecca to follow me. She ignored me and reached into the trash can. "Rebecca, get your ass back in the van," I whispered.

The hardheaded Rebecca ignored me, removed the trash, and ran back to the van with the garbage and the trash can lid. I got back in our van and prayed they had not noticed us. The Jamaicans looked around for a minute and talked to one another near the trash can. While waiting for them to leave, I crouched down in the van, sweating bullets. Rebecca was seemingly unfazed by their presence.

When they were gone, I asked Rebecca, "What the hell was that?"

She said, "We came here to steal their trash, so that was what I was doing."

"Rebecca, I appreciate your help," I said. "But this is not a damn kamikaze mission! We are not a suicide squad. Also, how the hell did you remain so damn calm? Did you take a sedative or something?"

Rebecca simply looked at me like a teenager who had just been scolded by a parent. She did not seem to have a clue about how dangerous her actions were. Lord knew I loved that kid! From that point on, I called her by her new nickname: Kamikaze.

CHAPTER 64

ROOKIE DETECTIVE

I learned that Jamaican and Nigerian drug dealers were extraordinarily clever and elusive. It took a concerted group effort to catch them. I was high on motivation but extremely short on help. I was confused as to what was going on. Working in the Major Narcotics Section was nothing like I had expected. My work was discouraging.

A lot of my frustration was due to poor leadership. I understood that I was the lowest man on the totem pole, and perhaps that was another factor that contributed to my colleagues' reluctance to assist me with my investigations. Lastly, I wondered if the issue was a problem in the system or if something more sinister was at work there.

I knew that for me to become successful, I had to develop a new strategy, so I chose a much easier target: greedy and less sophisticated American drug dealers. I knew I had to overcome the money barrier thrown at me by the lieutenant, and my analysis of the problem led me to believe that the best way to get the required money was to work with the feds. Therefore, I started getting suspects to meet me on federal property. The feds picked up the tab.

I learned to make new alliances. I worked with detectives from all races and ethnicities. I found one common denominator: black and Hispanic detectives and agents had almost the same challenges I had. I also learned to make alliances with prosecuting attorneys. Eventually, I was able to turn lemons into lemonade.

As an African American detective, you had to think and work outside the box. It was every man for himself. No one was going to work hard to make your black behind shine. I was likely brought into narcotics to help other investigators strengthen their cases. Black investigators helped conduct surveillance and did undercover work in black areas, but we could conduct covert operations a hundred times and still not get credit for the drugs seized in any case.

A little over a year after our Jamaican informant Desmond was deported, I sat on an interview panel for officer candidates for the narcotics division. A very familiar tall figure walked into the room and sat down. It was Detective Francis Francois, the same arrogant negro detective who gave me the blues when I first joined the Street Narcotics Section, the same person who talked trash to me when I was a rookie detective, saying, "You thought you were the shit at Hyattsville. You can't handle the fact that you are not shit here. You need to sit your rookie ass down." Now the genius was trying to get back into the unit.

The captain had already told everyone on the interview panel that he would never take Francois back into narcotics, but Francois was clueless. He had a better chance of surviving hell wearing gasoline drawers than getting back into the Narcotics Enforcement Division.

I asked Francois the first interview question. Unfortunately, my presence threw him off his game. He had temporary amnesia. He sat there for a few minutes and gathered his thoughts while swallowing probably the biggest piece of humble pie he had ever eaten in his life.

We took a break after the interview. I saw Francois talking to a detective in the hallway as he exited the interview room. Then he waited patiently for the sergeant and lieutenant from the interview panel to pass him in the hallway. The sergeant nodded at Francois, and Francois smiled back. Then the lieutenant and captain walked past him as if he was invisible.

"Do you think they're going to bring me back into the unit?" Francois eagerly asked. As much as I despised the boy, I did not have the heart to break his spirit. I told him we had not done our ratings yet. I wished him luck and wondered when in the hell he was going to get a clue. He could not have paid his way back into the unit. He had received his just desserts. He could have been a blessing to me instead of hindering me. Instead, the once arrogant detective was forced back into obscurity.

*****

It took time for police officers to develop what was called a sixth sense. In fact, not all officers developed a sixth sense. The sixth sense was an officer's ability to detect suspicious activity. It simply alerted you when danger was present or around the corner or if something was out of place. However, police officers were not the only people who had a sixth sense. Some criminals had it as well. These criminals posed a severe threat to undercover officers, because they always tuned in to all six senses when they encountered you.

I had always been amazed by criminals who had the sixth sense. When you came across these analytical criminals, you knew your safety could be in jeopardy. The fear of having your cover blown was always there. This was especially true when I worked street-level narcotics.

There might be five or six people in a group selling drugs. In that group, one of the dealers would likely recognize you from a previous arrest. All those suspects had the chance to see what we looked like, and then they had a second chance to study us when we testified against them in court. That was something in the back of your mind every time you made an undercover deal.

Most of us knew women had intuition. This was another thing we had to be aware of when working undercover. You put sixth sense and a woman's intuition together and you had one careful drug dealer. I found that out when my partner was buying from a Jamaican drug dealer who was a woman. An informant had already vouched for my partner's credibility as a drug dealer.

I arrived at Riverdale Plaza about fifteen minutes before the deal was supposed to go down to ensure that my partner negotiated the deal. I watched the female drug dealer pull up about ten minutes later. She was driving a beautiful red sports car. She circled through the parking lot about three times, checking out all the vehicles in the lot. By the time she was finished, I was thinking she was satisfied with what she had checked out in the parking lot, but I was wrong.

She then got out on foot and looked in every car in the parking lot. I was sitting in the passenger seat of my car, hoping to throw off suspicion. Instead, she poked her head into my car and questioned why I was sitting there. I told her I was waiting for my friend to come out of the House of Pancakes. I was astonished by the level of her countersurveillance.

Finally, she met with my partner and started the introductions. She looked him up and down, stared him in the eyes, and said, "There's just something about you. I don't know what it is. I don't trust you!" She continued. "I hate dealing with Americans, because all Americans do is set you up."

CHAPTER 65

UNDERCOVER BROTHER DETECTOR

A few months later, I was working undercover and interacting with a female drug dealer. She took me to meet her supplier. When we entered the dealer's house, the drug dealer was very polite and offered me something to drink. I sat down in her living room while the two of them retreated to the bedroom to talk. When they returned, the supplier had a large Doberman pinscher with her on a leash. She bent down and looked me in the eye and said, "My dog is going to sniff you out to determine if you're a cop."

One of my worst nightmares had come true. I was face-to-face with man's best friend but my worst enemy. I would have been more empowered if the supplier had pulled a gun on me, but instead, I sank into the cushions of the sofa with a big Doberman towering over me. Dogs could sense fear in a person, and unfortunately, I had plenty of it.

I was good at thinking on my feet, but not when it came to dogs, so I was unable to gather my thoughts for a few seconds. Once my mind cleared, my first instinct was to pull out my gun and give the dog gun face; but before I had a chance to respond, the woman started laughing and said, "I am just fucking with you." After that episode, I lost my appetite for catching the supplier, because I did not want to deal with that damn dog again. I came back into the office looking like a psycho.

One detective said, "Damn, Hicks, you look like you saw a ghost."

"Worse," I said. "I came face-to-face with a damn Doberman pinscher."

"Wait a minute," the detective said, growing excited. "You mean to tell me that your paranoid ass came face-to-face with a Doberman?"

I said, "Yes, that's what I am saying."

He started laughing all over the office. "I don't mean no harm to you, Hicks, but I would have paid a million dollars to have seen the expression on your face when lassie came out."

Another guy in my squad said, "Maurice is going to have nightmares for the next ten years."

I did not find either of their comments the least bit amusing.

My skirmishes with dogs did not end there. I obtained a search warrant for a drug dealer who had a Rottweiler. I told the SWAT team to beware of the dog. As the lead investigator, the unfortunate thing for me was that I would have to walk up to the door with the SWAT team to point out the suspect's door before they raided the house. This meant that there was a good possibility I would come face-to-face with the Rottweiler.

I tried to prepare for a possible confrontation with the dog. I remembered how quickly I drew and fired my weapon from my patrol duty belt, which I wore on all raids. I practiced with that holster at the firing range for years, and I felt rather good about getting my gun out and getting on target quickly.

On that day, my sergeant insisted I wear a larger vest, which would be too long for me to wear my standard-issue duty belt. I tried to make a case to him to use the same gun belt I always used. However, my sergeant insisted I wear the larger vest and the new holster issued with the vest. I had no problem wearing the vest, but I had a problem using a new holster that was not broken in yet. But he had the stripes; therefore, he won the battle.

We started on our journey to conduct the raid. The SWAT team sergeant was my old patrol sergeant. He already knew I had a fear of dogs, so when I told him about the Rottweiler, he laughed and said, "You're not going to pass out on me, are you?"

"Hopefully not," I replied.

We got out of the van and started walking single file toward the house. Two SWAT team officers carried their MP5 machine guns. The rest of the team removed their 9mm handguns and pointed them in alternate directions. I was positioned at the end of the line, directly behind the SWAT team sergeant. As two other SWAT team officers started up the steps of the house, the Rottweiler ran full speed in our direction, barking at us. The team immediately stopped advancing and moved out of the path of the dog.

I unsnapped my holster and began pulling at my gun as hard as possible, but I couldn't get my gun out of my holster. The dog was heading straight toward me. Just as the dog began to leap, I heard the MP5 being discharged. The SWAT team took the dog out. As usual, my instincts told me what I needed to know. I sensed the danger and tried to do what I could to keep myself from harm's way. I thanked God the SWAT boys were on point.

CHAPTER 66

UNDERCOVER BUY WITH THE JOLLY GREEN GIANT

My good friend Seth and I were dining at a local restaurant. I counted the number of cars filled with sixteen-year-old kids riding past, driving either a Mercedes-Benz or a BMW. Seth commented that drugs messed up a lot of good people.

"Hey, Moe," he then said. "Since you're always on the hunt for drug dealers, I got one for you. His name is Dylan. Here's his phone number. Tell him Becky Sue referred him to you. He's a big green dealer." Seth confided in me that a female member of the PCP ring had befriended his new girlfriend and had convinced her to experiment with PCP. The pain in his eyes touched my soul.

I looked at Seth. "They are going down!" I said.

"You must be out of your mind. You think a black man can infiltrate a European PCP ring?"

I answered yes to both. Later, I called Dylan.

"Hey, Dylan. This is Moe. Can I get a can of green from you?"

"Who gave you my number?" Dylan asked.

"Becky Sue."

"You must be a narc."

I thought, *Damn, Anthony gave me the worst possible name to drop*. "I ain't no narc," I said. "What made you say some bullshit like that?"

"We were beefing last week," Dylan explained. "The last thing she said before she left was that she was going to narc on me. I am not dealing with no narc."

"That is bullshit, man," I replied. "Fuck you." I hung up. I waited about three minutes, then called him back. "Dylan, I am sorry, man," I said in a country-sounding voice. "I am frustrated as hell! I've been calling everywhere, man, trying to get some green, but nobody ain't got none. I am just frustrated as hell," I told him again.

"Can you meet me at the Three Amigos?" Dylan asked.

"Yes, I can," I told him. "What time are you going to be there?" Dylan said twenty-five minutes. "What are you going to be wearing?" I asked. He said he could not tell me that. Then he asked me for my description. I said, "I'm black. You should be able to pick me out easy at that redneck joint. See you there. Ciao."

I arrived at the Three Amigos fifteen minutes later. Two other detectives covered me. Inside the bar, I walked over to a video game to kill time. Several scruffy-looking white men in their forties were staring at me. One white man wearing blue jeans and beige boots frowned at me and began rubbing his long brown and gray beard. He quickly chugged down a beer and squashed it with one hand. He burped loudly and began tapping his feet. My presence was infuriating him.

Two white waitresses in their midfifties descended upon me and asked if I wanted to buy a drink. I let them know I was waiting for a friend. One gave me the evil eye, walked over to another waitress, and began pointing at me. The bearded man rose to his feet and threw his giant cowboy hat on the table.

Dylan walked into the bar. I watched him for a few seconds, turned in his direction, and began my approach. Three cocktail waitresses surrounded me. The first waitress was very irritated. "Either you buy a drink," she said, "or you have to leave." The cowboy stood there with his hands on his hips, breathing fire. He was ready to pounce on me at any moment.

Unfortunately, the waitress had brought so much attention my way that Dylan was nowhere in sight when I got past them. I walked outside and scanned the parking lot—still no sign of Dylan. I paced the parking lot for about ten minutes. Then finally, I picked up the payphone and called Dylan's house. A woman answered the phone.

"Hey, this is Moe," I said. "Dylan was supposed to meet me here. I'm here now, but he did not show up. I need some green."

"He's out making drops," the woman said. "He calls me after every drop, so I can have him call you."

"Thanks. I'm at a phone booth. Take down this number."

About fifteen minutes later, the phone rang. It was Dylan.

"Dylan," I said, "I have been out here waiting for you for an hour. I thought you were going to take care of me. I need that green, man!"

"Can you meet me at the Valley Inn?" Dylan asked.

"What time?"

"In fifteen minutes."

"Do not let me down, man. I need that green," I said.

I arrived at the Valley Inn. I sat in my car for about twenty minutes and watched Dylan talk to several men in the parking lot. A uniformed police sergeant with an armful of tattoos was speaking to many of the bikers in front of the business. By that time, I was losing patience. The parking lot was beginning to fill up with white men riding their Harleys. I was the only African American person sitting in the parking lot. I stood out like a sore thumb.

I called over to Dylan. He came out of his drug-induced stupor momentarily and asked, "What's up, Moe?"

"Are you going to sell me the stuff or what, Dylan?" I asked.

Dylan said, "Oh, oh, oh, get in line. Everyone's coming to my house for green!"

I maneuvered my car to the back of about twelve cars, then followed Dylan to his home. I radioed my two cover officers to let them know where I was heading. I walked into the house last. I was taking my time to make a mental note of the exact address. I saw about fifteen people inside the modestly furnished apartment on the first floor when I walked in.

Dylan introduced me to everyone as if he had known me all his life. "This is my boy, Moe," he told one of his patrons.

"I ain't never seen you around here before," Dylan's patron said. "Most brothers do not use green."

"I have a hard time getting it. I'm from B-more," I said.

"Wow," the patron said, "that is unusual."

I was beginning to feel uneasy. The green bean seemed somewhat analytical. Something did not feel right. I was the only black person in a house filled with white PCP abusers. I thought for a moment. *What the hell is wrong with me? Why do I continue to put myself in these situations?* I hoped the PCP abuser would lose focus, as most PCP abusers often did. The freak show was like meeting with the most notorious villains in Gotham City. They had all violated the cardinal rule: never get high on your own supply.

Dylan started a conversation with all his guests from the Valley Inn, diverting green bean's focus. Dylan shook my hand and asked me to follow him outside the apartment. He said, "Moe, I am the best burglar in the world. I swear to God, man, that ain't no bullshit, man. I can steal everything in your house with my dress shoes on. And guess what? You would never hear me coming or leaving."

"It's good to take pride in your work, man," I said. "I respect that." But then I thought, *Note to self: notify station detectives about Dylan's impromptu confession.*

Dylan motioned for me to follow him. As we walked around the apartment complex, he began pointing out various apartment buildings. "Moe, if you need powder"—cocaine—"you go right there. Keith will take care of you. If you want rock cocaine, you go right there and see that nigger Rob." He quickly digressed. "Sorry about that, Moe. That does not include you."

"No offense taken, brother," I said. I could not wait to bust him after that, but I was patient. I tried to get Dylan refocused on our drug deal. "Am I going to get that can from you?" I asked.

"Oh, oh, oh," he said, "that's right. Let me make a phone call. I'm completely out."

I followed Dylan back into the house and observed as he dialed his supplier. Unfortunately, I missed the last two digits on the phone number. Once he had his supplier on the other end of the line, he said, "You need to get here quick. I have a house full of company.

And guess what? Everyone wants green!" Dylan turned around and faced his company. He slapped his hands and rubbed them together. "The stuff is on the way!" he said. He acted as if he had ordered a pizza.

I sat back down. Dylan's green bean friend resumed his discussion about my wanting to buy green. "Baltimore is a long way to travel for some green," he said.

"I must drive up here at least three days a week," I told him. "I wish you had somebody closer who could hook me up, because things are dry in Baltimore."

Suddenly, there was a knock on the door. Dylan opened it. I detected the unmistakable chemical smell of PCP. Two white women in their twenties entered the house and followed Dylan back into the bedroom. About eight of the twelve people in the apartment quickly converged on the bedroom. Because I was new to the group, I was reluctant to walk into the bedroom uninvited. Dylan eventually emerged from the bedroom and talked to his other guests in the living room.

I asked, "Dylan, am I going to get that green?"

"Oh, oh, oh yeah. Buy half a can and share it with me."

"I'm going to buy half a can and treat you to half of a can," I said.

"God bless you, man," Dylan said. "Give me the money."

Dylan took the money and walked into the bedroom. He emerged with a film canister, the PCP packed inside. "Dylan, I am going to stay in touch with you," I said. "I can save about twenty minutes travel time buying this from you. I normally drive to Bladensburg to get this. Your apartment is right off the parkway. Peace, man!" Dylan shook my hand.

By Wednesday that same week, I had my sights back on Dylan. I was highly interested in meeting as many of his friends as I could. I called Dylan and asked him to meet me somewhere in Riverdale. We met at a 7-Eleven near his house. Dylan exited his beat-up, dusty, dirty 1974 Dodge pickup truck, which sat beside my clean, shiny red Pontiac Firebird with me inside. I greeted Dylan like a long-lost friend.

"What is up with you, Dylan?"

"I got good news for you, brother," Dylan answered. "No waiting in line today. I got the shit right here with me."

"My man," I said. "That is the kind of service I am looking for." I gave Dylan the money, and he handed me a film canister of PCP.

"You want to smoke right here?" he asked. "I got some rolling papers."

That was the last thing I wanted to do. "No, man," I said. "I want to relax and enjoy this when I get back to B-more. I cannot afford to get stopped by the U.S. Park Police on the way home."

Dylan was a white man in his early thirties. He stood about six foot four with long brown hair. He smelled like cigarette smoke and looked like the poster boy for a lumberjack commercial. He sat down beside me. He was wearing a red-and-black checkered shirt and blue jeans.

Dylan pulled out a gigantic joint and lit it up. Just then, a marked county police car pulled up directly next to us, adjacent to where Dylan was sitting. I directed Dylan's attention to them. "Dylan," I said, "you might want to put that joint out."

Dylan took another puff of the joint, looked directly at me, wide-eyed, and then turned in the direction of the officers. He pointed at them and said, "Fuck 'em." Then he pulled out a giant Crocodile Dundee type of knife and said, "I will cut them motherfuckers up and saw them both in half!"

At that point, I realized my days of doing an undercover job with the green bean were numbered. He was out of control. That was just the beginning of the many nights Dylan lived rent-free in my head. I started having nightmares of him standing over me, smiling at me, while holding that gigantic knife over me. I would grab my gun in agony and click the trigger, only to find my gun was empty. The bad thing was, the nightmares and dangerous episodes were just getting started.

Lord Jesus, I thought, *I would hate to run into him on the streets while off duty.*

*****

I must have thought my hypothetical encounter with Dylan into existence. About two weeks later, I was walking with my fiancée, a walking representation of beauty. She had beautiful, flawless light skin. She was a black woman who could easily be mistaken for Asian or Latino. She was in her midtwenties, but she looked like she was eighteen. She had an hourglass figure and coal-black hair. To say she was easy on the eyes would be a serious understatement. No man on earth could have seen her and not done a double take.

After walking out of my fiancée's apartment building, I stepped on the street with her. I looked up and was horrified, because there was Dylan, the Jolly Green Giant, walking directly toward us. He was now in the path of my fiancée. I thought that when he saw my fiancée, he would immediately go on eyeball liberty. But instead, he looked at us briefly and waved as we passed each other. It was clear he was in a drug-induced stupor again. I did not think he realized who I was. He did not even look at my fiancée.

I breathed a sigh of relief, grabbed my fiancée's hand, and quickly ushered her to my car, which was parked nearby. She immediately started nagging. "Do you know him? How come you did not introduce me to him? I notice that you do not introduce me to certain people. Are you afraid to let people know you're with me?" Of course, I thought, *What idiot would not want to let people know he was with a beautiful girl?* But I temporarily ignored her. I backed the car up and quickly pulled out.

After I drove a few blocks away, I said, "That guy is a psychopath I am buying PCP from. Let me ask you a question. When that crazy bastard saws me in half, do you want him to saw you in half too? Baby, when I don't introduce you to somebody, there is a reason for that. Jesus, baby, please do not forget that your man works undercover."

Later that day, I met up with Dylan and pressed him to get in touch with someone who could get some liquid (PCP) to fix my dippers (cigarettes or marijuana dipped in PCP). He told me about a good friend who could get a bottle of liquid at a reasonable price. About a week later, Dylan had the deal set up. He called me and gave me the particulars. He told me the dealer's name was Josh. The name was not familiar to me, so I ran it through our local database and NADDIS, the DEA's database.

The screen lit up like a Christmas tree. I sat there smiling at the computer. Josh was under investigation for dealing drugs by both Maryland State Police and the Drug Enforcement Administration. I heard one detective whisper, "That Hicks is a strange bird." I was amped up. I was ready to make that bust.

I filled the sergeant in on the details of the undercover operation. I immediately detected resistance on his face.

"That's great, pal," the sergeant said. "But I want you to take someone with you."

"You know I like to work alone," I replied. "Druggies know that police normally work in teams, so they drop their guard when they see me by myself."

"Great, pal," Sergeant Martin said again. "But I want you to take somebody with you."

"Who, Martin?"

"What about Matt?"

"My God, Martin, a salt-and-pepper team? Please, Martin."

"The State Police and the feds want this guy. I want us to get this bust."

Martin was the ultimate micromanager. He was one person who did not need to be in a supervisory position. He did not understand how the drug culture worked. His way of operating was ideal for drug dealers. In his defense, he was responsible for my safety. His role was different from mine. We needed someone to reel us in at times, because we all focused exclusively on making the bust. But all his plans were flawed because they never incorporated flexibility. The drug trade entailed dealing with a lot of uncertainty. We often set up deals with people we had little information about. Often, we only had a nickname and a meeting location. That was the nature of the business.

*****

The day finally came when we met with Josh. He was a short, stocky white guy in his twenties. He stood about five foot four and weighed about 160 pounds. He had a reputation for being a good boxer. He was wearing a short black leather jacket. His face looked worn and had several scars. He approached the driver's side of my car and spoke to me.

"So you're a friend of Dylan's?" Josh asked.

"Yes. We've done a fair amount of business together," I said.

"Why do you need a whole bottle?" he asked.

"I got to travel to get mine," I replied. "This will save me some time and money."

"I'll start you with something small," he said. "And if everything is okay, I'll get you a bottle next time."

"I was hoping to get it this time," I told him. "I can get something small from Dylan."

"Okay. Well, have your boy check a dipper first," he said.

"Well, I'll give you the money for a dipper this time," I told him. "But next time, I am not coming out here unless you got a bottle for me."

Josh walked over to Murphy and handed him the dipper. A dipper was a marijuana-laced PCP joint. Murphy placed the dipper in the glove compartment. Josh stared at Murphy for a second, then said, "Who is this guy, man? He looks like 5-0."

I looked at Josh and said, "That is bullshit, man. If you're nervous about doing business together, that's one thing, but accusing him of being a narc is another."

"How can you be so sure?" Josh asked.

I replied, "Because he's my brother."

Josh looked at Murphy again and said to me, "I'm sorry, man. I do not sell drugs. Give me that dipper back." He walked over to Murphy and extended his hand.

I told Josh, "We've come too far not to get anything."

Murphy reached into the glove compartment of the car and gave the dipper back to Josh. After the deal fell apart, I shook my head at Murphy. "Why in the hell would you give him the dope back?" I asked. "We had him on a felony charge: an indefensible hand-to-hand deal. How in the hell are we supposed to explain this to Martin?"

I talked to Martin a few minutes later about the drug deal gone wrong. I reiterated, "That is why I like to work alone."

Later, I learned that Josh had picked up his mother several times from the county day care. His mother was a custodian there. During one of those visits, Josh saw Detective Murphy pick up his son from the county day care center while wearing his police badge on his belt. That was too close for comfort. We both had children in the county day care center.

Since Josh recognized my partner as a county police officer, it was time to shut the operation down. I decided to take out an arrest warrant on him. There was no way I would arrest the jolly green giant on my own.

CHAPTER 67

THE WRATH OF THE LIEUTENANT

In 1993, my friend Detective Miguel found himself on the Lieutenant's chopping block, which meant that the Lieutenant wanted to transfer him out of the unit. Miguel was an excellent detective who had distinguished himself consistently as a Major Narcotics Detective. A few months earlier, he had seized a large crate full of Thai sticks and cocaine. However, the Lieutenant was like Janet Jackson. His motto was, "What have you done for me lately!"

I wanted to help dislodge Miguel from the chopping block. But unfortunately, the Lieutenant liked to antagonize Miguel. I could tell it was getting under Miguel's skin. In addition to being an outstanding detective, Miguel was an excellent honest detective who always tried to do the right thing. Personally, Miguel was a good family man whom I respected. He had the perfect family life. Miguel was the perfect husband and perfect dad. He reminded me of Ward Cleaver on the old television show Leave It to Beaver. However, his career seemed to be taking a bit of a detour after the Lieutenant set his sights on him.

I was the rookie detective on the squad. Therefore, I usually got the case when Miguel had what the lieutenant called small PR cases. These were cases that some local politicians wanted us to handle. They were usually cases involving a low-level crack house. I always took these cases in stride because I was good at flipping small cases into more significant ones.

I started my drug enforcement career in Street Narcotics. Therefore, I had become an expert at convincing people to turn on their suppliers. Besides, each time I caught the culprits in PR cases, I gained favor with the lieutenant. But Miguel was a Major Narcotics detective all the way. He was appalled to have to take PR cases. Miguel was gunning for the big fish. He couldn't care less about the lieutenant's minor PR cases.

A few days later, the lieutenant came into the office and told people on my squad he was catching a lot of heat about someone dealing drugs out of his apartment complex. The bottom line was that the lieutenant was living there for free in exchange for providing security. Moreover, if the lieutenant could not grip the problem, he would lose his free apartment. He humbly asked if anyone on the squad could help him with his situation. Two detectives looked away from him and started fumbling with stuff on their desks.

I thought it was the perfect time for Miguel to maneuver off the lieutenant's shit list, but to my amazement, he said, "That sounds like a job for Street Narcotics." The lieutenant's face turned red. The 280-pound brawler stood in the middle of the office with his fists balled up, gritting his teeth. He looked like a boxer who was about to head into the boxing ring.

I calmly said, "No problem, Lieutenant. I will take care of it. What is the address?"

He temporarily looked at me and then stood there staring through Miguel. While still looking at him, the lieutenant said, "Follow me to my office, Moe."

I followed him to his office. My firecracker lieutenant sat in his chair for a second, staring into space. We all knew that the lieutenant had a hair-trigger temper. However, on that day, he looked humiliated. I took a second to console him. I said, "Don't worry, sir. I will take care of this in no time for you." I headed next door within ten minutes, grabbed one of my old squad members from Street Narcotics, and headed to the lieutenant's apartment complex.

I knocked on the door and identified myself as a detective. I asked the resident if I could come into the apartment to speak to them regarding an urgent matter. I explained that we had several complaints that someone was selling drugs out of her apartment and that I wanted to get to the bottom of the issue without having to cause the family any embarrassment. The woman assured me she was a hardworking woman and was not involved in selling drugs.

I asked her who else lived in the apartment. "Just my seventeen-year-old daughter," she said. She called her daughter into the living room. I showed her daughter my badge and identified myself as a police officer. She avoided eye contact with me. I asked her if she had invited anyone into the apartment while her mother was gone.

The daughter said, "No. Why?"

I said, "With the number of complaints I am receiving, something has to be going on here. If not, let us put this all to rest today."

I asked the hardworking woman if she would mind if I completed a quick search of her daughter's room, and she led me into the said bedroom. I noticed that the daughter's bed was full of teddy bears. First, however, I looked inside her closet. There was one teddy bear in the farthest corner on top of the closet. I asked the daughter why she did not have that teddy bear on the bed with the other teddy bears. She looked like she had seen a ghost. I grabbed the teddy bear in the closet and unzipped the back of the teddy bear. I looked back at my partner and pulled out a plastic bag containing about two and a half ounces of crack cocaine. The daughter started crying.

"How could you do this to your hardworking mother?" I asked.

"I work two jobs so that this child does not have to want for anything," the mother said.

"It looks like she is running a minor drug operation here, miss. It was probably good that we caught on before something terrible happened to her. These drug addicts and drug dealers can be ruthless," I said.

I then had the displeasure of breaking the mother's heart by taking her daughter into custody. Since her daughter was just a juvenile, I explained that she could pick her daughter up from the station in about two hours. It was a bitter sorrow for me. I headed back to the station and walked into the office.

The lieutenant asked, "You are back already? Did you look into the case like I asked?"

"Yes, sir," I replied. "I arrested a girl at the apartment and seized about two and a half ounces of rock cocaine."

He looked perplexed. "How in the hell did you do that?" he asked.

I hesitated for a few seconds. "I simply knocked on their door and asked for consent to search the apartment," I said.

"Damn, Moe, thank you," he said. He shook my hand and motioned me to come into his office. He picked up his phone to call the rental office at his apartment complex. "One of my men took care of that drug problem at that apartment a few minutes ago," he said.

The lieutenant put the phone down and smiled. He was now in a joyful mood. It was something I had not seen in a long time. I could tell he felt a little sentimental. I knew the whole situation was awkward for him. I picked up that he did not want me to see him looking vulnerable, so I said, "I have to take care of my prisoner, Lieutenant. Have a nice evening!" Then I left his office.

The next day, the lieutenant walked over to our squad with another PR case in his hand. He said, "Boys, I have another PR case that I need someone to take care of." I looked directly at him because I knew it was coming my way. The lieutenant came over to my desk but then turned toward Miguel's desk and threw the paper with the PR case in his face while saying, "Take this. You are not doing shit anyway!"

That almost pushed Miguel to his breaking point. He had it with the lieutenant's little innuendoes about his job performance. Miguel stood up. He prepared for battle with the lieutenant. The lieutenant just stood there waiting for Miguel to get froggy. He had a volatile temper of his own. He was not going to back down.

No, not the Italian Stallion. I picked up the PR and said, "Thank you, Lieutenant. He is going to take care of that for you." I was relieved when I saw the lieutenant robotically walking back toward his office like the terminator. *Whew, that was close.* A few minutes later, Sergeant Martin walked into the office and said, "Wow, the lieutenant is on fire today! Miguel, you need to work a case quick, fast, and in a hurry because the lieutenant is gunning for you."

Miguel got busy working on one of his sources. Luck was with him. He got a call from a patrol officer who had arrested a suspect on a felony drug trafficking warrant in New York City. He allegedly had several local drug connections. Miguel ran to the prisoner processing area and spoke to the potential informant: New York Rob.

About an hour later, Miguel called the sergeant and the rest of the squad down to the prisoner processing area to talk to Rob. He gave the sergeant the details of his plans to set up one of Rob's suppliers. I looked at the sergeant and wondered why he would let Miguel unhandcuff a wanted felony suspect and take him on the streets to make a drug deal. I thought, *No way!*

"Let's do it!" Sergeant Martin said.

I said, "What the F?"

Sergeant Martin would have done anything to help Miguel stay in the unit. Damn, that was his boy! I was just glad I did not have to make that call. However, I was also game to help my boy stay in the unit.

My nickname for Miguel's informant was New York Rob. New York Rob set up a drug deal with one of his suppliers. You all know who the sergeant chose to do the undercover: yours truly. Within an hour, Sergeant Martin, DEA agents, and the rest of our squad met near the DC border to go over the details of the drug bust. I was wearing my sporty new black-and-white New Balance athletic suit with purple letters and matching New Balance tennis shoes. There were twelve of us out there. A van full of SWAT officers pulled up to join the briefing.

We went over the details, including the bust signal and distress signals, and I talked to New York Rob and gave him the dos and don'ts of working undercover with me. The very dark-skinned African American DEA supervisor then told all his men to take a good look at me to ensure they knew I was the good guy. He asked one of the agents what Agent Poindexter's location was. No one seemed to know.

I watched as DEA agents and SWAT team members suited up. First, DEA agents put on their body armors and windbreakers with DEA written on the back. Next, my attention turned to the sounds of the SWAT team guys putting on their goggles and pulling the metal bolts back and forth on their MP5 machine guns. One pointed his rifle away from the team and looked out of his scope. Another SWAT team guy was twisting his body around and stretching. The Ninjas entered their unmarked van and headed off to the rendezvous point for the drug deal within a few minutes.

Within the next twenty minutes, the surveillance agents reported four carloads of people pulling up together and parking right near the store where I was supposed to make the drug deal. A few minutes later, the surveillance team reported that the men were all out of their cars and were checking out the other vehicles in the parking lot. Damn, the drug boys were doing countersurveillance on us. I thought, *These guys have their shit together.*

I wondered if that drug deal was going to be my last. I sat in my Jeep Cherokee for a few minutes. The rest of the squad studied my demeanor, trying to pick up clues about whether I was still going through with the drug deal. All the joking between the three squad members stopped, and there was silence for a few minutes.

My instincts told me to pull the plug on the operation. It sounded like a setup or perhaps a death trap. My instincts kept me alive on the streets. I hated to go against them. However, I promised Miguel I was going to come through for him.

Miguel was a great friend. He and his wife helped me with my son when I was a single parent. I looked at Miguel. He looked defeated. I knew the lieutenant would transfer him if he did not develop a significant drug seizure.

I looked at Miguel and said, "A deal is a deal, man. I am going to keep my promise."

The sergeant asked, "Are you still good with going through with this, pal?"

I wanted to say so badly, "You asshole. I know you would only try to talk me out of it if I backed out. I know you want your boy to succeed." Nevertheless, I reluctantly said, "I am still going through with it."

Sergeant Martin handed me a paper bag with thirty thousand dollars in drug buy money. New York Rob looked at the bag like a kid in a candy store. At around 3:00 p.m., I drove to the meeting point in a gray Jeep Cherokee with New York Rob riding shotgun. When I went to the parking lot to make the drug deal, I saw New York Rob's supplier, Commando.

Commando was a muscular Hispanic male in his twenties whose face and body were covered with tattoos. He was wearing a black tank top, blue jeans, and a black baseball cap twisted backward. When he saw New York Rob sitting in the front passenger seat of my vehicle, he smiled proudly, displaying a mouth full of gold and silver crowns.

There was a large paper bag sitting on top of a trash can. Commando came over to my vehicle and told me to meet him across the street in DC. That was an immediate red flag. I had learned in undercover school that moving to another location was dangerous, because suspects lured people to a place they were unfamiliar with and an area they could control. That pissed me off.

"I am not moving anywhere. We are going to do it right here or not at all," I said.

Commando looked around the parking lot and saw the DEA surveillance van. He pointed at the truck and said, "That is a DEA van. Are you DEA?"

I replied, "Why would you ask me some crazy shit like that?"

He repeated, "That is a DEA van."

I thought, *How does this thug know about the DEA van?* I said, "Okay. I guess I will take my business somewhere else."

Commando walked over to another man standing near the trash can and whispered something to him. Then he came back over to me and said, "Okay. The dope is on top of the trash can. Check it out."

I was in a dilemma. I had a wanted felony suspect in the vehicle with me and thirty thousand dollars in cash. New York Rob could easily take off with the car and the cash. On the other hand, Commando and his cohorts were standing on each side of the trash can, waiting for me to exit the vehicle. I thought they would try to execute me as soon as I approached the bag sitting on the trash can, so I scrutinized the men, looking for any signs of danger. They seemed relaxed.

I decided to remove the keys from the ignition and take the paper bag containing the thirty thousand dollars and stuff it as far as I could under the driver's seat. I took the car keys with me and walked toward Commando. I stopped in the middle of the parking lot and scanned it. I observed about ten Hispanic men dressed like Commando standing a few feet from him. I thought, *That is very clever.*

The hooligan standing closest to Commando was dressed differently. He was wearing a white wifebeater tank top and blue jeans. He had large biceps. I surmised that he was the brawler of the bunch. He marched to the beat of a different drum. He had an intense look on his face. He stared at me while I talked to Commando with a toothpick in his mouth.

I slowly walked over to the trash can. I paused for a second before opening the bag. There were ten other men out there; I was apprehensive. I peeked in the bag and observed a large baggie containing a rocky white substance. I gave the bust signal. Then I told Commando, "Wait for a second. I am going to get your money." I left the dope bag on top of the trash can and headed back toward my vehicle.

Suddenly, two of our Ninjas emerged from the van and ordered us to the ground. Commando and his companion lifted their hands. I wondered why they surrendered so quickly. Then I noticed a red laser beam on the center of their heads. Within a few seconds, SWAT and DEA agents had all the suspects surrounded. Before they could decipher a plan of escape, SWAT took all the suspects down to the ground. It was awe-inspiring work. A SWAT team guy grabbed me and put me gently on the ground. Patrons and merchants in the shopping center came outside, pointing at us and talking on their cell phones.

One DEA agent, who was later identified as Agent Poindexter, walked over to the SWAT team guy standing over me and guarding me. "You did not search him," he said. The SWAT officer insisted that he had properly searched me. "I watched you, and you did not search him," Agent Poindexter insisted. He began searching me and found my gun. He removed my weapon from my holster. "This motherfucker has got a gun!" the agent yelled. He kicked me in the side and rolled me over to finish his search. "This son of a bitch is wearing a vest too!" he yelled. He began rolling me all over the parking lot. I thought, *You might as well give them my name, rank, and badge number since you have blown my cover.*

The SWAT team supervisor and the DEA supervisor ran over to Poindexter and restrained him. Two SWAT officers picked me up and sat me in a detective's car. The DEA supervisor walked toward the back of the DEA van and motioned Agent Poindexter over to him. A few minutes later, Agent Poindexter came over to me and apologized.

I said, "You are a jerk! You fucked up my favorite jogging suit. Why didn't you listen to what the SWAT guy was telling you? You are an asshole, man. Do you know that?" He nodded. I was hot. I had no idea what the DEA did with the country boy. I only knew that he rose to number one on the DEA supervisor's shit list. The DEA supervisor was so embarrassed that he would not make eye contact with me. Finally, all the suspects were arrested. Miguel grabbed the giant paper bag, which contained a plastic bag that appeared to have over a kilo of crack cocaine.

"Miguel, I risked my life and took an ass-whipping for you. Are you happy now?"

Miguel said, "Yes, I am happy, Morty." That was his nickname for me.

I asked, "Happy about the arrest and seizure, or are you happy because you got a chance to see that backward country boy whipping my ass?"

He said, "Both! I am just kidding, man."

Miguel pulled out the paper bag containing the rocky white substance when we got to the station. When he looked at it, he began shaking his head.

"Don't tell me, Miguel. Is it what I think it is? Not that again," I said.

Miguel said, "Oh my God, not again. Fuckin' wax!"

Oh my God, this is the second case where I seized wax. They are going to start calling me the candlestick maker. He replied, "Damn, we called out an assist from DEA on this. If they find out about this, it won't be pretty." If DEA agents had known it was wax, they would probably still be telling that story to this day.

That is nothing, man. I told Miguel. "It is better to be called the candlestick maker than Malibu Barbie Man." Miguel agreed and laughed.

Miguel was not alone in his humiliation. I received a tip about a shipment of cocaine coming through UPS. I called UPS and had them seize a small box from the Virgin Islands. The security executive at UPS intercepted the package, and I obtained a search warrant to open the box.

I eagerly opened the box, unwrapped the tissue surrounding the box, and saw Malibu Barbie staring back at me. "You have got to be kidding me," I said. The security detective from UPS shook her head and started mumbling something under her breath. The following few times, when I asked her to intercept packages I suspected of containing drugs, she would say, "We are not after Malibu Barbie again, are we?" To say that was humiliating is an understatement. I am sure that I was the talk of the UPS Security team for quite a while.

True to form, I never gave up. I called the United States Postal Inspector's office and checked for packages going to the same address. I struck gold. I seized a large quantity of cocaine going to the same address. Unfortunately, my information was a little off. The package came from USPS and not UPS. However, I finally got my groove back and ditched the title Malibu Barbie man!

I figured since I almost gave myself a heart attack making the deal and got abused by DEA, I might as well try to have some fun. Police work could be tedious if you did not have a sense of humor. Two squad members handcuffed me and brought me into the prisoner processing area at the station, where Commando and his cohorts were being processed.

Commando was being fingerprinted at the time. He was bragging to the detective, saying that as soon as he got a call from "that punk New York Rob," he would burn him out of his money. He immediately called his boys to melt some wax so he could "burn the little punk." The officer holding me allowed me to poke my head into the room where Commando was being fingerprinted. Then of course, the officer fingerprinting him began prompting me to come into the room.

I said to Commando using a Jamaican accent I had perfected very well, "You do not know who I am, do you? Do you know who I'm connected to, boy? I'm with the Cali cartel, and you and your boys are going to be dealt with. My lawyer will get all of your addresses. You all will get a little visit from my Cali boys by next week, and I am just going to stand there and watch as they take care of business.

"You all messed with the wrong rude boy. You hear me, mon? You sold me wax. Now you must pay the price. You better pray you don't make bond," I said. Then I asked the officer who escorted me into the room, "Sir, can I have their names and addresses?"

"You threatened somebody in front of a police officer, and you got the nerve to ask me for their names? Are you out of your mind?" the officer said.

"Relax, mon! It will just be another group of drug dealers off the street for a while, sir. I am trying to make your jobs easier. What do you care?" I asked.

Commando stood there shaking. I thought the boy was going to break down and cry. Damn cartoon gangster. I could not help laughing. "I knew that boy's heart pumped Kool-Aid. This was why he brought almost a dozen people with him to cover the deal. Damn underachiever!" I told Miguel. *What real gangsters show up to a drug deal without their guns?*

The officer took me back to the room with Commando's friends. I started my rant again. "Somebody is going to run up on you guys and do a Rambo. It's going to be slow and painful. It's going to last a long time. You sell me wax, you pay the price. You try to take my money, I take your honey," I said. They looked at one another and tried to figure out what to do.

My squad members told Commando's men I was pretending to be a cartel member. Commando and his crew were relieved. The suspects were charged with possession with intent to distribute a noncontrolled, dangerous substance. They later told me in court that they did not know it was illegal to sell fake drugs. They all pleaded guilty and received probation. They learned an important lesson that probably saved their lives in the future.

Miguel wisely took control of his destiny. He decided to use his knowledge about drugs to help children. He became a dedicated Drug Resistance and Education Officer (DARE). It was the perfect next step for a good family man to make a difference in another way. I was happy for him.

Less than a year later, creme rose to the top once again. Miguel made his triumphant return to Major Narcotics. However, not as an investigator but in a new role as a Detective Sergeant. It was good to see something good happen for such a good person!

CHAPTER 68

THE ART OF DISCOURAGEMENT

At times, I felt horrible walking through the hallowed hallways of the Narcotics Enforcement Division. The lines had become blurred. I began to question who was my friend and who was my foe. Two storms were brewing in my life, and they both were gaining momentum: one was on the street, and the other conflict was with a few dream busters within my organization. I had to label it for what it was, spiritual warfare.

I had to work two years before I became eligible to take the sergeant's exam in my career. I felt torn between leaving the detective bureau and becoming a sergeant. I knew that I would not be allowed to conduct investigations personally once I was promoted to sergeant. However, I soon realized that my decision did not matter. God's will would be realized.

Sergeant Martin asked me if I was going to take the sergeant's test. I confirmed I was excited about taking it. However, I did not realize he had an ulterior motive for asking me. A few months later, Martin gave me my evaluation. I got a 96. I asked him why I did not get a 100. He told me that I was still a relatively new investigator and that I had a lot to learn. Therefore, I did not challenge him on the evaluation. I took the captain's advice and moved forward. I still held animosity for my sergeant, but I had no choice but to tolerate him. I had to respect the rank, but not the person.

I was talking to my old lieutenant from the Street Narcotics Section and one of the state's attorneys assigned to the narcotics division when my sergeant walked over and sat down to speak with the attorney. The lieutenant laughed as the sergeant sat down. "Look at what we have here," the lieutenant said, "a highly skilled Major Narcotics sergeant. Why don't you tell this fine attorney about your extensive knowledge of narcotics investigations?" Then he began laughing. "That would take about a fraction of a second," he said, "because you don't know shit."

I was shocked by the bluntness with which the lieutenant degraded my sergeant. I was almost embarrassed for him. But I thought it was interesting that my sergeant never defended himself. That was an indication to me that he knew that what the lieutenant was saying was true. I never worried about paying back the numerous injustices people like Sergeant Martin bestowed upon me. They always seemed to self-destruct.

*****

I was sitting at my desk one Friday at 5:07 p.m., awaiting the sergeant's list to be sent out via teletype, when the lieutenant walked over to my desk. "Congratulations. You just made sergeant," he told me. I was shocked. I made sergeant the first time I took the test.

I noticed that the clerk had posted something on the teletype board. I surmised it was the promotional list. After other investigators moved back from the board, I walked anxiously over to the board. Sergeant Stryker and Detective Miner stood behind me as I reviewed the list. I noticed that Miguel's name was on it. I continued to look for mine. Sergeant Stryker and Detective Miner began laughing very loudly. Then I realized the lieutenant had made a mistake. I died number one on the sergeant's list. I stared at the duo for a minute. Then James Brown's "Papa Don't Take No Mess" played in my head.

> Papa didn't cuss
> He didn't raise a whole lot of fuss
> But when we did wrong
> Papa beat the hell out of us

They both needed a beating, and they both deserved it. However, I had learned that violence was not the answer. I realized that Sergeant Martin had exploited my ignorance. I ranked nineteenth on the sergeant's list. My coworker Miguel ranked eighteenth. The evaluation score I received from Martin, the 96, had a devastating effect on the final composite score I received on my sergeant's test. It gave my good friend Miguel just enough competitive advantage to get promoted; only a fraction of a point separated us.

I learned a valuable lesson that day, a lesson I would never forget. Lowering an officer's evaluation score was an effective strategy for reducing their chances of achieving an elevated position within the department.

On Monday morning the following week, I woke up feeling defeated. At my lowest hour, my archenemies added salt to my wounds by laughing in my face. I gathered my strength and walked toward my office with my head down. As I passed Captain O'Connor's office, he noticed my demeanor and called me into his office. It was the first time I spoke to the captain. He directed me to have a seat.

"It is my understanding that you died number one on the sergeant's list," he began. "Every year, that list dies in front of somebody, and that person develops an attitude and never seems to make a comeback. Don't you be one of those people. You've demonstrated that you have the intelligence to be a sergeant, so bear down a little harder next time, and you will be a sergeant!"

I shook the captain's hand and thanked him. I was impressed that he took some time and interest in me and that he cared enough to encourage me. That was something I would never forget. He had nothing to gain by encouraging me. I was not a part of the clique in the office. I was just a young brother with no connections in the department. No wonder his compassion was so encouraging.

But justice prevailed, as my micromanaging old sergeant was transferred out of narcotics. Amid trying to sabotage my career, he met his demise. I began to feel more empowered to move my cases forward. Unfortunately, working with the new sergeant came with one major problem. His only goal in life was to study for the lieutenant's exam.

During the evening shift, Sergeant Mahoney would come to work at precisely five o'clock and sit in the parking lot and study for the exam for one or two hours. Again, I wondered why they were sending supervisors like him to narcotics. It was a toss-up between which sergeant the detectives respected the least, the old or the new sergeant.

No one on the squad had respect for the new sergeant, not even the rookie detectives. I was training a new detective at the time. He told me the sergeant was clueless and did not belong in narcotics. I concurred, but I also warned him not to be disrespectful to the sergeant. As our sergeant, he still could have a significant impact on our destiny in the narcotics division.

During our first raid with the new sergeant, our SWAT team sergeant, Hooks, ensured that Sergeant Mahoney knew they held no respect for him. I liked Sergeant Hooks. He was a real badass who did not take crap from anyone. He had no aspirations of getting promoted. Therefore, he said whatever the hell he wanted to say.

We were preparing to raid a house when Sergeant Hooks asked for an overview of what the team needed to expect when entering the home. It was my case, so I walked over with the sergeant. When Sergeant Mahoney began going over the raid details, Sergeant Hooks turned his back to Sergeant Mahoney and asked me to give him the case overview. I gave Sergeant Hooks a briefing. After the raid was over, Sergeant Hooks waved to the detectives and frowned at Sergeant Mahoney.

Sergeant Mahoney vented his frustration to me, saying, "That was very disrespectful. How dare he treat me like that? I'm a sergeant!"

"I would not push that issue if I were you," I said. "He's old-school SWAT. He learned his tactics in Vietnam. I would not want to be on the bad side of Sergeant Hooks. He could take you out, then claim post-traumatic stress from back in the day. You must earn his respect. He's not going to give it to you just because you're a sergeant," I said. "I earned his respect. That is why he chats with me. It was not that way when I first met him. I accepted it."

Sergeant Mahoney did not understand that sporting sergeant stripes did not automatically translate into respect.

CHAPTER 69

LONE WOLF DETECTIVE

No temptation has you in its power, but it is
common to human nature, and God is faithful
and will not allow you to be tempted beyond
your strength. But, when the temptation comes,
He will also provide the way of escape; so that
you may be able to bear it. No temptation has
taken you except what is common to man.
—1 Corinthians 10:13

I decided it was time for me to move forward. I retook the sergeant's exam. That morning, Sergeant Mahoney, my new narcotics sergeant, walked into the sergeant's office. Before he had a chance to put his briefcase down, Sergeant Stryker asked him how well I performed on the sergeant's exam. Sergeant Mahoney told him I scored a 91.

Sergeant Stryker jumped, banged his fist on his desk, and yelled at the top of his lungs, "Goddamn it!" He did everything in his power to discourage me. Now, his worst nightmare had come true, and now he would live to see me wearing sergeant stripes. When my sergeant communicated Sergeant Stryker's tirade to me, I decided that the best revenge would be to become a successful sergeant.

I knew I would likely be transferred out of the Narcotics Enforcement Division if I got promoted, but I found myself drawn back to the streets of Fifty-Fifth Avenue and the Bladensburg area. I was troubled that Barksdale and his cohorts still controlled the streets. I knew I had less than two years before I would receive my promotion to sergeant.

There seemed to be no end to the information Sergeant Stryker would withhold from me. At that point, I was hoping to obtain evidence that would show the lieutenant just how sinister and dangerous Sergeant Stryker's actions were.

The day finally came when an investigator called and told me Sergeant Stryker had called the office to inquire about a well-known drug dealer with a large cache of weapons in his house. Detective Johnson checked our internal database and found I had the suspect, Michael, under investigation. I had conducted about one month's worth of surveillance on his house.

Detective Johnson had told Sergeant Stryker I had the suspect under investigation. He also said he would let me know about the weapons Sergeant Stryker had mentioned, as I was still conducting surveillance on the house. Sergeant Stryker had told Johnson not to say anything to me about the information that had developed about Michael. Stryker figured that Johnson was a good old boy like him and would go along with his scheme. He was wrong. Detective Johnson was a good man.

Detective Johnson noted that he was troubled by what the sergeant had told him, and that was why he had decided to call me to let me know. I asked Detective Johnson a critical question: "Would you be willing to explain the entire episode to the lieutenant?" He agreed. I had to give him credit. It took a lot of courage to stand up to a powerful and well-connected sergeant.

I talked with Sergeant Mahoney about the incident, but he was reluctant to confront Sergeant Stryker, so I took the matter to the lieutenant. Sergeant Stryker had already been called into the lieutenant's office, and he waited for me and Sergeant Mahoney to arrive. I noticed that Detective Johnson was absent, and I inquired about his whereabouts. Another lieutenant, Lieutenant Freight, stated that we did not need him.

Sergeant Stryker confessed what he had done. He admitted that the office was competitive and that he sometimes withheld information from me about my cases.

I was shocked. I said to the lieutenant, "I cannot believe he admitted it. What are you going to do?"

"Nothing," the lieutenant said.

"You aren't going to do anything?"

He repeated, "Nothing."

I pointed my finger in Sergeant Stryker's face and told him he was a piece of crap. I told him I had no respect for him. He just sat there with a smirk on his face. I stormed out of the office, followed by my sergeant.

"You are out of control!" he said. "You need to have more respect for a sergeant."

"I don't give a damn about a sergeant who does not care about my safety, and I don't give a rat's ass about his rank! So if you're not going to do anything about him and if you're not going to stand up for me, I have no choice but to stand up for myself."

A few minutes later, my sergeant came over to my desk and tried to console me. He claimed that he did not realize Stryker went rogue. He had a different plan in mind. He asked me how I felt about dealing with all the problems in the division. I told him that I was enormously frustrated and that I feared for my safety.

A few hours later, the lieutenant asked what date I wanted to be transferred out of the unit. I was clueless as to what he was referring to. I asked him for clarification. He told me Sergeant Mahoney wrote up a memorandum stating I requested a transfer. I said, "You're kidding me!" The lieutenant handed me the memorandum Sergeant Mahoney wrote indicating that I requested a transfer. Instead of standing up to another sergeant, he took the path of least resistance and manipulated me into getting myself transferred.

I could not believe how quickly Sergeant Mahoney hung me out to dry. It reinforced my theory on why my rookie detective and another rookie detective on the squad had so little respect for him. I wanted to ask Mahoney if he was a man or a mouse. However, I already knew the answer to that question. I was at my wit's end. I said, "Fine! Go ahead. Submit your little false report."

*****

The next day, the captain waved at me and directed me into his office.

"I saw this request for transfer on my desk this morning," he said. "I was baffled by it. You're a veteran investigator, and you're on the sergeant's list, so why would you want to transfer?"

"I did not ask for a transfer," I said.

I went on to tell him about my frustration with Sergeant Stryker for withholding information indicating that a suspect in my case had a cache of weapons. I added that I was stunned by Sergeant Mahoney taking a personal conversation and using it to bait me into requesting a transfer.

What the captain did next totally took me by surprise. First, he tore up the transfer. "You're not going anywhere," he said. He asked me what other injustices I went through in the division. When I explained what was going on, he yelled, "Goddamn it! I knew the lieutenant was hiding a lot of stuff from me." Then he said, "Don't worry. From now on, nobody is going to fuck with you, including the lieutenant."

I left the captain's office rejuvenated. I looked forward to a sense of normalcy. The captain thwarted the sergeant's attempt to assassinate my character. I finally found an advocate at the top of the food chain. Now, I wondered what it would feel like to work in an environment free of degradation. I was ready to conquer the world.

After talking with the captain, I turned my attention to my other nemesis: The Barksdale Gang. Citizens in the Hyattsville/Bladensburg area were still under siege, and numerous murders allegedly perpetrated by the Barksdale Gang remained unsolved. Divine intervention must have played a hand in leading me to become engaged with the monumental task of trying to dismantle the county's most dangerous drug organization.

Kevin Barksdale headed the organization. He ascended from a lower-level drug dealer to a drug kingpin. His operation expanded beyond the borders of the Bladensburg area; it now included

Annapolis and Washington, DC. I ascended from a slick-sleeved patrol private to a detective in the Major Narcotics Section during the same time. The Barksdale case became the capstone project of my investigative career.

Unfortunately, I had to draw upon all my street wit, investigative expertise, and political capital to bring the organization to its demise. Barksdale, the organization's leader, was a formidable opponent. He possessed great instincts. Barksdale understood his rights, and he understood the limits of police authority. His ten-year skirmish with police detectives elevated his street IQ to the top of the Richter scale. With each arrest and each acquittal came enormous insight into the loopholes in the criminal justice system.

As with many gangsters, Barksdale idolized mafia figures Al Capone and John Gotti. The news media glorified gangsters. Their murder sprees seemed exciting and, at times, captivating. What was perhaps even more exciting to Barksdale was watching his hero gangsters rub their untouchable status in the eyes of the police and the feds. As one gangster in the movie *The Untouchables* told the police in court, "Watch how I beat the rap." That lifestyle was too alluring for Barksdale to retire from his life of crime.

Like most gangsters, Barksdale admired how Gotti successfully managed his criminal enterprise. Barksdale homed in on specific factors that kept Gotti out of jail. Gotti murdered anyone who stood in his path and ensured that any potential witnesses were murdered too. Gotti's most remarkable get-out-of-jail-free card was his attorney. His lawyer's skills far surpassed the skills of the best attorneys in the federal government, which forced the feds to strategize how to strip Gotti of his attorney.

Barksdale used the best practices of criminal enterprises and hired the best attorney in the county. His attorney was the president of the American Civil Liberties Union. His attorney also had political connections, which paid great dividends whenever he defended his clients in court. By my seventh year in the department, the Barksdale Gang had amassed an enormous track record of beating the rap. As a result, they were able to elude the long arm of the law, namely the best and brightest police officers and detectives working in the Baltimore-Washington metropolitan area. The Barksdale Gang seemed untouchable in the minds and hearts of prosecutors, and unfortunately, that fact only fueled Barksdale's obsession with power and domination.

While Barksdale faced off with his nemeses—law enforcement authorities—I was battling a nemesis of my own. I faced a small group of detectives, supervisors, and commanders I labeled the Negative Regime. These men immersed themselves in a sea of hate, pride, and arrogance. Their diabolic schemes soared to new heights. In their minds, my presence in the division was a threat to their sovereignty. I buckled up and prepared for the ride.

I started my investigation by checking our internal database to see if anyone in the division had the Barksdale Gang under investigation. I was amazed to discover that the coast was clear. I could start my research. Perhaps the other detectives had given up on catching the elusive gang. A review of our narcotics files revealed that two of our best narcotics detectives had tried numerous times to develop a case against Barksdale, but they failed each time. The files also showed that when one detective sent an informant to buy drugs from Barksdale, the informant was chased out of the house at gunpoint.

Barksdale and Pit Bull had been a thorn in my side since 1985. They controlled the drugs in my old patrol beat. The Barksdale Gang was believed to be responsible for the enormous surge of violent crimes in the area.

I could recall the first encounter I had with the Barksdale Gang when I was a rookie. We received a call for two men armed with guns. I pulled up to the scene; another patrol squad had already initiated a felony stop on Barksdale and his lieutenant. They searched his car and found shotgun shells and bullets all over the car but no weapons. They threw Barksdale's car keys on the roof of a nearby building. They hoped to discourage him from continuing his reign of terror on the community. They were wrong.

I recall asking my field training officer about Barksdale and his lieutenant, Pit Bull. I remembered my FTO saying, "Most of the knuckleheads down there work for Barksdale." On that same day, just a few hours later, I was called back to the Quincy Manor area for a second incident involving Barksdale carrying a gun. I was shocked to see him back on the same street. I initiated a high-risk stop targeting Barksdale and Pit Bull. "I know that bitch-ass, snitching-ass Beaver called you again," Barksdale said. "I will kill him as soon as I catch up with him." No drugs or weapons were found during this second traffic stop either.

A few months later, we responded to a call for a shooting, where we found Beaver suffering from several gunshot wounds. Officer Tripp arrived on the scene before me. Beaver was moaning from his injuries. He told Tripp, "Please hold my hand. I don't want to die."

Tripp bent down and held Beaver's hand. He tried to move Beaver to a different spot. "Stop moving him," another officer told him. "You're no doctor. You might paralyze him." Tripp stopped trying to move Beaver and attempted to stop the bleeding.

Later, I went to the emergency room to talk to Beaver. When I arrived, someone wearing a hospital gown and a mask walked up to me and said, "Moe."

I saw that it was Tripp. "What the hell are you doing wearing a hospital gown?" I asked.

"I'm here to get a dying declaration," he said.

Beaver said, "Barksdale shot me."

I did not know what the deal was with Tripp. He seemed as though he was trying to act more like a doctor than a cop. Fortunately, Beaver survived the shooting. Station detectives arrested Barksdale. I was summoned to court for the trial to testify regarding Barksdale's threat against Beaver. While driving to court on Largo Road, I looked at the car alongside me and saw Beaver in the back seat. Barksdale was driving the vehicle with Pit Bull riding shotgun. They were apparently on their way to court together. Barksdale waved to me as I passed them in my marked patrol car.

When Beaver got to court, he told the prosecutor he did not want to testify against Barksdale. The prosecutor declined to prosecute the case. The word on the street was that Barksdale promised to pay Beaver to drop the charge. Afterward, the prosecutor had ongoing conversations with Beaver about recharging Barksdale regarding the shooting. Beaver changed his mind several times but finally decided that he did not want to testify against Barksdale. He allegedly received some money from Barksdale to keep his mouth shut.

According to the detective who investigated Beaver's shooting, the prosecutor told Beaver he would tell Barksdale's lawyer that Beaver would testify anyway, even if he did not agree to testify. The prosecutor allegedly told Barksdale's defense attorney that Beaver was cooperating again. I do not know if the prosecutor said that, hoping Beaver would change his mind or if he said it to be spiteful. In any event, the information allegedly changed Beaver's fate.

Barksdale, assisted by three other hired guns, set out to ambush and kill Beaver. First, they stopped at a 7-Eleven to grab food and snacks for their stakeout. In the meantime, they identified a target of opportunity. They saw a man in the 7-Eleven wearing a nice leather coat and a pair of tennis shoes. They followed the victim out of the store.

Pit Bull allegedly forced the victim to the store's back and shot him in the back of the head. Barksdale returned to his car, leaving the other men to steal the victim's items. When Barksdale's men returned to the car, they had only the man's tennis shoes. Barksdale allegedly said, "All you idiots get from the guy is a pair of tennis shoes? You did not have enough common sense to get his leather jacket? Boy, you guys are pathetic. I am ashamed to ride with you guys."

At that stage in my career, I had mastered many of the intricacies of surveillance. I conducted early-morning surveillance around the area near Barksdale's drug operation. I located four spots that were ideal places for me to surveil my target. The problem was, there was a lot of foot traffic in the area. The traffic consisted primarily of crack addicts living in the area and drug buyers who parked their cars a block or so away. Their strategies prevented the police from seizing their vehicles.

I selected the perfect spot at the top of a hill to conduct my surveillance. As I intensified my surveillance on the street-level operation, I learned that the second-level members of the organization had moved back to the Bladensburg area to supervise street-level drug distribution there. Using binoculars, I observed the drug activity taking place directly in front of Pit Bull's house. Pit Bull was Barksdale's number one man. By then, things had changed for the better. My squad was functioning better as a team. We had a different sergeant and two motivated young detectives.

After three months of surveillance, I observed Pit Bull's brother Dante standing in front of Pit Bull's building, selling drugs. He had broken the golden rule: never get high on your own supply. Unfortunately, his mistake landed him back in street-level distribution.

With each drug deal, the possibility of the drug dealer being detected rose significantly, so I needed to capitalize on Dante's error in judgment. I sent Rebecca in to buy from Dante. Dante sold to Rebecca crack cocaine. Instantly, the forever faithful Detective Rebecca put me on the scoreboard. I was eternally grateful to her, as this represented the first crack in the Barksdale Gang's seemingly impenetrable fortress. At the time, Barksdale successfully ran his drug operation for eight years with total impunity.

The next day, I grew concerned about a filthy, drug-crazed, dark-skinned man in his thirties who kept circling my car at different locations where I was conducting surveillance on Fifty-Fifth Avenue. I figured he was either a lookout or a drug dealer or both. I sent two detectives out to purchase drugs from the man. He sold them crack. He was later arrested and taken back to the station. I interviewed him to cultivate him as an informant.

When the crack addict looked at me, he appeared very relieved. He said, "Man, I wondered why I kept seeing you sitting in your damn car at different locations around there. Damn, if I weren't so high and if I had figured out you were a cop, I would have taken out my piece and blown your head off your shoulders!" The addict's words shook me to my core. I was rolling the dice by sitting out there, but my instincts served me well.

Unbeknownst to me at the time, something had happened that would change the course of the investigation. A homicide sergeant was on the scene of a homicide that they believed Barksdale had ordered. When a homicide detective mentioned to the sergeant that Barksdale might be behind it, she went into hysterics. She started crying based on the mere mention of Barksdale's name. The homicide sergeant commented to the homicide detective that he was right, that people on the street were terrified of Barksdale. The detective told the sergeant that he and other homicide detectives had been telling that to homicide leadership for years.

CHAPTER 70

BACK TO THE GRAVEL PIT

No investigator could afford to put all his eggs in one basket. Therefore, I proceeded to work on other cases. I developed an informant who significantly changed my career. Kyle was the only informant I met who could effortlessly blend into any drug organization. He was worth his weight in gold.

I was excited when my informant told me about a drug dealer named Amari who had just moved to the county from New York City. He could move half a kilo to four kilos with a quick phone call. It was music to my ears because I knew it often took time for drug dealers to gain the trust of their suppliers. Amari trusted Kyle immensely.

We met with Amari at a restaurant parking lot in Riverdale. When he pulled up in a small compact car, he immediately shook my hand and engaged me in conversation. He did not examine my eyes, clothes, or gestures as most large-scale drug dealers did. Instead, he was entirely at ease. We discussed buying an ounce of crack cocaine for openers. Without hesitation, the drug boy sold me an ounce of crack cocaine, then pulled out of the parking lot slowly. To my amazement, he did not even check his rearview mirror. His carefree attitude confirmed that he was totally at ease.

I called my informant and asked him to contact the dealer and get me half a kilogram of cocaine. When my informant called the dealer, he told him it was okay to give me his phone number, so Amari, the drug dealer, and I spoke the next day. He told me he was heading to New York the next day, and he needed to know before he headed out if I still required half a kilo. I confirmed that I did. He said he was running out and would return at about seven o'clock at night.

I was extremely excited. Rarely did we get much notice. The scenario was perfect as long as my fearless leader, my sergeant, did not mess it up. The only problem this time was, my squad was working the day shift. My team was scheduled off at five o'clock, so I would have to depend on the help of the evening narcotics squad. Nevertheless, they had significant time to set up an operation on Amari's house.

Making the case was as easy as taking candy from a baby. My team knew who the dealer was, what he looked like, the vehicle he drove, where he lived, and the approximate time he was due to arrive. All we needed was to have enough detectives there to take him down. I briefed the evening narcotics sergeant and his squad and then headed out to Amari's house two hours before he would arrive. I had to pick a good spot to park my car, because he knew me but had no idea I knew where he lived. If Amari spotted me, nothing good could come of it.

The best-case scenario was, he would think I was a police officer. Worst-case scenario, he might think I was a drug dealer setting up to rob him. As the worst-case scenarios took up the bulk of my thoughts, I grabbed a walkie-talkie and asked what the other squad's estimated time of arrival (ETA) was. The assistant squad supervisor responded, "We will be there in twenty minutes."

One hour passed; no one appeared. Two hours later, still, no one appeared. I called again and asked where the squad was. This time, the supervisor came over the radio and said, "They're on their way now." I had given the evening narcotics squad a four-hour notice that Amari would be arriving home within two hours.

Another hour and thirty-eight minutes passed before I saw the suspect pull into his apartment complex. I slid down in the seat of my car and called the supervisor, asking whether the squad had seen the suspect pull up. There was radio silence. I called the assistant squad supervisor on the radio, but there was no response.

BACK TO THE GRAVEL PIT

Amari exited his vehicle, looked around, went to his trunk, and opened a Timberland shoebox. He closed the box, looked around again, and removed the package from the back of the vehicle. Looking around before removing the dope from the car was a universal sign I recognized immediately. It meant he was riding dirty (had drugs in his possession).

The street was very dark, except for the lights illuminating Amari's apartment building. I quickly opened my car door, then quietly closed it. I gave him another few seconds so he could check his surroundings. Just as I suspected, he took one more look to ensure no one was following him. Then he slowly walked toward his apartment building. I stepped up my pace. I was about twenty feet behind him when he reached for the entrance door. He opened the door, and the door shut behind him. I went for the door about a fraction of a second after he closed it, but the door was already locked. I quickly moved to the side of the door.

To my horror, Amari escaped. Lord knew I was hot. I wondered where the hell my backup was. I raced back to my car, got back on my radio, and asked the sergeant again where everybody was. He told me he was sorry the squad did not make it out on time. Damn saboteurs, they screwed me again. I called Sergeant Mahoney and asked him to deploy our team. He refused. Then I demanded that Sergeant Mahoney call the lieutenant to order the evening sergeant to stake out the scene. Again, he refused. I was hot as hell!

Because I was in my old patrol district, I called the station and asked the evening patrol squad to meet with me. They agreed to stop Amari if I could lure him out of the apartment building. I called the suspect for several hours. However, he did not return my calls. I sat back in my car, fuming, because I was on my own. I settled down the rest of the night with my eyes peeled on Amari's building. I called my sergeant back and asked him to ensure that I would be relieved by eight o'clock in the morning so I could attend a meeting at the Criminal Investigations Division at nine. I was not sure why the lieutenant wanted me there. My sergeant agreed; however, my relief did not arrive until eight thirty in the morning. I was sabotaged again.

I arrived for my meeting at 9:07 a.m. The chief of detectives, the commander of the Criminal Investigations Division (CID), the FBI group supervisor, a homicide sergeant, several homicide detectives, and several FBI agents were sitting around a large conference room table. The chief of detectives immediately chastised me for being late. I explained that I had been on a stakeout for eighteen hours and that I was screwed by my relief, who had arrived late.

The chief of detectives immediately snapped back to business. He gave an overview of a situation needing immediate attention. Frank, the chief of detectives, said he was briefed by the commander of homicide, who concluded that Barksdale had been committing murders for several years. Moreover, all supervisors seemed to agree that Barksdale was a significant threat to the community. Colonel Frank said, "I want this threat to the community eliminated as soon as possible." He looked at me and said, "Moe, let the lieutenant know what you need. I will make sure that you get it."

Lieutenant Colonel Frank was my former patrol lieutenant who rewarded me with a brand-new cruiser for being the top stat person at the Hyattsville station when I was still a private. He knew my work ethic. Colonel Frank further explained that the FBI offered to help us with human resources and other resources. I left the meeting wondering why Colonel Frank had asked me what I needed. First, I was a detective, not a sergeant. Secondly, I was assigned to Major Narcotics, not homicide.

I headed back to my narcotics squad. As soon as I walked in the door, my sergeant said, "Don't sit down. The lieutenant wants you in his office immediately." I braced myself in anticipation of being chastised for being late for my meeting at homicide. My lieutenant was a hot-tempered, aggressive, no-nonsense type of guy.

As I walked into his office, he seemed unusually calm. He told me to take a seat. He looked at me for a moment, then managed to get a partial smile out. He leaned back in his chair. I noticed that his demeanor began to change. He pointed at me and eventually began to speak. "I told you before. These motherfuckers here walk around with their chest out, thinking they are God's gift to narcotics! You know what? I received a call from the chief of detectives a few days ago. The chief of detectives said homicide told him about a big drug dealer who has been killing and ordering hits on people for years. They said he beats every murder, every shooting, and any case we put on him."

The lieutenant told me that the chief said sarcastically to him, "I know that one of your hotshot detectives has an active investigation on him since he has been a big drug dealer for many years. So tell me, Lieutenant, which one of your hotshots is investigating him? Because I know that with your four squads of Major Narcotics detectives, one of your detectives is actively working this boy. Now, Lieutenant, tell me who you have working this case."

The narcotics lieutenant went on to tell me that he sweat bullets following the question. He then asked the chief to hold on while he asked one of the clerks to run the suspect's name through the narcotics database. "Guess whose name came up on the computer as having an active investigation on him?" the lieutenant asked me. "It was you. I cannot tell you how relieved I was. I was even happier to see that you had already arrested some people in the organization. You helped me save face with the chief of detectives. When your fellow detectives found out homicide wanted me to send a narcotics detective to homicide, all these non-narc motherfuckers lined up to go."

He took a few seconds to calm himself. "A homicide sergeant in charge of the investigation specifically asked me to send Detective Miner. I told him no!" Finally, he stood up and walked toward me. "None of them was looking into the guy." Then he said, "I'm sending you because you deserve this. You are probably going to get promoted to sergeant within a year and a half, so I want you to go out with a bang." I thought for a moment and hoped I would not go out with a bang from someone's bullet.

The lieutenant shook my hand and said, "Good luck!" He sat on top of his desk in front of me. "I know you think that I did not stand up for you when Sergeant Stryker was pulling all of the childish bullshit on you. The reality was, he was friends with the chief of detectives at the time. Therefore, whatever discipline I would have taken against him would have been overruled," he said. That gave me some insight into the politics and power struggles I was unaware of in the unit. I gained a better understanding and appreciation for him as my leader. It must have taken a lot for him to admit that.

I headed to the sergeant's office. "How does it feel to be going to homicide?" he asked. I told him that catching those villains was my greatest passion. I quickly shifted the conversation back to the case from the previous night. My phone rang as I was about to explain to the sergeant how the evening squad screwed me. It was my fish on the hook, Amari.

He apologized for not meeting me the previous night. He told me he was exhausted after driving back from New York. He told me he could meet me at noon back at the restaurant on Baltimore Avenue. My sergeant watched my angry face turn into a grinch-like smile. He knew it was good news. "Let's saddle up the posse. Our boy is well-rested and ready to be busted," I said.

*****

Our squad quickly assembled in the parking lot of a local restaurant. I made sure everyone was in place before I drove in. I immediately made eye contact with the suspect as I entered the parking lot. I confirmed on my walkie-talkie that he was sitting in a blue compact car. The setup was so easy; even a rookie patrol officer could have taken him down.

I sat in my car for a few seconds and waited to see the unsuspecting drug dealer overwhelmed by a quick and organized takedown. Suddenly, Sergeant Mahoney drove up beside the suspect and pointed his 9mm handgun at him. The sergeant was in plain clothes. All the suspect could see was that a Hispanic-looking guy was pointing a gun at him. He tried to drive off. However, I heard brakes squealing and watched.

My colleagues quickly jumped out of their vehicles wearing blue jackets with Police written in yellow. They boxed Amari in the parking lot with military precision. They drew their weapons, raised their guns to eye level, and pointed their weapons at Amari. Amari promptly bailed out of his car and began running. Sergeant Mahoney threw his door open and tried to exit his vehicle to run after the suspect. However, he forgot to unbuckle his seat belt. The seat belt forced him back into the car. His gun fell to the ground. He struggled to reach his gun while still entangled in his seat belt.

"Yo, Sarge," I said. "Unbuckle your seat belt, man." *Where in the hell are they getting these sergeants from?* I thought. I joined three other detectives who were already in pursuit of the suspect. When the suspect was half a block away from the parking lot, he threw a bright-blue plastic baggie straight in the air. This case was almost too good to be true. I was amazed he did not throw the baggie into the bushes. I was even more surprised that he had picked the most easily identifiable color for the baggie to pack the cocaine in.

Amari was no match for the new, young, agile detectives on my squad. He was apprehended less than a block away. I retrieved the baggie, which contained about two and a half ounces of crack cocaine. Later, I obtained a search warrant for Amari's apartment. As soon as I walked into his bedroom, I saw the Timberland shoebox he had walked into the building with the previous night. Beside the box was a silver pie pan filled with crack cocaine. One piece of the pie was missing, but if I had reinserted the crack cocaine the suspect had thrown into the air, it would have fitted perfectly.

I came back into the station and walked into the interview room. The suspect was sitting there, shaking his head. He took a few seconds to speak. When he finally spoke, he said, "I'm glad you got me, man."

"Why?" I asked.

"You don't understand, man," he said. "This shit is a pain in the ass. People worry the shit out of me for the stuff, man. I go to clubs trying to meet a decent girl. Every time I think I meet somebody decent, they set me up to be robbed. I am sick of this shit, man. It seems like you cannot trust people anymore. All that these girls want to do is set you up," he said. "I try to be a good person, but everywhere I go, I meet women, and they try to set me up to be robbed. It's like you cannot meet any good people anymore."

I suggested that he should try a different occupation, one that would allow him to meet someone on the job. He seemed like a caring person; being successful in the drug business was difficult unless you were ruthless. "Man, once people in Maryland learn that you are from New York City, the first thing that comes to their minds is getting drugs for them at a lower price," he said.

Amari was convicted of transporting cocaine into the state and possession with the intent to distribute cocaine. He received a five-year sentence.

CHAPTER 71

TRANSFERRED TO HOMICIDE

I left Major Narcotics on a high note and started my new assignment on the Homicide Task Force. I teamed up with two homicide detectives. We shared notes about all the murders and other crimes we believed were tied to the Barksdale Gang. I went to the Central Records Division and pulled every document ever written on Barksdale and his cohorts. I also obtained every court record and newspaper article written on the Barksdale Gang.

Within two weeks, the Homicide Task Force became part of the FBI Safe Streets Task Force. I was now on my way to experiencing the odyssey of life in the FBI. The agency immediately sent me to the FBI Street Survival School located at the Marine Corps base in Quantico, Virginia. I arrived the evening before the class started. I brought my 10-speed along to ride around the base before the class began. I enjoyed the spring air, pedaling rapidly to see how fast I could make the bike go.

When I reached an enormous speed on the road, I stopped pedaling. I was moving so quickly and so stealthily that a deer standing in the road up ahead of me did not seem to hear me. I kept moving, waiting for the deer to sense my presence. When it became clear the deer was not going to detect me, I began braking and yelling. Just before I made contact with the deer, the animal saw me and ran away.

That was entirely too close for comfort. I rode my bicycle a little farther down the road and saw a blue sign with white letters.

Welcome to Hogan's Alley
City Limits
Caution: Law enforcement exercises in progress. Display of weapons, firing of blank ammunition, and arrests may occur. If challenged, please follow instructions.

I came across Hogan's Alley, a makeshift town the FBI used to test their agents' survival skills. The realistic looking town had a hotel, bank, barbershop, laundromat, deli, pool and several other businesses that an agent might expect to encounter in the real world. The secret to the town's realistic appearance was that Hollywood set designers helped the FBI construct the city. The FBI got the name Hogan's Alley from a comic book published in the late 1800s. It was a rough town full of bad guys.

As in any real town, you never knew what to expect. The FBI made it that way by hiring role players to interact with us in the city. Some role players might comply with our commands while other actors might resist our orders. The role players' reactions were typically based on how agents handled the scenarios.

While at the Street Survival School, I had a great time interacting with agents and other law enforcement officials from across the country. We strategized about the best way to approach different scenarios. By the second day, we were storming buildings and firing at various targets that popped up with men or women brandishing a variety of weapons. Some targets that popped up were supposed to be good guys while other targets represented bad guys.

I also went through extensive firearms training. The FBI firearms training was better than our firearms instruction in my police agency, so much so that I shot expert consistently after completing the FBI firearms training. After training, I headed to Baltimore to be deputized as a special agent with the FBI. I was then sent to a homicide investigators' school sponsored by the Army Criminal Investigation Division.

I had met my soon-to-be-wife, Rosie, a few years earlier, when I was a patrol officer. By the time she reconnected with me three years later, she was surprised to learn I was working in narcotics. We were married in 1991. We had 250 guests at our wedding, which included friends and family. We both had children from prior relationships. However, we also brought a beautiful baby girl into this world.

I was floating on air, living my best life. As for my wife, I was not sure if she knew what she was signing up for. My life lacked structure. I kept my wife in the dark about my undercover activities. She usually did not question what I was doing on the streets, but she started getting suspicious about why I spent enormous amounts of time conducting surveillance. My wife finally questioned me as to why I was working in homicide.

"What in the hell are you getting yourself into now?" she asked.

"They are a bunch of drug dealers that are killing people," I replied.

"Don't you care about anything else?" she asked.

"Of course I do, baby," I said.

She slammed the magazine she was reading on the table and ran upstairs. At that point, I realized the enormous toll my job was taking on her. I felt ashamed.

Once I was fully trained, I was back on the path to bringing down the Barksdale organization with renewed enthusiasm. But unbeknownst to Barksdale, the total weight of the FBI was swinging in his direction. As local officers on the Safe Streets Task Force, we were no longer bound by the jurisdictional constraints of working exclusively in Prince George's County. Now, the entire Baltimore Washington area was our playground. One of the most significant impediments for bringing down suspects was the lack of communication between law enforcement agencies. Now, we were all on one accord.

I became acquainted with my three FBI counterparts and my two associates from homicide. Agent Larry Stone was formally a fighter pilot. He was a brilliant man who spoke with a Southern accent. Stone had a photographic memory. He was pretty much a quiet guy if he had his coffee in the morning. However, he was not himself without his coffee.

Agent Kozlowski was an FBI agent who worked terrorism in Puerto Rico and Connecticut. He was an intelligent and very slender man who spoke almost exclusively in FBI lingo. Unfortunately, his overuse of FBI acronyms often left me confused about what he was talking about. Agent Joey Jackson was a very bright African American man who was previously a Drug Enforcement Administration chemist. He took most of our surveillance photographs.

Homicide detective Roger Covington was a short veteran detective who had nearly twenty years on the job. He saw just about everything one could see as a detective. Detective Monty Ferris had spent about the same amount of time in the department, and he believed he knew everything there was to know about homicide investigations.

Before long, I took the lead on the Barksdale case. I already had an enormous amount of historical knowledge about the Barksdale Gang. I had enough skirmishes and confrontations with them to understand their way of thinking in an up close and personal way. I could also recognize most of their voices over the telephone. Unfortunately, it had been quite a while since I interacted with members of the organization. Fortunately for us, Barksdale and his henchman were creatures of habit.

My comrades in homicide developed informants who gave us beneficial information. We were told that members of the Barksdale Gang were allegedly carjacking people for their vehicles, replating the cars with new vehicle identification numbers, and then selling the vehicles. I began looking into other people in the organization who were working for Barksdale in either Annapolis or Washington, DC. I became curious about the status of one of his early foot soldiers named Marty Cantor.

Marty was a light-skinned young kid whom I saw hanging out on a corner years earlier who said he could have me killed. I remembered telling him at the time that the only person whom he could have killed was himself. I urged him many times to stop dealing drugs for Barksdale. I knew he was ambitious, and he was determined to move up in the organization. Marty indeed began to rise in the ranks of the organization, and he vanished from the street corners. Instead, he was tasked with other responsibilities, such as picking up money and delivering drugs to the street dealers.

A few weeks into the investigation, I came across a police report showing that Barksdale and Pit Bull had allegedly conducted a ride-by shooting, then bailed out of the vehicle. Investigators recovered shell casings and latent fingerprints in the car. They also obtained the rental car agreement and determined that Marty Cantor was the person who rented the vehicle. Marty quickly became a person of interest for the investigators who were trying to confirm that Barksdale and Pit Bull were the ones who did the ride-by shooting.

In the meantime, Barksdale called Cantor and told him he would hook him up with a beautiful Puerto Rican girl who had all the right moves. Barksdale promised Cantor that the girl would rock his world and make him feel like he was in another galaxy. In addition, Barksdale told Cantor his job had all kinds of benefits.

According to a witness, what happened next was this: Barksdale drove Marty to Washington, DC, where they introduced him to a pimp named Joe, aka Rooster. Rooster gave Marty the key to an apartment where a gorgeous young Latina beauty was waiting to deliver on Barksdale's promise.

Marty was moaning within a few minutes as the Latin beauty gave him the ride of a lifetime. As she intensified her sexual activity, so did Marty's screams of ecstasy. It was a hot summer night. The apartment window, which faced the street, was slightly open, which put Marty's sexual escapades on display for all to see. After Marty's mission was complete, he fell fast asleep. Then he was startled by a knock on the door.

Barksdale and Pit Bull entered. They appeared to be anxious to talk to him. Pit Bull asked Marty to come out back to tell the homeys about his sexual escapade. Marty accompanied them to the back alley. He contemplated where he would begin the story. Then a gunman maneuvered behind him, placed the gun to the back of his head, and pulled the trigger. Within a few seconds, Marty's youthful existence came to an end. The killer disappeared into the night. There was no witness to link the rental car to Barksdale.

A neighbor who heard the shots called DC's police department. The prostitute quickly left the scene. During the preliminary investigation, officers determined that Marty was inside Rooster's apartment immediately before the murder. Detectives knocked on Rooster's door the next day and questioned him about Cantor's presence in his apartment before the murder.

DC homicide detective: Hey, Rooster. I need to talk to you.

Rooster: About what?

DC detective: Last night, there was a homicide near your favorite spot.

Rooster: Really, sir? I did not know that.

DC detective: I need to get that name, buddy.

Rooster: I wish I could help you, but my girls were not working there last night.

DC detective: About twelve witnesses told us that pretty boy was having the time of his life with your 'Rican girl before getting one to the back of the head.

Rooster: Sir, I wish I could help you.

DC detective: Okay. I will call Vice and let them know what's going on. You are going back to the broke brother that you used to be. We are going to have this chat with you every night until I get what I need.

CHAPTER 72

INTERROGATION AND SHOOTING OF THE PIMP

On day two, DC homicide detectives knocked on Rooster's door.

DC detective: Hey, Rooster. This is Detective Johnson. I need to talk to you.

Rooster: Man, please! I don't know anything.

Nonetheless, Rooster let the detectives into his apartment.

DC detective: Rooster, I will have to let some folks know how helpful you have been to the police in the past. The community needs to understand how you have been instrumental in helping narcotics cut down on the drug trade.

Rooster: Come on, man.

The DC homicide detectives worked Rooster hard every day. By the fifth day, Rooster's resistance was at an all-time low. One minute, he was being pressured daily by DC homicide; and the next minute, he was coping with daily interrogations from Barksdale about his contacts with the detectives from homicide.

DC detectives were slowly penetrating his armor. Rooster had survived in the prostitution business by giving the police information about a variety of crimes. Police knew pimps always had their ears to the ground. They knew what was going down on the streets, and so the detectives were relentless in asserting pressure on the rising guardian of the ladies of the night.

Rooster had ramped up his efforts during the year to shine the spotlight on his competitors, but now those same competitors had a competitive advantage. They were no longer under the microscope. Instead, Rooster was. In the end, the detectives generated enough heat on Rooster to halt his prostitution operation.

Perhaps these thoughts were foremost on Rooster's mind when Barksdale called him one particular day. Barksdale pressed him for any details he had about the murder investigation. Rooster's voice seemed different that day. Barksdale asked him what was wrong. "DC police keep sweating me!" Rooster yelled. "Man, y'all done brought all that heat down on me! I do not know, man. If they call me again, I might have to tell them something, man."

Barksdale's clever interview skills had served him well. In the past, he had employed those skills deliberately, because he needed to know how much information the police knew about him and whether Rooster was prone to caving under pressure. However, it was now clear Rooster had indeed cracked under pressure.

Barksdale calmly told him, "Rooster, don't worry about that, man. They don't have anything. You know what? I forgot to pay you for your services. Meet me at Kenilworth Avenue so that I can take care of you. I know you're hurting for money with them trying to fuck up your business and all."

Rooster made the critical mistake of agreeing to meet with Barksdale. While waiting for him, Rooster squeezed his six-foot-two, 350-pound body into a phone booth and called homicide detective Johnson. He told the detective that Barksdale and Pit Bull had taken Cantor out of the apartment in DC for a few minutes before the murder. He said he heard several shots in the back alley a few minutes later and assumed Barksdale and Pit Bull just killed him.

As the detective probed Rooster for more details, Rooster heard a vehicle drive at a high rate of speed. As he looked in the direction of the sound, he heard tires coming to a screeching halt. He watched in horror as Barksdale emerged from the driver's side with a large gun in his hand. Barksdale was careful to aim while Pit Bull emerged from the car's passenger side holding a handgun at eye level toward Rooster.

Rooster dropped the phone. Detective Johnson kept asking him if he was still there. Rooster tried to squeeze out of the phone booth, but it was too late. He pressed his body back inside the phone booth and pulled the door shut. At that point, all he could do was brace for impact.

Things appeared in slow motion. Glass began to fly. The bullets were coming from both sides of the phone booth. They started penetrating Rooster's body. All Detective Johnson could do was listen in horror to the sounds of gunshots and breaking glass.

*****

Rooster opened his eyes just as he was being loaded into an ambulance. The medics cut his clothes off as they transported him to the hospital. Rooster woke up about an hour later in the emergency room. As he awakened, he saw a doctor reviewing x-rays. Two nurses accompanied him.

The doctor told the nurses, "This is truly amazing."

Rooster asked, "How bad am I, Doc?"

The doctor replied, "Most of the bullets that hit you were lodged in your belly fat."

Rooster was staring at the x-rays just as the doctor said the bullets were lodged in his many layers of fat and failed to penetrate his vital organs. Unbeknownst to Barksdale, Rooster survived the encounter, but Barksdale had achieved his goal of discouraging any further cooperation with the police.

Marty was the second one of Barksdale's casualties I knew of personally. I wondered if he thought about my warnings concerning Barksdale as he lay bleeding in an alley in Washington, DC. My prophecy from years earlier came true. I told Marty that he could not get me killed and that the only person he was going to get killed was himself. As a result, the homicide case went cold. I knew Barksdale had merely whetted his appetite for murder. There were more to come.

*****

I took a black FBI agent named Joey Jackson with me to Fifty-Fifth Avenue to conduct surveillance. I wanted to identify some of Barksdale's other street-level drug dealers. I was in the driver's seat, and the FBI agent was in the passenger seat. I called out the vehicle tag numbers and descriptions of the drug dealers who were hanging out in the area.

We had been on surveillance for about an hour when I asked Agent Jackson if I could see his notes. When I read them, I was impressed by their level of detail. A few minutes later, I pulled out my microcassette recorder and started dictating notes.

The agent looked at me and asked, "What the hell is that?"

I said, "Lesson number one: always have a tape recorder with you to document your surveillance, because it will prevent you from having to look down while all these drug dealers surround you."

"Amusing, man," he said. "Very funny."

I saw a familiar face coming out of the apartment building I was surveilling when I looked around again. It was a street dealer I knew named Manny. Manny, aka Buckwheat, was a very dark-skinned street-level drug dealer. It was not clear whether his involvement in the drug trade was born out of financial necessity, lack of adequate job skills, or the camaraderie he enjoyed with his schoolmates, who were deeply immersed in the drug trade. Nevertheless, I believed that if Buckwheat had been placed in the right environment, he might have been able to free himself from the lifestyle of a street dealer.

I had arrested Buckwheat in uniform for selling drugs and had given him my version of the "I Have a Dream" speech. Buckwheat seemed somewhat intellectually challenged. He was the perfect pawn for the more sophisticated traffickers. Buckwheat also had a second problem: He liked to take out his lifelong frustrations on his girlfriend.

While smoking cigarettes and blowing the smoke in his girl-friend's face, he would frequently say, "There is one thing you can bank on in life, and that is, whenever you fuck up, I am going to kick your ass. So you are going to continue to get these ass-whippings."

Buckwheat was the same kid I used to rouse years earlier for going to school late and not carrying his schoolbooks. He had told me years earlier that selling drugs was all he knew how to do. He went on to say he was not book-smart.

We followed Buckwheat as he drove off. First, I reached into my jacket pocket and pulled out a little disposable Polaroid camera. Then I took a picture of Buckwheat's vehicle. The other agent laughed at me and said he could not believe I was using an instant camera to take a surveillance photograph. He reached into his bag and pulled out a Nikon long-lens camera.

"Lesson number one," he said, "a real detective needs to carry a real camera." Then he started taking multiple shots of Buckwheat's vehicle with his high-tech camera.

"You got my back," I said. "Good deal."

*****

Three days later, Agent Joey Jackson and I were riding down Fifty-Fifth Avenue when we saw Barksdale, Pit Bull, and five of their street-level drug dealers standing in front of Pit Bull's building.

"Joey," I said, "you have got to get this picture. Do you have your high-tech camera with you today?"

"It's right in the back of the van," Joey said.

"Great," I said. "I'm going to pull as close as I can to position you to get a good picture. I pray to God they don't see me."

Joey immediately retreated to the back of the van. Then I started to hear a cranking sound from the back.

"What is that awful noise?" I asked. "Joey, please hurry up!" I looked back and saw Joey setting up a stand with a lens as big as a stage light. "Joey, is that your new camera?"

"Yep."

"Do you have to shoot that out the front window?"

"Yep."

"I hope Jesus saves us both," I said. "And I hope they don't see that thing. They'll probably shoot this van up."

Joey set the camera up in a corner in the back of the van and started taking pictures. Then we eventually made good on our escape. When I saw the developed pictures, I was floating on air. "Damn, boy, you are my new superhero," I said while sifting through the large array of photographs. "Where is your cape, son? You got it going on?" He simply smiled.

The photographs provided an excellent depiction of a crime boss schooling his underlings. Barksdale appeared to be educating Pit Bull and five other street dealers on the ins and outs of drug dealing. I knew the photographs would be a thorn in Barksdale's side when we took him to court. Unbeknownst to Jackson, homicide detectives nicknamed him Agent Joey "Dirty Lens Cap" Jackson because some of his previous pictures were a bit blurry. Nevertheless, he distinguished himself again. As far as I was concerned, the boy was ready to work for National Geographic.

The next day, I met with task force members, and we discussed new information we had recently developed about the case. Homicide detectives developed an informant who told us about the carjackings Barksdale was conducting. He would carjack a vehicle, then replate it with new vehicle identification numbers. The description of one of the vehicles matched the car we found Buckwheat driving.

I had a daily ritual of going through all the police reports in the Quincy Manor area. As I began looking through police reports in the area of Fifty-Fifth Avenue, I discovered that Buckwheat was arrested in his carjacked vehicle with a large quantity of drugs and money a few days after the car was supposed to have been replated. Masquerading as auto theft detectives, homicide detectives of the task force decided to talk to Buckwheat about acquiring the vehicle.

Buckwheat informed the detectives that Pit Bull had sold the car and had given him the title. The detectives were surprised that he seemed to be telling the truth. They thought that for sure, Buckwheat was aware the vehicle was carjacked. However, I was not surprised, because I knew Buckwheat was not the sharpest tool in the shed.

The detectives told Buckwheat the vehicle was stolen. Buckwheat denied that the car was stolen and offered to have Pit Bull write him a letter explaining the circumstances surrounding the sale of the vehicle. Buckwheat called Pit Bull from his residence and informed him of the detectives' assertion.

"I am not going back to jail for nobody," Buckwheat told Pit Bull, but unfortunately, those words would come back to haunt him.

Pitbull replied, "No problem, Buckwheat. I'll get back to you on that."

Pit Bull later wrote Buckwheat a note telling him to stay close to home, because he might need to talk to him later. As soon as Buckwheat walked out of the door, Pit Bull called Barksdale.

"Man," Pitbull said, "what the fuck are we going to do? Buckwheat told the God damn police that I sold him the car. You know that they gave a description that matches both of us for the carjacking of that damn car."

Barksdale's method of problem-solving never changed: murder. "You know what we got to do," he said.

Pit Bull said, "Come on, man. He's been a friend for a long time."

Barksdale hung up the phone. Pit Bull called him back, but he did not pick up the telephone. Instead, Barksdale looked through some photographs and found a picture of Buckwheat. Then he got into his hooptie (beat up old car) allegedly headed toward Southeast Washington, D.C. and he picked up two shooters. Barksdale said, "You guys need some loot? I got a job for you. It will take you no more than an hour, and I will hook you up with an eighth of a kilo." The trio then headed toward Bladensburg, Maryland.

As Barksdale drove down Fifty-Fifth Avenue, he spotted Buckwheat sitting on the steps outside of a building. "There's the nigger right there," he said. The two villains carefully studied Buckwheat. Buckwheat looked relaxed. Unfortunately, he did not know what was lurking in the shadows.

Buckwheat had been sitting in front of his apartment building for about three hours when he observed what appeared to be a woman approaching him. As the person came closer, it seemed the person was a man wearing a wig. As the person drew closer still, Buckwheat determined that the man's facial features were familiar. Then as the person smiled, his identity became clear. Buckwheat realized it was Brandon, one of Barksdale's shooters.

Buckwheat's limited street wit finally kicked in. He made a quick dash for the apartment he shared with his girlfriend. Brandon started slowly following him. As Buckwheat reached his second-floor apartment, he began banging on the door fervently. His girlfriend was using the bathroom in the rear of the apartment and recognized his voice screaming, "Let me in this damn house!"

Fearing for her safety, she remained in the bathroom and contemplated her next course of action. As both the banging and screaming intensified, she made her way to the door. She slowly unlocked the door and pulled it until it hit the chain. As soon as the door was partially opened, Buckwheat pushed his arm through the opening and pulled on his girlfriend. She pulled away and started slamming the door on his arm until he pulled it out of the doorway. Then she locked the door again.

By then, the two shooters had allegedly caught up with Buckwheat. Buckwheat grabbed one of the bandits' guns, determined to survive. The second bandit yelled, "Step back!" then pulled the gun out of Buckwheat's hand. The suspect turned his gun sideways and fired a shot. Buckwheat reached into his pocket and tried to use his key to unlock the door. One villain said, "Oh no, what's wrong, Buckwheat? Your key doesn't work?" Buckwheat realized his worst nightmare had come true.

Earlier that day, something had happened that changed the course of Buckwheat's life. First, he had another argument with his girlfriend, and he reminded her that he could kick her ass anytime he felt like it and that there was nothing she could do about it. Then fearing for her safety, Buckwheat's girlfriend, Veronica, finally summoned the courage to change the locks.

A few seconds after Buckwheat tried to unlock the door to his apartment, only to find that his key did not work, his girlfriend heard a scuffle in the hallway. Buckwheat began to plead. "No, please don't do it!" Then three shots rang out in rapid succession—*bang,*

bang, bang. There was moaning and then praying. "Oh God, please help me." The sound of footsteps outside followed the sound of the entrance door being pushed open.

Veronica reached for the phone to call the police, but there was no dial tone. She was initially perplexed, but then it dawned on her that Buckwheat had refused to give her money to pay the telephone bill. Thus, he had unwittingly cut off his lifeline. Fearing what might await her outside, Veronica stared out the window, wondering what was the best way for her to help her dying boyfriend. Finally, about fifteen minutes later, she asked a man walking outside to call an ambulance for her boyfriend.

Members of the task force, including myself, went to the scene of Buckwheat's homicide and interviewed his girlfriend. The medical examiner had removed Buckwheat's bullet-ridden body away from the scene by the time I arrived. I searched Buckwheat's bedroom; I found a letter from Pit Bull stating he had sold Buckwheat his vehicle.

As I read the letter, I remembered my discussion with Buckwheat regarding Pit Bull. Buckwheat said he dealt with Pit Bull only because Barksdale was crazy. I remembered asking him if Pit Bull could control Barksdale. In the end, Pit Bull tried to deter Buckwheat from being murdered. For the first time, I came face-to-face with my failure to bring the Barksdale organization down. Buckwheat's homicide was not merely any shooting. The reality I preached to a younger Buckwheat was now staring me right in the face. My worst fears for him had come true. It was another gut-wrenching reality check.

The clock was ticking. I wondered how many more bullet-ridden bodies of kids I knew personally we would have to endure seeing before we brought the case to a close. Each interview and each interrogation brought me closer to solving the case. Unfortunately, each interview and each interrogation also brought the people I interviewed closer to danger. Knowing that whatever I did or did not do could determine if someone lived or died was a terrible way to live.

Each step of the investigation added more stress. Buckwheat's girlfriend was now in danger. I feared for her safety. My experience as an investigator in the case was much different from that of the other detectives and agents. I knew most of the people involved for about eight years.

*****

Four years later, Barksdale had enough of whom he referred to as "that bitch-ass, snitching-ass Beaver," so he allegedly gave a hit man a .357 Magnum and sent him to kill Beaver. The hit man's nickname was Ice. Barksdale left the details of the hit to him.

Ice dressed up as a maintenance man and knocked on Beaver's door, but Beaver knew that Barksdale's hit men were very clever. He slowly peeked out of the peephole on the door to his apartment. When he did not recognize the maintenance man, he pretended he was not home. He had been shot once already by Barksdale. Therefore, he was extremely cautious. Cleverly, Beaver survived the encounter.

One month later, Beaver let his guard down, just like Ice knew he would. Ice staked out Beaver's apartment. He finally caught Beaver in the parking lot and plunged a knife into his chest two times and then left him to die, but Beaver survived the stabbing. The next day, Ice met with Barksdale and gave him a rundown of the hit details.

"I gave you a .357 Magnum to take that boy out, but you stabbed the bammer, right? You are a fuckin' moron. Are you sure he is dead?" Barksdale asked.

"I told you. I think so," Ice replied.

"Give me back the gun, you fuckin' idiot. Why would you use a knife to kill somebody when I gave you a big-ass gun to do the job? What the fuck is wrong with you, man?"

Barksdale was constantly experiencing personnel problems. He was a brilliant criminal. However, he surrounded himself with a lot of cheap and unskilled labor. Barksdale snatched the gun out of Ice's hand and pointed the firearm sideways at Ice. "I should shoot you right now for fucking up the job, Ice. You are a fucked-up individual. I hope you know that."

Ice braced for the inevitable trigger pull, but instead, Barksdale straightened up the weapon and switched hands. He changed his shooting posture to a two-hand shooting position, raised the gun at eye level, and closed one eye. "Get the fuck out of here, you incompetent bastard!"

Ice raced to the door, but as he reached for the doorknob, Barksdale said, "Not so fast, you stupid motherfucker. One more thing before I let you go." He put the gun to the back of Ice's head and said, "If I find out that he is not dead, I am going to pay you a visit in that little-ass, hot-ass apartment you live in." Ice then left, and he fell off the radar for a while. He figured he was on the short list to be killed as well. Barksdale made a personnel change. He allegedly hired another hit man named Wayne.

Barksdale, Wayne, Pit Bull, and Barksdale's nephew Xavier discussed the best way to pull off the hit. Barksdale agreed to pay Wayne three thousand dollars for the job. He handed Wayne a shotgun but then grabbed the gun out of Wayne's hand and said, "No fuckups like the last guy." He handed Wayne back the shotgun. Wayne headed to Beaver's apartment.

It was a lovely spring day in April when Wayne arrived at Beaver's apartment complex. Beaver had grown tired of living in captivity, and it was too nice of a day for anyone to stay in the house. The weather was sunny, and it was about seventy degrees. In a few minutes, Beaver exited his apartment building and checked out his surroundings. The coast appeared to be clear. He walked toward a vehicle in the parking lot and heard footsteps behind him. As an added measure of caution, Beaver looked back one more time before opening his car door. Wayne emerged from behind a tree close to Beaver's car. He smiled and racked his shotgun.

Beaver took off running. Unfortunately, he was still recovering from his stab wounds from three weeks earlier. He started breathing heavily and holding the stab wound on his chest. Beaver knew that this time, he did not have the stamina to elude his antagonist. It was Barksdale's third attack on him. Before Beaver could get to the other end of the parking lot, Wayne grabbed him by the back of the shirt. He knocked Beaver on the ground and turned him over to see the look on his face. He told Beaver to get up and try to run. Wayne enjoyed playing with his prey.

Beaver struggled to his feet and tried to run, but Wayne ran in front of him and cut him off. Wayne stepped back a few feet, removed the shotgun from his shoulder, and aimed the shotgun at Beaver's chest. A few neighbors called the police, stating they heard a loud boom on the side of the apartment building. Wayne discharged his 12-gauge Remington into Beaver's chest, blowing him back several feet.

Wayne wanted to earn a few bonus points for the killing. He wanted to give a detailed report to Barksdale. So as Beaver lay there gasping for air while suffering from his previous stab wounds and from the shotgun blast to the chest, Wayne studied the last few minutes of his existence. Blood was trickling down one of Beaver's arms. He started gurgling. Wayne took the butt of the shotgun and started ramming it all over Beaver's head. When the police responded to the scene, they found Beaver's lifeless, pellet-ridden body lying on the grass near the parking lot.

The next day, Barksdale went to Wayne's house to get all the details of the murder. Wayne said, "You should have seen that bammer's facial expression when he saw me with that shotgun. Then the slow-ass bammer tried to run. I dropped that nigger with one blast and busted him in the head as he was coughing and wheezing and shit. Where's my three-thousand-dollar fee?" Barksdale laughed and handed him five hundred dollars. "This is all I get?" Wayne asked.

Barksdale laughed and said, "My estimate was a little off."

Wayne counted the money and left the apartment. He was immune to Beaver's suffering. He felt he had succeeded where others failed. Later, Barksdale and Pit Bull would both be questioned about the murder by the homicide division. Both would claim they knew nothing about it.

Barksdale and his associates were never charged nor convicted of Beaver's murder. Therefore, they should be presumed innocent until proven guilty in a court of law.

*****

In the year 1990, Barksdale walked into his apartment and smiled as he opened the safe in his bedroom closet. However, his smile dissipated when he discovered that the safe had been cleaned out. *Darn,* he thought. Fifty thousand dollars of his hard-earned drug money was gone.

Barksdale called his nephew and said, "Please tell me that you took the money out of the safe."

"I don't know what you are talking about," his nephew said.

Barksdale thought about how someone could have been bold enough to come into his home and take his money. He had to figure it out. He called Pit Bull and told him someone had stolen his money and asked him who he believed had taken it. Pit Bull was unsure. Ultimately, Barksdale surmised that the woman he last dated had set him up. Her ex-boyfriend Robert made his way onto the hit list.

The next day, Barksdale and Pit Bull staked out the soon-to-be victim's car and found him as he drove onto the street. Barksdale had three other people in different vehicles following the proposed victim. Once the proposed victim got into a secluded area, one of the men rear-ended his truck. Then they jumped out and pointed guns at the victim and kidnapped him.

One of the suspects drove the car into a wooded area. Once deep inside the woods, Barksdale directed one of his men to burn up the car to prevent the police from obtaining evidence regarding the murder. Barksdale's men shot the innocent victim in the head and left him for dead. Two weeks later, David, one of the men involved in the murder, was engaged in a shootout with DC Police Department. He was subsequently killed.

*****

Once news of Beaver's murder reached the ear of the assistant state's attorney, who had ratted Beaver out to Barksdale's attorney, he was seen at the bar of the Fraternal Order of Police, drinking heavily. He told the station detective who investigated the shooting that he messed up and probably got Beaver killed.

Once word spread on the street, Barksdale's underlings were gripped with fear. The message was clear: when you crossed Barksdale, you died. This was the beginning of Barksdale's killing spree. Unfortunately, still more was to come.

*****

The time to identify other members of Barksdale's organization came. We identified four new, very motivated seventeen-year-old street dealers who worked for the organization. After all, the friends the Barksdale Gang grew up with were still living there. Pit Bull could have personally supervised the distribution of the drugs, but I learned he used four juveniles to generate sales for him—Gerald, Melvin, Cliff, and Sticks.

Sticks was a very skinny, dark-skinned kid who was mesmerized by the lifestyle of Pit Bull and Barksdale. He was intrigued by every aspect of their being. He had dreams of becoming a large-scale trafficker. He longed to talk trash to the police as eloquently as his leaders did. He desired to have a team of youngins working for him.

He was thrilled by the cat-and-mouse game—being chased by the police. He derived his most excellent satisfaction from bailing out of stolen vehicles and leaving the police in the dust. He told his friends, "Oh, what a feeling it was to escape from the county police!"

He wanted to learn all that he could about the drug trade. He had a remarkably high opinion of himself, because he had surpassed his older brother in the drug trade. His ambition got Pit Bull's attention. He became a very valued employee.

Sticks had one significant personality flaw: he loved to talk about his illegal activities and ill-gotten gains to anyone who would listen. Unfortunately, when you worked for an organization that preferred to be shrouded in secrecy, this personality trait could be hazardous to your health.

Cliff seemed to be an intellectually challenged kid who was way over his head. He lacked street-savvy and common sense. As a result, he was an actual liability to the organization. Cliff's inability to reason well and problem-solve was also a liability to the organization.

Gerald was a very innocent-looking kid who could pass for thirteen although he was seventeen. Unfortunately, he had gotten a taste of the big cheese. Therefore, he no longer had an appetite for a minimum-wage job. He was now making up to five hundred dollars a day in drug sales. The prospect of working at McDonald's like some of his classmates did was unthinkable. Gerald's small stature equated to him being like a tuna surrounded by a large group of hungry sharks. I feared the kid was not going to make it out alive. Concerns about his safety would wear on my mind many nights.

Melvin was a streetwise kid who was a veteran street-level practitioner. He dealt drugs in the town of Upper Marlboro and its surrounding communities for years. Melvin understood the rules of the game. He had enormous potential. He also had a mind of his own. That meant he might aspire to branch out on his own if the time was right. Branching out on his own would not be tolerated by management, however.

When the Safe Streets Task Force members reviewed all the open murders and shootings on their books, I wondered how many of them were kids who hung out in the Quincy Manor area who had fallen prey to Barksdale's wrath. Not much later, we received a call from a DC police regarding a resident from Prince George's County who was killed in Southeast Washington.

*****

As the weeks and years passed, I kept reminding Cantor of our conversation every time I saw him. Cantor rose through the ranks of the organization. Therefore, he was no longer seen on street corners; instead, he was tasked with picking up money and delivering drugs to street-level dealers. Within one month from the start of my surveillance, I obtained a search warrant for the number two guy's apartment. Three or four days later, we were on our way to raid the apartment.

I exited the van with the SWAT team. We entered the building and tiptoed up to the third floor. The SWAT team looked more like military commandos than police officers. They were wearing helmets and eye protection, and a few were toting their machine guns.

After we reached the third floor, I pointed to the apartment. The SWAT team broke down the apartment door and stormed inside, yelling, "County police search warrant." Then there was an explosion. I recognized it as the sound of a flash-bang, a device SWAT used to disorient a suspect. The team leader gave the all-clear, and members of the task force entered the apartment and handcuffed a kid named Gerald. To my surprise, only one person was in the apartment: Gerald Jr. Ironically, his father, Gerald Sr., had called me several times over the previous two months. He was seeking advice on how to get his son out of the drug trade and away from Pit Bull.

Gerald was sitting on the bedroom floor, handcuffed. He was visibly shaken. Homicide detective Baird seized the opportunity to interrogate the kid. He walked into the bedroom with the kid and closed the door. About thirty minutes later, he came out of the bedroom, clearly frustrated that he could not extract any information from the kid.

"Did you get anything useful out of him?" I asked. He shook his head. I noticed that two FBI agents' eyes were fixated on our interaction, so I looked Detective Baird in the eyes and said, "He's not talking because he's more afraid of them than he is of us." Later, I brought the suspect into the interrogation room. Detective Baird insisted on taking the first crack at the interrogation. After all, he was homicide, and homicide knew everything there was to know about interrogation. Yeah, right!

Baird took the suspect into the interrogation room. He gleefully emerged about one hour later, saying, "Man, he is telling me everything. He is the main man. I knew I could break him!" I was bewildered that he thought the statement was good. If looks could kill, he would have been immediately destroyed. Our two assigned FBI agents looked intensely at the impending showdown between whom they referred to as the local guys. I could no longer contain my anger. I took the half-hearted and meaningless confession and threw it in Detective Baird's face, leaving all three of them in shock.

There was a misconception about what skills narcotics investigators had, because so much of what we did was unknown to the rest of the police department. Detective Baird soon discovered that he was not the only person who was skilled in interrogation. As a narcotics detective, I had mastered the art of flipping people. It was exceedingly difficult to do, because people in the hood were brainwashed not to cooperate with the police. I also had intimate knowledge about the organization's thinking, because I had arrested the top two people in the organization; and because I had spoken to them many times over the years, I had the men's backstory as well.

I opened the door of the interrogation room swiftly and quickly made contact with the suspect and said, "Look, man, my name is Detective Hicks, and I am only going to be here for a few seconds. What you decide here today is a matter of life and death. I am not Mr. Potato Head. I am going to warn you now that I do not want to hear that half-hearted crap that you gave that boy from Homicide. You are going to tell me what I want to hear. I want the truth, the whole truth, and nothing but the truth. If you don't give me that, you are going to be on your own. Save that stuff for them bammers down on Fifty-Fifth Avenue.

"I am going to give it to you quickly and simply. The people you work for are going to assume that you are down here snitching. Whether you are informing or not does not matter. They are not going to give you a chance to explain what happened. They are going to lure you somewhere and blow your head off.

"Nobody is going to be able to save you, son. You are just a dead man walking. You know what? I think that I am boring you. I want you to know, I am the only person in this entire world that can help you, and I am about to walk out that door."

I began walking out the door, but then I heard Gerald say, "Please don't leave, sir."

I turned around slowly, pointed at him, and said, "Who is the only person in this world who can help you?"

Gerald finally broke down. Tears began pouring down his face. He replied, "Only you can, sir!"

I thought, *What a terrible position for a seventeen-year-old.* It was agonizing as hell for me! His dad had been calling me back at narcotics asking me to help dislodge his son from Pit Bull's clutches. He had no idea at the time that I was the lead investigator on the case. I had spent hours over the past few months trying to explain how to convince his son to leave Pit Bull's apartment. But, of course, to no avail.

Fear fluttered in my stomach. Terror stabbed his father's heart while fear engulfed his son's body down to the soles of his shoes. I knew I would have the kid's blood on my hands if I had even the slightest miscalculation in judgment. I did not want his son's death nor his father's eternal heartbreak on my conscience.

My problem was, I had a soft spot for teenage kids. They were my youngest brother's age. I wanted to see them get out of the drug life; but the allure of large sums of cash, expensive cars, and beautiful women was magnetizing for these young men. This made the teenagers pawns in a risky game. Drug dealers would tell the young men they could get out of jail immediately by being released to their parents because they were juveniles, but the reality was much different.

Judges would not recommend kids who were sixteen and younger and who had drug distribution cases to remain in juvenile court. Instead, they ruled that there was no rehabilitation in the juvenile justice system for drug dealers. That meant many kids were charged and sentenced in the adult court. It also meant they were going to jail—real jail—and possibly do time in the prison.

After I finished my interrogation, I sat down at the interrogation table with Gerald, put my hand on his shoulder, and said, "You made the right decision, son. Now that you are on the right team, I'm going to do everything I can to help you." I shared with him that his father had called me several times to get him out of the gang.

When I took Gerald to meet his father at the station, I looked Gerald's father straight in the eyes and said, "What I am about to tell you is a matter of life and death. Your son was arrested in an apartment rented by an extremely dangerous man. He is going to assume your son provided us with information. Your son is probably on a list of people that Barksdale wants to eliminate.

"Please keep your son out of harm's way by any means necessary. If this were my son, I would be sending him to a relative's house out of town." Then I looked at Gerald and said, "Please do not go anywhere near that apartment, and please do not communicate with anyone associated with Pit Bull." After they left the station, I walked to the bathroom at the criminal investigations division. I stared at myself in the mirror.

Finally, I lost it. I yelled. "I don't need this scrap in my life! Crap in life." I rinsed my face with water. I grabbed some paper towels, dried my hands, and balled up the paper. Finally, I yelled, "Damn it!" I slammed the balled-up paper against the wall. I calmly picked up the discarded paper and slowly put it into the trash can. I looked back at myself in the mirror as if something had changed. Nothing had. The nightmare was real. I was being tortured emotionally. I knew that my mission was to save the kid from calamity. How I was going to accomplish my task remained a mystery to me. I took a deep breath and headed back into the office.

About one month later, FBI agent Kozlowski and I submitted our wiretap affidavit to the FBI's legal adviser. We were asking for permission to intercept phone calls at Barksdale's and Pit Bull's homes. It was the first step in getting approval before taking the wiretap affidavit to the attorney general. Agent Kozlowski and I sat down as the legal eagle carefully reviewed our one-hundred-page wiretap affidavit. He kept tapping his pen on the binder as he read through the pages. While he read the affidavit, we heard him say, "Particularly good. Good. Okay."

Finally, he put down the book containing the affidavit. He asked us an overly critical question: Did we have any specific information about Barksdale and Pit Bull using their telephones to sell drugs? We confessed that we did not. He shut the book and told us to come back when we had more information.

Agent Kozlowski was furious. He told me he would directly request the Department of Justice's legal adviser. "Don't you think this guy knows the other big shot that just reviewed it?" I asked. "I would imagine they conferred with each other about these matters." Kozlowski said he did not care. As soon as we arrived at the DOJ legal adviser's office, he said, "I heard there are some problems with this affidavit." I resisted the urge to look at Kozlowski to say, "I told you so."

We left the legal adviser's office with our tails between our legs. I did not have to be an FBI agent or a lawyer to know what would happen. I had learned about protocol and politics. I suggested we do a state wiretap affidavit, because for that, there was no requirement to have specific evidence about the telephone use. However, in the state affidavit for a wiretap, I could articulate that the suspects' phone usage to conduct illicit activity could be inferred based on my experience and training. Agent Kozlowski agreed, and we set out to get authorization through the state of Maryland to intercept the phone calls.

The investigation was no longer shrouded in secrecy. We had to rely on local prosecutors to get the tools we needed to complete the investigation. Once the affidavit was completed, a prosecutor named Linda, a friend of Sergeant Stryker, rode with us to get it signed by the state's attorney.

Out of the blue and without discussing any concerns she might have had; she dialed the chief of detectives from her cell phone. She told him I did not have enough experience to get the wiretap affidavit signed. Linda's actions were suspicious. She created the perfect storm to derail the months of work I put into the case. I wondered if the call would result in Barksdale getting another get out of jail free card. I wondered if justice would again be subverted for the Barksdale Organization.

I found myself in an awful dilemma. I did not want to give Linda any ammunition to complain about me to my superiors. I grabbed my head and began massaging my temples. Agent Stone glanced at me through the corner of his eyes. I felt compelled to fight for justice for people in the community affected by Barksdale and his cohorts. I tried desperately to conquer my frustration, but I felt my temperature continue to rise. I think that Stone sensed that I was about to blow. I realized that I had to revert to my training. It was a situation described by church folks where "Extra Grace (EG)" was required. I seemed to be working in an environment full of contradictions.

Stone, the lead FBI agent, was driving but had heard the entire conversation. He pulled the car over, and to my shock and absolute delight, he cursed Linda out. He told her she had no right to interfere with all the work we had done on the case. Linda went silent. I turned around and looked at her to take delight in the agony of her defeat.

What she did not know at that time was, the chief of detectives was my former patrol lieutenant. He held me in such high regard that he gave me a brand-new patrol car when I was still a private. The patrol car was my reward for making so many arrests while I was in uniform. He knew my work ethic and my uncompromising commitment to drug enforcement. He used to tease me about being a hound for narcotics.

Therefore, my saboteur's attempt to remove me from the case faced significant opposition from both ends of the spectrum. The agents had gotten a glimpse of the challenges I faced in the police department. Linda's scheme to sabotage me and remove me reached the ears of FBI agents. A female FBI agent confided in me that she overheard Sergeant Stryker tell a DEA agent not to share information with me on one of my cases.

Linda's and Sergeant Stryker's efforts to help my demise on the task force had the opposite effect. As a result of their misguided attempts, the FBI gave me a desk at their office. Therefore, I had an office in narcotics, in homicide, and at the FBI. I also had four other police officers assigned to me to help me with the case. Not bad for someone who was not even a police supervisor.

We were able to obtain authorization to tap the telephones at Barksdale's and Pit Bull's residences, and no sooner had we plugged into Pit Bull's phone, then I heard Pit Bull answer it. The person on the other end of the line asked, "Is any dope there for sale?" I was shocked by the openness with which Pit Bull and his client discussed the drug operation. Most drug dealers talked about drugs in code. Dealers rarely used the actual word in place of street terms for *drugs* over the phone. I knew we were in for a treat.

A few hours later, we intercepted a call that caused me some concerns. Pit Bull was on the phone with the number one guy,

Barksdale. He told him that he had spoken to Gerald and that Gerald denied telling the police anything. Pit Bull believed Gerald was lying. I asked another veteran homicide detective to come with me down to Fifty-Fifth Avenue to see the street operation. The operation had slowed down after we raided their apartment.

When I got within half a block of Pit Bull's apartment, I could not believe my eyes.

"Is that Gerald?" I asked the homicide detective sitting next to me.

"I'll be damned," he said.

I drove up next to Gerald and asked, "Gerald, do you remember our conversation? Is this your death wish?" I told Gerald to put his hands behind his back; he was under arrest for selling drugs. A couple of days earlier, I had sent an undercover officer to buy from Gerald, but I never charged him with the case. This time, I took him into custody. Then I contacted the assistant state's attorney. I asked her if she could get Gerald into a facility that was not in Prince George's County to prevent him from getting killed. She and her colleagues were able to help pull some strings, and they brought him into a tiny jail in a neighboring county.

I then called Gerald's father and let him know what was going on, but I could not tell him a call was intercepted between Pit Bull and Barksdale that indicated Pit Bull believed Gerald was lying. That essentially facilitated a death warrant for Gerald. Still, I was relieved to tell his father that he was safely off the streets and that he was reasonably safe in a jail in a small town. I spent about thirty minutes talking to Gerald's father on the phone. I listened to him pour his heart out. Gerald was taking his father through hell. Furthermore, his father's safety could also be in jeopardy because of his son's misguided behavior.

One week from the date when we started the wiretap on Barksdale's and Pit Bull's phones, we intercepted a phone call between Barksdale's two street-level dealers, Brandon George and Sterling White, after Annapolis City police stopped them. They both bailed out of the vehicle, but Brandon was the only person apprehended. The police detained Sterling White but then released him. After being released, he immediately walked a block to the stash house: the house of Barksdale's girlfriend. We listened intently to White's call to Barksdale.

"Hey, man, you will not believe what just happened," White said. "We got stopped by the police and bailed out of the car. You will not believe what Brandon did. He threw the drugs right in front of the police. I waited until I was around the corner before I threw mine."

Barksdale asked, "How much did he have?"

White said, "It was a big bag." He then told Barksdale that he gave the police his name and that the police let him go after.

Barksdale asked, "Did you give the police the correct name?"

"Yeah," White replied.

"What the fuck, man! I taught you better than that, man! What the fuck, man. You knuckleheads don't pay attention to shit. Now, this shit is going to cost me money."

Barksdale instantly went into problem-solving mode. He began dialing numerous bail bond agents. He then started calling other people, complaining that Brandon was not selling one pebble of crack when he got caught. Finally, he vented that Brandon was an underachiever.

The following week, Barksdale was determined to get the street-level drug operation back into full force. He was on a mission as he cruised down the streets of Annapolis, Maryland, driving a beat-up dark-brown four-door Volvo. He had three of his pharmaceutical salesmen riding with him. That caught the attention of an alert Anne Arundel patrol officer.

The replacements followed their training; they quickly bailed out of the vehicle and escaped. Barksdale remained in the car. He wasted no time asserting his rights and creating a distraction. With his pit bull sitting on his lap, he asked, "What are you pulling me over for?" The officer was stunned by Barksdale's arrogance. Then finally, he mentioned the fact that three men had just bailed out of Barksdale's car. "What the F that got to do with me?" Barksdale asserted. "I did not run."

He threatened to sic his dog on the officer, but his plan backfired. The officer arrested him for disorderly conduct and some minor traffic violations. Barksdale gave the officer a false name: Brandon Falls. The astute officer asked for the name of someone who could verify his name. He gave Pit Bull's name. We learned about the interaction between Officer Swanson and Pit Bull when we intercepted a phone call between the two men.

Swanson asked Pit Bull to describe Barksdale and to identify the person he had under arrest. "I have a guy under arrest who says he is a close friend of yours. He is about six foot four. He says you all have been best friends since high school. Can you tell me his name?" Officer Swanson asked. Crickets. The phone was silent for a few seconds.

"Ah, Marty Ball?" Pit Bull asked.

"Thank you, sir," Officer Swanson said and then hung up the telephone.

Pit Bull failed the test. Barksdale did not give the officer the name Marty Ball. Then his girlfriend came to the station and brought a Virginia driver's license in the name of Melvin Blevins. The name was also different from the name Barksdale had given to the police. The officer ran Barksdale's fingerprints and discovered his true identity.

CHAPTER 73

DRIVING WHILE BLACK
PHASE 1

I knew I would be tested in many ways as I embarked on my mission to bring the Barksdale Gang to justice. But first, I needed to gauge the intensity of Barksdale's street operation, so I drove my undercover vehicle down to Fifty-Third Place and Quincy Street, where I saw a Bladensburg police officer sitting in his car, staring at me. I made sure I came to a complete stop, signaled, and made a left-hand turn. The officer followed me. He followed me for about half a block before he pulled me over. I knew the officer was out of his jurisdiction when he initiated the stop because the area was my beat when I was a patrol officer.

The officer walked over to my car and asked for my driver's license and registration. When he approached me, I already had my hands on the steering wheel, and my police badge and ID card were in my hand. I was hot. I wanted to know why he was pulling me over for absolutely no reason. Before I handed the officer my ID, I told him I was a county police officer and wanted to know why I was being stopped. Instead, the officer began yelling at me, ordering me to get out of the car with my hands up.

The officer looked terrified. "What is wrong with you? Why are you shaking so badly?" I asked. He ordered me to put my hands on the hood of my car. He began searching me, but he missed the weapon in my shoulder holster. I was wearing a black Miami hoodie at the time and was perplexed that he did not feel my gun. He could barely hold the radio in his hand from his nervousness as he called for backup.

Two other Bladensburg police officers soon arrived on the scene. One burly white police officer told me it was in my best interest to stand still. The second police officer was a white female with whom I worked the streets in the past. I had backed her up many days in the town. Now, she was standing there as if she did not even know me.

I said, "Rebecca, I cannot believe you are just standing there, not even telling this man who I am."

She told me, "You better watch yourself, pal. I'd do exactly what the officer tells you to do."

I asked the officer and his two backup officers why I was stopped. No one seemed to have an answer. They began huddling together and talking. The officer who stopped me began searching my car. He removed my police wallet, which contained my badge and police identification card. He ran a warrant check on me for my police ID.

I protested, saying they jeopardized my safety by broadcasting my personal information. Every drug dealer and brother could have heard it. The burly white officer said, "Let me break this down to you, homeboy. Ninety percent of the people who commit crimes in this county are black. Therefore, ninety percent of the people we stop are black." I told him his statistics were bogus and asked for the source of that information.

The initial officer who stopped me called on his radio and asked for a county police supervisor. County police lieutenant Manny and an acting sergeant showed up a few minutes later. They spoke to the officer, pulled me aside, and asked me what was going on. I explained that the officer pulled me over for no reason and that the officers were out of their jurisdiction. I also let them know they still had not provided a rationale for pulling me over.

About three minutes later, I heard the dispatcher come over the radio. She said the tags did not belong to my car. I said, "Even if that is true, you do not have ESP. You could not have known that forty-five minutes ago when you pulled me over. This is my sergeant's car, and I had no idea the tags did not belong to the car."

Lieutenant Manny said, "Go ahead and leave."

I said, "I did not have to pull over to begin with."

The following day, I arrived at my desk at the FBI office at about nine o'clock. Before I could put my briefcase down, I received a call from the lieutenant, who wanted to see me immediately in his office. When I entered his office, the lieutenant told me he had a Bladensburg city police officer complaint. To my surprise, he seemed concerned.

I explained all the events surrounding my traffic stop in great detail, including the most devastating part of having my address discussed over the radio for every drug dealer and their brother to hear. I thought that would get the incredibly quiet and mellow lieutenant's dander up. However, I got a much different reaction.

"Maurice, I would have stopped you too," the lieutenant said.

"For what, sir?" I replied.

"I would have stopped you too," he repeated.

The lieutenant never explained why he would have stopped me; instead, he said he had concerns about my driving through drug areas and asserting my rights. "As a result," he said, "you are probably going to be pulled over a lot more. I am concerned about how you are going to react next time when the police stop you." I explained that if I were in the wrong, I would shut my mouth and be the humblest person on the face of the earth. Conversely, if I were stopped again for no reason, I would assert my rights again.

I guessed that answer was not satisfying, because I was called to the captain's office later in the day. By then, I had made a formal complaint against the Bladensburg police officer. I was naive enough to believe that the captain would be more empathetic to what I experienced. I was wrong again. The captain told me that he had concerns about how I handled the situation in Bladensburg and that the officer who stopped me was contemplating making a formal complaint against me.

The captain said, "You're on the sergeant's list, aren't you?"

I said, "Yes, I am."

The captain responded by saying, "You know, if they make a formal complaint about you, it will put your promotion in abeyance, which will prevent you from getting promoted until the investigation is over." He looked at me intensely, contemplating the best way to deal with the situation.

"You know what, sir? If being black is a crime, I will do the time. I am not backing down from my complaint."

He said, "Okay."

I figured that the situation presented an excellent opportunity for my commanders to take me out of homicide. Even better, they could use the complaint to justify taking me off the Safe Streets Task Force. So it was a win for my commanders, and it was a win for the Bladensburg police officers. There would be significant losers in this situation. Members of the community were stakeholders in the dangerous game of chance associated with dismantling the Barksdale Gang.

Nevertheless, even after my commanders recommended that the union president call me to convince me to drop the investigation, I held my ground. Years later, I would talk to a citizen who was almost in tears when he told me nearly the same story about the same officer who had stopped me. The officer treated him even worse, to the point where the man appeared devastated about the entire encounter.

Their bluff did not work, and they did not make a complaint against me. Instead, my commanders had a different strategy: they looked for a sellout to assist in the investigation. I remembered meeting with their lead investigator and a black investigator from a different town's police department. I knew that the Bladensburg lieutenant had asked the black investigator to be part of the investigation to be their token brother, aka token black man. His presence was supposed to give legitimacy to the investigation and to demonstrate that there was no racial bias.

At the beginning of the interview, their investigative lieutenant introduced me to the black man assisting with the investigation. The black detective proudly said he and the Bladensburg lieutenant had been friends for twenty years. I said, "Now I know why you are here, sir. You are here to clear their boy."

The detective asked me if I was offended as a citizen or as a black man. I thought that was the stupidest question he could have ever asked me. This was not about what offended me; this was about the officer's misuse of police power by pulling me over for no reason. It was also a matter of not extending me courtesy as a police officer.

I knew the outcome of the investigation from the moment I sat down in the police station. About two months later, a letter came that stated that the officer was justified in his stop and that he and the other officers had a right to search my car. In the end, there was no apology from anybody in their department. There was no acknowledgment of the lack of professional courtesy, nor was there any acknowledgment of the human decency not afforded to me.

The incident made me wonder whether black citizens were ever treated fairly under the authority of police officers. It was a fake investigation from the very beginning. They were little wannabe cowboys.

CHAPTER 74

DRIVING WHILE BLACK
PHASE 2

About two weeks later, I was conducting surveillance for the Barksdale case, sitting in the rear of the Briggs Chaney shopping center. It was the location of Pit Bull's new apartment. I had been sitting there no more than fifteen minutes when I saw a white man in his forties drive past me, giving me the evil eye. I figured he was a police officer. The location was in Montgomery County, a place where I did not know any other police officers. When the man spun around a second time and began staring at me again, I knew he was the police.

I headed out of the shopping center. Two unmarked units followed me. A few seconds later, the marked police car put his lights on and pulled me over. The officer approached my car. He was a young black officer in his early twenties. Identifying myself as a police officer, I showed him my badge and my police identification card.

I also showed him my FBI credentials. I explained to him that I was on a stakeout for a federal case. He looked in my car and observed my binoculars and my microcassette recorder. He shook my hand and told me to be safe. I drove off.

About half a mile down the road, I got pulled over again by the same white officer who initially saw me in the shopping center. When he walked over to my car, I explained that I had already been pulled over and that the officer checked me out and let me go.

"Now, I'm going to check you out," he said.

"Okay, sir," I said. "I understand. This is your jurisdiction. So what is the damn problem?" The brother checked me out and verified my credentials. "What else do you want from me?" I asked.

"Well," he replied, "we've had a lot of robberies in the area."

"Think about it, man," I told the officer. "If I were casing the joint, why would I do it from the back of a shopping center? If you noticed, my eyes were focused on the apartments behind the shopping center. Does that seem like someone who was casing the joint?"

He said, "Okay, man. I'm sorry."

"Even after I showed you my local and federal credentials, you still had it stuck in your mind because I'm black that I am still a criminal. Have a good day, sir!" I said.

At that point, my comrades in blue were becoming my most significant impediment to investigating the case. I sat there for a second, hoping some other Montgomery County police officer would not pull me over. At that moment, I reflected on my grandfather's prophecy that I would never be at peace as a black police officer. That was the irony of being a black police detective.

CHAPTER 75

DRIVING WHILE BLACK PHASE 3

I needed a reprieve from the hustle and bustle of working on the Barksdale case, so I drove my father-in-law, son, and wife to pick up our daughter in Martinsburg, West Virginia. The drive was easy with minimal traffic. I picked up our daughter and drove the family back toward Maryland. I noticed an orange racecar with 01 written on it passing me about one hundred miles per hour. I looked ahead and saw a Maryland state trooper working radar ahead. I looked at my father-in-law and said, "This boy is a trooper's delight. He's going to light that boy up and charge him with reckless driving." We were shocked that the trooper watched him but did not pull the vehicle over.

I continued to my destination, being careful not to exceed the speed limit. Then I looked in my rearview mirror and noticed that the state trooper was directly behind me. He followed my car for about ten miles. As soon as I signaled to get on I-270 south toward Washington, DC, the trooper turned on his lights and siren and pulled me over.

The trooper politely asked me where I was coming from and where I was heading. He wanted to know how long I was in West Virginia and for what purpose. I cooperated fully and answered all his questions. Then it dawned on me that he asked me questions to determine if I was a drug trafficker. I identified myself as a police officer and asked why he followed me for so long and pulled me over when I had been observing the speed limit. His answer took me by surprise. He admitted he was racially profiling me.

My mouth dropped. I told him I appreciated his honesty. However, I asked what facts had led him to profile a man with his family in the car. The trooper was honest again. He said he only saw me and my father-in-law. He did not see my wife and kids in the back seat. I sat in my car for a few minutes, holding the steering wheel, staring into space. I needed to build up the strength to control my anger.

My wife touched me on the shoulder. "Are you okay?" she asked.

"I am just trying to find a way to cope. I will be okay in a few minutes," I replied.

My father-in-law looked bewildered. "Take your time, son. I know it hurts," he said.

I wondered what the hell was going on in the law enforcement community. Did the police believe that only black people trafficked drugs? At one point, the most significant impediment to investigating the Barksdale Gang was not the gang's activities; it was the boys in blue. Nevertheless, I had to suck it up and move on. There was no time for a pity party. Lives were on the line. I had to put my big boy pants on and get back on the saddle. Oh well, that was the life of an officer of color.

I did not file a complaint against the trooper because I appreciated his honesty. However, the incident was still frustrating to me. The concept of white privilege was becoming front and center in my life regularly. It was the third time I was stopped while working the Barksdale case. The hunter had now become the hunted. I was overexposed to the negative experiences other law-abiding black men experienced daily. It was frustrating, humiliating, and disruptive. Most importantly, it was unfair.

Before leaving the scene, the trooper asked me what unit I worked for within the police department. I told the trooper I was a narcotics detective. He told me he aspired to be a narcotics detective. We all made mistakes. However, I hoped the trooper would learn from his experience.

CHAPTER 76

~~~~~

THE INVESTIGATION
DAY 7

We were anxious for something to happen. The surveillance team had been tailing Barksdale and his posse for about three and a half hours when Barksdale began blowing through red lights. He had work to do. He had a cadre of his most trusted villains, which meant he was looking for trouble. Barksdale was a streetwise drug dealer. He knew he had to clean himself up before engaging in any criminal activity. He succeeded in his endeavor.

I threw a hissy fit when I received word that the surveillance team had lost Barksdale and his gang. "What the hell?" I yelled after the discovery. I knew something big was going down. The surveillance team's nonchalant attitude about the situation only fueled my frustration. It happened to the best of us, but the timing was terrible. Typically, if an investigator lost a suspect, it occurred within the first few minutes. Barksdale was riding that deep for a reason.

Later, Barksdale was back on the telephone again. Fortunately for us, he wanted to discuss how he and his gang exercised dominion over their competition. But first, he needed to ensure that everyone took precautions to divest themselves of any evidence that might link them to whatever crime they committed, so he told Pit Bull, "Wash those clothes good." And then he said, "Somebody followed the shit out of me all day."

Pit Bull brushed Barksdale's comments off. Instead, he called several of Barksdale's associates. "Your boy is paranoid," he said. It reminded me of when Scarface's most trusted associate, Mano, brushed off his concerns about a surveillance van near their home. Mano said that they were not the only drug dealers on their street. Scarface replied, "That is a piss-poor attitude for someone who is the head of security." Barksdale's main henchmen had the same piss-poor attitude. Most drug dealers knew that when the police spent a lot of time following them, they considered them big fish.

We were perplexed about what was going on. The day after the surveillance team lost track of Barksdale, we received a break in the case. Barksdale frustrated our efforts to obtain incriminating evidence by phone. He used a variety of names when he talked on the phone, and he spoke in code. We wondered if he was as disciplined when discussing these same matters in person.

Barksdale certainly had a lot to talk about. His street-level operation consisted primarily of four to five sixteen- and seventeen-year-old kids whose main goal was chasing girls. They lacked the work ethic and commitment Barksdale had when he sold drugs on the street. He needed kids who could move products and think on their feet.

Cliff always seemed to have an excuse for not selling his portion of the cocaine. He expressed his frustration to Pit Bull about being caught and possibly being beaten by the county police. Pit Bull tolerated Cliff's actions, but they were unacceptable to Barksdale, so Barksdale decided an old-fashioned ass-whipping was the tool necessary to inspire Cliff.

Barksdale decided to personally meet with Cliff to pick up the proceeds for that day's drug sales. Once again, Cliff came up short. Barksdale's six-foot-four body frame towered over Cliff, who was five foot four. Barksdale gritted his teeth and poked Cliff on the forehead at the onset of the counseling session. He struggled to control his anger. A few seconds later, a loud slapping sound echoed off the building. "You stupid little motherfucker," Barksdale yelled. *Pow!* Barksdale slapped Cliff with everything he had. The slap caught Cliff off guard, and before he could recover from the first blow, *pow* again!

Barksdale followed up with a backhand slap to the other side of Cliff's face. He deemed it necessary to slap the taste out of Cliff's mouth, because the discipline was commensurate with the level of disrespect he felt. Cliff's fear of selling drugs in his neighborhood in Upper Marlboro was too much for Barksdale to bear. Cliff was working in an outpost. It was considered a dream job. I felt sorry for Cliff. I knew that the young man just did not have the skills to be an effective drug dealer.

It was out of character for Barksdale to deal directly with the lower echelon of his organization. It was akin to a general slapping one of his privates. Barksdale did not realize—or did not care—that Cliff may have had a learning disability. Moreover, Cliff lacked the courage and skill necessary to perform the job. Everyone knew selling drugs in Prince George's County came with risks, which everyone else was willing to take.

Barksdale began calling his associates to tell them how macho he was by disciplining Cliff. He was so fired up after slapping Cliff that he continued his conversation with Pit Bull when he called the Motor Vehicle Administration and was put on hold.

"All the little assholes want to do is malinger and chase fuckin' women," Barksdale told Pitbull. "Man, you do not know how thankful I am that I can always depend on you. I don't know what I would do if you started chasing women."

"You do not have to ever worry about me," Pit Bull replied, "because I don't fuck with them women." Pit Bull was gay. At least Barksdale was an equal opportunity employer.

Finally, Barksdale made an error. I was fuming when I heard Barksdale bragging about how he slipped away from the FBI surveillance team. He eluded the police long enough to exact revenge on his competition. According to Barksdale's intercepted phone call, he drove past a drug area in Annapolis, Maryland, that he controlled and noticed several other people working his corner. Barksdale gave one of them the evil eye. Just about everyone who knew Barksdale's reputation knew the evil eye meant that an attack was imminent.

To Barksdale's delight, the rival drug dealer motioned to him and signified that he was carrying a weapon. Barksdale backed up his vehicle and smiled. "You are playing with yours, but I am real with my shit," he said. The gesture by Barksdale's competitor was just what Barksdale longed for. It was a reason to annihilate his competition.

Barksdale returned later that day with a car full of his posse, and they were all strapped (carrying weapons). Like a squad leader in an infantry unit, Barksdale sought to launch the attack with a superior weapon, setting the firefight stage. He figured that once the leader was taken out, his soldiers would flee. The situation presented an excellent opportunity for Barksdale's team to show their courage under fire.

Barksdale handed the shotgun to Sticks, the youngest member of the posse. He then directed Sticks to take out the posse with the shotgun while they laid cover fire. At the last minute, Barksdale changed his mind. He believed he needed to be the one who initiated the firefight. He snatched the shotgun back from Sticks. Then there was a loud sound. *Bam!* The shotgun discharged, striking Barksdale's foot. Barksdale quickly retreated and limped back to his vehicle. "Do not just stand there. Start shooting!" he exclaimed. The posse lifted their guns and began shooting at the rival gang. When the smoke settled, the rival gang escaped unharmed.

"You fuckin' idiots!" Barksdale yelled. "You all embarrassed the fuck out of me." Barksdale removed his sock and inspected his gunshot wound. "Get me the fuck out of here before they come back with their gats!" He was embarrassed that his foot soldiers did not have the common sense to engage the enemy when he went down. The mistake was another indication that personnel changes were in order.

We obtained enough information to obtain eight search warrants relating to the Barksdale Gang. First, however, we needed to identify Barksdale's supplier before we shut the operation down. A glimmer of hope ignited our efforts when we noticed that Barksdale had paged a phone number in New York City. We knew his supplier lived in New York. A few minutes later, he received a callback from an Asian man named Chang. When Barksdale started talking in code, we knew he was talking to his supplier.

"You got one of those joints for me?" Barksdale asked.

Chang became very excited. "Yes, yes, yes," he said. "It is ready for you to pick up."

A few minutes later, one of Barksdale's henchmen called his girl-friend and said, "Get your baby and pack your bag. We have some business to take care of in New York."

Members of the task force inferred that Barksdale was going to New York. The FBI was supposed to have a surveillance team ready to go. I sat down with the agent involved in the case and the assistant special agent in charge (ASAC) of the office to discuss updates. The timing was perfect.

I asked the ASAC who would be involved in the surveillance of Brandon during his trip to New York. He said, "Nobody," and continued with the meeting. At the end of the session, he asked, "That was a good meeting, wasn't it?" I tried my best to contain my anger, which had been festering the entire span of the forty-five-minute meeting.

The ASAC could see the anger on my face. "What?" he asked.

I had to let it out. "This is bullcrap, man! You were all supposed to have this covered. Instead, you all have this carefree attitude about the whole thing. That was the most important time for you all to be on point. You all are dropping the ball. Suppose they get caught in another jurisdiction? Suppose they get robbed? Our whole case will be in jeopardy," I said.

"Don't get mad at us," the ASAC replied.

"By the way, we spend more time meeting than working," I told him. "We have meetings to have meetings. You all seem to be happiest when you all are meeting."

"Well, damn, Maurice," he said, "excuse us."

I had reasons for being angry. Lives were on the line. I worked hard to gain the trust of the people in the community who shared information about the Barksdale Gang. I promised their safety. By that time, I had amassed a small army of informants. I had just about every person I could muster involved in the intelligence loop. They gathered information from numerous locations occupied by the Barksdale Gang. I had everyone from landscapers, grocers, barbers, and maintenance personnel gathering intelligence on the Barksdale Gang. I left no stone unturned.

I wondered whether I went overboard with the ASAC. I had a bad habit of letting things fester and then blow up. I was known for going from zero to one hundred when I was agitated or provoked. Even though I was a tranquil person, my coworkers referred to me as the quiet storm. My good friend Hunter often said I turned into a pit bull when I was provoked. Luckily for me, the ASAC was a former NYPD detective. He was a cool white guy with a lot of swag. He knew what it was like to be a passionate local detective. He laughed the whole thing off.

Barksdale called Pit Bull's apartment and identified himself with the fake name Bono. He talked with Pit Bull for a while and then hung up. Later, when he tried to reach Pit Bull again, he received a busy signal. That meant Sticks was using both lines. Barksdale was at his wit's end. Everything seemed to be going wrong. On top of that, he was being followed by people he did not recognize.

Pit Bull had a nonchalant attitude about Barksdale's surveillance. He told everyone that Barksdale was paranoid for thinking that everyone was following him. Barksdale's attack against his competitors was sloppy and uncoordinated. He was trying to coordinate a drug run to New York but could not get through to Pit Bull. Sticks was walking on thin ice. Barksdale had a hair-trigger temper, which was escalating every moment.

Barksdale called Pit Bull again, and again, the phone line was busy. He called back a third time. This time, Sticks answered the phone. Barksdale used another fake name and asked where Pit Bull was. Sticks told him he did not know. "Stay off the motherfucking phone!" Barksdale demanded. Like in most organizations, good help was hard to find. To Barksdale's frustration, he relied on a labor force that did not take the drug dealing business as seriously as he did. As a result, he knew distancing himself from the acquisition of the drugs was important.

Barksdale gave Brandon detailed instructions regarding how to take a young woman and a baby to a specific address in New York to buy half a kilo of cocaine and bring it back to him. He instructed

Brandon not to contact him by phone under any circumstances for the duration of the trip. The plan went downhill from the start.

When Brandon arrived in New York, he immediately called Barksdale and asked, "Can you give me that address again?"

"Did I not tell you not to call me, you stupid motherfucker?" Barksdale replied.

Brandon said, "Okay. Can you just give me the address again?"

Brandon then heard a dial tone. Barksdale had hung up. Barksdale called Pit Bull again, but nobody picked up the phone. He called again, and Sticks picked up the phone. Barksdale asked him whether Pit Bull was there. Sticks told him to hang on. When he came back on the telephone, by that time, Barksdale was about to detonate.

"You are one hardheaded little motherfucker. I told you to stay off the motherfucking phone!" Barksdale said.

Sticks handed Pit Bull the phone. "Can you give this dumbass the street address of New York Connect and then put the address on his pager?"

Pit Bull said, "No problem."

"I am going to kill that hardheaded little motherfucker. He stays on that motherfucking phone!" Barksdale said.

Pit Bull fell silent. He recognized that Sticks had ignited a ticking time bomb, which was subjected to go off any minute. Barksdale was back in a very dark place. Pit Bull knew to keep his distance from him whenever he got like that. Stick's lifespan was now uncertain. Barksdale's plan was going off the rails. When he handed the coordination of the shipment to Pit Bull, it came with inherent risks. Pit Bull had loose lips. He was nowhere near as cautious as Barksdale.

Barksdale called Pit Bull again using a different name. This time, he told Pit Bull, "Call Brandon and tell him to handle the shit right."

Just then, Pit Bull received a collect call from Brandon in New York. He told Barksdale, "I will call you back. That dumbass is now calling me collect from Penn Station."

Then Pit Bull clicked over to the other line. Brandon asked him for the address of the supplier in New York. Pit Bull gave him the street name and told him he would put the street number on his pager. Again, I was impressed that Pit Bull followed Barksdale's explicit instructions.

About thirty minutes later, Brandon called Pit Bull again and repeated the New York source's full address, defeating the entire strategy of not giving the address over the phone. Brandon expressed his frustration about not being able to find the supplier's address. He asked several cabdrivers if they were familiar with the address, but none knew.

Then Brandon asked Pit Bull, "Is Brooklyn different from Manhattan?" I was listening to the call with another detective. We looked at each other and high-fived. Pit Bull asked Brandon exactly where he was located. Brandon told him he was in Manhattan.

"What the fuck are you doing in Manhattan when you are supposed to be in Brooklyn?" Pit Bull asked.

"My bad," Brandon said. "Thanks, Pit Bull."

We could hear Brandon's girlfriend talking and the sound of her baby crying in the background. Barksdale called Pit Bull's house again to get a status report on Brandon. He received another busy phone signal. Finally, Barksdale got through to Sticks on his next attempt. "Your ass is mine when I see you," he told Sticks. "I swear to God, you are going to pay."

Later that night, Pit Bull was heard talking to a friend on the phone. He told his friend that Sticks was dead and gone. There was silence for a few seconds on the phone. Then finally, Pit Bull's friend asked what had happened to Sticks. "Sticks is dead and gone. Barksdale killed him," Pit Bull said.

The FBI agents notified the ASAC of Pit Bull's phone conversation with his friend. All hell broke loose. It created a five-alarm fire for the feds. The ASAC started reporting to people up the FBI's chain of command. Finally, he demanded we shut the entire operation down and arrest Barksdale.

My head was spinning. The situation was a calamity, because we had not developed enough information to charge Barksdale. The incident rocked my world. Nevertheless, I pleaded with the task force members to keep the wiretap going. Agent Kozlowski explained that

FBI leadership adhered to a fear-based model. No one wanted to make a decision that might negatively affect their careers. Therefore, the agency became plagued by indecision. It was now more advantageous to take the path of least resistance.

We were on edge. Two days went by without any phone chatter regarding Brandon's whereabouts. I was beginning to believe we were not going to seize Barksdale's drug shipment. I felt defeated and overwhelmed. I retreated home for some much-needed relaxation, but I had only been home for less than an hour when I received a phone call from North Carolina. My uncle told me my grandfather, who was the greatest and most influential person in my life, had just died.

I sat back in my chair and stared at the wall. My wife asked what was going on. I gave her the bad news. She hugged me and asked me if there was anything she could do. I shook my head and returned to an almost comatose state. I struggled to find a coping mechanism. I decided to focus on how my grandfather would have wanted me to handle his departure. I knew he would have said, "Maurice, be strong, because I lived the best life that I could."

It seemed surreal. The wise man was gone! But I had to be strong, and I needed to reconcile his departure with God. Meanwhile, certain events related to the Barksdale case that we could never have anticipated began to unfold.

Before embarking on his journey to New York, Barksdale provided Brandon with explicit instructions regarding avoiding police detection during his trip. Brandon's role was to supervise and protect a young lady named Angel during their journey to pick up drugs. Most importantly, Brandon was to avoid any interaction with Angel during the trip. That would allow her to be the fall girl if authorities caught her. Barksdale chose to create the appearance of a young woman traveling alone with her child to visit the child's father in New York. He related the plan exclusively to Brandon, not Angel, so she could not link him to the shipment.

*****

Brandon and Angel walked into the Greyhound bus station together. They went to separate lines to pay for their tickets, but Brandon forgot to give Angel the money to pay for hers. Angel stepped out of the line and asked Brandon for the money.

"I told you not to have any contact with me!" Brandon yelled.

"How am I supposed to pay for the ticket with no money?" Angel asked.

Brandon gave Angel a handful of money. New York City detectives were observing them the whole time. The detectives waited until the duo was in line to board the bus before confronting Brandon. They asked Brandon if they could talk to him. "I am too busy to talk," Brandon replied. He and Angel boarded the bus together. Brandon smiled as the Greyhound bus departed from the bus station. It was a close call, but now they were free.

When the Greyhound bus arrived in Washington, DC, Brandon slowly and cautiously exited the bus. He checked the station for DC Interdiction detectives. Brandon did not recognize anyone as a detective. He sighed with relief. After he took a few steps, however, two men emerged from behind a wall. Brandon did not know that the New York detectives from earlier had given DC Interdiction detectives a heads-up. Brandon and Angel were heading their way.

The DC detectives took note of Brandon. Brandon kept looking back toward the Greyhound bus. As the men walked in Brandon's direction, he turned back around and stared straight ahead. His behavior seemed unnatural to the detectives. Brandon stumbled as he reached the curb. He remembered that his orders were to protect the shipment. Stickup boys often lurked in the bus depot. Brandon felt compelled to keep Angel in sight. He looked back at the bus and made eye contact with her.

Angel stopped as soon as she exited the bus. Then she began looking for Brandon. Noticing that the two men who were initially walking toward Brandon were now out of sight, she started walking toward him. Brandon and Angel began walking together. Suddenly, the same two men who had been following Brandon reappeared. Brandon whispered in Angel's ear, then quickly walked away. One of the two men followed him. The other man approached Angel.

As Brandon's pursuer approached him, Brandon saw a badge hanging from the man's belt. He stopped and placed his hands against the wall. The detective removed his badge from his belt and said, "That isn't necessary. Please put your hands down. My name is Officer Chaney. I am with DC Police Department. I just want to talk to you for a second. Please relax." The detective was laying the legal groundwork for a proper interdiction stop. He made Brandon aware that he was not detaining him.

"Do you know that girl over there?" the detective asked. "The girl with the baby?"

Brandon replied, "No, sir, I do not know her."

Meanwhile, the other detective approached Angel. He asked her if she knew Brandon, the person he was pointing to. Angel told the detective they just visited New York together. The smiling and friendly detective politely asked Angel if he could check her diaper bag. Politeness was a great way to facilitate the cooperation of a subject. Once, I was profiled by a Maryland state trooper who was trained in interdiction. I was amazed by how he finessed me into answering his questions before I realized what his motives were.

The detective questioning Angel secured consent to search her diaper bag. Angel did not want to offend the polite detective by telling him no. The detective removed half a kilogram of cocaine from the diaper bag, and both Angel and Brandon were arrested. Like I mentioned earlier, Washington Metropolitan Police patrol officers and detectives were sharp as tacks. I was impressed by the excellent communication between New York detectives and DC detectives. They solidified our case.

Angel's arrest created a liability that Barksdale's organization could not afford. The young woman quickly rose to number one on Barksdale's hit list. Things began moving swiftly. Later, within two hours after I was notified of my grandfather's death, Sergeant Stryker informed me that the case against Barksdale was solidified. Moreover, he relayed that Brandon was just arrested in DC with half a kilogram of cocaine.

Brandon was sent to a DC jail with no bond after their arrests while Angel was transferred to a halfway house. We intercepted several of Barksdale's phone calls the next day that directed his men to determine where Angel was incarcerated. One of his associates called back and provided Angel's location. At the end of the call, Agent Kozlowski and I looked at each other and said simultaneously, "They are going to kill her."

We both raced to the nearest telephone and tried to call someone to intervene in Angel's pending execution. Kozlowski called the halfway house directly while I called the office of Prince George's County state's attorney. Managers at the halfway house told Agent Kozlowski that they could not give him information regarding who was staying there. Kozlowski asked the manager to look out of the window to see if she could see anybody hanging around there. She reported seeing two men in their twenties hanging in front of the building. We held our breath, hoping Barksdale's associates would not reach her before we did. If this scenario did not play out right, Angel's six-month-old infant could be motherless within a few minutes.

The following day, I attended a strategy meeting regarding the Barksdale case. In addition, I informed the task force and my lieutenant that I was leaving the next day to attend my grandfather's funeral. With Angel's safety and my grandfather's funeral occupying my mind, I scrambled to prepare eight search warrants for a judge's signature. With the help of Agent Kozlowski and one other narcotics detective, we prepared to execute the eight search warrants simultaneously.

My new lieutenant called me into his office and said, "I hate to have to tell you this, but we cannot wait until you return from your grandfather's funeral. We're going to hit all the locations while you're out of town." After that, I did not have any fight left in me. I just walked out of his office. I told my homicide supervisor and task force members about the lieutenant's decision. The supervisor told me, "We are not going to do a damn thing without you here." It was a much-needed support, as I was at a low point in my life.

I left an extensive to-do list for my FBI comrades to ensure that all the addresses on the search warrants were correct. I sat at my desk at the FBI office and looked over the search warrants to ensure that I did not miss anything. Then I heard a thunderous banging coming from near the rear exit of the offices. I began walking toward it. I thought some lunatic was trying to break into the FBI's offices. The sound kept getting louder as I walked toward the back.

There, I saw Agent Stone drawing his arm back and striking the copy machine. Stone wasn't himself without his coffee. He was still wailing on the machine as I walked up. He was hitting the copy machine with all his might. I ran over and restrained him, then asked him what was wrong. He gritted his teeth and pointed at the machine, and said, "Goddamn it! Every other FBI office has copy machines that will do everything for you but give you a fuckin' head job! Ours won't even copy papers." I liked working with Stone because he was an effective, no-nonsense guy. He had a mind like a steel trap. He was blessed with almost total recall.

I told Stone, "Please give me whatever you need to be copied. I will take it back to the Criminal Investigations Division and have the papers copied, sorted, and stapled for you in no time."

He smiled and said, "Thank you, Maurice."

*****

A few hours later, I boarded the elevator with Agents Kozlowski and Stone. A white woman in her late fifties boarded the elevator with us and then pushed the button to get off the elevator the next floor down. Agent Stone said to the woman, "Goddamn it. Can't you walk down one flight of fucking stairs?" The lady did not respond to Stone but quickly walked out of the elevator when the doors opened.

Agent Kozlowski said, "Stone, you are an FBI agent. You cannot talk to people like that."

Agent Stone said, "Shut up, asshole."

Stone did not have his coffee that morning. Stone was not himself when he did not have his coffee. I thought coffee deprivation and the pressure of the case had taken their toll on him. I checked with my sergeant on the status of the flowers that were supposed to be sent to my grandfather's funeral just before heading to the Baltimore/ Washington International Airport. Sergeant Johnson broke the bad news to me. Sergeant Stryker's relentless campaign of discouragement had reached a new low. He refused to send flowers to my grandfather's funeral.

I contributed money to the flower fund in the narcotics division for over five years. However, Stryker never sent flowers to my family for any occasion. My sergeant said Stryker refused to send flowers because my grandfather was not my immediate family. I explained that my grandfather raised me. He said Stryker laughed about that and still said no.

The more I pursued peace with Sergeant Stryker, the more he pursued war. I realized I could not change his relentless attacks on my spirit. I could only change the way I responded to his misdeeds. I sought an antidote for my emotional distress. I was now unplugged from my primary power source: my grandfather. So I searched my mind for scriptures that would reenergize me and release my mind from the fiery furnace of affliction.

I reflected on Psalm 43:1–2: "Vindicate me, O God, and plead my cause against an ungodly nation; rescue me from deceitful and wicked men. You are God my stronghold." I had to focus on God's ability to help me rather than my ability to help myself. I was desperate for spiritual nourishment as I departed for my grandfather's funeral in North Carolina.

I reached the deputy state's attorney a few hours later and joined a three-way call to the halfway house. I listened as the bureaucrats at the halfway house told the deputy state's attorney they needed something in writing. At that point, I lost my patience and felt compelled to intervene. "You will be able to sign the paperwork in Angel's blood if you do not act soon!" I interjected.

I still did not know Angel's fate as I boarded my plane from Baltimore to Philadelphia, where I had a connecting flight on a small commuter plane to Raleigh, North Carolina. It was the first time I ever flew on such a small plane. Within twenty minutes after liftoff, we were flying through the worst thunderstorm I had ever experienced in my life.

I grabbed the armrest and braced myself as the plane shook and dipped. Every few seconds, the plane shook violently and descended in altitude. I wondered if the tiny aircraft would reach its destination.

I wondered what would become of the Barksdale case if I did not make it through the storm. I found myself more concerned about Barksdale's victims than my safety. At that point, I realized how emotionally invested I was in the case.

*****

Over the next two days, I visited family in Burgaw, North Carolina, whom I had not seen in over twenty years. They all told me the same thing about my grandfather. They said my grandfather would pull out a picture of me that he kept in his shirt pocket every day. He would show everyone my picture and would tell them how proud he was of me. When my cousin shared this with me, I took a few minutes to compose myself. My cousin looked directly at me and said, "When he died sitting at the kitchen table, he still had your picture in his shirt pocket."

By the end of the day, I was emotionally overwhelmed. I fought hard to hold back the flood of tears coming down my face. I reflected on a conversation my grandfather had with me while I was in my early twenties. He revealed to me that he was not my biological grandfather. I realized just how blessed I was to have such a good man in my life. He was a good man who treated me like I was his son. May God bless him and every other man like him who stepped up to the plate and made a positive difference in someone's life.

Unfortunately, I lost an enormous source of strength and encouragement. Now, I had to reflect on his philosophies and teachings to guide me out of the hellhole of the Narcotics Enforcement Division. I was both hurt and disappointed that my grandfather did not live long enough to see the fruits of his labor. He did not live long enough to see me make sergeant. He would have been so proud of me.

CHAPTER 77

THE MURDER OF TONY CLARK

Many people in the neighborhood saw that high-level drug dealers were living their best life, but unfortunately, the reality was that drug dealers often lived dangerous lives. Danger usually peeked its ugly head around every corner. Drug barons and their associates were often targeted for robbery. Barksdale's girlfriend was no exception.

On a spring day in 1987, Tony Clark followed Barksdale's girlfriend Sharonda as she walked into her apartment. He pointed his pistol at her and began slapping her on the face, yelling, "Come here, you dumb bitch. You're going to do all kinds of things for me tonight, you fine motherfucker. I've got to give you an ass-whipping first so you'll know what time it is. Your boyfriend done fucked up and left you all alone. Do not worry. Big Daddy is going to give you some good loving, and then you are going to tell me everything I want to know about that punk-ass Barksdale."

Sharonda was fortunate. Clark did not intend to rape her. His interest was only in that mean green (money). He knew Barksdale had plenty of cash stashed in Sharonda's apartment. Sharonda watched in horror as Clark tied her up. She was probably thinking, *This is not what I envisioned my relationship would be like.* Clark fled the scene with a little less than thirty thousand dollars—not a bad investment for fifteen minutes of work. But Clark made a fatal error. He robbed a woman who knew him by name.

When the news reached Barksdale's ear, Barksdale knew he had to get his hands dirty. The robbery was personal, which meant the resolution had to be swift and personal as well. First, he needed to send a message not to attack his woman. But more importantly, he had to let everyone know that the theft of his ill-gotten gains would not be tolerated.

Barksdale and one of his business associates started their reconnaissance near the metro station adjacent to Clark's house. Barksdale could not believe his luck when he saw Clark walking toward his apartment. He immediately ran up the hill and allegedly shot Clark in the head. Although Barksdale allegedly had an insatiable appetite for murder, the alleged murder of Clark seemed to me to be Barksdale's first kill. Barksdale was never charged nor convicted of the murder of Tony Clark.

Barksdale soon deduced that he was at the end of his reign. He knew that the comfortable lifestyle he had become accustomed to was on the verge of collapse. There was a sudden change in his demeanor. This was his come-to-Jesus moment. He desperately wanted to change his fate. Barksdale started calling his faithful assassins and encouraging them to accompany him to church. He even started researching legitimate occupations. Barksdale was looking for the quickest exit out of his business, but old habits were hard to break.

In the summer of 1993, the moment of truth finally arrived. The FBI, the Maryland State Police, the Prince George's County Police and the Prince George's County Sheriff's department assembled to plan simultaneous raids in Prince George's County, Howard County, and Anne Arundel County. Unfortunately, one of the raids executed took place close to Pit Bull's apartment.

The channel Investigation Discovery televised a true-crime series called *Fear Thy Neighbor*. Unfortunately, a scenario was unfolding that would give them a new episode. Sixty-five-year-old Mr. Grady had good reason to fear his neighbor. Unfortunately, he had the misfortune of living next door to Pit Bull's apartment, Barksdale's drug operation epicenter.

If Mr. Grady had known the reputation shared by Barksdale and his associates, he would have been better prepared for what was to come next. To the dismay of his wife, Mr. Grady decided to supplement his disability checks by selling crack cocaine. Pit Bull also used Mr. Grady's apartment to store drugs when the police raided his apartment. Mr. Grady also performed car repairs to make additional money on the side.

Grady was a novice at selling drugs. He expressed his frustration to Pit Bull regarding his difficulties in making a profit by selling crack cocaine. To add to his woes, Pit Bull was overcharging him for the cocaine he sold him.

"Why do your prices keep going up?" Grady asked.

"Because there is a shortage," Pit Bull replied. He offered to cut the cocaine for Mr. Grady to help him make a profit. In addition to selling drugs, Pit Bull just developed a new skill: manipulating vulnerable adults.

As soon as the sun rose that morning, heavily armed SWAT team members battered their way into Mr. Grady's apartment. Grady and his wife rubbed their eyes and looked up at the several men pointing their weapons at them. His wife started praying as agents yelled, directing Grady to get dressed for his trip to jail. Grady was charged with cocaine distribution charges and released the next day.

Before Grady could get himself settled back home, the phone rang. It was Barksdale who had escaped the raid at his home. Barksdale needed to know Grady's state of mind. He wasted no time.

"How are you doing, old man?" he asked. Agent Kozlowski and I listened to the call, so naturally, I hoped Grady would not say anything to set Barksdale off. The following words that I heard sent chills down my spine.

"Man," Grady said, "I was about to go crazy after being in jail for over six hours. I cannot take that, man. I do not know how you all do it. The police questioned me about you all for several hours, but I did not tell them anything. If them police ask me about you all again, I am going to tell them something. I am never going back to that place again!"

Agent Kozlowski and I looked at each other in disbelief. Had our ears deceived us, or had we just heard a vulnerable older man tell the infamous Barksdale he would say to the police what they wanted to know? I was frustrated. I wondered how many more people we would need to scramble around for to ensure their protection. But Grady was not a cooperating witness. He was on his own. The worst part about the situation was, Barksdale and one of his henchmen avoided capture during the simultaneous raids. Nevertheless, I tried to think positively. Perhaps Barksdale and Jungle Jim were on their way out of town.

Barksdale was frustrated. So many people to eliminate, and so little time. He must have been experiencing sensory overload. He did not have the luxury of going back to his apartment to pick up his belongings, because we had raided his apartment, and that was a wise choice since we had an undercover FBI agent renting the apartment next door. He needed to raise money for his defense attorney and defense attorneys for his associates. The feds were on his trail. Police officers in Prince George's County and Anne Arundel County were looking for him. The worst part for him was, they knew him by his real name. The most capable fugitive agents were looking for him.

We needed to turn up the heat even higher on Barksdale. People under pressure made mistakes. We needed to find Barksdale and Jungle Jim quickly before they could leave a bloody trail behind them. Fortunately, when Barksdale and Jungle Jim disappeared off our radar, it allowed the FBI to do what they did best: track fugitives. My partner, Agent Stone, was a former fugitive agent. I was anxious to see my tax dollars go to work. I wanted to watch Stone do his fugitive thing.

Stone knew that one of the quickest ways to obtain information was to cater to people's love for money, so the FBI put out a five-thousand-dollar reward for information relating to Barksdale's arrest and the arrest of Jungle Jim.

The next day, Grady received a call from Jungle Jim. He wanted to know if Mr. Grady needed to make some extra money. Mr. Grady was in desperate need of money. He needed to hire an attorney. So Jungle Jim hired Grady to fix his car. Grady was not thinking clearly. He needed to avoid any contact with Barksdale's associates.

Jungle Jim met with alleged terminators Rob and Ronnie to devise a strategy to shoot Grady. However, when the time came to put their plan in motion, Rob had a change of heart. He did not want the murder of a senior citizen on his conscience. Jungle Jim was furious. A potential witness was no longer willing to participate in the murder. It was a loose end and an unnecessary complication.

Jungle Jim rounded up a friend named Ronnie and drove to Grady's apartment. Then Jungle Jim knocked on the door as Ronnie stood a slight distance behind him. As soon as Grady opened the door, Jungle Jim yanked him into the hallway. He waited a few moments. He needed to hear the old man beg for his life.

Grady pleaded desperately with Jungle Jim. He tried to explain that he would take the charge the police had slapped on him. But instead, Jungle Jim replied, "This is what you get for being a snitch, you dumb old man." He put the handgun to the back of Grady's head. Popping sounds echoed through the building. Then four more shots were fired in rapid succession. A scream followed each shot.

Then Jungle Jim straddled Grady's body and began picking up the spent shell casings. He was not going to leave any evidence behind. Ronnie put some of the shell casings in his shirt pockets. Then they ran out of the building under the backdrop of the deafening screams of Mrs. Grady, which people would never forget. No one dared to call the police until the men were far away from the building. Then Grady's wife called the police. She was too terrified to come into the hallway. When the police and ambulance arrived, it was too late. Mr. Grady was already dead.

Jungle Jim needed to tie up any loose ends immediately, so after leaving the residence, he contacted Rob by phone. Jungle Jim seemed unusually composed when they spoke, so Rob figured he did not follow through with his plans to execute Grady. Later, Ronnie joined Jungle Jim when he picked up Rob and handed him a glass jar. Rob watched as the two other men threw the spent shell casings from the shooting into the jar. Finally, it became clear to Rob that Jungle Jim had carried out his plan. Jungle Jim gave Rob the jar and directed him to bury the jar in the woods. Rob was satisfied that he had redeemed himself in Jungle Jim's eyes.

The next day, Jungle Jim picked up Rob and Ronnie again. He handed Ronnie a gun and gave him his game plan for the day. They were going to stick up somebody. Ronnie drove to a location in Bladensburg. Jungle Jim gave him and Rob a description of the person they were looking to rob. Rob was in the driver's seat. Jungle Jim crouched down in the rear passenger seat. Ronnie was seated in the front. They waited for their victim to appear.

Jungle Jim pointed out the window and showed Ronnie a man walking down the street. He said, "That's our mark!" Jungle Jim then shot Ronnie in the back of the head. Blood splattered all over the rear window and the front and back seats of the car. Rob almost soiled his pants. He jumped out of the car and started removing particles of Ronnie's brain from his clothing. Jungle Jim picked up Ronnie's gun from the floor of the vehicle. He pulled Ronnie out of the driver's seat and dumped his body on the street.

Ronnie had been duped. The whole thing was a setup. Jungle Jim had given Ronnie an empty gun. Rob knew Jungle Jim was leaving nothing to chance. He knew he was slated to be Jungle Jim's next victim. Jungle Jim pointed his gun at Rob. "Get your stupid ass back in the car, right here up front," he said. Rob inadvertently left his rifle in the back seat. At that point, he figured the gun was probably empty.

Jungle Jim took over the wheel and began driving away from the scene. He was silent and had a mad look in his eyes. Jungle Jim was confused about how to proceed next while Rob was trying to clear the images of the murder out of his head. Jungle Jim knew that Rob was soft and was nowhere as streetwise as Ronnie. He was more manageable prey. Rob knew he had to act quickly to survive.

When Jungle Jim reached the next traffic light on Landover Road, Rob leaped out of the vehicle and started running zigzag. Rob was not a streetwise hoodlum, but he was a military movie buff. He knew it was difficult to hit a moving target. Jungle Jim did not have time to search for him. Jungle Jim knew he was already hot, and he was covered with blood. Most importantly, the police were looking for him. Most of the officers in his police district knew him by name. So it was time for Jungle Jim to get out of dodge.

Jungle Jim had failed to think the murder plot through. Nevertheless, there was a living witness to the aftermath of the shooting, a witness who knew the location of incriminating evidence. Rob would later lead my colleagues to the jar containing the shell casings. Oh well, haste makes waste.

CHAPTER 78

THE FBI TAKES CONTROL

When I despair, I remember that all through
history, the way of truth and love have always won.
Of course, there have been tyrants and murderers,
and they can seem invincible for a time, but in
the end, they always fall. Think of it—always.
—Mahatma Gandhi

Special Agent Stone updated me on his strategy to apprehend
Barksdale and Jungle Jim. He focused on the fugitives' habits. We
knew Jungle Jim loved his alcohol, and Barksdale loved his women.
It did not take a rocket scientist to figure out that a man turned to his
woman for support when he was down on his luck. By this time, we
had shut down the wiretap. As a result, we no longer had the luxury
of listening to their phone calls.

We knew Jungle Jim had family in Ohio. One month later, the
FBI traced a phone call from a phone booth next to a bar in Ohio to
the house of Jungle Jim's mother. Stone said he laughed when they
traced the call. The caller had to be Jungle Jim, because he knew how
much the boy loved his liquor. Indeed, FBI agents in Ohio apprehended Jungle Jim at the bar next to the phone booth.

One month later, a tipster called into the FBI office and provided a possible location for Barksdale. Armed with the information,
FBI agents surrounded the building in question, then watched as

Barksdale, his girlfriend, and one of his new villains walked out of the building. They headed toward a car in the parking lot. A small army of heavily armed FBI agents wearing blue windbreakers with the letters FBI written in bright-yellow letters suddenly surrounded the trio.

Barksdale blocked out the sounds of the hyped-up agents shouting commands at him at gunpoint as he searched for a way to escape. He looked at his bodyguard for help. Barksdale was shocked. His bodyguard was supposed to engage the feds or distract them as he made his escape, but the fear must have been overwhelming. This time, it was not the local police pursuing him but members of the Federal Bureau of Investigation.

Barksdale's mind flashed back to the good old days when he would outrun well-polished rookie police officers fresh out of the academy. His escape plans always served him well, and he taught these same skills to his subordinates. Now, he had to demonstrate that he still had the skills needed to escape. Barksdale had an advantage for several reasons. First, he knew that the feds did not have K-9 dogs. Second, he knew the FBI agents were good guys, protectors of civil rights. Third, there was only one alternative: run like hell! After all, he was in his early twenties, and he was in the best shape of his life. He knew his six-foot-four frame was far superior than that of his aging pursuers.

If the local police were the ones chasing him, his escape options would have been limited. Veteran patrol officers were skilled at apprehending fleeing felons. They surround the area, formed a perimeter, and called for K-9. Barksdale knew the rules of the game. If the county police's K-9 dog caught him, the dog would repay him for the old and new things he had done wrong. But if the Prince George's County cowboys were forced to chase him, he would get street justice in the form of a wood shampoo.

Agents lunged toward Barksdale with the veracity of a lion while Barksdale gracefully leaped away. His strides were twice as long as those of his pursuers. He looked back at the pursuing agents, smiling while his Air Jordans made their way through the slippery grass. The agents looked at the agile twenty-six-year-old in disbelief. Then they quickly closed the gap between them. The agents were locked in on their prey.

Barksdale's arrogance began to fade as he noticed the enormous determination of his pursuers. To his chagrin, he was being chased by three agents who were distance runners. They longed to test their running skills against Barksdale's. The hill in the rear of the apartment complex where the chase occurred was an obstacle Barksdale did not anticipate. He was not familiar with the topography of the area. He began to slip and slide on the slippery grass as he started his descent off the hill. This gave the slightly overweight FBI agents an edge.

Barksdale fell on the grass. He found himself surrounded by three agents, one of whom appeared to have an itchy trigger finger. Agent Stone carefully aimed his handgun. He always enunciated when he spoke with his Southern accent. "Goddamn it," he said, "if you move a muscle, I am going to blow you away."

There was no misreading Stone's face; it would have been his last if Barksdale had made a wrong move. He would be the last person who would receive the benefit of the doubt in a deadly confrontation. At last, Barksdale was in custody.

As the three agents worked their way back to Barksdale's car, they suddenly realized they had left Special Agent Kozlowski alone to confront Barksdale's bodyguard during their quest to apprehend Barksdale. They had no idea Agent Kozlowski was facing a deadly encounter.

Agent Kozlowski pointed his gun at Barksdale's bodyguard, Dante, and yelled for him to show him his hands. In response, Dante started lowering his hands. He needed to make a calculation. Should he blast his way out? The agent was alone. A young woman was sitting next to him. The agent might be afraid to engage him with an innocent bystander sitting so close to him. Dante's instinct was to escape, but he needed to get past the agent first.

He had never encountered a federal agent, yet this one agent was his only barrier to freedom. He knew the feds rarely lost a case. Engaging him was too risky, but Dante had another weapon at his disposal, a pit bull. Dante threw the pit bull out of the driver's window and gave the dog the command to attack Agent Kozlowski. Kozlowski, a dog lover, chose to run from the dog to avoid shooting him. Still, the dog continued a relentless attack on him. The dog chased Agent Kozlowski around Barksdale's vehicle three times.

Finally, the slender and physically fit Agent Kozlowski jumped on the hood of the car. The pit bull pursued him onto the hood. Agent Kozlowski then jumped on top of the vehicle with the pit bull chasing behind him. Finally, Agent Kozlowski shot the dog through the neck. The shot went through the dog's neck, through the top of the car, and between Dante and Barksdale's girlfriend, who were still sitting next to each other in the back seat of the vehicle. The round then went into the trunk of the car. The dog fell off the hood of the car. It had seen its last attack.

The agent was still not out of danger. He still had to confront Dante. Agent Kozlowski jumped down from the hood of the car and reengaged Dante at gunpoint. Dante was still counting his lucky stars that the agent's bullet missed him by less than a quarter of an inch. He knew it was time to surrender.

As the other agents emerged from the top of the hill, they saw the dead dog lying on the ground and Agent Kozlowski patting Dante down. One agent ran to assist Kozlowski. The agent watched as Agent Kozlowski removed a loaded 9mm handgun from Dante's waistband. He then realized why Dante seemed so desperate to escape. He had an outstanding warrant for murder. The manhunt was finally over. Finally, finally, all our suspects were in custody.

I was still on vacation when the news came in regarding Barksdale's arrest. I arrived at the station just as Agent Joey Jackson got Barksdale out of the car at the Criminal Investigations Division. The agent got some papers out of his car. I grabbed Barksdale by the arm to secure him, and the agent rifled through his car, looking for documents.

"You just had to say you got me, Hicks," Barksdale said.

"It's not even like that," I said. "I just did not want you to escape."

I walked them into the building. Then I retreated home for the last few days of my vacation.

CHAPTER 79

THE NIGHTSTALKER

Unbeknownst to the residents of Bowie, Maryland, as they slept peacefully, a man was monitoring their every move. He used a tape recorder to document the time people came home, the time they left home, who lived in their homes, and the time their lights went out. The man's demonic ambition, if fully realized, would change the course of their lives forever.

Unfortunately, police commanders at the Prince George's County Police Department were pursuing all the wrong angles. Their theory was, the suspect was probably a contractor familiar with the houses being built.

In June 1994, the assailant identified his first victim. Then on August 12, 1994, a day that a particular family would never forget, a man who was fast asleep was awakened by a violent blow to his head. As the man opened his eyes, he felt the barrel of an assault weapon being inserted into his mouth. The man who inserted the gun was wearing a big black ski mask, a black shirt, black pants, and black combat boots. In addition to having an assault rifle, he also had a crossbow and arrows in a quiver slung over his other arm.

The man forced the victim to get down on his knees and crawl to the next bedroom, where he threw the man a long piece of rope and told him to tie himself up. The suspect asked the man whether his wife would be upset if he woke her up. The victim stated she would. The suspect gagged the man with a T-shirt and tissues he got from the nightstand. Then he disappeared from the room, returning with the victim's wife. The man's wife was crying uncontrollably.

The couple told the suspect he was welcome to steal all their money. At that point, the suspect forced the husband to lie down on the bed. Then he threw the man's wife on top of him. The rapist put a blindfold over the victim's eyes. Then he began assaulting the woman, raping her while the husband lay underneath. First, the assailant told her that if she fought him, he would kill her. Then he taunted her by telling her he had AIDS. Finally, he asked the victim if she had AIDS, and she told him yes hoping this would discourage him.

The woman asked to go to the bathroom, at which time the assailant allowed her to loosen her blindfold. She tripped over the crossbow upon returning to the bedroom. The assailant talked to the woman for nearly twenty minutes about his life and his future. He confided in her, telling her he did not know why he did these things. He further added that he wanted to be in a good relationship and wanted a good job. He did not realize he was giving information that could be used to lead to his capture. The assailant also asked the woman to show him her security system.

I could only imagine the feeling of helplessness the man must have experienced while watching another man rape his wife while he lay helplessly on the bed underneath. The incident undoubtedly held long-term emotional and psychological consequences for both of them. Unfortunately, their goal at that point was just to survive the encounter.

After the man finished the assault, he pulled his pants up, picked up his crossbow, and placed it in a bag. He stated that he had good news: he was going to leave. However, he told the husband he had terrible news for him: he was going to shoot him. The man put his head down on a pillow as the suspect raised an AK-47 assault rifle, but the rifle would not engage. He made the man's wife escort him to the townhouse basement, but he left through the shattered sliding door.

The following day, a man began knocking on doors in the neighborhood. He asked the homeowners if they needed an alarm system. The man passed out posters encouraging homeowners to purchase new alarm systems. The flyers contained articles discussing how the assailant who was terrorizing the community could defeat his victims' alarm systems. The poster said, "Do not let this happen to you. A woman was recently assaulted in a large home. Call me. It is happening in our neighborhood. The assailant shot a dog."

On September 5, 1993, the assailant pursued his next victim. Again, he followed his regular pattern of deactivating the alarm system, cutting the glass on the sliding door, and then taking the telephone off the hook to prevent the victim from calling the police. He was again wearing his burglar attire: the all-black outfit and a nylon mask. As usual, he was carrying his AK-47 assault rifle and his crossbow with arrows.

This victim was alone. She was a graduate student at the University of Maryland who was majoring in psychology. The female victim woke up and saw her assailant standing in the darkness of her bedroom doorway. He was dressed in all black with a crossbow and an AK-47 assault rifle. The next thing she knew, she was being dragged off the bed.

The assailant tied up her hands and feet, gagged her, and blindfolded her with duct tape. Finally, he told her he was going to rape her. Fear gripped her throat. She could feel nothing but blind terror. She tried to squirm away from him, but her efforts were unsuccessful because her hands and feet were bound. He repeatedly raped the victim. Shockingly, she had the presence of mind to rub his face to determine the amount of hair the suspect had on his face. They talked, and the victim convinced the suspect that he needed help and that she was willing to assist him in finding help. Next, she convinced him to take her work phone to call her. The assailant demanded her wallet and said he wanted something to remember her by. He took her phone number and ran out of the room.

The assailant left a pair of scissors to allow the victim to cut herself free when he left. The victim marked where the assailant's head fell in relation to a poster on her wall to determine the suspect's height. She untied herself and looked out of the window. She was able to see her assailant drive off in a small gray vehicle.

I was no longer assigned to the Criminal Investigations Division, so I had no idea I was about to be thrust into the middle of such a high-profile case. I was in a good space. I had just wrapped up a two-and-a-half-year investigation working with the FBI. I was returning from vacation. I had taken the entire summer off to spend time with my family. I took my wife to the Bahamas, and I took my whole family to Disney World. I was relieved to escape the toxic atmosphere of the Narcotics Enforcement Division for such a long time.

After my vacation, I had another two-week reprieve from the division. I went to homicide school and then followed it up with a week of in-service training. While sitting in my in-service training class, my lieutenant walked past the classroom and saw me. When the class broke out for lunch, I saw him standing by the door. He quizzed me regarding how long I had been away from the division. After that, I knew the jig was up. "You're coming back to the division as soon as in-service is over." The honeymoon was over. It was time to get back to the real world.

On my first day back, my lieutenant told me the captain wanted to speak to me. He walked me into the captain's office. Captain O'Connor, my previous captain, once gave me a safety net. He talked me into remaining in the division when I was at my lowest point. It was a time when my new sergeant, a cartoon character, went rogue on me and wrote a memo up saying I wanted to be transferred. Captain O'Connor renewed my spirit and assured me there would be hell to pay if anyone tried to harass me, including the lieutenant.

The new captain had fallen under the spell of my nemesis. He was frustrated about his failed attempts to break my indomitable spirit. He wanted me to know he was the new sheriff in town. It was clear he was now the commander of what I called the Negative Regime. He had plans for me. He knew precisely how to extinguish the enormous positive energy I contained within me.

The captain took a few seconds to gather his thoughts. He chose his words carefully. Finally, he said, "You are about to be promoted to sergeant within the next few months, correct?"

"Hopefully, sir," I replied.

"Well, we do not want to lose your slot in Major Narcotics when you leave," he said. "So if you don't mind, I am going to put you in the Intelligence Unit."

"What?" I asked. "You're putting me back in Street Narcotics?" Technically, the Intelligence Unit fell under Street Narcotics. The sergeant reassured me I would not be conducting street-level drug investigations. I waited a few seconds to answer to gauge his enthusiasm for transferring me. I wanted to quote an old cereal commercial and say, "Silly Rabbit, Trix Are for Kids." Then I said, "It's your division, sir. You can put me anywhere you want."

On the way out of the captain's office, I noticed Sergeant Stryker's eyes locked on me. He had a smirk on his face. He looked as satisfied as any man could be. He had gone rogue to the point of no return. He experienced the full effect of my reaction to the transfer.

It was astonishing that I was transferred to the Intelligence Unit after taking down the person deemed by the news media as the most dangerous man in county history. There was no "Thank you" and no "Job well done." Instead, I was given a transfer.

My detractors were gleaming with joy regarding my exile from Major Narcotics. At that point, I was at my wit's end from dealing with their never-ending, hate-induced ritual of planning my demise. I was treading water, waiting until my promotion to sergeant came through. Although my commanders were ecstatic, I did not challenge my transfer out of Major Narcotics. They were unprepared for God's blessings upon me in my new assignment. Unbeknownst to them, they were positioning me for a triumphant return to the main stage.

On my first day in the Intelligence Unit, I was in good spirits. My sergeant, the native Baltimorean who was also a former Baltimore City police officer, was a sharp station detective who worked the beat I had when I was a patrol officer. I also knew both of my two coworkers; we came from the same station. Detective McQuade worked intelligence, and Detective Brody worked gambling cases.

When I walked into the office, Detective Brody was talking to Detective McQuade and Sergeant Dixon. Brody had his feet propped on his desk. He was wearing a white T-shirt and beige shorts. The Lieutenant told me that he was tired of hearing his war stories. The sergeant and several other detectives were huddled around him. The huddle was familiar. I thought differently. It was more likely a story about his sexual conquests.

But despite Brody's need to express the intimate details of his sex life, I liked and admired him. He was a well-respected detective who worked gambling cases. I looked forward to going out on gambling raids with him.

Detective McQuade was a nice and humble guy who had a reputation for being an excellent intelligence officer, so I was in good company. McQuade greeted me with a handshake and told me he was happy I was on the sergeant's list. He confided in me that although he loved doing intelligence work, he longed for the day when he could answer the phone by saying, "Sergeant McQuade." He certainly deserved it. I would have been delighted to see him get promoted.

I told him I was disappointed because I previously died number one on the sergeant's list. However, I said to him that it ended up being a blessing in disguise. It allowed me to work on the type of cases I loved working on.

I figured I would add some new investigative skills to my résumé before I got promoted. Brody obtained a search warrant for suspected gambling activities at a notorious house for large-level gambling a few days later. I was excited because I had never been on a gambling raid before. However, I was surprised we did not use our SWAT team to execute the raid, and I asked Brody why that was the case. He told me most gamblers were nonviolent people.

Brody knocked on the door. When the occupant opened the door, Brody calmly showed his badge. The occupant waved for us to come in. Our sergeant and two other detectives walked into the house and yelled, "This is a raid. Everybody, put your hands up!"

Brody called it right. Everyone in the house seemed amused about the raid and not angry. Brody collected notes about wins and losses. I noticed several personalized license plates affixed to the wall throughout the house. The plates displayed words like Gambler 1, Gambler 2, Poker 1, and Poker 2. I alerted Brody, who took pictures of the plates.

Brody paced around the house, looking both bewildered and frustrated. When I queried him about the change in his demeanor, he told me something was not right. "There isn't that much money here," he said. Confident detectives had a sixth sense for crimes they were investigating, a fact I found amazing. Brody picked up a stick he saw lying by the window, and he raised one end of the rod to a ceiling tile. Then he pushed the tile upward. Stacks of money fell from the ceiling. They kept falling and falling, and I said, "Oh my God, Brody, you are blessed. Out of all the ceiling tiles in the house, you picked the exact one where the money can be found."

*****

I was elated while sitting at my desk and reading the following article in the newspaper. It was titled, "The County's Most Dangerous Man Arrested." After all, I beat the odds. My hateful coworkers, although still envious, had to acknowledge a few facts: I managed the investigation of a criminal who eluded the best of the best detectives. Barksdale eluded homicide and narcotics as well as station-level detectives for a decade. Finally, my tour of duty with the FBI was over. I was heading back to the gravel pit.

But my feeling of joy as I sat in my chair, reading the newspaper, was short-lived. My sergeant nervously walked in. I very much liked my new sergeant in the Intelligence Unit. He was a native Baltimorean too. He was also a former Baltimore City police officer. We shared a lot of stories about growing up and being with the police in Baltimore.

"What's going on there now?" I asked. He explained that a guy with an AK-47 was raping women in Bowie. The community was in an uproar. The rapist was primarily targeting single white women living in large homes in Bowie. I was bewildered as to what the case had to do with us. After all, rape investigations were handled by the Sexual Assaults Unit in our Criminal Investigations Division. Sergeant Dixon got right to the point. The chief wanted people with surveillance expertise to stake out the Bowie area during the midnight shift.

Two hours later, I found myself driving around Bowie, looking for a needle in a haystack. There was no description of the suspect because he wore a mask. On day three, I was transferred to the day shift based on a new lead. I began my surveillance at 9:00 a.m. My supervisor called me at about 5:00 p.m. and told me to stand by. The suspect was on the phone with one of his victims. I had a four-hour battery with no charger. My radio had been in operation for eight hours. Technically, the battery was supposed to be dead.

The plan was for us to follow the suspect from Washington, DC, back to Maryland. Once in Maryland, our Emergency Services Team, aka SWAT, would take him down. I arrived on the scene three minutes later. Detectives traced the call to the phone booth at Young's Carryout located at 5929 East Capitol Street in Washington, DC. The suspect was on the phone with one of his rape victims. I was the first and only African American detective on the scene.

The first thing I noticed was the four phone booths at the site. However, only one person was using the phone. This was undoubtedly an unexpected blessing. The shopping center was an open-air drug market. About eight young black men in their twenties were selling drugs. The man using the phone was about forty years old and had dark skin. In addition, he sported a small Afro and a beard.

I knew that the rapist's last victim had the remarkable presence of mind to feel her assailant's face through his nylon mask. She also made it a point to observe where the rapist's head fell in relation to a poster on the wall as he ran out of her bedroom. She managed to untie herself and place a mark on the poster to identify his height. The description of the rapist matched the man in the phone booth almost perfectly.

The man had a giant smile on his face as he continued to engage in his conversation with the victim. He was enjoying his conversation with his prey. But at the faint sound of a police siren in the distance, he suddenly hung up the phone. Then after the sound faded, he redialed the call. A full forty-seven minutes later, the suspect was still on the phone. It was time enough for a small army of police detectives from Maryland to arrive on the scene.

The suspect looked so satisfied that I thought he was going to light up a cigarette. He seemed to be very much in control. That was until the sound of a siren in the distance became audible. The suspect slammed the phone down and walked into a convenience store. He stayed there for a few minutes. Once the sound of the sirens dissipated, he quickly got back on the phone again.

We all waited for him to get into a vehicle in the parking lot beneath the phone booth. I was looking forward to handing the takedown over to SWAT, because they had rifles and better body armor than we did. But then I began to think of the many things that could go wrong. I was relieved when two other African American detectives radioed me that they had arrived on the scene. I directed them to get out on foot if the suspect decided to run.

The sight of the detectives on foot gave me a temporary sense of relief. I knew that if anything went wrong, I was going to be the fall guy. I was now the official eyes and ears of the operation. The sight of any white person would have been a dead giveaway. They were the police. I braced myself and watched intently as the suspect hung up the telephone. I depressed the transmit button on my radio and prayed my radio battery was not as dead as a doorknob.

CHAPTER 80

THE CONTINUING SAGA OF THE NIGHTSTALKER

I was able to transmit four words before my radio started to die. "He's on the move!" I exclaimed. To everyone's amazement, the suspect ascended some concrete steps that provided access to entirely different streets. I immediately radioed the information. "This guy is going to get away. There is no immediate vehicle access to the street he's on."

The Criminal Investigations Division captain came over the radio. "Don't follow him. Do not take him down. Wait for the Emergency Services Team (AKA SWAT)," he said.

"You don't understand. This guy is about to get away," I replied.

I turned off my radio, then left my car double-parked in the parking lot. I hurried past the group of drug dealers in the parking lot and waved to the two detectives on foot. I quickly ascended the concrete stairs and observed the suspect bopping from side to side while shaking hands with several of his homeboys along the way. Then he walked into a house. One of the detectives pulled up in an undercover vehicle. I leaned into the car and told him to let the captain know the suspect was in a house. I told him the suspect was about to get away if we did not act soon.

The detective cautiously keyed on his radio and said, "Captain, Detective Hicks advised the suspect is in a house. Hicks is recommending we take the suspect down on the first opportunity."

In response, the captain advised, "Take him down as soon as possible."

Just then, the suspect emerged from the house. He walked down the street, along the driver's side of the vehicles. He jumped inside the sixth car on the road and attempted to start his car. Detective Franklin yelled, "Police! Freeze!" He put the barrel of his 9mm semi-automatic right next to the left side of the suspect's head.

The suspect attempted to turn the key in the ignition. I aimed my 9mm Beretta at the right side of his head and yelled, "If you turn the key, I am going to kill you." Just then, Detective Brady pointed his 9mm at the suspect from the front windshield, yelling, "You move this car; you are a dead man."

Suddenly, I heard a yell from a nearby home. It was his mother. "Please don't kill my baby!" The suspect looked at the three of us and started trembling. Then he froze in horror. He was the proverbial deer caught in the headlights. Our shock and awe tactics served us well. Before contemplating his next move, Franklin opened the car door and yanked him onto the ground. We quickly handcuffed him, and almost on cue, we observed a marked DC police cruiser drive up and stop right in front of us.

We quickly ushered the assailant in the back seat of a black female DC police officer's car. She did not seem the least bit concerned about the suspect; it was business as usual for her. The female DC police officer smiled and looked back at the suspect. "You are not getting any more sex tonight. Somebody might be getting your stuff tonight," she said. The suspect kept looking at us. He was in total amazement that we caught him.

I breathed a sigh of relief. As I entered the Criminal Investigations Division, the Captain asked, "The Chief wants to know who else was with you when you went hands-on with the guy?" I provided the name of the two detectives. The captain laughed and said. "It seems no matter how often they throw you down in narcotics, you always manage to land on your feet and keep running. I just smiled. I was shocked that the captain was aware of my challenges in narcotics.

We had the car impounded back to our jurisdiction. We had a detective follow the vehicle back to the criminal investigations division to ensure there would be no issue regarding the chain of custody. At that point, we obtained a search warrant for the car. We found the black bag that all the victims described. We also found an AK-47 assault rifle with armor-piercing rounds, the mask used during the rape, the duct tape, the knife, the crossbow, and the arrows he used to commit the crimes. The car also contained the tape recorder he used to tape his conversation with the victim at the phone booth. On the tape, he also had surveillance notes documenting what times the lights went out at his victims' homes.

The rapist used his crimes to create fear in the community to scare them into buying a new alarm. The rapist had recently been fired from an alarm company. Therefore, he created a market for his alarm installation business. That is why he asked the victims about their alarm systems. We also found flyers in his vehicle that advised customers, "There was a rapist on the loose." He thereby demonstrated a need to buy his alarm systems. He went back to the same neighborhoods where he committed the crimes and tried to sell them new alarms.

Two DNA samples linked the suspect to the crimes. In addition, one of the victim's wallets was found in the car. As a result, the suspect was charged with 44 counts of 1st-degree rape, first-degree sex offense, robbery, false imprisonment, and weapons charges.

The next day the police chief had a press conference where he displayed all the evidence seized from the vehicle's trunk for news the media to photograph. I looked at the two detectives who helped me take the suspect down and gave them a high five. I was floating on cloud nine.

That joy proved to be short-lived. By the next day, I was going through a living hell. I did not realize it, but since the arrest was made outside of our jurisdiction, it caused the case to come under enormous legal scrutiny. It was fright night for real. I had orchestrated the arrest, setting myself up perfectly to be the fall guy for the case. That was not the only thing that had me worried. All the evidence seized was now in jeopardy.

I met with the Deputy State's attorney, who was prosecuting the case a few days later. She asked me and the other two detectives who apprehended the suspect if we could identify him again if we saw him. They both said no. If I were the prosecutor, I would have freaked out. However, not Deb. She was cool as a cucumber. She turned around, looked at me, and asked if I could identify him. I said, "Absolutely!" Then it dawned on me; I was the only witness who was able to put the final nail in his coffin. If I screwed the case up, I could forget getting my Sergeant stripes.

Deb asked me if my commanders received permission from the DC police chief before going into DC. I told her that I did not know. Of course, I assumed that the Captain secured approval. She told me to check with my commanders. I spoke to my Captain, and I asked him if he had secured the permission; his face turned red. "Don't come to me with that bullshit; let the lawyers fight it out!" He replied. I wondered whose side he was on.

I met with Deb again and let her know the Captain's response. Furthermore, she was very calm. I told her I had been Deputized as an FBI Agent to work the Barksdale case. She researched and found that my federal credentials only gave me jurisdiction for the Barksdale case. To use the Captain's words, "The lawyers had to fight it out."

The judge scheduled a hearing for the lawyers to fight it out in court. The bout was between the Deputy State's Attorney and the Chief Public Defender. In court, Deb deployed every legal justification imaginable. She finally asserted that I had the right to make a citizen's arrest in DC at a minimum. The case survived the evidence suppression hearing and was scheduled for trial. It was clear that getting a conviction would be a steep and heavy lift walking uphill. Nevertheless, it was another burden for me to bear.

I knew that my testimony had to be on point at trial. So, I went back to the scene of the suspect's arrest three times and studied every detail of the area. Then, finally, when the first day of the trial rolled around, I walked into the courtroom. There were a bunch of news reporters gathered inside.

As I walked toward the witness stand to take the oath, the suspect looked at me with a big grin and said, "How are you doing today, detective?" His words took me by total surprise. I looked at the judge and the suspect's attorney, and I finally answered, "I am doing good." Then, I took the witness stand and explained how the entire surveillance unfolded.

Deb pointed to a whiteboard that contained several pictures of the scene. She walked over to the witness stand, handed me a pointer, and asked me to describe each crime scene picture. At that point, I was glad that I had taken the initiative to study the area. After I went back to the witness stand, I noticed that someone was sketching me. Next, the public defender grilled me about the crime scene and asked me what authority I had to make the arrest. That question had my stomach in knots. All I could say was that I feared that if we did not get him that day that he would rape other women. Finally, my torture was over. The defense counsel finally ran out of questions. I glanced at the jury quickly to gauge their receptiveness to my testimony. They all had poker faces. No relief there. I headed out of the courtroom. A group of reporters immediately swarmed me.

That night, I was playing with my children when the nightly news came on. They began talking about the trial. A few seconds before the report ended, a sketch of me flashed across the screen. I said, "Oh my God. My daughter was sitting on my lap. She asked, "What is wrong, daddy? I fell silent. My wife asked, "What is wrong, honey?" I slowly turned in her direction and said, "They just showed a sketch of me at the trial on television. I was still working undercover at that time. "There goes my cover," I replied.

A few days later, Deb called and said, "The judge ruled on the issue of your arrest." Okay, give it to me straight." I said. I braced myself for what was to come next. "The judge ruled that the arrest of the rapist was illegal and that you had no legal justification to stop him under D.C. law." He added that a person could only make a citizen's arrest for a felony in D.C.

I told her, "I only have myself to blame for this one. They have wanted me to screw up for a long time. I guess they finally got their wish." She said, "The judge ruled that you had every right to detain for the interest of public safety at least briefly until D.C. authorities arrived. He added that your brief detention was reasonable under the circumstances." The person whom the news media dubbed the crossbow rapist was convicted of rape. He received three life sentences.

This AK-47 rifle, crossbow, arrow, mask, knife, and duct
tape were recovered from the trunk of the serial rapist.

CHAPTER 81

THE COLOMBIAN CONNECTION

Two weeks later, every narcotics detective in the division was assigned to work a wiretap case with Major Narcotics. Detectives in the narcotics division were expecting a drug shipment, the mother lode. The lead investigator was my archenemy. He was an extremely well-known and well-respected detective in the region. You would have thought he invented narcotics investigations.

Just about everyone agreed he was the main person who professionalized narcotics investigations. He expected great results. He convinced our captain, the Drug Enforcement Administration (DEA), the FBI, and the Bureau of Alcohol, Tobacco, and Firearms (ATF) that the case would yield dividends for all of them. All the agencies came on board and participated in the investigation.

At about four thirty that day, my sergeant walked toward my desk, looking distressed. "What is going on now, Sarge?" I asked. He explained that a sergeant from the Gardena Police Department had intercepted a package containing drugs and had allowed the box to proceed to our jurisdiction for future investigation.

"You know you're the only one in the division that isn't working Detective Miner's wiretap case," he said.

I replied, "And?"

"The Major Narcotics lieutenant gave it to me to handle," he replied. "I do not know what the hell he wants to do on short notice.

This case is time-sensitive, and we don't have anyone to work it." He braced himself for my inevitable, brief tirade.

"Let me get this straight," I said. "The captain transferred me out of Major Narcotics after I worked a case for almost three years that they took credit for. They held a press conference on that case and a second conference on the crossbow rapist case. Now, they want me to investigate a narcotics case with no help. Unbelievable!

"No worries, Sarge. I got you. You know, I still love locking up drug dealers. I will go down to homicide and get some of the other FBI task force detectives and take care of this. I want you to know that the only reason I'm doing this is that I have mad love for you since you are from Baltimore." As he started walking back to his desk, I smiled and said, "Stay black, man!"

"You watch too many Spike Lee movies," he said.

Less than an hour later, I was able to assemble a team to work the case. When I walked over to the sergeant's office to let him know I had assembled a team, he was on the phone with his wife. A few minutes later, he told me his wife told him one of her best employees at the bank was arrested for selling drugs. The suspect asked my sergeant's wife for help because he knew she was married to a Prince George's County sergeant.

I asked, "What did you tell her, Sarge?"

"That I would speak to the detective who arrested him," he said. The sergeant said that he met him and that he was a good guy. The sergeant's phone rang again, and he spoke to his wife. "You're kidding me," he said. "Okay. I'll call you right back." He turned to me. "Good news. Guess who arrested my wife's employee."

"I give up, Sarge," I replied. "Who locked up the scumbag?"

"It was you." He then asked me if I could give him a break.

"Sarge," I said, "I don't mean no harm, but there is only one way for someone to get a break from Detective Hicks. They must give me a bigger fish, one with at least 125 grams of cocaine—minimum, to be exact."

When the sergeant dropped the suspect's name, I yelled, "That little demon! The only break I'm going to give him is to break my foot off in him."

The sergeant said, "Oh my God, come on, man. I feel bad for the guy. He lives in Howard County. He's a real low-key guy who doesn't bother anybody." He looked intensely at me as he noticed a change in my demeanor.

I took a moment to calm myself down. Then I took on a more quiet but severe tone. I said, "Sarge, don't let that selfish little yuppie fool you, man. He is bad news. He dared to sell drugs out of a single parent's house who had a three-month-old baby. He had all these crackheads knocking on her door, asking for drugs. She would call him to sell drugs to the customer.

"You should have seen all the zombies coming in and out of her sparsely furnished apartment. You should have seen him when I did the undercover operation. He was in his world. He seemed to be getting his jollies out of manipulating that young girl. The answer is no, Sarge. He is going down! I don't even want him to snitch for me."

"Lord Jesus," the sergeant replied. "You are hard-core."

I could tell the sergeant was going to make another attempt to get me to change course. I turned my attention back to my importation case. Once word got out, I seized four kilos of cocaine. Sergeant Stryker and his little henchman started scheming how they could steal the case from me. I was sitting at my desk when my lieutenant came over to me and asked me if he could see my four kilograms of cocaine. That was the most unusual request I had ever heard. *Why in the world would the lieutenant even ask me something so simple?* I thought.

"Sir, we are about to deliver these drugs tomorrow morning," I said. "I don't want to reopen the box, because I'm already concerned that the suspects will be suspicious because it has bite marks on it from the drug dog in California." He told me Detective Miner believed the drugs belonged to his case. "Lieutenant, let's be realistic here," I said. "I'm investigating two American drug dealers from Gardena, California, in their connection to a cartel in Colombia. Conversely, he's investigating a Jamaican drug gang. There is no connection other than the one inside his Vulcan mind. I am not catering to his insecurities!" The lieutenant walked out of the room.

A captain from another division had been listening to our conversation. He laughed and said, "That boy is going crazy over there. He can't stand the fact that you're outshining him. You aren't even assigned to Major Narcotics anymore, but you're still seizing more drugs than him." I was satisfied the matter was over, and I went back to my desk to strategize the delivery of the four kilos. The lieutenant came back in and said he wanted to see the cocaine.

I said, "This is my case, this mass seizure. This is evidence. He's not going to see it!"

"What if I want to see it?" the lieutenant asked.

I said, "Excuse me, sir?"

"You heard me," he said. "I want to see it. Show me the dope." The room grew quiet. Everybody in the office was looking to see how I was going to respond.

"Yes, sir," I told the lieutenant. I hesitated for a second. "How are you—or anyone else—going to link this dope to his suspect, sir?" I asked. The lieutenant gave me a nasty look. "No problem, sir!" I exclaimed. "Fuckin' jerk," I said.

"What was that?" the lieutenant asked.

"Nothing, sir," I replied. "Fuckin' jerk," I whispered again.

The lieutenant put his hands on his hips like a father about to scold his son. We were testing each other's patience. We walked over to the evidence room together. I removed the box from the evidence locker and showed the cocaine to the lieutenant.

"See?" I asked. "The drug cartel's name is written on it. See the mustard and pepper in the box? They were attempting to throw off the drug dog. When have you ever known Jamaicans to ship drugs like that?"

The lieutenant said simply, "Thanks, buddy."

I said, "You're welcome, sir."

I held my frustration in with every ounce of my strength. When my sergeant shut the door, I exploded. "Fucking spineless jellyfish!" He let the little commie bastard coach him into having me open my evidence! I couldn't stand Miner and his little snake sergeant. They were lower than whale manure!

The next day, I went down to the UPS depot in Maryland and picked up the box containing the four kilograms of cocaine the Gardena Police Department had intercepted. I obtained a search warrant for the package inside. I reached for a pair of scissors on my desk and briefly examined the box and then yelled, "Damn it!"

The sergeant and two detectives ran over to my desk and asked what was wrong. "Their stupid little dog bit all over this box. What the hell? If they see those bite marks, they're going to be suspicious. I wish they had used the type of dogs that just sit when they alert on the package."

Nonetheless, I devised a plan to deliver the package. I even convinced the sergeant to work undercover for me. He came to the hotel to provide the box. We staked out the hotel lobby. A young man in his early thirties was pacing around the lobby. As soon as the sergeant walked into the hotel carrying the package, the young man perked up. When the sergeant told the hotel clerk he had a delivery for Jefferson, the suspect walked quickly over to the hotel lobby phone and picked up the receiver.

The hotel phone rang, and the hotel lobby clerk answered it. The hotel clerk advised that Mr. Jefferson was on the phone and inquired about the package. The sergeant took the phone and offered to bring the box to the caller's room. The caller told the undercover police sergeant to leave it with the hotel clerk. The suspect then got on the house phone again.

Another male came down the elevator, and I had the other suspect in the hotel lobby. A few minutes later, a female employee walked from behind the hotel desk and met with the two men. All three of them boarded the elevator together. I loved setting up surveillance. It helped us put the pieces of the puzzle together.

We waited for two hours for someone to pick up the package, but no one ever came back to retrieve the box. Therefore, the sergeant took the box back and called off the operation. He declared that the surveillance was a lost cause because the suspects had been spooked. The undercover sergeant gave the hotel manager a card for

Mr. Jefferson, stating to have the package redelivered. But of course, they never called back.

*****

On Monday morning, I told the sergeant I was heading back to the hotel.

He asked, "For what?"

I said, "I want to lock somebody up for this case."

He laughed and said, "Good luck!"

When I arrived back at the hotel, I asked the manager for the phone records. I specifically asked him to let me know if any phone was placed in Gardena, California. He told me he did not have the phone call records. That aroused my suspicion, because I knew hotels gave their customers an itemized list of their calls at checkout. I made a mental note and started interviewing the clerk who worked the previous Friday.

I introduced myself as Detective Hicks of the Major Narcotics Section. The clerk looked extremely nervous. I shook his hand and noticed his palms were sweating. I asked him if anyone by the name of Mark Jefferson was listed as a guest there. Mark Jefferson was the intended recipient of the box I intercepted at the UPS depot. He answered no without even checking the records. That also aroused my suspicion. I looked him straight in his eyes and asked, "What the hell are you hiding?"

The clerk took a deep breath and admitted he had lied about there not being a Mark Jefferson. He handed me the hotel registration card. It showed where he put a line through the name Mark Jefferson. He confessed that he knew two big drug dealers were staying at the hotel under that name. I went back to the manager and told him he and the clerk were part of a drug conspiracy. He became nervous and told me he was afraid to say he knew who I was looking for because he and his family lived at the hotel.

Finally, he told me the room where they were staying. The clerk also said to me that the two men came there regularly. He told me they always got a corner room to check the parking lot for surveillance at the hotel. I asked for uniformed officers to come to the hotel to assist us. As a result, two patrol officers and two detectives went to the room where the two men stayed. At the same time, I headed to the prosecutor's office to get a grand jury subpoena to obtain the phone and hotel registration records.

The two men were still there, and to my amazement, eventually, they came out of their room. I turned around and went back to the hotel. I found out that the two men in the room were the same men who mailed the package from California. I placed both men under arrest for possession with intent to distribute four kilograms of cocaine and for importing over twenty-eight grams of cocaine into the state.

I obtained a search warrant for the hotel room. I could not find anything related to drugs. However, there was about five thousand dollars worth of clothes in the room. I also found two brand-new computers and scanners. However, there were no receipts for anything in the room. That also aroused my suspicion.

One item I found was from Montgomery Ward. The store was close by, so I went there. Unfortunately, they could not track the person who purchased the item, but they confirmed the package was purchased the day after the men arrived. They also told me the person bought an extended warranty for the item.

As a customer, I remembered anyone who purchased an extended warranty put their name in a warranty book, so I asked to see that book. It was there where I found the name of the person who used the credit card to purchase the item. To make a long story short, I charged the two suspects with several thefts and turned several other theft cases over to other local detectives.

Further investigation revealed that the DEA previously arrested one of the suspects and had a prior arrest with the United States Marshal Service. Both suspects were convicted of all charges. One suspect received a five-year sentence, and the other suspect received a ten-year sentence.

My partner's face is blocked out to conceal his identity. Four kilograms of cocaine seized in New Carrollton, Maryland. The cocaine was labeled with the name of the Colombian drug cartel. The box contained pepper and mustard to throw off the scent from the drug detection dogs.

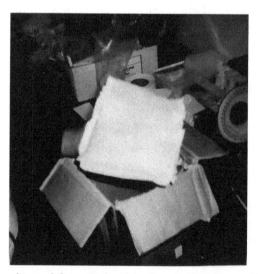

This box was shipped from Colombia, South America to Bladensburg, Maryland. The box contained a total of one kilogram of cocaine. 250 grams of cocaine was compressed on each side of the box.

CHAPTER 82

THE AGONY OF DEFEAT

It's been a long, long time coming, But I
know a change gonna come.
—Sam Cook

My four-kilogram seizure whetted my appetite to work more
significant drug cases. I was on the hunt for bigger game. I analyzed
my investigative strategies and concluded I was doing undercover
buys for other agencies as a favor, earning only a small return on
my investment. Moreover, I was conducting undercover work for
small-level drug cases and neglecting the time I should have devoted
to working on more significant cases. I realized I was being used by
some of the agencies I worked with.

I had several cases for the Postal Inspector's Office, so when I
learned that the postal inspectors were throwing me the small fish
by conducting undercover buys from their employees, then giving
white investigators in my same office large shipments of cocaine,
I was livid. I called the supervisory agent for the Postal Inspector's
Office and said, "I have a question for you. Why would you call me
to do these low-level undercover buys from employees, but you never
call me when you get large shipments of drugs?"

The supervisory agent claimed he did not know I was interested
in those types of cases. "Look, man," I said, "I could have referred
you to Street Narcotics for all those cases. However, I did these cases

strictly as a favor to you. So now could you do me a favor? Whenever you have a large shipment of drugs coming in, I need you to call me." The supervisory agent apologized and assured me he would let me know when the next shipment of drugs was intercepted.

My timing could not have been better. A few weeks after our phone conversation, he told me they intercepted twelve kilograms of cocaine destined for our county. I entered the information into our database as an active investigation. I was floating on air, thinking about seizing a large load of cocaine. When I went back to my desk, the office was eerily quiet. I heard Sergeant Stryker and Detective Miner whispering something about a case.

The next day, I learned that Miner's squad was working a case with U.S. Customs involving the seizure of ten kilograms of cocaine. As I would later learn, the problem was that U.S. Customs did not share the address where the cocaine was being shipped. Just when I thought things could not get any better, I received a call from the Postal Inspector's Office supervisor telling me U.S. Customs had seized an additional ten kilograms being shipped to the same address. Now my seizure had multiplied to twenty-two kilograms.

I briefed my sergeant and prepared to coordinate the delivery of the twenty-two kilos of cocaine. When the customs detectives came into the office, they gave Sergeant Stryker the address to deliver the drugs. I had to get a front-row seat to watch Sergeant Stryker's facial expression as the clerk entered the suspect's name and address into the computer. He received the shock of his life when he saw my name flashing in red letters, saying Active Investigation. He sat there staring at the computer in disbelief. I walked out of the room.

We coordinated the case with U.S. Customs and the Postal Inspector's Office, seized twenty-two kilograms of cocaine, and arrested a couple of Colombians. But when our monthly stat sheet came out the next month, I could not believe my eyes. I was not given credit for the seizure of any of the drugs. Just to spite me, the lieutenant credited the seizure to Sergeant Stryker and my sergeant. I went completely off.

I said to my sergeant, "What kind of twisted bullcrap is this? I followed the rules, which are clear. If you have a case listed in the computer as active, you get credit for the drug seizure. Can you explain to me how two sergeants get credit for seizing dope? All the previous stat sheets don't even contain the sergeants' names." My sergeant urged me to calm down. "This is bullcrap!" I said again.

They could not stand to see a black man succeed, so I knocked on the lieutenant's door, but before I had a chance to say anything, he said, "Hicks, I don't want to hear it." Discrimination was so systemic within the division that it seemed like it would never end. It seemed like every time I took a bite out of crime, the police department took a bite out of me.

CHAPTER 83

THE BREAKTHROUGH

My breakthrough finally came. My bureau chief called to notify me I was on the list for promotion to sergeant. My dream had come true while the Negative Regime's worst nightmare was realized. Now I could implement a vision for the community. I had the distinct pleasure of being the only person in the Narcotics Enforcement Division to get promoted to sergeant during the promotion cycle. Oh, what a feeling that was!

My promotion and transfer were effective in ten days. I looked forward to socializing and reminiscing at my goingaway party with my good friends in the division, and I asked my sergeant for the date of my goingaway party. When I saw his face after I asked the question, I knew something was amiss. Sergeant Stryker rained on my parade, delivering his final blows. His five-year bout to triumph over my infectious positive attitude culminated in the canceling of my goingaway party. He also conveniently forgot to order me the customary plaque for my service in narcotics.

I stewed over the revelation while sitting at my desk. Then finally, I stood up and made a beeline for the sergeant's office. My sergeant observed my demeanor. He intercepted me before I reached the door. "I know it hurts," he said before I could speak a word. "But don't do anything that would jeopardize your promotion." I knew his intervention blessed me. If I had cut loose on my antagonist, I would have lost all self-control. My success, I decided, would be my revenge.

I eagerly anticipated receiving the official notification of my promotion to sergeant. I wanted official notice of my promotion because my lieutenant verbally notified me of my promotion during the previous promotional cycle. Then I found out a few minutes later that I died number one on the sergeant's list. At 4:30 p.m., the promotion list was released by our teletype system. I stared momentarily as I read the teletype: "Promoted to the rank of sergeant, Maurice R. Hicks Sr."

I felt truly blessed. God allowed me to prevail under extremely difficult circumstances. I wanted to be a sergeant in the Narcotics Enforcement Division. When detectives in the Narcotics Enforcement Division and our Criminal Investigations Division were promoted, it was common to promote experienced detectives to detective sergeant and leave them in the same detective units as supervisors.

I immediately went to my personnel file to ensure all my training certificates and commendations were in the file. The captain saw me in the clerk's office and asked me why I was looking at my personnel file. I explained that I wanted to ensure any commanders considering me for their division had accurate qualifications. The captain laughed and told me no one would be looking at my file. He explained no one cared what I did in the department. I looked at the veteran clerk, who shook her head, agreeing with the captain.

On the way out of the office, I ran into my friend and fellow detective Herman. He shook my hand, smiled, and said, "Congratulations, brother. Where do you think you are heading?" I told him I hoped I could stay in narcotics. He asked if I had made the captain aware I wanted to stay there. I told him no. He urged me to take the items in my personnel file to the captain and express my interest in remaining in narcotics, but I was very reluctant to talk with the captain. After all, my last two cases were profiled on the news by the commander of Investigative Services.

Against my better judgment, I knocked on the door of the captain's office. He motioned for me to come in. I told him I was interested in the open sergeant's position. Then I placed a large stack of papers on his desk containing numerous letters of commendation for narcotics cases and several training certificates for narcotics investigations.

He frowned and turned his head to the side. "I pretty much know your qualifications," he said. "But we're not going to keep you here." I tried to make eye contact with him, but he would not look directly at me. So finally, I slowly gathered my papers from his desk and walked out of his office.

My buddy Herman was waiting for me. He smiled and said, "How did it go, brother?"

"I can't believe that I let you talk me into this!" I replied. "I knew I shouldn't have done it. I just played myself. I made myself look like a blinking idiot by asking him for a job. I felt like a damn imbecile." I had given the captain a final opportunity to extinguish my fire. A piece of scripture came to mind as I tried to make sense of the situation: "Do not be too anxious for anything."

A few days later, I ran into my former boss, who was the chief of detectives. When he saw me, he said, "Congratulations on your promotion, Moe. You had some great years here. Where do you think you're headed for your new assignment?" I told him that I hoped to stay in narcotics but that the captain told me otherwise. I asked him if he felt I did an excellent job in narcotics.

"I remember how good you were at catching those drug dealers when you were still a rookie," he said. I asked him why that was not good enough for me to stay in narcotics. "I am not going to interfere with any of my commander's decisions." I realized I was still clueless. There was no justice for me there. I had to accept that. I held my head down and just walked away. It was so defeating.

Later, I told my coworker Rebecca about the incident.

"What?" she said. "Just yesterday, I saw the chief of detectives at the FOP Lodge bragging about how good of a detective you are."

I said, "Get the fuck out of here!"

She insisted that he had told her how proud he was of me. I was perplexed why my haters in narcotics insisted on keeping me from returning to narcotics. My sergeant said they told him I had too strong of a personality as a detective, and they thought I would be even more challenging to manage as a sergeant. But I knew there was more to the story. I did not know it at the time, but my transfer out of the division was divine intervention. It kept me out of the clutches of the Negative Regime.

Within three days, I picked myself back up, marched on, and accepted my fate. Then I shifted my attention to getting back into uniform and sporting my new sergeant stripes. Fortunately, the Negative Regime could not control where I chose to focus my thoughts. The good thing was, I was still a sergeant, which meant I would have a chance to implement my vision. Naturally, at that point, I figured I would be heading to a patrol station. To me, being a patrol sergeant was the real deal.

I picked up the new uniform shirts with my sergeant stripes and awaited confirmation regarding my new assignment. Nothing could keep me down for long. I had something the vultures did not have: a deeply rooted faith in the Almighty God. Man did not control my fate; only God could do that.

I was flying on a natural high as I made my triumphant return to the Hyattsville station. I chose to focus on the fact that I had the distinction of being the only detective to be promoted out of the Narcotics Enforcement Division for that two-year promotion cycle. I learned that several other newly promoted sergeants were also being transferred to the Hyattsville station.

Several sergeants told me they were going to get the ACTION Team sergeant's slot. Sergeant Stryker demonstrated a skill many other supervisors and commanders bragged about: the talent to F with people whenever they felt like it. I spoke to a few retirees who still bragged about their continued ability to F with officers even during their retirement.

I learned a valuable lesson from that experience. The best revenge was to be successful. As my grandfather always told me, "A man can plan his steps, but the Lord determines all outcomes." Or as the deodorant commercial says, "Never let them see you sweat."

I felt good that I was leaving narcotics on the highest note possible. I led a federal task force that dismantled county history's most dangerous drug organization in my last year alone. I apprehended a serial rapist, and I seized several millions of dollars of cocaine. But unfortunately, those accomplishments were achieved under the duress by people who rebuked me instead of supporting me. My commanders refused to nominate me for awards acknowledging my work on the Barksdale case and for the apprehension of the crossbow rapist.

I was curious about my new assignment. I was happy to be back at the Hyattsville station. I had worked at Hyattsville before being transferred to narcotics. I expected to be assigned back to patrol. However, my new station commander was my old captain from narcotics. My new commander had been promoted to the rank of major.

He was the person who came to my rescue when the Negative Regime was tormenting me. I had a glimmer of hope that he would put me in charge of the station-level narcotics unit (the ACTION Team). However, the good old boy network was set to prevail. The commander promised the job to an old friend who was already at the station. However, in the commander's haste to go to Mardi Gras, he forgot to make personnel decisions for the station before leaving. Therefore, the decision was left to the captain.

The captain asked about the qualifications of all the sergeants at the station. At the time, he was told I had just been promoted out of narcotics. The captain stated that I was the most qualified person for the job. The next day, I learned I would become the officer in charge of the ACTION Team. I would coordinate narcotics investigations for the entire station.

God blessed me with the best of both worlds. I was able to coordinate narcotics investigations, and I was allowed to moonlight. The moonlighting jobs added another twenty thousand to thirty thousand dollars per year in extra income. In addition, my wife and I were expecting our third child together. Therefore, the job was a Godsend.

As soon as the word got out about my new position, I became public enemy number one among the sergeants at the station. As the officer in charge of the ACTION Team, I met with every sergeant in the station and deployed their officers to help us on certain days. The first sergeant I met was a 25-year veteran police Sergeant named Sergeant O'Donnell. His arms were covered with tattoos. The Lieutenant introduced him to me. He said, "Sergeant O'Donnell, I want you to meet Sergeant Hicks. You and your men will be reporting to him on overlap days."

I reached out my hand to shake his. He just looked at my hand, crossed his arms, and turned back around to look at the lieutenant. He did not utter a word. I quickly moved my hand back to my side and tried to make eye contact with him. He avoided eye contact with me; instead, he began talking to one of his men. He succeeded in expressing his disapproval for my getting the job. It was unheard of for a newly promoted sergeant to be given a supervisory position in a specialty unit at the station level.

The lieutenant and I were walking back to his office when I ran into the former ACTION Team sergeant, who had been promoted to lieutenant. He attempted to introduce me to a lieutenant whom I referred to as Lieutenant Benedict. However, Lieutenant Benedict told him he was busy and would catch up with me later when he started the introduction.

I saw Lieutenant Benedict three times that week. Every time I saw him, I asked him for the keys to my office. Each time, he acted as if he did not hear me. Finally, on the fourth time I passed him in the station, I asked him for the keys again. He turned his face as he passed me and almost hit his face against the wall. I complained to my lieutenant that he failed to acknowledge me or give me the keys to my office.

Lieutenant Benedict came to my office the next day and said, "I think we got off on the wrong foot. Were you ever in narcotics? Because I cannot remember seeing you there." I knew that was bait. I knew he was a close friend of a member of the Negative Regime. He was insinuating that I was way beneath him concerning my investigative skills. I had a witty come-back prepared for such an occasion. However, I held it back. I knew God would be my vindicator. I knew that he would feel the wrath of God like many of my other enemies. I later learned that his payback would come more swiftly than initially anticipated. Although unrelated to that incident, the wrath he experienced was much more personal.

I decided not to retaliate against Benedict. Instead, I decided to pull out my sword. It was not the sword that cuts you. Instead, my sword was the word of God. In the words of Michelle Obama, "When they go low, we go high."

I said, "You were the rude person to me, sir." But, unfortunately, the little respect for him had utterly disintegrated by then. He finally relinquished the keys to my office. But then, he proceeded to do everything to undermine my authority even though I worked to bring to justice the same person he could never catch as a narcotics detective, Barksdale.

Benedict did his best to drill into my investigators' heads that I was not qualified to be their supervisor. However, he would soon learn what a motivated Marine could do. My light would shine brighter than he could ever imagine. We, as a team, achieved a level of success in the job that he never dreamed of. I was later awarded the prestigious Veterans of Foreign Wars award for my role as the Officer in Charge of the ACTION Team.

CHAPTER 84

NO WITNESS, NO CASE

God never ceased to amaze me. He always showed me favor in my life. A few weeks after my conversation with Lieutenant Benedict, I received a second surprise. The assistant United States attorney on the Barksdale case wrote a letter of commendation to the police chief regarding my work on the Barksdale case. He also requested I be assigned to his office for six months while his team prepared to take the case to trial in federal court.

The United States Attorney's Office selected Harvard-trained assistant United States attorney Robert McGahn and Rebecca Weinstein to present the government's case. Barksdale's choice for an attorney was stunningly clever. First, he chose Baltimore's best and brightest attorney, Courtland Johnson. Barksdale and his associates were initially charged in Prince George's County Circuit Court. The attorney fee for the case was estimated to be between forty and fifty thousand dollars. However, the state case was dropped after Barksdale's organization was charged in federal court.

The state's case was now over. The fee covered only the state case. The new federal case cost would cost Barksdale an estimated sixty or seventy thousand dollars. A price that taxpayers likely ended up paying for.

Like gangster John Gotti, Barksdale never relied solely on an attorney to facilitate his get-out-of-jail-free card. Instead, he knew no bounds when it came to intimidating people. For example, he sent threatening letters to the Prince George's County executive and a newspaper reporter with the *Prince George's County Journal* after he wrote about Barksdale's arrest.

Barksdale set his sights on a new and high-profile target: assistant United States attorney Rebecca Weinstein. She received an up close and personal glimpse of the fear people in the community still faced from Barksdale. After presiding over a two-week evidence suppression hearing against Barksdale, I noticed Rebecca was much quieter than usual. Instead, she spoke in a very calm tone as she explained she received multiple pages to Harmony Cemetery, the same cemetery Barksdale discussed sending his enemies to while he was on the phone. Rebecca fought hard to dispense her fear and move on with the trial. However, the fear still lingered as the trial progressed. For the first time in her career as a federal prosecutor, she had to be escorted by a United States marshal for personal protection.

Barksdale's mind went into overdrive. He was facing a life sentence in prison. His analytical mind went to work to try to identify potential weaknesses in his organization. A light bulb went off in his head. He correctly surmised that investigators would target the women in the organization first. His greatest threat was his girlfriend at the time, Fantasia. He knew that the best man to eliminate threats was Antoine.

Antoine previously demonstrated his skills in witness intimidation. Thus, he knew exactly the right tone to strike to discourage Fantasia from testifying against Barksdale effectively. Barksdale contacted Antoine and put his plan into place. Fantasia knew Barksdale would do anything to get out of prison. However, since she had criminal exposure herself, she agreed to testify against Barksdale in court. She was staying at her aunt's house until the trial began. Meanwhile, Antoine started questioning Fantasia's neighbors and friends. Finally, he reported her disappearance back to Barksdale.

Fantasia was lying low at her aunt's house. She felt safe there. Only a few of her trusted associates knew where her auntie Patty lived. One night, as the clock ticked past midnight, Fantasia drifted into a deep sleep. She needed to escape from the enormous stress she was under. She awakened to the presence of someone near her bedroom window. She heard footsteps outside her bedroom door. Then a knock came on the door.

Fantasia partially opened the door, which had a chain. There stood Antoine. Fantasia had seen him only once. She knew Barksdale deployed him on only the most sensitive assignments. Barksdale's henchman had a sinister grin on his face. "Surprised to see me, baby girl?" he asked. "I know you are not snitching on my boy."

Fantasia tried to remain calm, but fear and trembling besieged her. The horror of what Antoine possibly had in store for her overpowered her mind. It became difficult for her to think or to speak. She knew her name appeared on the witness list to testify against Barksdale. But Fantasia was streetwise. She knew she had to develop a logical explanation for why her name had appeared on the witness list.

She smiled at Antoine and said, "Those feds must think that I am crazy. There is no way I am going to testify against my man. They threatened me by telling me they would put my name on the witness list if I did not cooperate. I told them to go ahead. I guess they did it."

Antoine shook his head. "I am glad to hear that, baby girl, because I would hate for something to happen to you."

Antoine was cautious about what he communicated verbally. He feared the feds might have Fantasia wired up, so he handed her a note. The note said, "You testify, you die!" Then he took the note back and drove off operating a white Nissan Maxima.

Fantasia closed the door and began to hyperventilate. Her midnight rendezvous with the death angel was the last straw. As far she was concerned, Barksdale had demonstrated that no one was beyond his reach. Fantasia wondered whether she had selected the wrong team. If she took the jail time, at least she might live to see a brighter day. Now death was staring her in the face. As she lay awake in bed, she wondered if other henchmen were lying in wait for her outside her aunt's residence.

The following day, Fantasia called FBI special agent Kozlowski. Her voice was coarse and unrecognizable, and she was crying uncontrollably. Agent Kozlowski asked her what was wrong. It took about ten seconds for Fantasia to finally get words out of her mouth.

"He sent that crazy-ass guy to kill me last night," she said. "I almost died last night! He came right here to my aunt's house. He was creeping near my bedroom window. I don't know how he found me. I'm going to die!"

Agent Kozlowski used his quiet, soothing voice to calm her down. "Fantasia," he said, "if the man wanted you dead, you would be dead. You need to find another place to stay immediately. Make sure you tell me where you are and nobody else."

We all wondered whether Fantasia would live long enough to provide her testimony against Barksdale. I feared she would be our first female homicide victim. We needed to find the man who had threatened her as quickly as possible. We needed to send him a message telling him not to intimidate our witnesses. But we did not have enough information to determine the stalker's identity.

Barksdale developed a backup plan in the event that Antoine's visit to Fantasia did not prove persuasive enough. On the first day of the trial, a mysterious African American man slithered into the federal courthouse in Baltimore and took a front-row seat at Barksdale's trial. FBI agents, United States marshals, and the judge noticed that the man immediately began making scary faces at the cooperating witnesses testifying against the Barksdale Gang. Barksdale dispatched both day and night stalkers to carry out his wicked schemes.

The judge stopped the trial and asked the FBI agents to come forward. The judge told the agents to sit beside the court intruder to discourage him from intimidating their witnesses. The agents flanked the provocateur. But unfortunately, he was unfazed, and he continued to make scary faces at each witness who took the witness stand.

Agent Kozlowski returned to the office and told me about the mysterious man sitting in court, intimidating witnesses. The prosecutor asked me to begin escorting witnesses to the courtroom to testify. I was perplexed as to why the judge allowed the man to disturb the sanctity of the courtroom. Kozlowski explained to me that the judge could not bar the man from a public courtroom.

I took the liberty of peeking inside the courtroom after escorting one of our witnesses. I immediately recognized the court provocateur. He was one of Barksdale's most loyal subjects, Antoine. I recalled that Antoine had a prior conviction for witness intimidation.

Later, when Antoine exited the courtroom, I approached him and said, "What's up, Antoine?"

He replied, "What's up, Hicks?"

"What are you doing down here in Baltimore?" I asked.

"I'm just here to support a friend," he said.

"You and Barksdale are still close?" I asked. "That's cool, man. I'll catch you another time."

Antoine boarded the elevator. I quickly took the stairs and inconspicuously began following him. To my delight, the two case agents, Stone and Kozlowski, were just entering the building as Antoine exited it. I told them I was tailing the suspect from the courtroom. Surveillance saw Antoine leave in a white Nissan Maxima, the same type of vehicle Fantasia observed her stalker leave in. Later, FBI agents showed Fantasia a photograph of Antoine. We confirmed Antoine, the courtroom intimidator, was the same man who had threatened Fantasia.

Agent Kozlowski and I slapped hands. Then Kozlowski said, "We're going to get this little bastard." He and I both had hero syndrome. We took Antoine's intimidation of Fantasia and the rest of our witnesses personally. I was glad Kozlowski had Antoine in his sights. Kozlowski had a law degree. Therefore, I knew his paperwork would be airtight. I replied, "I can't wait to see the look on his face when the FBI shows up on his doorstep." I was as happy as a pig in the mud.

Agent Kozlowski promptly obtained a federal arrest warrant for Antoine for witness intimidation. He also obtained a search warrant for Antoine's residence. Our goal was to find the note he had handed to Fantasia to review it. He immediately took the letter back. We executed the search warrant on Antoine's place, but we could not find the written message he showed Fantasia. As a result, Antoine was arrested for federal witness intimidation.

CHAPTER 85

THE PERFECT MOUTHPIECE

Witness testimony was an essential component of any criminal case. We assembled a group of witnesses to corroborate the physical evidence and telephone conversations we intercepted during the wiretap. The federal prosecutors watched and listened as our witnesses meticulously testified about the illegal activities of the Barksdale Gang. After the first break in our witnesses' testimony, Barksdale's attorney, Courtland Johnson, convinced the judge to grant him administrative subpoena power. Armed with authority, Johnson began to discredit our witnesses one by one.

Barksdale's girlfriend, Fantasia, already took the witness stand, appearing calm and composed. She testified that Barksdale was the head of a criminal enterprise and that Barksdale used her apartment in Annapolis to stage his drug operation. Her testimony was clear and concise. Then it was time for Attorney Johnson to conduct his cross-examination. Johnson immediately laid into her.

"So, Fantasia, you want the court to believe that you are credible when you state you sold drugs for my client, correct?"

"Yes," Fantasia replied.

"Have you ever lied on a federal, state, or local government application?" Johnson asked.

Fantasia replied, "No, sir."

Johnson picked up a document on his desk and handed it to the bailiff to present to the judge. The clerk marked the exhibit and handed it back to the bailiff to give to the judge. Johnson passed the document to Fantasia.

"Can you tell me what this is?" Johnson asked.

Yes," Fantasia answered. "It is my application for welfare."

Johnson asked her whether the signature on the document was her signature. Fantasia confirmed it was. Johnson asked Fantasia to flip the paper over and to read a note on the back that she had left for Barksdale. Fantasia read the first part of the note, which seemed insignificant to her. She was asked to keep reading. The remainder of the message read, "I can't wait for you to get home so I can suck that big, fat pickle."

Fantasia slapped the microphone on the witness stand. She was suddenly transformed into a hostile witness. Johnson had succeeded in rattling her cage. He brought out a side of Fantasia that the jury had not yet seen. Barksdale's inside scoop regarding Fantasia's alleged welfare fraud paid dividends to his defense. Johnson demonstrated to the court that Fantasia had allegedly lied on her welfare application, thereby committing welfare fraud, an allegation that damaged her credibility as a witness against Barksdale.

Although Fantasia was humiliated on the witness stand, she nonetheless succeeded in inflicting damage on Barksdale. She corroborated information provided by other witnesses and conversations intercepted during the wiretap.

Witness Kindred Campbell took the stand next. He believed Barksdale was responsible for his cousin Beaver Johnson's death. However, Campbell was testifying for a different purpose. He had sold Barksdale drugs for over ten years. Campbell's methodical testimony told the story of Barksdale's rise to stardom in the organization. Then the court recessed, during which time Attorney Johnson faxed a subpoena to the Motor Vehicle Administration.

When the trial resumed, Johnson began his cross-examination of Campbell. First, he asked Campbell if he had ever lied on any official documents. Campbell replied no. Johnson showed him two different driver's licenses with Campbell's face on the permits and two other names. He was busted for lying.

Next, seventeen-year-old street dealer Sticks was called to the witness stand. Again, we expected Johnson to annihilate the kid like he did the previous two witnesses. Agents waited for Johnson to rip the kid into shreds. Instead, Barksdale watched closely as Sticks made his way to the witness stand. Once Sticks took the witness stand, he smiled as the federal prosecutor began to question him.

Sticks explained in detail the exact dates and times he met with Barksdale and Pit Bull. He told the court exactly how much dope he was given to sell, how much he made, and how much money he made for the Barksdale Gang. He explained how he used the skills he learned from the Barksdale Gang to elude law enforcement authorities. For example, Sticks told the court he learned the art of bailing out of vehicles to avoid apprehension. His testimony was so vivid and spoken with a clear and inviting voice that the jury could imagine being there.

None of the attorneys was able to find any legal documents to discredit Sticks. Nonetheless, Johnson began a slow, methodical cross-examination of the witness. He figured, if anyone could break a witness down, it was him. As Johnson went over the details of Sticks's testimony, he asked if he had heard the details correctly. Sticks repeated his testimony and gave Johnson a more detailed account than he showed during his direct examination. This time, Sticks described each outfit of every member of the Barksdale Gang during each interaction, right down to their tennis shoes. Each time Johnson paraphrased Sticks's testimony, Sticks would correct him and remind him of precisely what he had said in his earlier testimony.

After multiple unsuccessful attempts to discredit Sticks's testimony, Johnson reminded Sticks that he injured his head years ago, which might have affected his memory. Sticks reassured Johnson that his brain was fine and that he vividly remembered all the details of the conversations he recounted. Sticks's excitement over his interactions with the Barksdale Gang unmasked the enormity of Barksdale's negative influence over him. Four other defense attorneys meticulously cross-examined Sticks. However, none of them could lay a glove on him. His testimony was airtight. Sticks left the courtroom unscathed. He outwitted a team of the best defense attorneys I ever met.

I felt the weight of the world on my shoulders as I sat in the United States Attorney's Office, waiting for my turn to testify in the Barksdale case. I was the affiant on both wiretaps and all nine search warrants. I was the primary vehicle of ensuring justice was obtained for all of Barksdale's victims. His previous attorney annihilated the best and most seasoned detectives in court. I knew that if my testimony was contradicted in any way, it would be disastrous for the case; and if the case were thrown out, all our witnesses would be in jeopardy.

I knew that Sergeant Stryker, Detective Miner, and members of the Negative Regime in narcotics were hoping I would lose the case in court. I would be questioned about certain events that occurred as far back as ten years earlier in court. The FBI agent who was the co-affiant on the wiretap affidavit did not testify during the trial. He sat at the trial table with the prosecutors and was a spectator during the entire trial. I walked into the United States Attorney's Office wearing my dark-blue suit, a white shirt, and matching blue-and-white tie.

"Are you a preacher or a damn policeman?" one agent asked me.

Another agent said, "You look like someone who is about to preach the gospel."

I replied, "I am about to preach the gospel. I am going to tell the jury that them there boys been sinning!"

The joke lightened my mood. I felt like a preacher. I had a solid duty to stand firmly for people who were weaker than me. I then proudly took the witness stand wearing my blue preacher suit. After I finished the direct testimony, the prosecutor allowed me to address an error during the investigation. I misidentified the voice of a codefendant who was charged in the case. The prosecutor's strategy removed fuel from the defense attorneys' fire.

I carefully braced myself for the inevitable attacks during cross-examination. I was immediately bombarded by a flurry of questions from five different defense attorneys. Each attorney represented one of the members of the organization who were on trial. I took my time and thought carefully before answering questions from each attorney. Each attorney chose an angle by which to poke holes in my testimony.

I knew Attorney Johnson would zero in on a surveillance photo of Barksdale, Pit Bull, and several street-level dealers together in front of Pit Bull's house. I knew it was a rare and incriminating photograph. When Agent Joey Jackson and I saw the group gathering in front of the house, I encouraged Agent Jackson to take the pictures.

It had been said that a picture was worth a thousand words. This was true with these photographs. It showed Barksdale talking to the group in a circle. All eyes were trained on him. He appeared to be using verbal cues and hand gestures to explain something to them. Barksdale looked like a teacher, and the street-level drug dealers looked like students who were eager to learn.

Attorney Johnson wanted to point out what the photograph did not show. I testified that I was present when the pictures were taken. I explained what I believed was going on in the photos. During cross-examination, Johnson asked me a simple question: "Do you see any illegal activity going on in the photograph?"

I had to admit that no illegal activity could be observed in the photograph. Johnson did a great job of getting me to admit that. However, the picture spoke for itself. After three days on the witness stand, I was pleased to leave it unscathed by the defense counsel.

The case was sent to the jury. The outcome of the case was now in their hands. The jury was selected from the citizens of Baltimore City. But unfortunately, they did not know the toll Barksdale and his gang had on Prince Georgians.

I always found it difficult to read the faces of the jury. To any reasonable person, the evidence was overwhelmingly in our favor. Nonetheless, I wondered what my life would be like if Barksdale prevailed in the case. I knew I would be the fall guy. My commanders would quickly distance themselves from me. The chief of police and the chief of detectives both knew I was the lead investigator on the case. I wondered how the loss would affect my life and my career.

What would I tell the families of Gerald and Sticks? Their lives and their families' lives would surely be in imminent danger. Would

Barksdale emerge even more violent if he was set free? These questions lingered in my mind.

Like many other arrogant drug dealers, Barksdale took the stand in his defense. That was a risky move. Most defense attorneys discouraged their clients from taking the witness stand. However, I was sure Barksdale's overbearing personality convinced his attorney he would testify regardless of his attorney's recommendations.

Barksdale's defense was that he was a heroin dealer, not a cocaine dealer. Moreover, a small amount of heroin was recovered earlier from his girlfriend's house in Annapolis. That fact, he believed, would bolster his claim. Barksdale urged his codefendants by letter to stay strong and stick together during the trial. Now federal prosecutors were using Barksdale to seal Pit Bull and Brandon's fate. Barksdale corroborated most of the evidence the prosecutors presented against his codefendants.

Two task force members were sitting in the courtroom when members of the jury began filing back into the courtroom. Suddenly, there was a loud commotion. First, there was yelling followed by a punch. Jungle Jim had struck Barksdale in the face, but an alert task force member noticed that Jim winked at Barksdale before the blow. The two had conspired to fake a fight. It would have been a perfect reason to cause a mistrial. However, the wink before the punch gave it away.

Prosecutors put Detective Baird on the witness stand to describe what he had observed. The judge polled the jury to see how much of the charade they had observed. The poll revealed that no one saw what had happened, but they surmised that Jungle Jim possibly punched Barksdale. None of the jury stated that their deliberations would be affected by what they observed. The attempt to cause a mistrial failed. However, Barksdale and Jungle Jim established grounds for an appeal if they were convicted.

*****

"Hicks," Barksdale said while sitting on the witness stand, "tell the court how you harassed me at Chuck E. Cheese while I was with my family. I told Hicks to come outside. I was going to kick his ass. Hicks followed me outside, and when I was about to kick his ass, several officers met me outside, and they all jumped me."

It was a great but fictional story. The truth was this: I was moonlighting at Chuck E. Cheese when Barksdale walked in, saw me, and immediately walked out with his daughter and another child. I followed him outside to see what car he was driving. Barksdale also asked me to tell the jury how many times my boys from the county police used to kick his ass.

If Barksdale received street justice from the county police, it certainly was not from me. I never struck Barksdale nor any of his associates. I believe that Barksdale hoped his testimony would convince the jury he had already received his punishment. Then he moved on to a new tactic. Barksdale wanted the jury to envision the hardship he had endured in prison. "While you all are in your homes, I am sitting in jail with cockroaches crawling all over my face," he told the jury.

Barksdale was very clever. I was amazed by how many angles he used to try to ensure his acquittal. Unfortunately, Barksdale was not a model prisoner. While in jail, awaiting trial, a petite Prince George's County correctional told FBI agents that without provocation, Barksdale attacked him. He alleged that Barksdale began punching him several times all over his body. The attack lasted several minutes before anyone could come to the officer's aid. Due to pending federal charges, Barksdale was never charged with the assault on the correctional officer. Therefore, he should be presumed innocent until proven guilty.

Finally, Barksdale was transferred to the Baltimore City jail. While Barksdale was there, he allegedly caused a miniature riot by leading a revolt because of his frustration about receiving a bologna sandwich.

After a thirteen-week trial, Barksdale's fate rested in the jury's hands. The United States attorney for Baltimore entered the courtroom flanked by several assistant United States attorneys. Barksdale was not charged with any murders. However, prosecutors presented evidence regarding the violence used by the Barksdale Gang while operating their criminal enterprise.

I listened carefully as the jury rendered its verdict on six drug charges. We all stood there in disbelief as they declared Barksdale not guilty of the six counts of drug trafficking in the indictment. Barksdale was convicted on only a single count of possession with the intent to distribute cocaine. Unfortunately, the jury was unable to reach a verdict on one charge against him. I hoped the trial judge would do what the jury failed to do: hold Barksdale accountable for his alleged murderous drug rampage.

The judge allowed Barksdale to address the court at his sentencing. Barksdale took the witness stand while carrying a thick black binder. No one could have imagined he would continue his bizarre rant for more than three hours. Barksdale started out by insulting both prosecutors in the case. I won't dignify his disparaging words here. Next, he talked about Agent Stone and Agent Kozlowski. Barksdale told the jury, "The agents who were chasing me had on too-tight jeans and too-little T-shirts." He and members of the jury busted out laughing. Next, he turned his attention to me. He said, "Detective Hicks and your one-hundred-page wiretap affidavit, you sellout!"

He quickly digressed and said, "You are not a sellout, because you did it because you wanted to do it." He pointed at African American FBI agent Joey Jackson and said, "You are the sellout." He turned his attention back to me and said, "Look at what they did with you, Hicks. They used you, and then they benched your ass!" I wanted to say, "Amen to that," because he was right. Moreover, after the case was over, Agent Stone received a $2,500 bonus for his work on the case. He took the other agents involved in the case out to dinner to celebrate. That was a custom in the FBI. Although I worked 2 ½ years on the case and worked six months in the United States preparing for trial, I was not invited to the celebration.

Barksdale went on to talk about the history of the FBI spying on black leaders. This was also true. However, Barksdale was not a poster boy for civil rights. He was now a convicted drug dealer. I could not understand how he could draw parallels between himself and civil rights leaders. Next, Barksdale turned his attention to the trial judge. He told the judge, "You are the hanging judge. If you had it your way, you would invite the entire family to watch my execution."

The judge showed enormous patience and allowed Barksdale to let out all his frustrations. Any reasonable person would have used restraint when addressing the judge personally. However, Barksdale was hot-tempered and used to getting his way. It was hard for him to fathom his fate might be held in someone else's hands. Barksdale began crying. I was shocked to see that a man who had negatively made an impact on many lives felt sorry for himself. I thought of all the grieving mothers whose lives were affected by Barksdale's ten-year reign of terror.

Two and a half years after I initiated the investigation, Barksdale and Pit Bull received life sentences. Brandon received a thirty-year sentence. In addition, several underlings received sentences of six months to one year. Jungle Jim AKA the Murder Boy was acquitted of all charges. Barksdale cut him off from receiving drugs at the beginning of our case. Barksdale told Jungle Jim, he cut him off because he "Missed a connect fucking with him." That became Jim's saving grace. Jungle Jim was charged with the murder of Pit Bull's elderly neighbor Grady. Witness Rob gave the jar with the spent shell casings from the murder to task force members. Jungle Jim's prints were found on the glass jar. The Murder Boy was acquitted of Grady's murder. However, Jungle Jim was convicted of another murder and sentenced to twenty-five years in prison. When he was released a few years ago, however, he, too, was murdered.

One other top Barksdale associate was acquitted on a gun charge in federal court but was convicted in state court for another weapons charge related to the case.

CHAPTER 86

ANTOINE'S SENTENCING

With the prominent members of the Barksdale Gang sentenced, prosecutors brought Antoine's witness intimidation case to trial in federal court. When I walked into the courtroom at the start of the three-day trial, Pit Bull was astonished to see me wearing my uniform. "Damn, Hicks," he said, "you made sergeant." I smiled at him and gave him the thumbs-up as I walked toward the witness stand.

My relationship with Pit Bull was peculiar. He admired me as a professional African American police officer. He saw my diligence, and he also saw my compassion. He admired that I maintained my professionalism and that I never got sucked into using excessive force.

Barksdale's defense attorney worked diligently to put a dent in my armor. Attorney Johnson argued that prosecutors could not prove Antoine had any connection to Barksdale. But I took the witness stand, determined to put the final nail in Antoine's coffin. I testified that I stopped Barksdale and Antoine together about eight years earlier. Barksdale's defense attorney, Johnson, laughed and asked me how I could be sure of what I said. I presented a field interview report I wrote when I was a patrol private eight years earlier. It showed that I stopped Barksdale and Antoine. They were together.

The defense attorney, Johnson, stared at the field interview report in disbelief. He was astonished that I not only documented Barksdale and Antoine's contact from so long ago but that I also pulled the report and brought it to trial. My diligence as a patrol officer provided the lynchpin for connecting the two conspirators. This connection had implications for both Antoine and Barksdale.

Antoine was found guilty and was slapped with a fourteen-year prison term in Fort Leavenworth, Kansas. He also received eight years of backup time for a parole violation for a prior conviction relating to witness intimidation. So much for rehabilitation. That quick, short-term surveillance on Antoine at the federal courthouse paid more significant dividends than I ever imagined, but more importantly, we sent a message to anyone wishing to intimidate any of our witnesses that we were going to pursue each of them vigorously.

Despite insurmountable obstacles, I coordinated the investigative talents of numerous law enforcement officers and agents to dismantle an organization operated by what the news media described as "The most dangerous man in county history." I was elated. I was able to obtain justice for the twelve or so men who allegedly lost their lives because of the violence associated with the Barksdale Gang, and I was also able to do so while keeping my soul intact.

The Barksdale Gang was never convicted of any murders. Therefore, Barksdale, Pit Bull, and other murder and shooting suspects mentioned in this book are presumed innocent of the murders and shootings contained herein until proven guilty. However, our documentation of the organization's drug dealing, and the violence associated with the organization is what sealed their fate.

Members of the Negative Regime repeatedly denied all requests to grant me any recognition for dismantling the Barksdale Gang and apprehending the Crossbow Rapist. Commanders in the Narcotics Enforcement Division and Criminal Investigations Division denied me recognition for those two significant cases several times. Notwithstanding, God was able to use me spectacularly. God demonstrated that one person could make a difference. But, as always, God revealed that he had the last say.

Three years later, the County Executive hired a new and very astute police chief from an outside police agency. The new chief heard about the Barksdale Gang Investigation and the Crossbow rapist case. He ordered that all the people associated with the case be recognized. Three years later, at the rank of Lieutenant, I received the

Chief's Award of Merit for both cases. I also received an award from the FBI for both cases.

As I progressed in rank, I faced more personal and professional challenges than I could have ever dreamed of. I would go through a new phase where I would not only deal with adversaries on the street but also with enemies from within.

These weapons recovered were during an unrelated drug raid.

EPILOGUE

I rode an emotional roller coaster as I entered the hallowed halls of the Criminal Investigations Division. My home life was a wreck. My baby brother had just been gunned down in the cold, harsh streets of Baltimore. Meanwhile, I was amid another battle. I was being summoned to the office of the chief of detectives. I knew they were looking for a fall guy. They knew my guard was down. That created a perfect opportunity for him and his cohorts to torment me. I wondered about their motives. They appeared anxious. They relished any opportunity to put a dent in my spiritual armor. There was no doubt in my mind that they fantasized about the day they would devise a scheme by which I would meet my demise.

I glanced up momentarily and noticed the assistant commander standing near the door with his arms folded across his chest. A short distance behind him stood the commander. My mind was preoccupied, trying to figure out what had triggered my baby brother to depart from being an honor student to entering a life of crime. I knew my commanders would derive enormous satisfaction from breaking down the quiet native Baltimorean. They despised me because I was not a subservient commander. I studied their behavior and struck back at them with intellect, not aggression. I had learned earlier in my career the pitfalls of fighting them through aggression.

I took a moment to gather my composure. I knew I needed to be suited up mentally and spiritually to withstand the subsequent tsunami my commanders would throw my way. My commander hastily explained he had orders to take me to see the chief of detectives.

"See me for what?" I asked.

He pretended to look bewildered. "I have no idea, Maurice."

I knew that whatever was going down, my commanders were the chief architects of the plan. They gleefully marched me down the hallway toward the headquarters building. My commander walked on the left side while the captain (assistant commander) was on the right. I felt like a lamb being led into the slaughterhouse.

The captain became increasingly anxious as we reached the headquarters building. He questioned me as we ascended the head-quarters stairs. He demanded to know why detectives in the division were in an uproar. I remained silent. I knew the captain well enough to know he was trying to bait me into a premature confrontation.

As I entered the deputy chief's sparsely furnished office, I could feel the tension in the air. The chief detective's executive officer opened the inner door and told me to have a seat. I knew the executive officer from my patrol days. He was a good man. I could tell he wanted no part in whatever was going down. He mumbled something to me that I could not hear as I entered the room. He deliberately avoided eye contact with me.

There were two chairs directly in front of the chief detective's desk and a sofa to the right. As I attempted to sit on the couch, the chief detective pointed to a chair next to the wall and said, "Sit right here where I can see you." His words surprised me. He was treating me as if I was a child. Until that point, he had nothing but positive things to say about me. I wondered where the change was coming from. Suddenly, it dawned on me that the assistant commander was the acting commander for about two weeks. That gave him ample time to burn the chief detective's ear.

My commanders quickly grabbed their chairs and placed them beside mine, blocking me into the corner. The executive officer closed the door and reinforced the blockade with his chair. I knew then that this was a planned attack. I smiled, and I thought, *They do not know who they are messing with.* So I chuckled for a moment. *What a waste. These guys are a bunch of military wannabes.*

I was a hard-core police veteran who had seen just about all there was to see on the streets. I had engaged in hand-to-hand combat with PCP abusers and gang members in the city of Baltimore and Prince George's County. I had arrested murderers, robbers, and drug kingpins. Naturally, therefore, my commanders were as intimidating to me as cartoon characters.

The chief detective initially sat in his seat, staring at me. His body appeared to be larger than usual. He had a large bump on the side of his face. Everything about him was repulsive. He was trying to engage me in some sort of twisted psychological warfare. Then without warning, he stood up and thrust his body at me. He braced his arms on his desk and leaned his head toward mine. All his gestures were drenched with hate. I showed no fear. My rage was ignited. I was longing for the battle to start.

The deputy chief's eyes momentarily glanced away from me as he scanned his comrades. He needed reassurance that he had an attentive audience. Within a few seconds, our eyes naturally gravitated back to one another. We locked gazes like rams locking horns. This was the grand showdown. The chief detective was determined to teach his subordinate commanders the art of degradation. Although he was the bureau chief, he pretty much ran the department.

A glance at some of the photographs hanging in his office told me justice would never prevail. One picture showed a younger commander, captain, and deputy chief smiling and profiling with a freshly captured bass about twenty years ago. I looked at the photograph and then looked back at the deputy chief, the commander, and the captain with a smirk on my face. That was the last straw; the chief detective could no longer maintain his silence.

"There are a lot of racial problems in this division," the chief detective began. "And we have discovered you are at the center of it all." To me, it seemed like the pot calling the kettle black. I sat there for a few seconds, I was trying to maintain my composure. The longer I sat there, the more I felt my temperature rise. I looked down momentarily. I thought of how my grandfather warned me of men who were addicted to power.

Slowly, I raised my head. I looked at the chief of detectives and his cronies with my bloodshot eyes. They looked terrified. They knew I was about to explode. It was time for a showdown, something the deputy chief did not expect. I knew I would not have another chance to do what needed to be done. He did not realize I had a cure for his provocative tirade. I needed to send him a clear message that his behavior would not be tolerated. I knew my words needed to strike him with surgical precision. What I was about to do was unthinkable, namely standing up to a high-ranking commander on his turf. They needed to understand that I was no longer a rookie police officer. Instead, now I was career PD. I would not be their sacrificial lamb, fall guy, or anything else. I wanted to use Janet Jackson's lyrics from her control album and say, "That was a long ago!" They were about to see a side of me that they had never seen before.

I scanned the room again, finding the executive officer, assistant commander, and the commander waiting to watch my destruction. They were probably hoping I would become violent. My words were slow but insidious as I began my rant. "You are trying to blame racial problems on me. There are no problems in my section. Most of the problems are in homicide. When the brothers complained about racial problems, I told them to give you a chance, but you never solved any problems."

"I'll bet you will not find a single person in my section—female, black, white, Hispanic, Puerto Rican, Haitian, or anyone from the Zulu nation—that would say anything negative about me or my section. All of my people know I care about them, and I run a tight ship. I don't tolerate any discrimination. If you want to find the problem, sir, you should look in the mirror. You are the problem!"

I pointed to the photographs in his office. "I see all your pictures in here. You all have probably been friends since high school. There is no justice here. This is the most racially oppressive environment I have ever worked in my entire freaking life. I did not create this hostile work environment. I am just working in it!"

The deputy chief gritted his coffee-stained large teeth and said, "Let me tell you something, son. Your education means nothing to me, your performance means nothing to me, and your credentials mean nothing to me."

I asked, "What in the hell means anything to you, sir?"

He was speechless. He then yelled, "Get the hell out of my office!"

"I will as soon as your boys release me from this damn corner," I replied.

His cronies slid their chairs back. I walked toward the door. As soon as I reached for it, the chief detective said, "I am going to have to do something to get you out of that hostile environment."

I replied, "Well, excuse me for living! It's your world, sir. I am just living in it."

I met my untimely demise in the Criminal Investigations Division. However, no one could ever stop my anointing. I was blessed with the ability to turn negatives into positives. Their actions inspired me to write my second book. Stay tuned for another collection of exciting and fast-paced stories of policing in the Baltimore-Washington metropolitan area. See how I learned how to adapt and overcome.

BIBLIOGRAPHY

Sondervan. 1973. The Holy Bible. The New International Version.

James and Twigg. (1992, September). Police officer shot, wounded at Flag House high-rise Plainclothesman ambushed at Southeast Baltimore complex. https://www.baltimoresun.com/news/bs-xpm-1992-09-19-1992263007-story.html

ABOUT THE AUTHOR

Photograph by Jackie Hicks, Fond Memories Photography

Maurice Hicks is a decorated twenty-year Maryland law enforcement veteran. He worked undercover narcotics investigations for five years and served as the lead investigator of the FBI Safe Streets Task Force for almost three years. Maurice received numerous awards and commendations during his Baltimore City and Prince George's County tenure. Some of these accolades include two Chief's Awards of Merit and a Veterans of Foreign Wars Award.

Mr. Hicks earned a master's degree in management from Johns Hopkins University, a bachelor's degree in criminology from the University of Maryland, and an associate degree in general studies from Baltimore City Community College. Maurice has worked at the University of Maryland Global Campus for over twenty-two years. He has served in various capacities at the University, including adjunct associate professor, course chair, and peer mentor.

Maurice worked in various capacities in law enforcement, including Special Assistant to the Director of Public Safety, Executive Officer, Patrol Officer, Patrol Sergeant, Patrol Commander, Detective, Detective Sergeant, and Detective Lieutenant. Additionally, he worked at several detective units within the police department, including street narcotics, major narcotics, intelligence, robbery, and homicide. Additionally, Maurice has worked for many years as a private investigator in the states of Nevada and Maryland. He earned a Certified Protection Professional (CPP) certification in October 2006. Maurice is the father of five children and has seven grandchildren.

Printed in the USA
CPSIA information can be obtained
at www.ICGtesting.com
LVHW090317010624
781673LV00001B/21

9 798885 050869